C# 7 and .NET: Designing Modern Cross-platform Applications

The Open Source revolution of .NET Core

Mark J. Price
Ovais Mehboob Ahmed Khan

BIRMINGHAM - MUMBAI

C# 7 and .NET: Designing Modern Cross-platform Applications

First Published: December 2018

Production Reference: 1201218

Published by Packt Publishing Ltd.
Livery Place, 35 Livery Street
Birmingham, B3 2PB, U.K.

ISBN 978-1-78995-669-6

www.packtpub.com

`mapt.io`

Mapt is an online digital library that gives you full access to over 5,000 books and videos, as well as industry-leading tools to help you plan your personal development and advance your career. For more information, please visit our website.

Why Subscribe?

- Spend less time learning and more time coding with practical eBooks and Videos from over 4,000 industry professionals

- Improve your learning with Skill Plans built especially for you

- Get a free eBook or video every month

- Mapt is fully searchable

- Copy and paste, print, and bookmark content

Packt.com

Did you know that Packt offers eBook versions of every book published, with PDF and ePub files available? You can upgrade to the eBook version at `www.packt.com` and as a print book customer, you are entitled to a discount on the eBook copy. Get in touch with us at `customercare@packtpub.com` for more details.

At `www.packt.com`, you can also read a collection of free technical articles, sign up for a range of free newsletters, and receive exclusive discounts and offers on Packt books and eBooks.

Contributors

About the Authors

Mark J. Price is a Microsoft Certified Solutions Developer (MCSD), Microsoft Specialist: Programming in C#, and Episerver Certified Developer, with more than 20 years of educational and programming experience. Since 1993, Mark has passed more than 80 Microsoft programming exams, and he specializes in preparing others to pass them too. His students range from professionals with decades of experience to 16-year-old apprentices with none. He successfully guides all of them by combining educational skills with real-world experience in consulting and developing systems for enterprises worldwide. Between 2001 and 2003, Mark was employed full-time to write official courseware for Microsoft in Redmond, USA. His team wrote the first training courses for C# while it was still an early alpha version. While with Microsoft, he taught "train-the-trainer" classes to get Microsoft Certified Trainers up-to-speed on C# and .NET. Currently, Mark creates and delivers classroom and e-learning training courses for Episerver's Digital Experience Cloud, the best .NET CMS for Digital Marketing and E-commerce. He is an Episerver Certified Developer (ECD) on Episerver CMS. In 2010, Mark studied for a Postgraduate Certificate in Education (PGCE). He taught GCSE and A-Level mathematics in two London secondary schools. He holds a Computer Science BSc Hons. degree from the University of Bristol, UK.

Ovais Mehboob Ahmed Khan is a seasoned programmer and solution architect with over 14 years of software development experience. He has worked in organizations across Pakistan, the USA, and the Middle East. Currently, he is working for a government entity based in Dubai. A Microsoft MVP, he specializes mainly in Microsoft .NET, the cloud and web development. He has published technical articles on MSDN, TechNet, personal blog, and has authored two other books published by Packt: JavaScript for .NET Developers and Enterprise Application Architecture with .NET Core.

About the Reviewers

Dustin Heffron is a software engineer by day and an independent game developer by night. He has over 10 years of experience programming in various languages, eight of which have been in working with C# and .NET. Currently, Dustin develops tools to automate and test medical instruments at Becton Dickinson. He is also the cofounder and CEO for SunFlake Studios. Dustin has a long history of reviewing for Packt, including *XNA 4.0 Game Development by Example: Beginner's Guide, C# 6 and .NET Core 1.0: Modern Cross-Platform Development*, and the video tutorial series *XNA 3D Programming by Example*. He also coauthored the video tutorial series *XNA 3D Toolkit* with *Larry Louisiana*.

Efraim Kyriakidis is a skilled software engineer with over 10 years of experience on developing and delivering software solutions for diverse customers and projects. He's well-versed in all stages of the software development lifecycle. His first acquaintance with computers and programming was a state of the art Commodore 64, back in the '80s as a kid. Since then he has grown and received his Diploma from Aristotle University Thessaloniki in Greece. Throughout his career, he mainly worked with Microsoft technologies, using C# and .NET since .NET 1.0. He currently works for Siemens AG in Germany as a software developer.

Jalpesh Vadgama has been working on technologies like .NET such as MVC, ASP.NET Core, Web Forms, and REST APIs for over 14 years now. Experienced in open source server-side technologies such as Node.js, he has worked with frameworks such as jQuery, Knockout.js, Angular, React.js and Vue. He has been awarded the Microsoft MVP award six times for his technical contribution to .NET and has delivered over 50 Enterprise-level applications using .NET technologies. He has also been using software development methodologies such as Agile, Scrum, and Waterfall for quite a while.

Packt Is Searching for Authors Like You

If you're interested in becoming an author for Packt, please visit authors.packtpub.com and apply today. We have worked with thousands of developers and tech professionals, just like you, to help them share their insight with the global tech community. You can make a general application, apply for a specific hot topic that we are recruiting an author for, or submit your own idea.

Table of Contents

Preface

C# is a widely used programming language, thanks to its easy learning curve, versatility, and support for modern paradigms. It is used to create desktop apps, background services, web apps, and mobile apps. Also, the .NET Core is open sourced and is compatible with Mac OS and Linux apart from Windows. Thus, there is no limit to what you can achieve with C# and .NET Core.

This Learning Path is your one-stop solution for building powerful cross-platform apps with C# 7 and .NET Core 2.0. It begins with the basics of C# and object-oriented programming and explores features of C#, such as tuples, pattern matching, out variables, and so on. You will explore .NET Standard 2.0 class libraries, ASP.NET Core 2.0, and learn how to create professional websites, services, and applications. You will become familiar with mobile app development using Xamarin.Forms and learn to develop high performing applications by writing optimized code with various profiling techniques.

By the end of this Learning Path, you will have all the knowledge required to build modern, cross-platform apps using C# and .NET.

Who This Book Is For

This Learning Path is designed for developers who want to gain a solid foundation with C# and .NET Core, and want to build cross-platform applications. To gain maximum benefits from this Learning Path, you must have the basic knowledge of C#.

What This Book Covers

Chapter 1, *Controlling the Flow and Converting Types*, talks about writing code that makes decisions, repeats a block of statements, and converts between types, and writing code defensively to handle errors when they inevitably occur. You will also learn the best places to look for help.

Chapter 2, *Writing, Debugging, and Testing Functions*, is about following the Don't Repeat Yourself (DRY) principle by writing reusable functions, and learning how to use debugging tools to track down and remove bugs, monitoring your code while it executes to diagnose problems, and rigorously testing your code to remove bugs and ensure stability and reliability before it gets deployed into production.

Chapter 3, *Building Your Own Types with Object-Oriented Programming*, discusses all the different categories of members that a type can have, including fields to store data and methods to perform actions. You will use OOP concepts, such as aggregation and encapsulation. You will learn the C# 7 language features such as tuple syntax support and out variables, and C# 7.1 language features such as default literals and inferred tuple names.

Chapter 4, *Implementing Interfaces and Inheriting Classes*, explains deriving new types from existing ones using object-oriented programming (OOP). You will learn how to define operators and C# 7 local functions, delegates and events, how to implement interfaces of the base and derived classes, how to override a type member, how to use polymorphism, how to create extension methods, and how to cast between classes in an inheritance hierarchy.

Chapter 5, *Understanding and Packaging .NET Standard Types*, presents .NET Core 2.0 types that are part of .NET Standard 2.0, and how they are related to C#. You will learn how to deploy and package your own apps and libraries.

Chapter 6, *Using Common .NET Standard Types*, discusses the .NET Standard types that allow your code to perform common practical tasks, such as manipulating numbers and text, storing items in collections, and implementing internationalization.

Chapter 7, *Working with Files, Streams, and Serialization*, talks about interacting with the filesystem, reading and writing to files and streams, text encoding, and serialization.

Chapter 8, Improving Performance and Scalability Using Multitasking, discusses allowing multiple actions to occur at the same time to improve performance, scalability, and user productivity. You will learn about the C# 7.1 `async Main` feature, and how to use types in the `System.Diagnostics` namespace to monitor your code to measure performance and efficiency.

Chapter 9, *Building Web Sites Using ASP.NET Core Razor Pages*, is about learning the basics of building websites with a modern HTTP architecture on the server-side using ASP.NET Core. You will learn the new ASP.NET Core feature known as Razor Pages that simplifies creating web pages for small websites.

Chapter 10, *Building Web Sites Using ASP.NET Core MVC*, is about learning how to build large, complex websites in a way that is easy to unit test and manage with teams of programmers using ASP.NET Core. You will learn about startup configuration, authentication, routes, models, views, and controllers in ASP.NET Core MVC.

Chapter 11, *Building Web Services and Applications Using ASP.NET Core*, explains building web applications with a combination of a modern frontend technology, such as Angular or React, and a backend REST architecture web service using ASP.NET Core Web API.

Chapter 12, *Building Windows Apps Using XAML and Fluent Design*, talks about learning the basics of XAML that can be used to define the user interface for a graphical app for the Universal Windows Platform (UWP), and applying principles and features of Fluent Design to light it up. This app can then run on any device running Windows 10, Xbox One, and even Mixed Reality devices such as HoloLens.

Chapter 13, *Building Mobile Apps Using XAML and Xamarin.Forms*, discusses introducing you to taking C# mobile by building a cross-platform app for iOS and Android. The client-side mobile app will be created with Visual Studio for Mac using XAML and Xamarin.Forms.

Chapter 14, *Understanding .NET Core Internals and Measuring Performance*, discusses the core concepts of .NET Core, including the compilation process, garbage collection, building highly-performant .NET Core applications utilizing multiple cores of the CPU, and publishing an application using a release build. We will also explore the benchmarking tool that is highly used for code optimization and provides results specific to in-memory objects.

Chapter 15, *Data Structures and Writing Optimized Code in C#*, outlines the core concepts of data structures, the types of data structure, and their advantages and disadvantages, followed by the best possible scenarios to which each data structure is suited. We also learn about the Big O notation, which is one of the core topics to consider when writing code and helps developers check the quality of the code and performance. Lastly, we will look into some best practices and cover topics such as boxing and unboxing, string concatenation, exception handling, `for` and `foreach`, and delegates.

Chapter 16, *Designing Guidelines for .NET Core Application Performance*, showcases some coding principles that make application code look clean and easy to understand. If the code is clean, it offers other developers a way to understand it completely and helps in many other ways. We will learn some basic design principles that are considered to be part of the core principles when designing applications. Principles such as KISS, YAGNI, DRY, Separation of Concerns, and SOLID are highly essential in software design, and caching and choosing the right data structure have a significant impact on performance, and can improve performance if they are properly used. Lastly, we will learn some best practices that should be considered when handling communication, resource management, and concurrency.

Chapter 17, *Memory Management Techniques in .NET Core*, outlines the underlying process of how memory management is done in .NET. We will explore the debugging tool, which can be used by developers to investigate the object's memory allocation on the heap. We will also learn about memory fragmentation, finalizers, and how to implement a dispose pattern to clean up resources by implementing the IDisposable interface.

Chapter 18, *Microservices Architecture*, looks at the most quickly evolving software architecture for developing highly performant and scalable applications for the cloud based on microservices. We will learn some of the core fundamentals of the microservices architecture, its benefits, and patterns and practices used when designing the architecture. We will discuss certain challenges faced when decomposing enterprise applications into the microservices architecture style and learn patterns such as API composition and CQRS in order to address them. Later in the chapter, we will develop a basic application in .NET Core and discuss the solution's structure and the components of microservices. Then we will develop identity and vendor services.

To Get the Most out of This Book

The readers should be equipped with the following configurations of the environment:

1. Visual Studio 2017 on Windows 10
2. Visual Studio for Mac on macOS
3. Visual Studio Code on Windows 10 or macOS
4. Visual Studio 2015/2017 Community Edition
5. .NET Core

The best version of Windows to use is Microsoft Windows 10 because you will need this version to create Universal Windows Platform apps in Chapter 12, *Building Windows Apps Using XAML and Fluent Design*. Earlier versions of Windows, such as 7 or 8.1, will work for the other chapters.

The best version of macOS to use is Sierra or High Sierra because you will need macOS to build iOS mobile apps in Chapter 13, *Building Mobile Apps Using XAML and Xamarin.Forms*. Although you can use Visual Studio 2017 on Windows to write the code for iOS and Android mobile apps, you must have macOS and Xcode to compile them.

Download the Example Code Files

You can download the example code files for this book from your account at `www.packt.com`. If you purchased this book elsewhere, you can visit `www.packt.com/support` and register to have the files emailed directly to you.

You can download the code files by following these steps:

1. Log in or register at `www.packt.com`.
2. Select the **SUPPORT** tab.
3. Click on **Code Downloads & Errata**.
4. Enter the name of the book in the **Search** box and follow the onscreen instructions.

Once the file is downloaded, please make sure that you unzip or extract the folder using the latest version of:

- WinRAR/7-Zip for Windows
- Zipeg/iZip/UnRarX for Mac
- 7-Zip/PeaZip for Linux

The code bundle for the book is also hosted on GitHub at `https://github.com/PacktPublishing/Csharp7-and-.NET-Designing-Modern-Cross-platform-Applications`. In case there's an update to the code, it will be updated on the existing GitHub repository.

We also have other code bundles from our rich catalog of books and videos available at `https://github.com/PacktPublishing/`. Check them out!

Download the color images

We also provide a PDF file that has color images of the screenshots/diagrams used in this book. You can download it here: `https://www.packtpub.com/sites/default/files/downloads/Csharp7_and_dotNet_Design_Modern_Cross_Platform_Applications.pdf`

Conventions Used

Code words in text, database table names, folder names, filenames, file extensions, pathnames, dummy URLs, user input, and Twitter handles are shown as follows: "We have statically imported the `Console` type so that we can simplify calls to its methods such as `WriteLine`."

A block of code is set as follows:

```
using System;

namespace Packt.CS7
{
    public class Person
    {
    }
}
```

When we wish to draw your attention to a particular part of a code block, the relevant lines or items are set in bold:

```
<Project Sdk="Microsoft.NET.Sdk>

  <PropertyGroup>
    <OutputType>Exe</OutputType>
      <TargetFramework>netcoreapp2.0</TargetFramework>
  </PropertyGroup>

  <ItemGroup>
    <ProjectReference
      Include="../PacktLibrary/PacktLibrary.csproj" />
  </ItemGroup>

</Project>
```

Any command-line input or output is written as follows:

```
cd PacktLibrary
dotnet new classlib
cd ..
cd PeopleApp
dotnet new console
```

Bold: New terms and important words are shown in bold. Words that you see on the screen, for example, in menus or dialog boxes, appear in the text like this: "This rule is known as **Banker's Rounding**..."

 Warnings or important notes appear like this.

 Tips and tricks appear like this.

Get in Touch

Feedback from our readers is always welcome.

General feedback: If you have questions about any aspect of this book, mention the book title in the subject of your message and email us at customercare@packtpub.com.

Errata: Although we have taken every care to ensure the accuracy of our content, mistakes do happen. If you have found a mistake in this book, we would be grateful if you would report this to us. Please visit www.packt.com/submit-errata, selecting your book, clicking on the Errata Submission Form link, and entering the details.

Piracy: If you come across any illegal copies of our works in any form on the Internet, we would be grateful if you would provide us with the location address or website name. Please contact us at copyright@packt.com with a link to the material.

If you are interested in becoming an author: If there is a topic that you have expertise in and you are interested in either writing or contributing to a book, please visit authors.packtpub.com.

Reviews

Please leave a review. Once you have read and used this book, why not leave a review on the site that you purchased it from? Potential readers can then see and use your unbiased opinion to make purchase decisions, we at Packt can understand what you think about our products, and our authors can see your feedback on their book. Thank you!

For more information about Packt, please visit packt.com.

1
Controlling the Flow and Converting Types

This chapter is about writing code that makes decisions, repeats blocks of statements, converts between types, handling exceptions, and checking for overflows in number variables.

This chapter covers the following sections:

- Selection statements
- Iteration statements
- Casting and converting between types
- Handling exceptions
- Checking for overflow

Selection statements

Every application needs to be able to select from choices and branch along different code paths. The two selection statements in C# are `if` and `switch`. You can use `if` for all your code, but `switch` can simplify your code in some common scenarios.

Using Visual Studio 2017

Start Microsoft Visual Studio 2017. In Visual Studio, press *Ctrl* + *Shift* + *N* or choose **File | New | Project...**.

In the **New Project** dialog, in the **Installed** list, select **Visual C#**. In the list at the center, select **Console App (.NET Core)**, type the name SelectionStatements, change the location to C:\Code, type the solution name Chapter03, and then click on **OK**.

Using Visual Studio Code on macOS, Linux, or Windows

If you have completed the previous chapters, then you will already have a Code folder in your user folder. If not, create it, and then create a subfolder named Chapter03, and then a sub-subfolder named SelectionStatements.

Start Visual Studio Code and open the /Chapter03/SelectionStatements/ folder.

In Visual Studio Code, navigate to **View | Integrated Terminal**, and then enter the following command:

```
dotnet new console
```

The if statement

The if statement determines which branch to follow by evaluating a Boolean expression. The else block is optional. The if statement can be nested and combined. Each Boolean expression can be independent of the others.

The code

Add the following statements inside the Main method to check whether this console application has any arguments passed to it:

```
if (args.Length == 0)
{
    WriteLine("There are no arguments.");
}
else
{
    WriteLine("There is at least one argument.");
}
```

As there is only a single statement inside each block, this code *can* be written without the curly braces, as shown in the following code:

```
if (args.Length == 0)
  WriteLine("There are no arguments.");
else
  WriteLine("There is at least one argument.");
```

This style of the `if` statement is not recommended because it can introduce serious bugs, for example, the infamous *#gotofail* bug in Apple's iPhone operating system. For 18 months after Apple's iOS 6 was released, it had a bug in its **Secure Sockets Layer (SSL)** encryption code, which meant that any user running Safari to connect to secure websites, such as their bank, were not properly secure because an important check was being accidentally skipped: `https://gotofail.com/`

Just because you can leave out the curly braces, doesn't mean you should. Your code is not "more efficient" without them, instead, it is less maintainable and potentially more dangerous, as this tweet points out:

 Chris Adamson @invalidname · May 26
Had a colleague remove my {} surrounding a 1-line if clause today. No, not angry. It's on his conscience now. #gotofail

    🔁 10   ⭐ 15   •••

Pattern matching with the if statement

A feature introduced with C# 7 is **pattern matching**. The `if` statement can use the `is` keyword in combination with declaring a local variable to make your code safer.

Add the following statements to the end of the `Main` method. If the value stored in the variable named `o` is an `int`, then the value is assigned to the local variable named `i`, which can then be used inside the `if` statement. This is safer than using the variable named `o` because we know for sure that `i` is an `int` variable and not something else:

```
object o = "3";
int j = 4;

if(o is int i)
{
    WriteLine($"{i} x {j} = {i * j}");
}
else
```

```
{
    WriteLine("o is not an int so it cannot multiply!");
}
```

Run the console application and view the output:

```
o is not an int so it cannot multiply!
```

Delete the double-quote characters around the "3" value so that the value stored in the variable named o is an int type instead of a string type and then rerun the console application and view the output:

```
3 x 4 = 12
```

The switch statement

The switch statement is different from the if statement because it compares a single expression against a list of multiple possible cases. Every case is related to the single expression. Every case must end with the break keyword (like case 1 in the following code) or the goto case keywords (like case 2 in the following code), or they should have no statements (like case 3 in the following code).

The code

Enter the following code after the if statements that you wrote previously. Note that the first line is a label that can be jumped to and the second line generates a random number. The switch statement branches based on the value of this random number:

```
A_label:
  var number = (new Random()).Next(1, 7);
  WriteLine($"My random number is {number}");
  switch (number)
  {
    case 1:
      WriteLine("One");
      break; // jumps to end of switch statement
    case 2:
      WriteLine("Two");
      goto case 1;
    case 3:
    case 4:
      WriteLine("Three or four");
      goto case 1;
    case 5:
```

```
    // go to sleep for half a second
    System.Threading.Thread.Sleep(500);
    goto A_label;
  default:
    WriteLine("Default");
    break;
} // end of switch statement
```

Good Practice
You can use the `goto` keyword to jump to another case or a label. The `goto` keyword is frowned upon by most programmers but can be a good solution to code logic in some scenarios. Use it sparingly.

In Visual Studio 2017, run the program by pressing *Ctrl + F5*.

In Visual Studio Code, run the program by entering the following command into **Integrated Terminal**:

```
dotnet run
```

Run the program multiple times to see what happens in various cases of random numbers, as shown in the following output from Visual Studio Code:

```
bash-3.2$ dotnet run
My random number is 4
Three or four
One
bash-3.2$ dotnet run
My random number is 2
Two
One
bash-3.2$ dotnet run
My random number is 1
One
```

Pattern matching with the switch statement

Like the `if` statement, the `switch` statement supports pattern matching in C# 7. The case values no longer need to be literal values. They can be patterns.

Add the following statement to the top of the file:

```
using System.IO;
```

Add the following statements to the end of the `Main` method:

If you are using macOS, then swap the commented statement that sets the `path` variable and replace my username with your user folder name.

```
// string path = "/Users/markjprice/Code/Chapter03";
// macOS
string path = @"C:\Code\Chapter03"; // Windows
Stream s = File.Open(
  Path.Combine(path, "file.txt"),
  FileMode.OpenOrCreate);

switch(s)
{
    case FileStream writeableFile when s.CanWrite:
      WriteLine("The stream is to a file that I can write to.");
      break;
    case FileStream readOnlyFile:
      WriteLine("The stream is to a read-only file.");
      break;
    case MemoryStream ms:
      WriteLine("The stream is to a memory address.");
      break;
    default: // always evaluated last despite its current position
      WriteLine("The stream is some other type.");
      break;
    case null:
      WriteLine("The stream is null.");
      break;
}
```

Note that the variable named `s` is declared as a `Stream` type.

You will learn more about the `System.IO` namespace and the `Stream` type in Chapter 7, *Working with Files, Streams, and Serialization*. You can read more about pattern matching at the following link:
`https://docs.microsoft.com/en-us/dotnet/csharp/pattern-matching`

In .NET, there are multiple subtypes of `Stream`, including `FileStream` and `MemoryStream`. In C# 7 and later, your code can more concisely both branch, based on the subtype of stream, and declare and assign a local variable to safely use it.

Also, note that the `case` statements can include a `when` keyword to perform more specific pattern matching. In the first `case` statement in the preceding code, `s` would only be a match if the stream was `FileStream` and its `CanWrite` property was true.

Iteration statements

Iteration statements repeat a block either while a condition is true or for each item in a group. The choice of which statement to use is based on a combination of ease of understanding to solve the logic problem and personal preference.

Use either Visual Studio 2017 or Visual Studio Code to add a new console application project named `IterationStatements`.

In Visual Studio 2017, you can set the solution's start up project to be the current selection so that the current project runs when you press *Ctrl + F5*.

The while statement

The `while` statement evaluates a Boolean expression and continues to loop while it is true.

Type the following code inside the `Main` method:

```
int x = 0;
while (x < 10)
{
    WriteLine(x);
    x++;
}
```

Run the console application and view the output:

```
0
1
2
3
4
5
6
7
8
9
```

The do statement

The do statement is like while, except the Boolean expression is checked at the bottom of the block instead of the top, which means that it always executes at least once.

Type the following code at the end of the Main method and run it:

```
string password = string.Empty;
do
{
    Write("Enter your password: ");
    password = ReadLine();
} while (password != "secret");
WriteLine("Correct!");
```

You will be prompted to enter your password repeatedly until you enter it correctly, as shown in the following output:

```
Enter your password: password
Enter your password: 12345678
Enter your password: ninja
Enter your password: asdfghjkl
Enter your password: secret
Correct!
```

As an optional exercise, add statements so that the user can only make ten attempts before an error message is displayed.

The for statement

The for statement is like while, except that it is more succinct. It combines an initializer statement that executes once at the start of the loop, a Boolean expression to check whether the loop should continue, and an incrementer that executes at the bottom of the loop. The for statement is commonly used with an integer counter, as shown in the following code:

```
for (int y = 1; y <= 10; y++)
{
    WriteLine(y);
}
```

Run the console application and view the output, which should be the numbers 1 to 10.

The foreach statement

The `foreach` statement is a bit different from the other three iteration statements. It is used to perform a block of statements on each item in a sequence, for example, an array or collection. Each item is read-only, and if the sequence is modified during iteration, for example, by adding or removing an item, then an exception will be thrown.

Type the following code inside the `Main` method, which creates an array of string variables and then outputs the length of each of them:

```
string[] names = { "Adam", "Barry", "Charlie" };
foreach (string name in names)
{
    WriteLine($"{name} has {name.Length} characters.");
}
```

Run the console application and view the output:

```
Adam has 4 characters.
Barry has 5 characters.
Charlie has 7 characters.
```

Technically, the `foreach` statement will work on any type that implements an interface called `IEnumerable`. An interface is a contract and you will learn more about them in `Chapter 4`, *Implementing Interfaces and Inheriting Classes*.

The compiler turns the `foreach` statement in the preceding code into something like this:

```
IEnumerator e = names.GetEnumerator();
while (e.MoveNext())
{
    string name = (string)e.Current; // Current is read-only!
    WriteLine($"{name} has {name.Length} characters.");
}
```

 Due to the use of an iterator, the variable declared in a `foreach` statement cannot be used to modify the value of the current item.

Casting and converting between types

You will often need to convert between different types. For example, data input is often done into a text field, so it is initially stored in a variable of the `string` type, but it then needs to be converted into a date, or time, or number, or some other data type, depending on how it should be stored and processed.

Casting has two varieties: **implicit** and **explicit**. Implicit casting happens automatically and it is safe, meaning that you will not lose any information. Explicit casting must be performed manually because it may lose information, for example, the accuracy of a number. By explicitly casting, you are telling the C# compiler that you understand and accept the risk.

Add a new console application project named `CastingConverting`.

Casting from numbers to numbers

Implicitly casting an `int` variable into a `double` variable is safe.

Casting numbers implicitly

In the `Main` method, enter the following statements:

```
int a = 10;
double b = a; // an int can be stored in a double
WriteLine(b);
```

You cannot implicitly cast a `double` variable into an `int` variable because it is potentially unsafe and would lose data.

In the `Main` method, enter the following statements:

```
double c = 9.8;
int d = c; // compiler gives an error for this line
WriteLine(d);
```

In Visual Studio 2017, press *Ctrl + W, E* to view the **Error List**, as shown in the following screenshot:

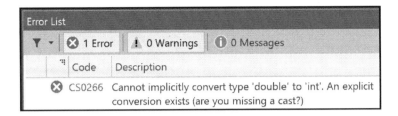

In Visual Studio Code, either view the **PROBLEMS** window, or enter the `dotnet run` command, which will give the following output:

```
Compiling Ch03_CastingConverting for .NETCoreApp,Version=v1.1
/usr/local/share/dotnet/dotnet compile-csc
@/Users/markjprice/Code/Chapter03/Ch03_CastingConverting/obj/
Debug/netcoreapp1.1/dotnet-compile.rsp returned Exit Code 1
/Users/markjprice/Code/Chapter03/Ch03_CastingConverting/Program.cs(14
,21): error CS0266: Cannot implicitly convert type 'double' to 'int'.
An explicit conversion exists (are you missing a cast?)
Compilation failed.
    0 Warning(s)
    1 Error(s)
Time elapsed 00:00:01.0461813
```

Casting numbers explicitly

You must explicitly cast a `double` variable into an `int` variable using a pair of round brackets around the type you want to cast the `double` type into. The pair of round brackets is the **cast operator**. Even then, you must beware that the part after the decimal point will be trimmed off without warning.

Modify the assignment statement for the d variable, as shown in the following code:

```
double c = 9.8;
int d = (int)c;
WriteLine(d); // d is 9 losing the .8 part
```

Run the console application and view the output:

```
10
9
```

We must perform a similar operation when moving values between larger integers and smaller integers. Again, beware that you might lose information because any value too big will get set to –1!

Enter the following code:

```
long e = 10;
int f = (int)e;
WriteLine($"e is {e} and f is {f}");
e = long.MaxValue;
f = (int)e;
WriteLine($"e is {e} and f is {f}");
```

Run the console application and view the output:

```
e is 10 and f is 10
e is 9223372036854775807 and f is -1
```

Using the convert type

An alternative to using the casting operator is to use the System.Convert type.

At the top of the Program.cs file, type the following code:

```
using static System.Convert;
```

Add the following statements to the bottom of the Main method:

```
double g = 9.8;
int h = ToInt32(g);
WriteLine($"g is {g} and h is {h}");
```

Run the console application and view the output:

```
g is 9.8 and h is 10
```

 One difference between casting and converting is that converting rounds the double value up to 10 instead of trimming the part after the decimal point.

The `System.Convert` type can convert to and from all the C# number types as well as Booleans, strings, and date and time values.

Rounding numbers

You have now seen that the cast operator trims the decimal part of a real number and that the convert methods round up or down. However, what is the rule for rounding?

In British primary schools, children are taught to round *up* if the decimal part is .5 or higher and round *down* if the decimal part is less.

Enter the following code:

```
double i = 9.49;
double j = 9.5;
double k = 10.49;
double l = 10.5;
WriteLine($"i is {i}, ToInt(i) is {ToInt32(i)}");
WriteLine($"j is {j}, ToInt(j) is {ToInt32(j)}");
WriteLine($"k is {k}, ToInt(k) is {ToInt32(k)}");
WriteLine($"l is {l}, ToInt(l) is {ToInt32(l)}");
```

Run the console application and view the output:

```
i is 9.49, ToInt(i) is 9
j is 9.5, ToInt(j) is 10
k is 10.49, ToInt(k) is 10
l is 10.5, ToInt(l) is 10
```

Note that the rule for rounding in C# is subtly different. It will round *up* if the decimal part is .5 or higher and the nondecimal part is odd, but it will round *down* if the nondecimal part is even. It always rounds *down* if the decimal part is less than .5.

This rule is known as **Banker's Rounding,** and it is preferred because it reduces bias. Sadly, other languages such as JavaScript use the primary school rule.

Good Practice

For every programming language that you use, check its rounding rules. They may not work the way you expect!

Converting from any type to a string

The most common conversion is from any type into a `string` variable, so all types have a method named `ToString` that they inherit from the `System.Object` class.

The `ToString` method converts the current value of any variable into a textual representation. Some types can't be sensibly represented as text so they return their namespace and type name.

Add the following statements to the bottom of the `Main` method:

```
int number = 12;
WriteLine(number.ToString());
bool boolean = true;
WriteLine(boolean.ToString());
DateTime now = DateTime.Now;
WriteLine(now.ToString());
object me = new object();
WriteLine(me.ToString());
```

Run the console application and view the output:

```
12
True
27/01/2017 13:48:54
System.Object
```

Converting from a binary object to a string

When you have a binary object that you want to store or transmit, it is best not to send the raw bits, because you never know how those bits could be misinterpreted, for example, by the network protocol transmitting them or another operating system that is reading the store binary object.

The safest thing to do is to convert the binary object into a string of safe characters. Programmers call this **Base64** encoding.

The `Convert` type has a pair of methods, `ToBase64String` and `FromBase64String`, that perform this conversion for you.

Add the following statements to the end of the `Main` method:

```
// allocate array of 128 bytes
byte[] binaryObject = new byte[128];

// populate array with random bytes
(new Random()).NextBytes(binaryObject);

WriteLine("Binary Object as bytes:");
for(int index = 0; index < binaryObject.Length; index++)
{
    Write($"{binaryObject[index]:X} ");
}
WriteLine();

// convert to Base64 string
string encoded = Convert.ToBase64String(binaryObject);

WriteLine($"Binary Object as Base64: {encoded}");
```

 By default, an `int` value would output assuming decimal notation, that is, base10. You can use format codes such as `index:X` to format the value using hexadecimal notation.

Run the console application and view the output:

```
Binary Object as bytes:
B3 4D 55 DE 2D E BB CF BE 4D E6 53 C3 C2 9B 67 3 45 F9 E5 20 61 7E 4F 7A 81
EC 49 F0 49 1D 8E D4 F7 DB 54 AF A0 81 5 B8 BE CE F8 36 90 7A D4 36 42 4 75
81 1B AB 51 CE 5 63 AC 22 72 DE 74 2F 57 7F CB E7 47 B7 62 C3 F4 2D 61 93
85 18 EA 6 17 12 AE 44 A8 D B8 4C 89 85 A9 3C D5 E2 46 E0 59 C9 DF 10 AF ED
EF 8AA1 B1 8D EE 4A BE 48 EC 79 A5 A 5F 2F 30 87 4A C7 7F 5D C1 D 26 EE
Binary Object as Base64:
s01V3i0Ou8++TeZTw8KbZwNF+eUgYX5PeoHsSfBJHY7U99tUr6CBBbi+zvg2kHrUNkIEdYEbq1H
OBWOsInLedC9Xf8vnR7diw/QtYZOFGOoGFxKuRKgNuEyJhak81eJG4FnJ3xCv7e+KobGN7kq+SO
x5pQpfLzCHSsd/XcENJu4=
```

Parsing from strings to numbers or dates and times

The second most common conversion is from strings to numbers or date and time values. The opposite of `ToString` is `Parse`. Only a few types have a `Parse` method, including all the number types and `DateTime`.

Add the following statements to the `Main` method:

```
int age = int.Parse("27");
DateTime birthday = DateTime.Parse("4 July 1980");
WriteLine($"I was born {age} years ago.");
WriteLine($"My birthday is {birthday}.");
WriteLine($"My birthday is {birthday:D}.");
```

Run the console application and view the output:

```
I was born 27 years ago.
My birthday is 04/07/1980 00:00:00.
My birthday is 04 July 1980.
```

 By default, a date and time value outputs with the short date and time format. You can use format codes such as D to output only the date part using long date format. There are many other format codes for common scenarios.

One problem with the `Parse` method is that it gives errors if the string cannot be converted.

Add the following statements to the bottom of the `Main` method:

```
int count = int.Parse("abc");
```

Run the console application and view the output:

```
Unhandled Exception: System.FormatException: Input string was not in
a correct format.
```

To avoid errors, you can use the `TryParse` method instead. `TryParse` attempts to convert the input string and returns `true` if it can convert it and `false` if it cannot. The `out` keyword is required to allow the `TryParse` method to set the count variable when the conversion works.

Replace the `int count` declaration with the following statements:

```
Write("How many eggs are there? ");
int count;
string input = Console.ReadLine();
if (int.TryParse(input, out count))
{
    WriteLine($"There are {count} eggs.");
}
else
{
```

```
        WriteLine("I could not parse the input.");
}
```

Run the application twice. The first time, enter 12. You will see the following output:

```
How many eggs are there? 12
There are 12 eggs.
```

The second time, enter twelve. You will see the following output:

```
How many eggs are there? twelve
I could not parse the count.
```

> You can also use the Convert type; however, like the Parse method, it gives an error if it cannot convert.

Handling exceptions when converting types

You've seen several scenarios when errors have occurred when converting types. C# calls this, *an exception has been thrown.*

Good practice is to avoid writing code that will throw an exception whenever possible, perhaps by performing if statement checks, but sometimes you can't. In those scenarios, you must catch the exception and handle it.

As you have seen, the default behavior of a console application is to display details about the exception in the output and then stop running the application.

You can take control over how to handle exceptions using the try statement.

The try statement

Add a new console application project named HandlingExceptions.

When you know that a statement can cause an error, you should wrap that statement in a try block. For example, parsing from a string to a number can cause an error. We do not have to do anything inside the catch block. When the following code executes, the error will get caught and will not be displayed, and the console application will continue running.

In the `Main` method, add the following statements:

```
WriteLine("Before parsing");
Write("What is your age? ");
string input = Console.ReadLine();
try
{
    int age = int.Parse(input);
    WriteLine($"You are {age} years old.");
}
catch
{

}
WriteLine("After parsing");
```

Run the console application and enter a valid age, for example, 43:

```
Before parsing
What is your age? 43
You are 43 years old.
After parsing
```

Run the console application again and enter an invalid age, for example, kermit;

```
Before parsing
What is your age? kermit
After parsing
```

The exception was caught, but it might be useful to see the type of error that occurred.

Catching all exceptions

Modify the `catch` statement to look like this:

```
catch(Exception ex)
{
    WriteLine($"{ex.GetType()} says {ex.Message}");
}
```

Run the console application and again enter an invalid age, for example, `kermit`:

```
Before parsing
What is your age? kermit
System.FormatException says Input string was not in a correct format.
After parsing
```

Catching specific exceptions

Now that we know which specific type of exception occurred, we can improve our code by catching just that type of exception and customizing the message that we display to the user.

Leave the existing `catch` block, but add the following code above it:

```
catch (FormatException)
{
    WriteLine("The age you entered is not a valid number format.");
}
catch (Exception ex)
{
    WriteLine($"{ex.GetType()} says {ex.Message}");
}
```

Run the program and again enter an invalid age, for example, `kermit`:

```
Before parsing
What is your age? kermit
The age you entered is not a valid number format.
After parsing
```

The reason we want to leave the more general `catch` below is that there might be other types of exceptions that can occur. For example, run the program and enter a number that is too big for an integer, for example, `9876543210`:

```
Before parsing
What is your age? 9876543210
System.OverflowException says Value was either too large or too small  for
an
Int32.
After parsing
```

Let's add another catch for this new type of exception:

```
catch(OverflowException)
{
    WriteLine("Your age is a valid number format but it is either too big or
small.");
}
catch (FormatException)
{
    WriteLine("The age you entered is not a valid number format.");
}
```

Rerun the program one more time and enter a number that is too big:

```
Before parsing
What is your age? 9876543210
Your age is a valid number format but it is either too big or small.
After parsing
```

 The order in which you catch exceptions is important. The correct order is related to the inheritance hierarchy of the exception types. You will learn about inheritance in `Chapter 3`, *Building Your Own Types with Object-Oriented Programming*. However, don't worry too much about this—the compiler will give you build errors if you get exceptions in the wrong order anyway.

Checking for overflow

Earlier, we saw that when casting between number types, it was possible to lose information, for example, when casting from a `long` variable to an `int` variable. If the value stored in a type is too big, it will overflow.

Add a new console application project named `CheckingForOverflow`.

The checked statement

The `checked` statement tells .NET to throw an exception when an overflow happens instead of allowing it to happen silently.

We set the initial value of an `int` variable to its maximum value minus one. Then, we increment it several times, outputting its value each time. Note that once it gets above its maximum value, it overflows to its minimum value and continues incrementing from there.

Type the following code in the `Main` method and run the program:

```
int x = int.MaxValue - 1;
WriteLine(x);
x++;
WriteLine(x);
x++;
WriteLine(x);
x++;
WriteLine(x);
```

Run the console application and view the output:

```
2147483646
2147483647
-2147483648
-2147483647
```

Now, let's get the compiler to warn us about the overflow using the `checked` statement:

```
checked
{
    int x = int.MaxValue - 1;
    WriteLine(x);
    x++;
    WriteLine(x);
    x++;
    WriteLine(x);
    x++;
    WriteLine(x);
}
```

Run the console application and view the output:

```
2147483646
2147483647
Unhandled Exception: System.OverflowException: Arithmetic operation
resulted in an overflow.
```

Just like any other exception, we should wrap these statements in a `try` block and display a nicer error message for the user:

```
try
{
    // previous code goes here
}
catch(OverflowException)
{
```

```
    WriteLine("The code overflowed but I caught the exception.");
}
```

Run the console application and view the output:

```
2147483646
2147483647
The code overflowed but I caught the exception.
```

The unchecked statement

A related keyword is `unchecked`. This keyword switches off overflow checks within a block of code.

Type the following statement at the end of the previous statements. The compiler will not compile this statement because it knows it would overflow:

```
int y = int.MaxValue + 1;
```

Press *F6* or enter the `dotnet run` command to build and notice the error, as shown in the following screenshot from Visual Studio 2017:

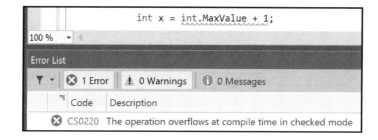

Note that this is a **compile-time** check. To disable compile-time checks, we can wrap the statement in an `unchecked` block, as shown in the following code:

```
unchecked
{
    int y = int.MaxValue + 1;
    WriteLine(y); // this will output -2147483648
    y--;
    WriteLine(y); // this will output 2147483647
    y--;
    WriteLine(y); // this will output 2147483646
}
```

Run the console application and view the output:

```
2147483646
2147483647
The code overflowed but I caught the exception.
-2147483648
2147483647
2147483646
```

Of course, it would be rare that you would want to explicitly switch off a check like this because it allows an overflow to occur. But, perhaps, you can think of a scenario where you might want that behavior.

Looking for help

This section is about how to find quality information about programming on the web.

Microsoft Docs and MSDN

The definitive resource for getting help with Microsoft developer tools and platforms used to be **Microsoft Developer Network** (**MSDN**). Now, it is **Microsoft Docs**:
https://docs.microsoft.com/

Visual Studio 2017 is integrated with MSDN and Docs, so if you press *F1* inside a C# keyword or type, then it will open your browser and take you to the official documentation.

 In Visual Studio Code, pressing *F1* shows the **Command Palette**. It does not support context-sensitive help.

Go to definition

Another useful keystroke in both Visual Studio 2017 and Visual Studio Code is *F12*. This will show what the public definition of the type looks like by reading the metadata in the compiled assembly. Some tools will even reverse-engineer from the metadata and IL code back into C# for you.

Enter the following code, click inside `int`, and then press *F12* (or right-click and choose **Go To Definition**):

```
int z;
```

In the new code window that appears, you can see that `int` is in the `mscorlib.dll` assembly; it is named `Int32`; it is in the `System` namespace; and `int` is therefore an alias for `System.Int32`, as shown in the following screenshot:

```
MetadataAsSourceProject                         System.Int32

  Assembly mscorlib, Version=4.0.0.0, Culture=neutral, PublicKeyToken=b77a5c561934e089

  using ...

  namespace System
  {
      ... public struct Int32 : IComparable, IFormattable, IConvertible, IComparable<Int32>
      {
          ... public const Int32 MaxValue = 2147483647;
          ... public const Int32 MinValue = -2147483648;
```

>

Microsoft defined `int` using a `struct` keyword, meaning that `int` is a value type stored on the stack. You can also see that `int` implements interfaces such as `IComparable` and has constants for its maximum and minimum values.

In the code editor window, scroll down to find the `Parse` methods and in Visual Studio 2017, you will need to click on the small box with a plus symbol in them to expand the code like I have done in the following screenshot:

```
//
// Summary:
//     Converts the string representation of a number to its 32-bit signed integer equivalent.
//
// Parameters:
//   s:
//     A string containing a number to convert.
//
// Returns:
//     A 32-bit signed integer equivalent to the number contained in s.
//
// Exceptions:
//   T:System.ArgumentNullException:
//     s is null.
//
//   T:System.FormatException:
//     s is not in the correct format.
//
//   T:System.OverflowException:
//     s represents a number less than System.Int32.MinValue or greater than System.Int32.MaxValue.
public static Int32 Parse(string s);
```

In the comment, you will see that Microsoft has documented what exceptions might occur if you call this method (ArgumentNullException, FormatException, and OverflowException).

Now, we know that we need to wrap a call to this method in a try statement and which exceptions to catch.

Stack Overflow

Stack Overflow is the most popular third-party website for getting answers to difficult programming questions. It is so popular that search engines such as DuckDuckGo have a special way to write a query to search the site.

Go to >DuckDuckGo.com and enter the following query:

```
!so securestring
```

You will get the following results:

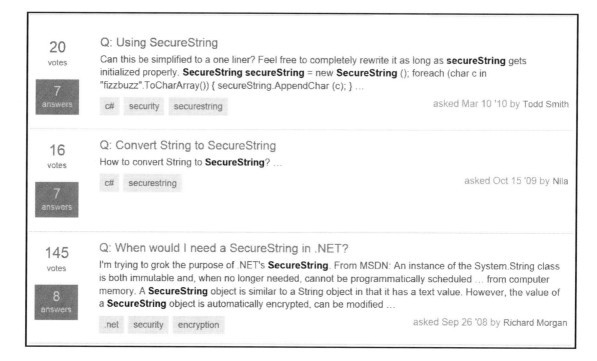

Google

You can search **Google** with advanced search options to increase the likelihood of finding what you need.

For example, if you are searching for information about `garbage collection` using a simple Google query, you will see a Wikipedia definition of garbage collection in computer science, and then a list of garbage collection services in your local area, as shown in the following screenshot:

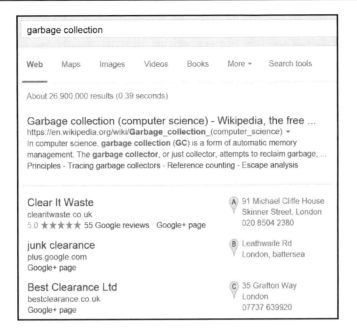

We can improve the search by restricting it to a useful site such as Stack Overflow, as shown in the following screenshot:

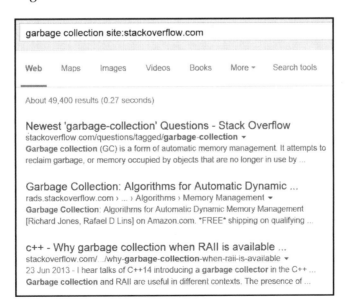

We can improve the search even more by removing languages that we might not care about such as C++, as shown in the following screenshot:

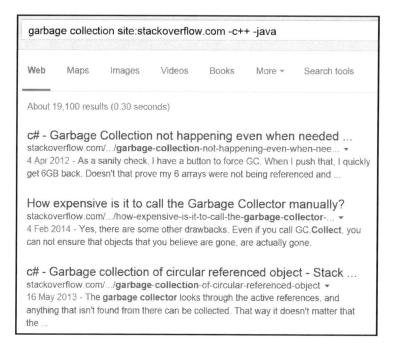

Subscribing to blogs

To keep up to date with .NET, an excellent blog to subscribe to is the official *.NET Blog* written by the .NET engineering teams. (`https://blogs.msdn.microsoft.com/dotnet/`).

Design patterns

A **design pattern** is a general solution to a common problem. Programmers have been solving the same problems over and over. When the community discovers a good reusable solution, we call it a design pattern. Many design patterns have been documented over the years.

Navigate to the following link to read about common design patterns:

`https://en.wikipedia.org/wiki/Software_design_pattern#Classification_and_list`

Microsoft has a group called *patterns & practices* that specializes in documenting and promoting design patterns for Microsoft products.

Good Practice
Before writing new code, search to see if someone else has already solved the problem in a general way.

Singleton pattern

One of the most common patterns is the **Singleton** pattern. Examples of Singleton in .NET are the `Console` and `Math` types.

Read more about the Singleton pattern
at: `https://en.wikipedia.org/wiki/Singleton_pattern`

Summary

In this chapter, you learned how to branch and loop, how to convert between types, how to catch exceptions, and most importantly, how to find help.

You are now ready to learn how to track down bugs in your code and squash them!

2
Writing, Debugging, and Testing Functions

This chapter is about writing functions to reuse code, debugging logic errors during development, logging exceptions during runtime, and unit testing your code to remove bugs and ensure stability and reliability.

This chapter covers the following topics:

- Writing functions
- Debugging during development
- Logging during runtime
- Unit testing

Writing functions

A fundamental principle of programming is **Don't Repeat Yourself (DRY)**.

While programming, if you find yourself writing the same statements over and over, then turn those statements into a function. Functions are like tiny programs that complete one small task. For example, you might write a function to calculate sales tax and then reuse that function in many places in a financial application.

Like programs, functions usually have inputs and outputs. They are sometimes described as black boxes, where you feed some raw materials in one end and a manufactured item emerges at the other. Once created, you don't need to think about how they work.

Let's say that you want to help your child learn their times tables, so you want to make it easy to generate a times table for a number, such as the 12 times table:

```
1 x 12 = 12
2 x 12 = 24
...
12 x 12 = 144
```

You previously learned about the `for` statement, so you know that `for` can be used to generate repeated lines of output when there is a regular pattern, like the 12 times table, as shown in the following code:

```
for (int row = 1; row <= 12; row++)
{
    Console.WriteLine($"{row} x 12 = {row * 12}");
}
```

However, instead of outputting the 12 times table, we want to make this more flexible, so it could output the times table for any number. We can do this by creating a function, also known as a **method**.

Writing a times table function

Create a solution/folder named `Chapter04`, and add a new console application project named `WritingFunctions`.

Modify the template file as shown in the following code:

```
using static System.Console;

namespace WritingFunctions
{
    class Program
    {
        static void TimesTable(byte number)
        {
            WriteLine($"This is the {number} times table");
            for (int row = 1; row <= 12; row++)
            {
                WriteLine(
                    $"{row} x {number} = {row * number}");
            }
        }

        static void RunTimesTable()
```

```
    {
        Write("Enter a number between 0 and 255: ");
        if (byte.TryParse(ReadLine(), out byte number))
        {
            TimesTable(number);
        }
        else
        {
            WriteLine("You did not enter a valid number!");
        }
    }

    static void Main(string[] args)
    {
        RunTimesTable();
    }
}
}
```

Note the following:

- We have statically imported the `Console` type so that we can simplify calls to its methods such as `WriteLine`.
- We have written a function named `TimesTable` that can have a `byte` value passed to it named `number`.
- The `TimesTable` function uses a `for` statement to output the times table for the number passed to it.
- We have written a function named `RunTimesTable` that prompts the user to enter a number, and then calls the `TimesTable` method, passing it the entered number. It includes handling for dealing with the scenario where the user does not enter a valid number.
- We call the `RunTimeTable` function in the `Main` method.

> The function named `TimesTable` has one input: a parameter named `number` that must be a `byte` value. `TimesTable` does not return a value to the caller, so it is declared with the `void` keyword before its name.

Run the console application, enter a number, for example, 6, and view the output:

```
Enter a number between 0 and 255: 6
This is the 6 times table:
1 x 6 = 6
2 x 6 = 12
3 x 6 = 18
4 x 6 = 24
5 x 6 = 30
6 x 6 = 36
7 x 6 = 42
8 x 6 = 48
9 x 6 = 54
10 x 6 = 60
11 x 6 = 66
12 x 6 = 72
```

Writing a function that returns a value

The previous function performed actions (looping and writing to the console), but it did not return a value.

Let's say that you need to calculate sales tax or **valued-added tax (VAT)**. In Europe, VAT rates range from 8% in Switzerland to 27% in Hungary. In the United States, state sales taxes range from 0% in Oregon to 8.25% in California.

Add another function to the `Program` class named `SalesTax`, with a function to run it, as shown in the following code, and note the following:

- The `SalesTax` function has two inputs: a parameter named `amount` that will be the amount of money spent, and a parameter named `twoLetterRegionCode` that will be the region the amount is spent in
- The `SalesTax` function will perform a calculation using a `switch` statement, and then return the sales tax owed on the amount as a `decimal` value; so, before the name of the function, we have declared the data type of the return value
- The `RunSalesTax` function prompts the user to enter an amount and a region code, and then calls `SalesTax` and outputs the result.

```
static decimal SalesTax(
  decimal amount, string twoLetterRegionCode)
{
  decimal rate = 0.0M;
  switch (twoLetterRegionCode)
  {
```

```
      case "CH": // Switzerland
        rate = 0.08M;
        break;
      case "DK": // Denmark
      case "NO": // Norway
        rate = 0.25M;
        break;
      case "GB": // United Kingdom
      case "FR": // France
        rate = 0.2M;
        break;
      case "HU": // Hungary
        rate = 0.27M;
        break;
      case "OR": // Oregon
      case "AK": // Alaska
      case "MT": // Montana
        rate = 0.0M;
        break;
      case "ND": // North Dakota
      case "WI": // Wisconsin
      case "ME": // Maryland
      case "VA": // Virginia
        rate = 0.05M;
        break;
      case "CA": // California
        rate = 0.0825M;
        break;
      default: // most US states
        rate = 0.06M;
        break;
    }
    return amount * rate;
}

static void RunSalesTax()
{
    Write("Enter an amount: ");
    string amountInText = ReadLine();
    Write("Enter a two letter region code: ");
    string region = ReadLine();
    if (decimal.TryParse(amountInText, out decimal amount))
    {
        decimal taxToPay = SalesTax(amount, region);
        WriteLine($"You must pay {taxToPay} in sales tax.");
    }
    else
    {
```

```
            WriteLine("You did not enter a valid amount!");
    }
}
```

In the `Main` method, comment the `RunTimesTable` method call, and call the `RunSalesTax` method, as shown in the following code:

```
// RunTimesTable();

RunSalesTax();
```

Run the console application, enter an amount and a region code, and view the output:

```
Enter an amount: 149
Enter a two letter region code: FR
You must pay 29.8 in sales tax.
```

Can you think of any problems with the `SalesTax` function as written? What would happen if the user enters a code of UK? How could you rewrite the function to improve it?

Writing mathematical functions

Although you might never create an application that needs to have mathematical functionality, everyone studies mathematics at school, so using mathematics is a common way to learn about functions.

Formatting numbers for output

Numbers that are used to count are called **cardinal** numbers, for example, 1, 2, and 3. Numbers that are used to order are **ordinal** numbers, for example, 1st, 2nd, and 3rd.

We will write a function named `CardinalToOrdinal` that converts a cardinal `int` value into an ordinal `string` value; for example, it converts 1 into 1st, 2 into 2nd, and so on, as shown in the following code:

```
static string CardinalToOrdinal(int number)
{
    switch (number)
    {
        case 11:
        case 12:
        case 13:
```

```
      return $"{number}th";
    default:
      string numberAsText = number.ToString();
      char lastDigit =
        numberAsText[numberAsText.Length - 1];
      string suffix = string.Empty;
      switch (lastDigit)
      {
        case '1':
          suffix = "st";
          break;
        case '2':
          suffix = "nd";
          break;
        case '3':
          suffix = "rd";
          break;
        default:
          suffix = "th";
          break;
      }
      return $"{number}{suffix}";
  }
}

static void RunCardinalToOrdinal()
{
  for (int number = 1; number <= 40; number++)
  {
    Write($"{CardinalToOrdinal(number)} ");
  }
}
```

Note the following:

- The CardinalToOrdinal function has one input: a parameter of the int type named number, and one output: a return value of the string type
- A switch statement is used to handle the special cases of 11, 12, and 13
- A nested switch statement then handles all other cases: if the last digit is 1, then use st as the suffix, if the last digit is 2, then use nd as the suffix, if the last digit is 3, then use rd as the suffix, and if the last digit is anything else, then use th as the suffix
- The RunCardinalToOrdinal function uses a for statement to loop from 1 to 40, calling the CardinalToOrdinal function for each number and writing the returned string to the console, separated by a space character

In the `Main` method, comment the `RunSalesTax` method call, and call the `RunCardinalToOrdinal` method, as shown in the following code:

```
// RunTimesTable();
// RunSalesTax();

RunCardinalToOrdinal();
```

Run the console application and view the output:

```
1st 2nd 3rd 4th 5th 6th 7th 8th 9th 10th 11th 12th 13th 14th 15th 16th 17th
18th 19th 20th 21st 22nd 23rd 24th 25th 26th 27th 28th 29th 30th 31st 32nd
33rd 34th 35th 36th 37th 38th 39th 40th
```

Calculating factorials with recursion

The factorial of 5 is 120, because factorials are calculated by multiplying the starting number by one less than itself, and then by one less again, and so on, until the number is reduced to 1, like this: *5 x 4 x 3 x 2 x 1 = 120*.

We will write a function named `Factorial` that calculates the factorial for an `int` passed to it as a parameter. We will use a clever technique called **recursion**, which means a function that calls itself.

Recursion is clever, but it can lead to problems, such as a stack overflow due to too many function calls. Iteration is a more practical, if less succinct, solution in languages like C#. You can read more about this at the following link:
https://en.wikipedia.org/wiki/Recursion_(computer_science)#Recursion_versus_iteration

Add a function named `Factorial`, as shown in the following code:

```
static int Factorial(int number)
{
    if (number < 1)
    {
        return 0;
    }
    else if (number == 1)
    {
        return 1;
    }
    else
```

```
    {
        return number * Factorial(number - 1);
    }
}

static void RunFactorial()
{
    Write("Enter a number: ");
    if (int.TryParse(ReadLine(), out int number))
    {
        WriteLine(
            $"{number:N0}! = {Factorial(number):N0}");
    }
    else
    {
        WriteLine("You did not enter a valid number!");
    }
}
```

Note the following:

- If the input number is zero or negative, Factorial returns 0.
- If the input number is 1, Factorial returns 1, and therefore stops calling itself.
- If the input number is larger than one, Factorial multiplies the number by the result of calling itself and passing one less than the number. This makes the function recursive.
- RunFactorial prompts the user to enter a number, calls the Factorial function, and then outputs the result, formatted using the code N0, which means number format and use commas to show thousands with zero decimal places.

In the Main method, comment the RunCardinalToOrdinal method call, and call the RunFactorial method.

Run the console application several times, entering various numbers, and view the output:

```
Enter a number: 3
3! = 6
Enter a number: 5
5! = 120
Enter a number: 31
31! = 738,197,504
Enter a number: 32
32! = -2,147,483,648
```

Factorials are written like this: 5!, where the exclamation mark is read as *bang*, so 5! = 120, that is, *five bang equals one hundred and twenty*. Bang is a good name for factorials because they increase in size very rapidly, just like an explosion. As you can see in the previous output, factorials of 32 and higher will overflow the `int` type because they are so big.

Debugging an application during development

In this section, you will learn how to debug problems at development time.

Creating an application with a deliberate bug

Add a new console application project named `Debugging`.

Modify the template code to look like this:

```
using static System.Console;

namespace Debugging
{
    class Program
    {
        static double Add(double a, double b)
        {
            return a * b; // deliberate bug!
        }

        static void Main(string[] args)
        {
            double a = 4.5; // or use var
            double b = 2.5;
            double answer = Add(a, b);
            WriteLine($"{a} + {b} = {answer}");
            ReadLine(); // wait for user to press ENTER
        }
    }
}
```

Run the console application and view the output:

```
4.5 + 2.5 = 11.25
```

There is a bug: `4.5` added to `2.5` should be `7` and not `11.25`!

We will use the debugging tools in Visual Studio 2017 or Visual Studio Code to squash the bug.

Setting a breakpoint

Breakpoints allow us to mark a line of code that we want to pause at to find bugs. Click on the open curly brace at the beginning of the `Main` method and press *F9*.

A red circle will appear in the margin bar on the left-hand side to indicate that a breakpoint has been set, as shown in the following screenshot:

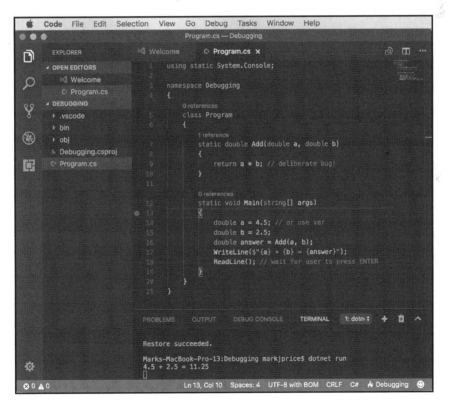

Breakpoints can be toggled with *F9*. You can also left-click in the margin to toggle the breakpoint on and off, or right-click to see more options, such as remove, disable, or edit the breakpoint.

In Visual Studio 2017, go to **Debug | Start Debugging,** or click on the **Start** toolbar button, or press *F5*.

In Visual Studio Code, go to **View | Debug,** or press *Shift + Cmd + D*, and then click on the **Start Debugging** button, or press *F5*.

Visual Studio starts the console application executing and then pauses when it hits the breakpoint. This is known as **break mode**. The line that will be executed next is highlighted in yellow, and a yellow arrow points at the line from the gray margin bar, as shown in the following screenshot:

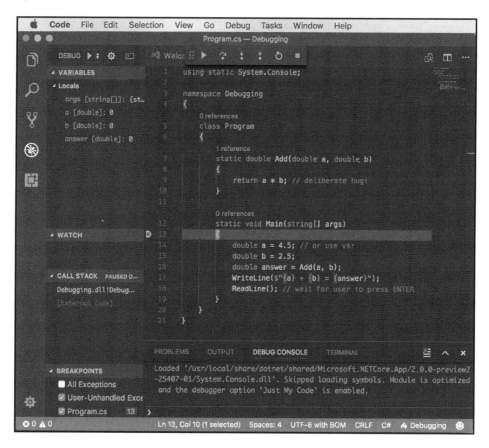

The debugging toolbar

Visual Studio 2017 enables some extra toolbar buttons to make it easy to access debugging features. Here are a few of those:

- **Continue**/*F5* (green triangle): This button will run the code at full speed from the current position
- **Stop Debugging** / *Shift + F5* (red square): This button will stop the program
- **Restart**/*Ctrl* or *Cmd + Shift + F5* (circular black arrow): This button will stop and then immediately restart the program
- **Step Into** / *F11*, **Step Over** / *F10*, and **Step Out** / *Shift + F11* (blue arrows over dots): This button will step through the code in various ways

The following screenshot illustrates Visual Studio 2017's extra toolbar buttons:

The following screenshot illustrates Visual Studio Code's extra toolbar buttons:

Debugging windows

Visual Studio 2017 makes some extra windows visible so that you can monitor useful information, such as variables, while you step through your code. If you cannot find one of these windows, then, in Visual Studio 2017, navigate to **Debug | Windows**, and then select the window you want to view, as shown in the following screenshot:

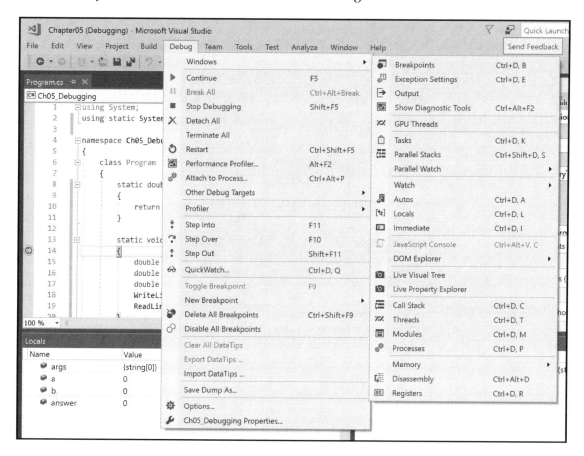

 Most of the debug windows are only available when you are in the break mode.

In Visual Studio Code, the windows are all in the **Debug** view on the left-hand side, as shown in the earlier screenshot.

The **Locals** windows in Visual Studio 2017 and Visual Studio Code, show the name, value, and type for any local variables. Keep an eye on this window while you step through your code, as shown in the following screenshots:

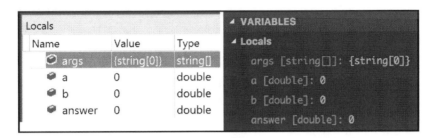

The basic Visual Studio 2017 **Immediate Window** and Visual Studio Code **DEBUG CONSOLE** also allow live interaction with your code.

For example, you can ask a question such as, "What is 1+2?" by typing 1+2 and pressing *Enter*, as shown in the following screenshot:

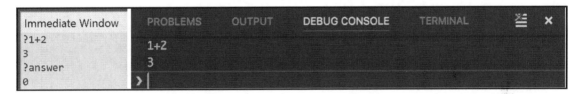

Stepping through code

In Visual Studio 2017, navigate to **Debug | Step Into**, or in both Visual Studio 2017 and Visual Studio Code, click on the **Step Into** button in the toolbar, or press *F11*.

The yellow highlight steps forward one line, as shown in the following screenshot:

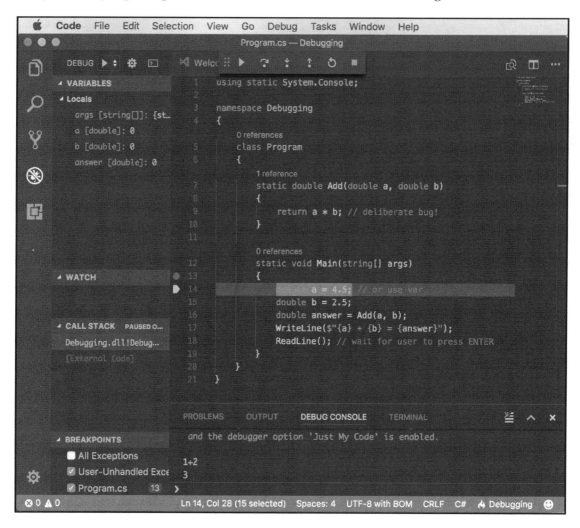

Go to **Debug** | **Step Over** or press *F10*. The yellow highlight steps forward one line. At the moment, you can see that there is no difference between using **Step Into** or **Step Over**.

Press *F10* again so that the yellow highlight is on the line that calls the Add method:

```
                    0 references
    12              static void Main(string[] args)
  ● 13              {
    14                  double a = 4.5; // or use var
    15                  double b = 2.5;
  ▶ 16                  answer = Add(a, b);
    17                  WriteLine($"{a} + {b} = {answer}");
    18                  ReadLine(); // wait for user to press ENTER
    19              }
    20          }
    21      }
```

The difference between **Step Into** and **Step Over** can be seen when you are about to execute a method call. If you click on **Step Into**, the debugger steps *into* the method so that you can step through every line in that method. If you click on **Step Over**, the whole method is executed in one go; it does *not* skip over the method.

Click on **Step Into** to step inside the method. If you are using Visual Studio 2017, hover your mouse over the multiply (*) operator. A tooltip will appear, showing that this operator is multiplying a by b to give the result 11.25. We can see that this is the bug. You can pin the tooltip by clicking on the pin icon, as I have done here:

```
  ⇨                 static double Add(double a, double b)
  ⊯               {  ≤ 20ms elapsed
                      return a * b;        ● a * b 11.25
                  }
```

 Visual Studio Code does not have the hover-over-operator and pin features, but it does have a hover-over-variable feature. If you hover your mouse pointer over the a or b parameters, a tooltip appears showing the current value.

Fix the bug by changing * to +.

We now need to stop, recompile, and restart, so click on the red square **Stop** button or press *Shift + F5*.

If you rerun the console application, you will find that it now calculates correctly.

Customizing breakpoints

In Visual Studio 2017, you can right-click on a breakpoint and choose advanced options, such as **Conditions...**, as shown in the following screenshot:

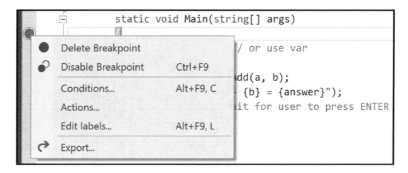

The conditions for a breakpoint include an expression that must be true and a hit count to reach for the breakpoint to apply.

In the example, as you can see in the following screenshot, I have set a condition to only apply the breakpoint if both the answer variable is greater than 9 and we have hit the breakpoint three times:

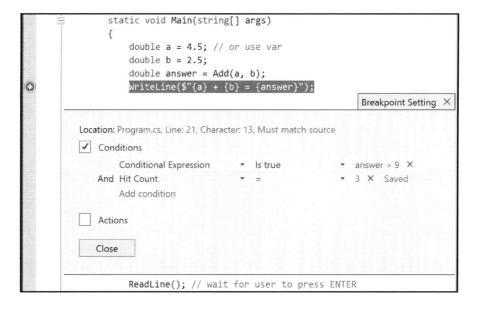

Visual Studio Code has similar, but more limited customization options.

You have now fixed a bug using some debugging tools.

Logging during development and runtime

Once you believe that all the bugs have been removed from your code, you would then compile a release version and deploy the application so people can use it. But no code is bug-free, and during runtime unexpected errors can occur.

End users are notoriously bad about noticing what they were doing when an error occurs, so you should not rely on them accurately providing useful information to fix the problem.

Therefore, it is good practice to add code throughout your application to log what is happening, and especially when exceptions occur, so that you can review the logs and use them to trace the issue and fix the problem.

There are two types that can be used to add simple logging to your code: `Debug` and `Trace`. `Debug` is used to add logging that gets written during development. `Trace` is used to add logging that gets written during both development and runtime.

Instrumenting with Debug and Trace

You have seen the use of the `Console` type and its `WriteLine` method to provide output to the console window. We also have a pair of types named `Debug` and `Trace` that have more flexibility in where they write out to.

The `Debug` and `Trace` classes can write to any **trace listener**. A trace listener is a type that can be configured to write output anywhere you like when the `Trace.WriteLine` method is called. There are several trace listeners provided by .NET Core, and you can even make your own by inheriting from the `TraceListener` type.

Writing to the default trace listener

One trace listener, the `DefaultTraceListener` class, is configured automatically and writes to Visual Studio 2017's **Output** pane, or to Visual Studio Code's **Debug** pane. You can configure others manually using code.

Add a new console application project named `Instrumenting`.

Modify the template code, as shown in the following code:

```
using System.Diagnostics;

namespace Instrumenting
{
    class Program
    {
        static void Main(string[] args)
        {
            Debug.WriteLine("Debug says, I am watching!");
            Trace.WriteLine("Trace says, I am watching!");
        }
    }
}
```

Start the console application with the debugger attached.

In Visual Studio 2017's **Output** window, you will see the two messages. If you cannot see the **Output** window, press *Ctrl + W + O* or navigate to **View | Output**. Ensure that you select the **Show output from: Debug** option, as shown in the following screenshot:

```
'dotnet.exe' (CoreCLR: clrhost): Loaded 'C:\Program Files\dotnet\shared\Microsoft.NETC
'dotnet.exe' (CoreCLR: clrhost): Loaded 'C:\Program Files\dotnet\shared\Microsoft.NETC
Debug says, I am watching!
Trace says, I am watching!
The program '[8948] dotnet.exe' has exited with code 0 (0x0).
```

In Visual Studio Code, the **DEBUG CONSOLE** will output the same two messages, mixed with other debugging information like loaded assembly DLLs, as shown in the following screenshot:

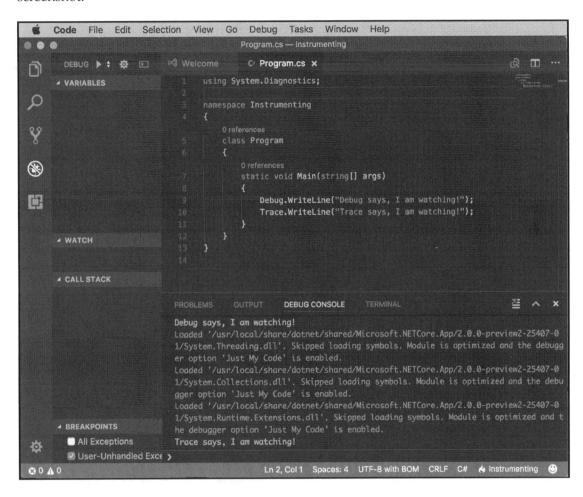

Configuring trace listeners

Now, we will configure another trace listener that will write to a text file.

Modify the template code to look like this:

```
using System.Diagnostics;
using System.IO;

namespace Instrumenting
{
    class Program
    {
        static void Main(string[] args)
        {
            // write to a text file in the project folder
            Trace.Listeners.Add(new TextWriterTraceListener(
            File.CreateText("log.txt")));

            // text writer is buffered, so this option calls
            // Flush() on all listeners after writing
            Trace.AutoFlush = true;
            Debug.WriteLine("Debug says, I am watching!");
            Trace.WriteLine("Trace says, I am watching!");
        }
    }
}
```

Run the console application without the debugger, and open the file named log.txt, as shown in the following screenshot:

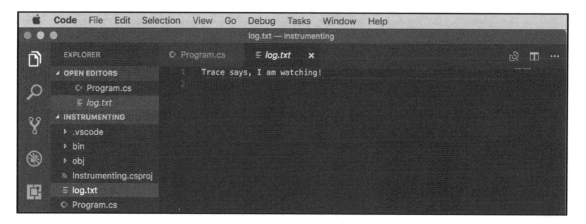

When debugging, both `Debug` and `Trace` are active and will show their output in the **Output / DEBUG CONSOLE** window. When running without debugging, only the `Trace` output is shown. You can therefore use the `Debug.WriteLine` calls liberally throughout your code, knowing they will be stripped out automatically when you compile the release version of your application.

Switching trace levels

The `Trace.WriteLine` calls are left in your code even after release. So, we need a way to control when they are output. We can do this with a trace switch.

The value of a trace switch can be set using a number or a word. For example, the number 3 can be replaced with the word Info, as shown in the following table:

Number	Word	Description
0	Off	This will output nothing
1	Error	This will output only errors
2	Warning	This will output errors and warnings
3	Info	This will output errors, warnings, and information
4	Verbose	This will output all levels

Add some statements to the end of the `Main` method to create a trace switch, set its level using a passed command line parameter, and then output the four trace switch levels, as shown in the following code:

```
var ts = new TraceSwitch("PacktSwitch",
  "This switch is set via a command line argument.");

if (args.Length > 0)
{
    if (System.Enum.TryParse<TraceLevel>(args[0],
        ignoreCase: true, result: out TraceLevel level))
    {
        ts.Level = level;
    }
}

Trace.WriteLineIf(ts.TraceError, "Trace error");
Trace.WriteLineIf(ts.TraceWarning, "Trace warning");
Trace.WriteLineIf(ts.TraceInfo, "Trace information");
Trace.WriteLineIf(ts.TraceVerbose, "Trace verbose");
```

In Visual Studio Code, in **Integrated Terminal**, enter `dotnet run info` to run the console application and ask to output up to Info (3) level, and then open the file named `log.txt`, as shown in the following screenshot:

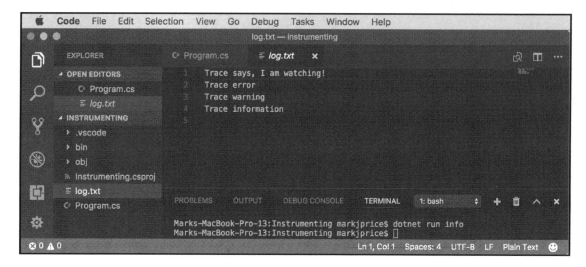

In Visual Studio Code, in **Integrated Terminal**, enter `dotnet run 1`, to run the console application and ask to output up to Error (1) level, and then open the file named `log.txt`, and note that this time, only `Trace error` is output from the four levels.

In Visual Studio 2017, in **Solution Explorer**, right-click on **Instrumenting** project, and click on **Properties**. Click on the **Debug** tab, and enter `info` in the **Application arguments** box, as shown in the following screenshot:

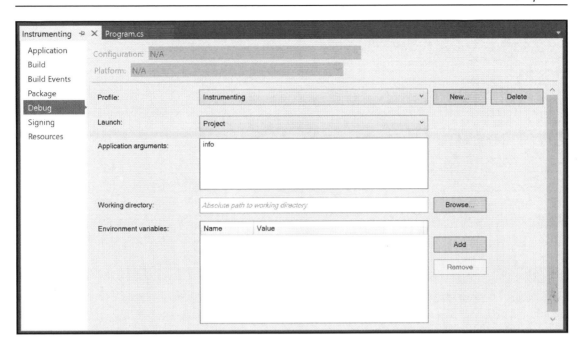

Press *Ctrl* + *F5* to run the console application, and then open the file named `log.txt`, as shown in the following screenshot:

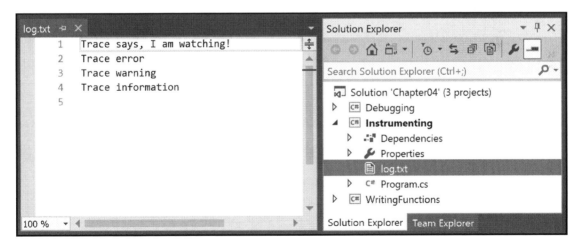

If no argument is passed, the default trace switch level is Off (0), so nothing is output.

Unit testing functions

Fixing bugs in code is costly. The earlier a bug is discovered, the less expensive it will be to fix. Unit testing is a great way to find bugs early in the development process. Some developers even follow the principle that programmers should create unit tests before they write code. This is called **Test Driven Development (TDD)**.

 You can learn more about unit testing at the following link:
`https://docs.microsoft.com/en-us/dotnet/core/testing/`
You can learn more about TDD at the following link:
`https://en.wikipedia.org/wiki/Test-driven_development`

Microsoft has a proprietary unit testing framework known as MS Test, which is closely integrated with Visual Studio. However, to use a unit testing framework that is compatible with .NET Core, we will use the third-party framework **xUnit.net**.

Creating a class library that needs testing with Visual Studio 2017

In Visual Studio 2017, add a new **Class Library (.NET Standard)** project named `CalculatorLib`, as shown in the following screenshot:

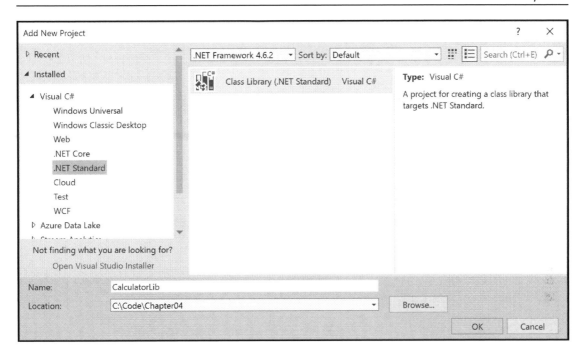

In Visual Studio 2017, in the **Solution Explorer** window, right-click on the Class1.cs file and choose **Rename**. Change its name to Calculator. You will be prompted to rename all references. Click on **Yes**.

Modify the code to look like this (note the deliberate bug!):

```
namespace Packt.CS7
{
    public class Calculator
    {
        public double Add(double a, double b)
        {
            return a * b;
        }
    }
}
```

Creating a unit test project with Visual Studio 2017

In Visual Studio 2017, add a new **xUnit Test Project (.NET Core)** project named `CalculatorLibUnitTests`, as shown in the following screenshot:

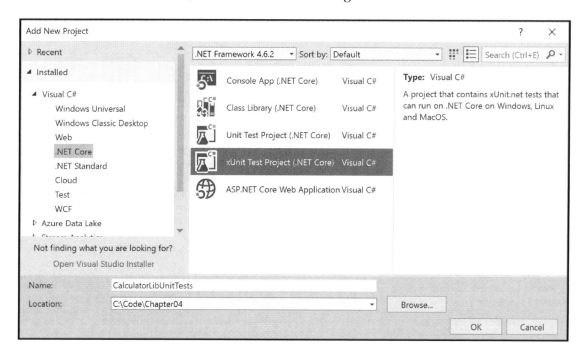

In **Solution Explorer**, in the `CalculatorLibUnitTests` project, right-click on **Dependencies**, and choose **Add Reference...**. In the **Reference Manager** window, select the checkbox for `CalculatorLib`, and then click on **OK**, as shown in the following screenshot:

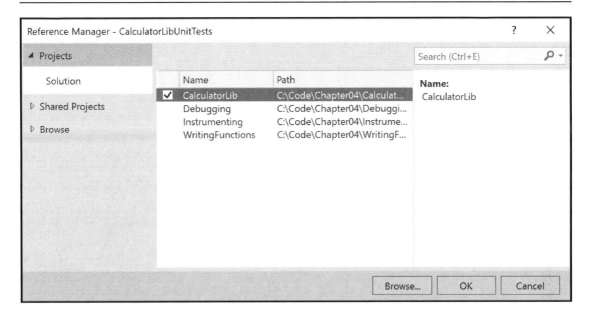

In the **Solution Explorer** window, right-click on the `UnitTest1.cs` file and choose **Rename**. Change its name to `CalculatorUnitTests`. Click on **Yes** when prompted.

Creating a class library that needs testing with Visual Studio Code

Inside the `Chapter04` folder, create subfolders named `CalculatorLib` and `CalculatorLibUnitTests`.

In Visual Studio Code, open the `CalculatorLib` folder, and enter the following command in the **Integrated Terminal** window:

```
dotnet new classlib
```

Rename the file named `Class1.cs` to `Calculator.cs`, and modify the file to look like the following code (note the deliberate bug!):

```
namespace Packt.CS7
{
    public class Calculator
    {
        public double Add(double a, double b)
        {
```

```
            return a * b;
        }
    }
}
```

Enter the following command in the **Integrated Terminal** window:

```
dotnet build
```

Open the `CalculatorLibUnitTests` folder, and enter the following command in the **Integrated Terminal** window:

```
dotnet new xunit
```

Click on the file named `CalculatorLibUnitTests.csproj`, and modify the configuration to add an item group with a project reference to the `CalculatorLib` project, as shown highlighted in the following markup:

```xml
<Project Sdk="Microsoft.NET.Sdk">

  <PropertyGroup>
    <TargetFramework>netcoreapp2.0</TargetFramework>
    <IsPackable>false</IsPackable>
  </PropertyGroup>

  <ItemGroup>
    <PackageReference Include="Microsoft.NET.Test.Sdk"
                      Version="15.5.0-preview-20171012-09" />
    <PackageReference Include="xunit" Version="2.3.0" />
    <PackageReference Include="xunit.runner.visualstudio"
                      Version="2.3.0" />
  </ItemGroup>

  <ItemGroup>
    <ProjectReference Include=
      "..\CalculatorLib\CalculatorLib.csproj" />
  </ItemGroup>

</Project>
```

 You can search Microsoft's NuGet feed for the latest `Microsoft.NET.Test.Sdk` at the following link: https://www.nuget.org/packages?q=Microsoft.NET.Test.Sdk

Rename the file named `UnitTest1.cs` to `CalculatorUnitTests.cs` and the class to `CalculatorUnitTests`.

Writing unit tests

In Visual Studio 2017 or Visual Studio Code, open the file named
`CalculatorUnitTests.cs`, and then modify the code to look like this:

```
using Packt.CS7;
using Xunit;

namespace CalculatorLibUnitTests
{
    public class CalculatorUnitTests
    {
        [Fact]
        public void TestAdding2And2()
        {
            // arrange
            double a = 2;
            double b = 2;
            double expected = 4;
            var calc = new Calculator();
            // act
            double actual = calc.Add(a, b);
            // assert
            Assert.Equal(expected, actual);
        }
        [Fact]
        public void TestAdding2And3()
        {
            // arrange
            double a = 2;
            double b = 3;
            double expected = 5;
            var calc = new Calculator();
            // act
            double actual = calc.Add(a, b);
            // assert
            Assert.Equal(expected, actual);
        }
    }
}
```

A well-written unit test will have three parts:

- **Arrange**: This part will declare and instantiate variables for input and output
- **Act**: This part will execute the unit that you are testing
- **Assert**: This part will make one or more assertions about the output

Running unit tests with Visual Studio 2017

In Visual Studio 2017, navigate to **Test** | **Windows** | **Test Explorer**, and then navigate to **Build** | **Build Solution**, or press *F6*. Note that two tests have been discovered but not yet run, as shown in the following screenshot:

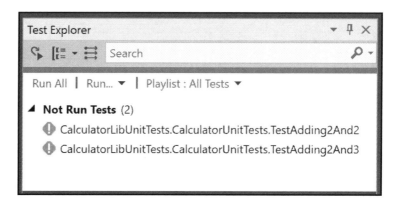

In **Test Explorer**, click on **Run All**.

Wait for a few seconds for the tests to complete, as shown in the following screenshot. Note that one test passed and the other failed. This is why it is good to write multiple tests for each unit:

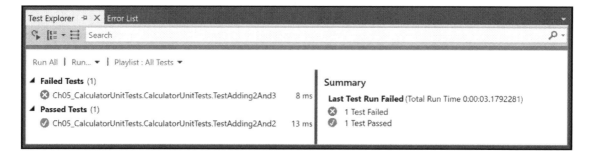

Clicking on a test shows more details and, from there, we should be able to diagnose the bug and fix it:

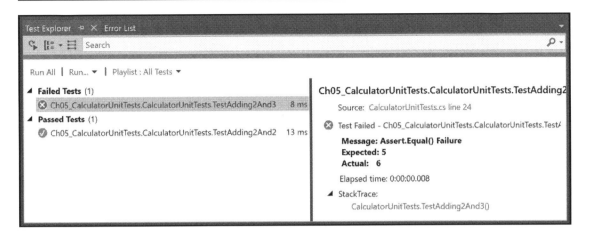

Fix the bug in the Add method, and then rerun the unit tests to see that the bug is now fixed, as shown in the following screenshot:

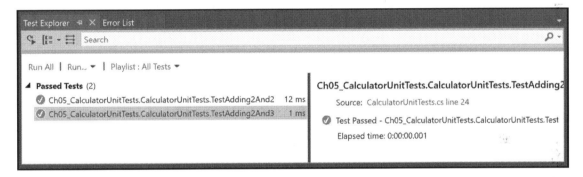

Running unit tests with Visual Studio Code

In Visual Studio Code, open the Chapter04 folder.

In **Integrated Terminal**, enter the following command:

```
cd CalculatorLibUnitTest
dotnet test
```

You should see the following results:

Fix the bug in the `Add` method, and then rerun the unit tests to see that the bug is now fixed, as shown in the following screenshot:

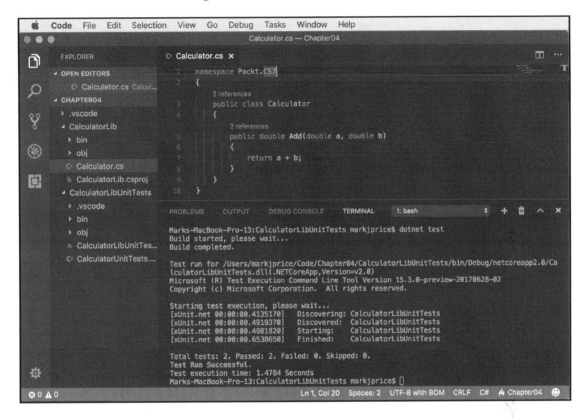

Summary

In this chapter, you learned how to use the Visual Studio debugging and diagnostic features, and unit tested your code.

In the next chapter, you will learn how to build your own types using object-oriented programming techniques.

3
Building Your Own Types with Object-Oriented Programming

This chapter is about making your own types using **object-oriented programming** (OOP). You will learn about all the different categories of members that a type can have, including fields to store data and methods to perform actions. You will use OOP concepts such as aggregation and encapsulation. You will also learn about C# 7 language features, such as tuple syntax support and `out` variables, and C# 7.1 language features, like inferred tuple names and default literals.

This chapter will cover the following topics:

- Talking about OOP
- Building class libraries
- Storing data with fields
- Writing and calling methods
- Controlling how parameters are passed
- Splitting classes using partial
- Controlling access with properties and indexers

Talking about OOP

An object in the real world is a thing, such as a car or a person. An object in programming often represents something in the real world, such as a product or bank account, but can also be something more abstract.

In C#, we use `class` (usually) or `struct` (rarely) to define each type of object. You can think of a type as being a blueprint or template for an object.

Object-oriented programming concepts are briefly described here:

- **Encapsulation** is the combination of the data and actions that are related to an object. For example, a `BankAccount` type might have data, such as `Balance` and `AccountName`, as well as actions, such as `Deposit` and `Withdraw`. When encapsulating, you often want to control what can access those actions and the data.
- **Composition** is about what an object is made of. For example, a car is composed of different parts, such as four wheels, several seats, and an engine.
- **Aggregation** is about what is related to an object. For example, a person could sit in the driver's seat and then becomes the car's driver.
- **Inheritance** is about reusing code by having a subclass derive from a **base** or **super** class. All functionality in the base class becomes available in the derived class.
- **Abstraction** is about capturing the core idea of an object and ignoring the details or specifics. Abstraction is a tricky balance. If you make a class more abstract, more classes would be able to inherit from it, but there will be less functionality to share.
- **Polymorphism** is about allowing a derived class to override an inherited action to provide custom behavior.

Building class libraries

Class library assemblies group types together into easily deployable units (DLL files). Apart from when you learned about unit testing, you have only created console applications to contain your code. To make the code that you write reusable across multiple projects, you should put it in class library assemblies, just like Microsoft does.

Good Practice
Put types that you might reuse in a .NET Standard class library to enable them to be reused in .NET Core, .NET Framework, and Xamarin projects.

Creating a class library with Visual Studio 2017

Start Microsoft Visual Studio 2017. In Visual Studio, press *Ctrl + Shift + N*, or go to **File | New | Project....**

In the **New Project** dialog, in the **Installed** list, expand **Visual C#**, and select **.NET Standard**. In the center list, select **Class Library (.NET Standard)**, type **Name** as `PacktLibrary`, change **Location** to `C:\Code`, type **Solution name** as `Chapter05`, and then click on **OK**, as shown in the following screenshot:

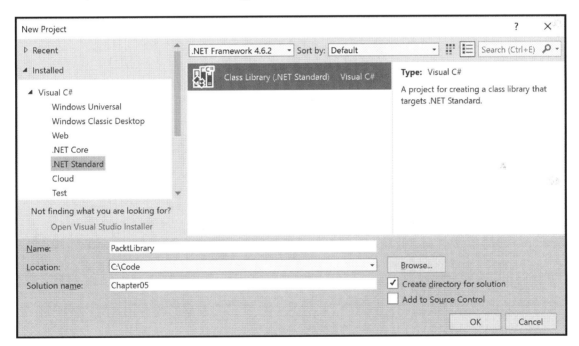

Make sure you choose a **Class Library (.NET Standard)** and *not* a **Console App (.NET Core)**!

In **Solution Explorer**, right-click on the file named `Class1.cs` and choose **Rename**. Type the name as `Person`. When you are prompted to rename all other references to the class, click on **Yes**.

Creating a class library with Visual Studio Code

To create a class library with Visual Studio Code, follow these steps:

1. Create a folder named `Chapter05` with a subfolder named `PacktLibrary`.
2. Start Visual Studio Code and open the `PacktLibrary` folder.
3. View **Integrated Terminal** and enter the following command:

   ```
   dotnet new classlib
   ```

4. In the **EXPLORER** pane, rename the file named `Class1.cs` to `Person.cs`.
5. Click on `Person.cs` to open it, restore packages, and change the class name to `Person`.

Defining a class

In either Visual Studio 2017 or Visual Studio Code, change the namespace to `Packt.CS7`, because it is important to put your classes in a logically named namespace. In this, and the next chapter, we will learn about OOP and most of the new language features of C# 7.0 and 7.1.

Your class file should now look like the following code:

```
using System;

namespace Packt.CS7
{
    public class Person
    {
    }
}
```

Note that the C# keyword `public` is applied before `class`. This keyword is called an **access modifier**, and it allows all code to access this class. If you do not explicitly apply the `public` keyword, then it would only be accessible within the assembly that defined it. We need it to be accessible outside the assembly too. This type does not yet have any members encapsulated within it. We will create some soon.

Members can be fields, methods, or specialized versions of both. They are described here:

- **Fields** are used to store data. There are also three specialized categories of field, as shown in the following bullets:
    - **Constants**: The data in this field never changes
    - **Read-only fields**: The data in this field cannot change after the class is instantiated
    - **Events**: This refers to methods that you want to call automatically when something happens, such as clicking on a button
- **Methods** are used to execute statements. You saw some examples when you learned about functions in `Chapter 3`, *Writing, Debugging, and Testing Functions*. There are also four specialized categories of method, as shown in the following bullets:
    - **Constructors**: These are the methods that execute when you use the `new` keyword to allocate memory and instantiate a class
    - **Properties**: These are the methods that execute when you want to access data
    - **Indexers**: These are the methods that execute when you want to access data
    - **Operators**: These are the methods that execute when you want to apply an operator

Instantiating a class

In this section, we will make an **instance** of the `Person` class, which is known as **instantiating** a class.

Referencing an assembly using Visual Studio 2017

In Visual Studio 2017, add a new console application project named `PeopleApp` to your existing `Chapter05` solution.

Make sure you add a **Console App (.NET Core)** and *not* a **Class Library (.NET Core)**!

Right-click on the solution, choose **Properties**, set **Startup Project** to **Single startup project**, and choose **PeopleApp**.

This project needs a reference to the class library we just made.

In **Solution Explorer**, in the **PeopleApp** project, right-click on **Dependencies** and choose **Add Reference...**.

In the **Reference Manager - PeopleApp** dialog box, in the list on the left-hand side, go to **Projects | Solution**, select the PacktLibrary assembly, and then click on **OK**, as shown in the following screenshot:

In **Solution Explorer**, expand **Dependencies** in both projects to show the class library's dependence on .NET Standard, and the console application's dependence on **PacktLibrary** and .NET Core, as shown in the following screenshot:

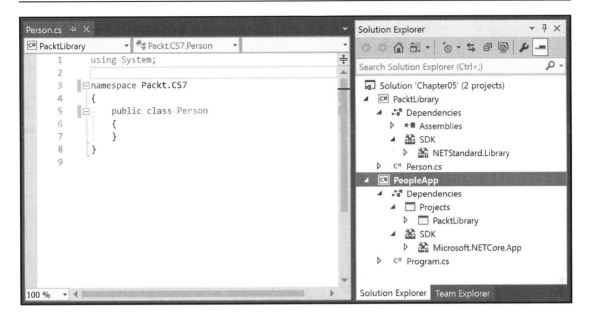

Referencing an assembly using Visual Studio Code

Create a subfolder under `Chapter05` named `PeopleApp`.

In Visual Studio Code, open the `PeopleApp` folder.

In **Integrated Terminal**, enter the following command:

```
dotnet new console
```

In the **EXPLORER** pane, click on the file named `PeopleApp.csproj` and add a project reference to `PacktLibrary`, as shown highlighted in the following markup:

```
<Project Sdk="Microsoft.NET.Sdk>

  <PropertyGroup>
    <OutputType>Exe</OutputType>
      <TargetFramework>netcoreapp2.0</TargetFramework>
  </PropertyGroup>
```

```
  <ItemGroup>
    <ProjectReference
      Include="../PacktLibrary/PacktLibrary.csproj" />
  </ItemGroup>

</Project>
```

In Visual Studio Code, in **Integrated Terminal**, enter the following commands:

```
dotnet restore
dotnet build
```

Both the `PacktLibrary` and `PeopleApp` projects will compile into DLL assemblies, as shown in the following screenshot:

Importing a namespace

In both Visual Studio 2017 and Visual Studio Code, at the top of the `Program.cs` file, type the following code to import the namespace for our class and statically import the `Console` class:

```
using Packt.CS7;
using static System.Console;
```

In the `Main` method, type the following code to create an instance of the `Person` type using the `new` keyword. The `new` keyword allocates memory for the object and initializes any internal data. We could use `Person` in place of the `var` keyword, but the use of `var` involves less typing and is still just as clear:

```
var p1 = new Person();
WriteLine(p1.ToString());
```

 You might be wondering, "Why does the `p1` variable have a method named `ToString`? The `Person` class is empty!" You are about to find out.

Run the console application, using *Ctrl + F5* in Visual Studio 2017, or entering `dotnet run` in Visual Studio Code, and view the output:

Packt.CS7.Person

Managing multiple projects with Visual Studio Code

If you have multiple projects that you want to work with at the same time, either open a new window by navigating to **File | New Window** or press *Shift + Cmd + N*, or open a parent folder that contains the project folders that you want to work with.

If you choose to open a parent folder, be careful when executing commands in the Terminal because they will apply to whatever the current folder is.

In Visual Studio Code, open the `Chapter05` folder, and then in Terminal, enter the following command to change the directory to the console application project, as shown in the following screenshot:

```
cd PeopleApp
```

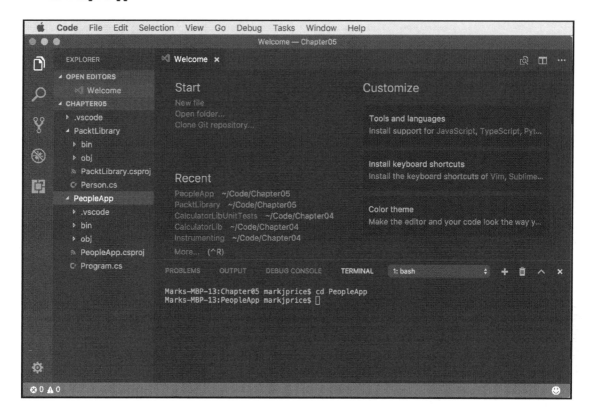

Inheriting from System.Object

Although our `Person` class did not explicitly choose to inherit from a type, all types indirectly inherit from a special type named `System.Object`. The implementation of the `ToString` method in the `System.Object` type simply outputs the full namespace and type name, as shown in the preceding output.

Back in the original `Person` class, we could have explicitly told the compiler that `Person` inherits from the `System.Object` type, like this:

```
public class Person : System.Object
```

 When class B **inherits** from class A, we say that A is the **base** or **super** class and B is the **derived** or **subclass**. In this case, `System.Object` is the base or super class and `Person` is the derived or subclass.

You can also use the C# type alias keyword `object`:

```
public class Person : object
```

Modify your `Person` class to explicitly inherit from `object`. Then, click inside the keyword and press *F12*, or right-click on the `object` keyword and choose **Go to Definition**.

You will see the Microsoft-defined `System.Object` type and its members. You do not need to understand any of this yet, but notice that it has a method named `ToString`, as shown in the following screenshot:

```
namespace System
{
    public class Object
    {
        public Object();

        ~Object();

        public static bool Equals(Object objA, Object objB);
        public static bool ReferenceEquals(Object objA, Object objB);
        public virtual bool Equals(Object obj);
        public virtual int GetHashCode();
        public Type GetType();
        public virtual string ToString();
        protected Object MemberwiseClone();
    }
}
```

 Good Practice
Assume other programmers know that if inheritance is not specified, the class will inherit from `System.Object`.

Storing data with fields

Next, we will define some fields in the class to store information about a person.

Defining fields

Inside the `Person` class, write the following code. At this point, we have decided that a person is composed of a name and a date of birth. We have encapsulated these two values inside the person. We have also made the fields public so that they are visible outside the class itself:

```
public class Person : object
{
    // fields
    public string Name;
    public DateTime DateOfBirth;
}
```

 You can use any type for a field, including arrays and collections such as lists and dictionaries. These would be used if you need to store multiple values in one named field.

In Visual Studio 2017, you might want to click, hold, and drag the tabs for one of your open files to arrange them so that you can see both `Person.cs` and `Program.cs` at the same time, as shown in the following screenshot:

In Visual Studio Code, you can click on the **Split Editor** button or press *Cmd* + \, and then close one copy of the duplicated file editor so that you have two files open side by side, as shown in the following screenshot:

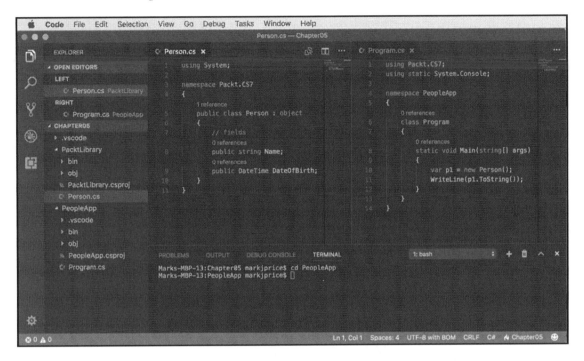

Understanding access modifiers

Note that, like we did with the class, we applied the `public` keyword to these fields. If we hadn't, then they would be `private` to the class, which means they are accessible only inside the class.

There are four access modifier keywords, and one combination of keywords, that you can apply to a class member, such as a field or method. Part of encapsulation is choosing how visible the members are:

Access Modifier	Description
private	Member is accessible inside the type only. This is the default.
internal	Member is accessible inside the type and any type in the same assembly.
protected	Member is accessible inside the type and any type that inherits from the type.
public	Member is accessible everywhere.
internal protected	Member is accessible inside the type, any type in the same assembly, and any type that inherits from the type.

Good Practice
Explicitly apply one of the access modifiers to all type members, even if you want to use the default, which is `private`. Also, fields should usually be `private` or `protected`, and you should then create `public` properties to get or set the field values. This provides more control.

At the top of `Program.cs`, import the `System` namespace, if it is missing, as shown in the following code:

```
using System;
```

Inside the `Main` method, change the code to look like this:

```
var p1 = new Person();
p1.Name = "Bob Smith";
p1.DateOfBirth = new System.DateTime(1965, 12, 22);
WriteLine($"{p1.Name} was born on {p1.DateOfBirth:dddd, d MMMM  yyyy}");
```

Run the application and view the output:

```
Bob Smith was born on Wednesday, 22 December 1965
```

You can also initialize fields using a shorthand object initializer syntax using curly braces.

Add the following code underneath the existing code to create another new person. Notice the different format code for the date of birth when writing to the console:

```
var p2 = new Person
{
    Name = "Alice Jones",
    DateOfBirth = new  DateTime(1998, 3, 17)
};
WriteLine($"{p2.Name} was born on {p2.DateOfBirth:d MMM yy}");
```

Run the application and view the output:

```
Bob Smith was born on Wednesday, 22 December 1965
Alice Jones was born on 17 Mar 98
```

Storing a value using the enum keyword

Sometimes, a value needs to be one of a limited list of options. For example, a person may have a favorite ancient world wonder. Sometimes, a value needs to be a combination of a limited list of options. For example, a person may have a bucket list of ancient world wonders they want to visit. We can store this data using an enum type.

An enum type is a very efficient way of storing one or more choices because, internally, it uses the int values in combination with a lookup table of string descriptions.

In Visual Studio 2017, add a new class to the PacktLibrary project named WondersOfTheAncientWorld by pressing *Shift + Alt + C* or going to **Project | Add Class....**

In Visual Studio Code, add a new class to the project by selecting PacktLibrary, clicking on the **New File** button in the mini toolbar, and entering the name WondersOfTheAncientWorld.cs, as shown in the following screenshot:

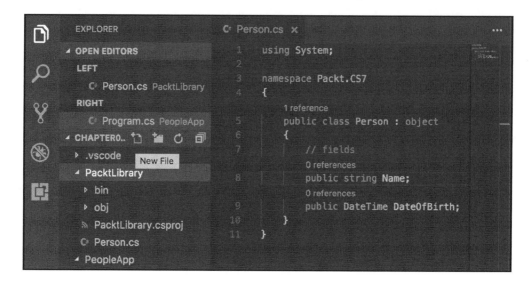

Modify the WondersOfTheAncientWorld.cs class file to make it look like this:

```
namespace Packt.CS7
{
    public enum WondersOfTheAncientWorld
    {
        GreatPyramidOfGiza,
        HangingGardensOfBabylon,
        StatueOfZeusAtOlympia,
        TempleOfArtemisAtEphesus,
        MausoleumAtHalicarnassus,
        ColossusOfRhodes,
        LighthouseOfAlexandria
    }
}
```

In the Person class, add the following statement to your list of fields:

```
public WondersOfTheAncientWorld FavouriteAncientWonder;
```

Back in the `Main` method of `Program.cs`, add the following statements:

```
p1.FavouriteAncientWonder =
  WondersOfTheAncientWorld.StatueOfZeusAtOlympia;
WriteLine($"{p1.Name}'s favourite wonder is {p1.FavouriteAncientWonder}");
```

Run the application and view the additional output:

Bob Smith's favourite wonder is StatueOfZeusAtOlympia

For the bucket list, we could create a collection of instances of the enum, but there is a better way. We can combine multiple choices into a single value using **flags**.

Modify the enum to look as shown in the following code. Note that I have used the left shift operator (<>) to set individual bits within the flag. I could also have set the values to 1, 2, 4, 8, 16, 32, and so on:

```
namespace Packt.CS7
{
    [System.Flags]
    public enum WondersOfTheAncientWorld : byte
    {
        None = 0,
        GreatPyramidOfGiza = 1,
        HangingGardensOfBabylon = 1 << 1, // i.e. 2
        StatueOfZeusAtOlympia = 1 << 2, // i.e. 4
        TempleOfArtemisAtEphesus = 1 << 3, // i.e. 8
        MausoleumAtHalicarnassus = 1 << 4, // i.e. 16
        ColossusOfRhodes = 1 << 5, // i.e. 32
        LighthouseOfAlexandria = 1 << 6 // i.e. 64
    }
}
```

 We are assigning explicit values for each choice that would not overlap when looking at the bits stored in memory. We must also mark the enum type with the `System.Flags` attribute. Normally, an enum type uses an `int` variable internally, but since we don't need values that big, we can make it more efficient by telling it to use a `byte` variable.

If we want to indicate that our bucket list includes the *Hanging Gardens* and *Mausoleum at Halicarnassus* ancient world wonders, then we would want the 16 and 2 bits set to 1. In other words, we would store the value 18:

64	32	16	8	4	2	1	0
0	0	1	0	0	1	0	0

In the Person class, add the following statement to your list of fields:

```
public WondersOfTheAncientWorld BucketList;
```

Back in the Main method of PeopleApp, add the following statements to set the bucket list using the | operator (logical OR) to combine the enum values. We could also set the value using the number 18 cast into the enum type, as in the comment:

```
p1.BucketList = WondersOfTheAncientWorld.HangingGardensOfBabylon |
WondersOfTheAncientWorld.MausoleumAtHalicarnassus;
// p1.BucketList = (WondersOfTheAncientWorld)18;
WriteLine($"{p1.Name}'s bucket list is {p1.BucketList}");
```

Run the application and view the additional output:

```
Bob Smith's bucket list is HangingGardensOfBabylon,
MausoleumAtHalicarnassus
```

Good Practice

Use the enum values to store combinations of discreet options. Derive an enum type from byte if there are up to eight options, from short if there are up to 16 options, from int if there are up to 32 options, and from long if there are up to 64 options.

Storing multiple values using collections

Let's add a field to store a person's children. This is an example of aggregation because children are instances of a class that is related to the current person, but are not part of the person itself.

We will use a generic `List<T>` collection type, so we need to import the
`System.Collections.Generic` namespace at the top of the `Person.cs` class file:

```
using System.Collections.Generic;
```

The angle brackets after the `List<T>` type is a feature of C# called
generics that was introduced in 2005 with C# 2.0. It's just a fancy term for
making a collection **strongly typed**, that is, the compiler knows more
specifically what type of object can be stored in the collection. Generics
improve the performance and correctness of your code. Strong typed is
different from **statically typed**. The old `System.Collection` types are
statically typed to contain weakly typed `System.Object` items. The
newer `System.Collection.Generic` types introduced in 2005 are
statically typed to contain strongly typed `<T>` instances. Ironically, the
term *generics* means a more specific static type!

Then, we can declare a new field in the `Person` class:

```
public List<Person> Children = new List<Person>();
```

Notice that we need to ensure the collection is initialized to a new instance of a collection
before we can add items to the collection.

In the `Main` method, add the following code:

```
p1.Children.Add(new Person { Name = "Alfred" });
p1.Children.Add(new Person { Name = "Zoe" });
WriteLine(
  $"{p1.Name} has {p1.Children.Count} children:");
for (int child = 0; child < p1.Children.Count; child++)
{
    WriteLine($"  {p1.Children[child].Name}");
}
```

Run the application and view the output:

```
Bob Smith has 2 children:
  Alfred
  Zoe
```

Making a field static

The fields that we have created so far have all been instance members, meaning that a copy of each field exists for each instance of the class that is created.

Sometimes, you want to define a field that only has one copy that is shared across all instances. These are called **static** members.

In the `PacktLibrary` project, add a new class named `BankAccount`. Modify the class, as shown in the following code:

```
namespace Packt.CS7
{
    public class BankAccount
    {
        public string AccountName;
        public decimal Balance;
        public static decimal InterestRate;
    }
}
```

 Each instance of `BankAccount` will have its own `AccountName` and `Balance` values, but all instances will share a single `InterestRate` value.

In `Program.cs` and its `Main` method, add the following code, where we will set the shared interest rate and then create two instances of the `BankAccount` type:

```
BankAccount.InterestRate = 0.012M;
var ba1 = new BankAccount();
ba1.AccountName = "Mrs. Jones";
ba1.Balance = 2400;
WriteLine($"{ba1.AccountName} earned {ba1.Balance *
BankAccount.InterestRate:C} interest.");
var ba2 = new BankAccount();
ba2.AccountName = "Ms. Gerrier";
ba2.Balance = 98;
WriteLine($"{ba2.AccountName} earned {ba2.Balance *
BankAccount.InterestRate:C} interest.");
```

Run the application and view the additional output:

```
Mrs. Jones earned £28.80 interest.
Ms. Gerrier earned £1.18 interest.
```

 :C is a format code that tells .NET to use the currency format for the numbers. In Chapter 6, *Using Common .NET Standard Types*, you will learn how to control the culture that determines the currency symbol. For now, it will use the default for your operating system installation. I live in London, UK, hence my output shows British Pounds (£).

Making a field constant

If the value of a field will never *ever* change, you can use the const keyword and assign the value at compile time.

Inside the Person class, add the following code:

```
// constants
public const string Species = "Homo Sapien";
```

Inside the Main method, change the code to look like this. Note that, to read a constant field, you must write the name of the class, not the name of an instance of the class:

```
WriteLine($"{p1.Name} is a {Person.Species}");
```

Run the application and view the additional output:

```
Bob Smith is a Homo Sapien
```

Examples of the const fields in Microsoft types include System.Int32.MaxValue and System.Math.PI because neither value will ever change, as you can see in the following screenshot:

```
(constant) int int.MaxValue = 2147483647
Represents the largest possible value of an int. This field is constant.

(constant) double Math.PI = 3.1415926535897931
Represents the ratio of the circumference of a circle to its diameter, specified by the constant, π.
```

Good Practice

Constants should be avoided for two important reasons: the value must be known at compile time, and it must be expressible as a literal string, Boolean, or number value. Every reference to the `const` field is replaced with the literal value at compile time, which will, therefore, not be reflected if the value changes in a future version.

Making a field read-only

A better choice for fields that should not change is to mark them as read-only.

Inside the `Person` class, write the following code:

```
// read-only fields
public readonly string HomePlanet = "Earth";
```

Inside the `Main` method, add the following code statement. Notice that, to get a read-only field, you must write the name of an instance of the class, not the type name, unlike `const`:

```
WriteLine($"{p1.Name} was born on {p1.HomePlanet}");
```

Run the application and view the output:

```
Bob Smith was born on Earth
```

Good Practice

Use read-only fields over the `const` fields for two important reasons: the value can be calculated or loaded at runtime and can be expressed using any executable statement. So, a read-only field can be set using a constructor or a field assignment. Every reference to the field is a live reference, so any future changes will be correctly reflected by calling code.

Initializing fields with constructors

Fields often need to be initialized at runtime. You do this in a constructor that will be called when you make an instance of the class using the `new` keyword. Constructors execute before any fields are set by the code that is using the type.

Inside the `Person` class, add the following highlighted code after the existing read-only `HomePlanet` field:

```
// read-only fields
public readonly string HomePlanet = "Earth";
public readonly DateTime Instantiated;

// constructors
public Person()
{
    // set default values for fields
    // including read-only fields
    Name = "Unknown";
    Instantiated = DateTime.Now;
}
```

Inside the `Main` method, add the following code:

```
var p3 = new Person();
WriteLine($"{p3.Name} was instantiated at  {p3.Instantiated:hh:mm:ss} on
{p3.Instantiated:dddd, d MMMM  yyyy}");
```

Run the application and view the output:

```
Unknown was instantiated at 11:58:12 on Sunday, 12 March 2017
```

You can have multiple constructors in a type. This is especially useful to encourage developers to set initial values for fields.

Inside the `Person` class, add the following code:

```
public Person(string initialName)
{
    Name = initialName;
    Instantiated = DateTime.Now;
}
```

Inside the `Main` method, add the following code:

```
var p4 = new Person("Aziz");
WriteLine($"{p4.Name} was instantiated at
{p4.Instantiated:hh:mm:ss} on {p4.Instantiated:dddd, d MMMM yyyy}");
```

Run the application and view the output:

```
Aziz was instantiated at 11:59:25 on Sunday, 4 June 2017
```

Setting fields with default literal

A new language feature introduced in C# 7.1 is default literals.

For example, if you had some fields in a class that you wanted to initial to their default type values in a constructor, you could use `default(type)`, as shown in the following code:

```
using System;
using System.Collections.Generic;
using Packt.CS7;

public class ThingOfDefaults
{
    public int Population;
    public DateTime When;
    public string Name;
    public List<Person> People;

    public ThingOfDefaults()
    {
        Population = default(int); // C# 2.0 and later
        When = default(DateTime);
        Name = default(string);
        People = default(List<Person>);
    }
}
```

You might think that the compiler ought to be able to work out what type we mean without being explicitly told, and you'd be right, but for the first 15 years of the C# compiler's life, it didn't.

Finally, with the C# 7.1 compiler, it does, as shown in the following code:

```
using System;
using System.Collections.Generic;
using Packt.CS7;

public class ThingOfDefaults
{
    public int Population;
    public DateTime When;
    public string Name;
```

```
    public List<Person> People;

    public ThingOfDefaults()
    {
        Population = default; // C# 7.1 and later
        When = default;
        Name = default;
        People = default;
    }
}
```

But if you try to use this new C# 7.1 keyword, Visual Studio 2017 and Visual Studio Code both currently give a compile error, as shown in the following screenshot:

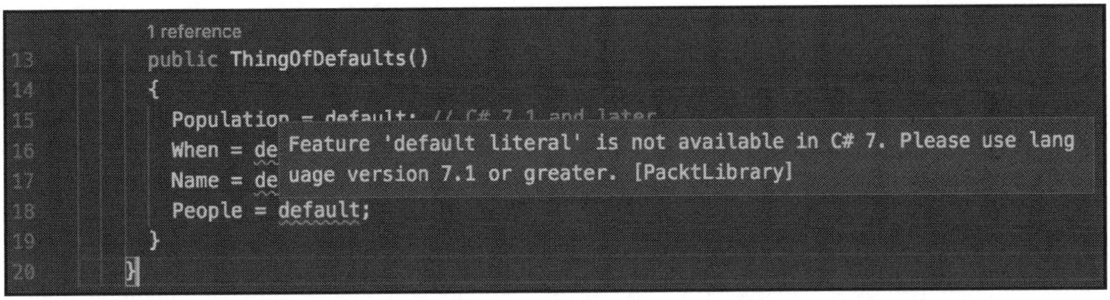

To tell the Visual Studio 2017 and Visual Studio Code to use the C# 7.1 compiler, open `PacktLibrary.csproj`, and add a pair of `<PropertyGroup>` elements for the `Release` and `Debug` configurations, as shown in the following markup:

```
<PropertyGroup
Condition="'$(Configuration)|$(Platform)'=='Release|AnyCPU'">
  <LangVersion>7.1</LangVersion>
</PropertyGroup>

<PropertyGroup Condition="'$(Configuration)|$(Platform)'=='Debug|AnyCPU'">
  <LangVersion>7.1</LangVersion>
</PropertyGroup>
```

You can replace `<LangVersion>7.1</LangVersion>` with `<LangVersion>latest</LangVersion>` if you always want to use the latest C# compiler for a project. For example, early in 2018, Microsoft plans to release C# 7.2.

Constructors are a special category of method. Let's look at methods in more detail.

Writing and calling methods

Methods are type members that execute a block of statements.

A method that performs some actions, but does not return a value indicates this by showing that it returns the `void` type before the name of the method. A method that performs some actions and returns a value indicates this by showing that it returns the type of that value before the name of the method.

For example, you will create two methods:

- `WriteToConsole`: This will perform an action (writing a line), but it will return nothing from the method, indicated by the `void` keyword
- `GetOrigin`: This will return a string value, indicated by the `string` keyword

Inside the `Person` class, statically import `System.Console`, and then add the following code:

```
// methods
public void WriteToConsole()
{
    WriteLine($"{Name} was born on {DateOfBirth:dddd, d MMMM yyyy}");
}

public string GetOrigin()
{
    return $"{Name} was born on {HomePlanet}";
}
```

Inside the `Main` method, add the following code:

```
p1.WriteToConsole();
WriteLine(p1.GetOrigin());
```

Run the application and view the output:

```
Bob Smith was born on Wednesday, 22 December 1965
Bob Smith was born on Earth
```

Combining multiple values with tuples

Each method can only return a single value that has a single type. That type could be a simple type, such as `string` in the previous example, a complex type, such as `Person`, or a collection type, such as `List<Person>`.

Imagine that we want to define a method named `GetTheData` that returns both a `string` value and an `int` value. We could define a new class named `TextAndNumber` with a `string` field and an `int` field, and return an instance of that complex type, as shown in the following code:

```
public class TextAndNumber
{
    public string Text;
    public int Number;
}

public class Processor
{
    public TextAndNumber GetTheData()
    {
        return new TextAndNumber
        {
            Text = "What's the mean of life?",
            Number = 42
        };
    }
}
```

Alternatively, we could use tuples.

Tuples have been a part of some languages such as F# since their first version, but .NET only added support for them in .NET 4.0 with the `System.Tuple` type. It was only in C# 7 that the C# language added syntax support for tuples.

While adding tuple support to the C# 7 language, .NET also added a new `System.ValueTuple` type that is more efficient in some common scenarios than the old .NET 4.0 `System.Tuple` type.

`System.ValueTuple` is not part of .NET Standard 1.6, and therefore not available by default in .NET Core 1.0 or 1.1 projects. `System.ValueTuple` is built-in with .NET Standard 2.0, and therefore, .NET Core 2.0.

Defining methods with tuples

First, we will define a method that would work in C# 4 or later. Then we will use the new C# 7 language support.

Inside the `Person` class, add the following code to define two methods, the first with a return type of `System.Tuple<string, int>` and the second with a return type using C# 7 syntax:

```
// the old C# 4 and .NET 4.0 System.Tuple type
public Tuple<string, int> GetFruitCS4()
{
    return Tuple.Create("Apples", 5);
}

// the new C# 7 syntax and new System.ValueTuple type
public (string, int) GetFruitCS7()
{
    return ("Apples", 5);
}
```

Inside the `Main` method, add the following code:

```
Tuple<string, int> fruit4 = p1.GetFruitCS4();
WriteLine($"There are {fruit4.Item2} {fruit4.Item1}.");

(string, int) fruit7 = p1.GetFruitCS7();
WriteLine($"{fruit7.Item1}, {fruit7.Item2} there are.");
```

Run the application and view the output:

```
There are 5 Apples.
Apples, 5 there are.
```

Naming the fields of a tuple

To access the fields of a tuple, the default names are `Item1`, `Item2`, and so on.

You can explicitly specify the field names. Inside the `Person` class, add the following code to define a method:

```
public (string Name, int Number) GetNamedFruit()
{
    return (Name: "Apples", Number: 5);
}
```

Inside the `Main` method, add the following code:

```
var fruitNamed = p1.GetNamedFruit();
WriteLine($"Are there {fruitNamed.Number} {fruitNamed.Name}?");
```

Run the application and view the output:

```
Are there 5 Apples?
```

Inferring tuple names

If you are constructing a tuple from another object, you can use a new feature introduced in C# 7.1 called **tuple name inference**.

Let's create two tuple things, made of a `string` and `int` value each, as shown in the following code:

```
var thing1 = ("Neville", 4);
WriteLine(
  $"{thing1.Item1} has {thing1.Item2} children.");
var thing2 = (p1.Name, p1.Children.Count);
WriteLine(
  $"{thing2.Item1} has {thing2.Item2} children.");
```

In C# 7, both things use the `Item1` and `Item2` naming schemes. In C# 7.1, the second thing would infer the names `Name` and `Count`, as shown in the following code:

```
var thing2 = (p1.Name, p1.Children.Count);
WriteLine(
  $"{thing2.Name} has {thing2.Count} children.");
```

 Just like all C# 7.1 language features, you will need to modify `PeopleApp.csproj` to instruct the compiler to use 7.1 or latest.

Deconstructing tuples

You can also deconstruct tuples into separate variables. The deconstructing declaration has the same syntax as named field tuples, but without a variable name for the whole tuple. This has the effect of splitting the tuple into its parts and assigning those parts to new variables.

Inside the `Main` method, add the following code:

```
(string fruitName, int fruitNumber) = p1.GetFruitCS7();
WriteLine($"Deconstructed: {fruitName}, {fruitNumber}");
```

Run the application and view the output:

```
Deconstructed: Apples, 5
```

 Deconstruction is not just for tuples. Any type can be deconstructed if it has a **Deconstructor** method. You can read about this at the following link:
https://docs.microsoft.com/en-us/dotnet/csharp/tuples#deconstruction

Defining and passing parameters to methods

Methods can have parameters passed to them to change their behavior. Parameters are defined a bit like variable declarations, but inside the parentheses of the method.

Inside the `Person` class, add the following code to define two methods, the first without parameters and the second with one parameter:

```
public string SayHello()
{
    return $"{Name} says 'Hello!'";
}

public string SayHelloTo(string name)
{
    return $"{Name} says 'Hello {name}!'";
}
```

Inside the `Main` method, add the following code:

```
WriteLine(p1.SayHello());
WriteLine(p1.SayHelloTo("Emily"));
```

Run the application and view the output:

```
Bob Smith says 'Hello!'
Bob Smith says 'Hello Emily!'
```

Overloading methods

When typing a statement that calls a method, IntelliSense should show useful tooltips in both Visual Studio 2017 and Visual Studio Code, with the appropriate language extension installed.

In Visual Studio 2017, you can press *Ctrl* + *K, I* or go to **Edit** | **IntelliSense** | **Quick Info** to see quick info of a method, as shown in the following screenshot:

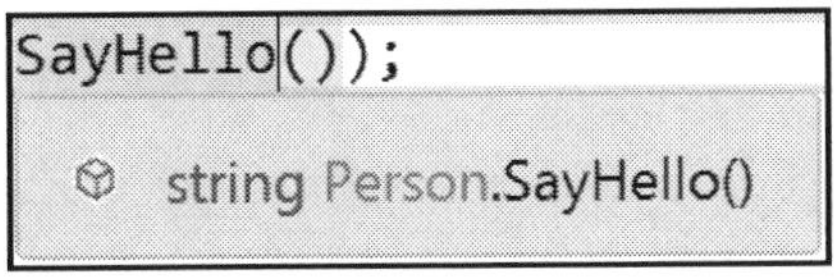

```
SayHello());

    ⬡   string Person.SayHello()
```

Here is the `SayHelloTo` method's quick info:

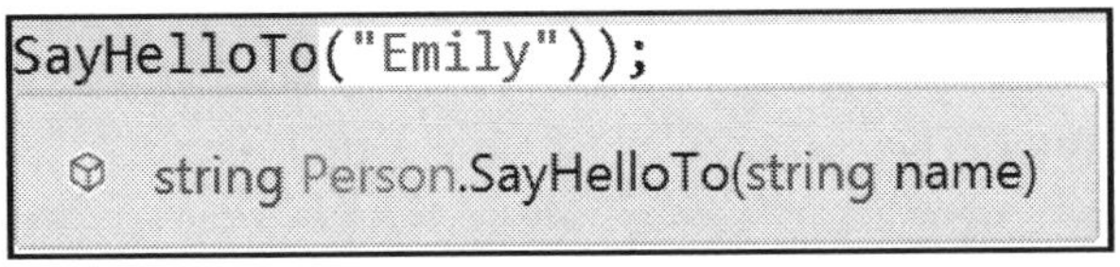

```
SayHelloTo("Emily"));

    ⬡   string Person.SayHelloTo(string name)
```

Instead of having two different method names, we could give both methods the same name. This is allowed because the methods each have a different signature. A **method signature** is a list of parameter types that can be passed when calling the method.

In the `Person` class, change the name of the `SayHelloTo` method to `SayHello`. Now, when you view the quick info for the method, it tells you that it has one additional overload:

```
SayHello("Emily"));
```

⬡ string Person.SayHello(string name) (+ 1 overload)

Good Practice
Use overloaded methods to simplify your class by making it appear to have fewer methods.

Optional parameters and named arguments

Another way to simplify methods is to make parameters optional. You make a parameter optional by assigning a default value inside the method parameter list. Optional parameters must always come last in the list of parameters.

There is one exception to optional parameters always coming last. C# has a `params` keyword that allows you to pass a comma-separated list of parameters of any length as an array. You can read about `params` at the following link:
https://docs.microsoft.com/en-us/dotnet/csharp/language-referenc
e/keywords/params

You will now create a method with three optional parameters.

Inside the `Person` class, add the following code:

```
public string OptionalParameters(string command = "Run!",
   double number = 0.0, bool active = true)
{
    return $"command is {command}, number is {number}, active is {active}";
}
```

Inside the `Main` method, add the following code:

```
WriteLine(p1.OptionalParameters());
```

Watch IntelliSense's **Quick Info** appear as you type the code, and you will see a tooltip, showing the three optional parameters with default values, as shown in the following screenshot:

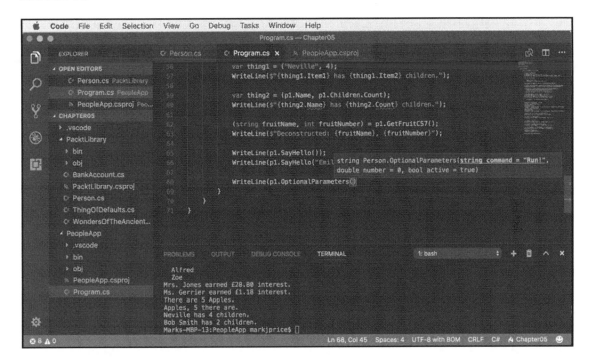

When you run the application, you will see the following output:

```
command is Run!, number is 0, active is True
```

In the `Main` method, add the following line, which passes a `string` value for the `command` parameter and a `double` value for the `number` parameter:

```
p1.OptionalParameters("Jump!", 98.5);
```

Run the application and see the output:

```
command is Jump!, number is 98.5, active is True
```

The default values for `command` and `number` have been replaced, but the default for `active` is still `true`.

Optional parameters are often combined with naming parameters when you call the method, because naming a parameter allows the values to be passed in a different order than how they were declared.

In the `Main` method, add the following line, which passes a `string` value for the `command` parameter and a `double` value for the `number` parameter but using named parameters, so that the order they are passed through can be swapped around:

```
p1.OptionalParameters(number: 52.7, command: "Hide!");
```

Run the application and see the output:

```
command is Hide!, number is 52.7, active is True
```

You can even use named parameters to skip over optional parameters.

In the `Main` method, add the following line that passes a `string` value for the `command` parameter using positional order, skips the `number` parameter, and uses the named `active` parameter:

```
p1.OptionalParameters("Poke!", active: false);
```

Run the application and see the output:

```
command is Poke!, number is 0, active is False
```

Controlling how parameters are passed

When a parameter is passed into a method, it can be passed in one of three ways:

- By **value** (this is the default): Think of these as being *in-only*
- By **reference** as a `ref` parameter: Think of these as being *in-and-out*
- As an `out` parameter: Think of these as being *out-only*

In the `Person` class, add the following method:

```
public void PassingParameters(int x, ref int y, out int z)
{
    // out parameters cannot have a default
    // AND must be initialized inside the method
    z = 99;

    // increment each parameter
    x++;
    y++;
    z++;
}
```

In the `Main` method, add the following statements to declare some `int` variables and pass them into the method:

```
int a = 10;
int b = 20;
int c = 30;
WriteLine($"Before: a = {a}, b = {b}, c = {c}");
p1.PassingParameters(a, ref b, out c);
WriteLine($"After: a = {a}, b = {b}, c = {c}");
```

Run the application and see the output:

```
Before: a = 10, b = 20, c = 30
After: a = 10, b = 21, c = 100
```

When passing a variable as a parameter by default, its current *value* gets passed, *not* the variable itself. Therefore, x is a copy of the a variable. The a variable retains its original value of 10. When passing a variable as a `ref` parameter, a *reference* to the variable gets passed into the method. Therefore, y is a reference to b. The b variable gets incremented when the y parameter gets incremented. When passing a variable as an `out` parameter, a *reference* to the variable gets passed into the method. Therefore, z is a reference to c. The c variable gets replaced by whatever code executes inside the method. We could simplify the code in the `Main` method by not assigning the value 30 to the c variable, since it will always be replaced anyway.

In C# 7, we can simplify code that uses the `out` variables.

Add the following statements to the `Main` method:

```
// simplified C# 7 syntax for out parameters
int d = 10;
int e = 20;
WriteLine($"Before: d = {d}, e = {e}, f doesn't exist yet!");
p1.PassingParameters(d, ref e, out int f);
WriteLine($"After: d = {d}, e = {e}, f = {f}");
```

 In C# 7, the `ref` keyword is not just for passing parameters into a method, it can also be applied to the return value. This allows an external variable to reference an internal variable and modify its value after the method call. This might be useful in advanced scenarios, for example, passing around placeholders into big data structures, but it's beyond the scope of this book.

Splitting classes using partial

When working on large projects with multiple team members, it is useful to be able to split the definition of a complex class across multiple files. You do this using the `partial` keyword.

Imagine we want to add a new method to the `Person` class without having to ask another programmer to close the `Person.cs` file. If the class is defined as `partial`, then we can split it over as many separate files as we like.

In the `Person` class, add the `partial` keyword, as shown highlighted in the following code:

```
namespace Packt.CS7
{
    public partial class Person
    {
```

In Visual Studio 2017, navigate to **Project | Add Class...** or press *Shift + Alt + C*. Enter the name `Person2`. We cannot enter `Person` because Visual Studio 2017 isn't smart enough to understand what we want to do. Instead, we must now rename the new class to `Person`, change the namespace, and add the `public partial` keywords, as shown in the following code:

```
namespace Packt.CS7
{
    public partial class Person
    {
```

In Visual Studio Code, click on the **New File** button in the `PacktLibrary` folder in the **Explorer** pane and enter a name of `Person2.cs`. Add statements to the new file, as shown in the following code:

```
namespace Packt.CS7
{
    public partial class Person
    {
    }
}
```

 The rest of the code we write for this chapter will be written in the `Person2.cs` file.

Controlling access with properties and indexers

Earlier, you created a method named `GetOrigin` that returned a `string` containing the name and origin of the person. Languages such as Java do this a lot. C# has a better way: **properties**.

A property is simply a method (or a pair of methods) that acts and looks like a field when you want to get or set a value, thereby simplifying the syntax.

Defining read-only properties

In the `Person2.cs` file, inside the `Person` class, add the following code to define three properties:

- The first property will perform the same role as the `GetOrigin` method using the property syntax that works with all versions of C# (although, it uses the C# 6 and later string interpolation syntax)
- The second property will return a greeting message using the C# 6 and later, the lambda expression (=>) syntax
- The third property will calculate the person's age

Here is the code:

```
// property defined using C# 1 - 5 syntax
public string Origin
{
    get
    {
        return $"{Name} was born on {HomePlanet}";
    }
}

// two properties defined using C# 6+ lambda expression syntax
public string Greeting => $"{Name} says 'Hello!'";

public int Age => (int)(System.DateTime.Today
    .Subtract(DateOfBirth).TotalDays / 365.25);
```

In the `Main` method, add the following code. You can see that, to set or get a property, you treat it like a field:

```
var sam = new Person
{
    Name = "Sam",
    DateOfBirth = new DateTime(1972, 1, 27)
};
WriteLine(sam.Origin);
WriteLine(sam.Greeting);
WriteLine(sam.Age);
```

Run the application and view the output:

```
Sam was born on Earth
Sam says 'Hello!'
46 // if executed between 27 January 2018 and 27 January 2019
```

Defining settable properties

To create a settable property, you must use the older syntax and provide a pair of methods—not just a `get` part, but also a `set` part.

In the `Person2.cs` file, add the following code to define a `string` property that has both a `get` and `set` method (also known as *getter* and *setter*). Although you have not manually created a field to store the person's favorite ice-cream, it is there, automatically created by the compiler for you:

```
public string FavoriteIceCream { get; set; } // auto-syntax
```

Sometimes, you need more control over what happens when a property is set. In this scenario, you must use a more detailed syntax and manually create a `private` field to store the value for the property:

```
private string favoritePrimaryColor;
public string FavoritePrimaryColor
{
    get
    {
        return favoritePrimaryColor;
    }
    set
    {
        switch (value.ToLower())
        {
            case "red":
            case "green":
            case "blue":
                favoritePrimaryColor = value;
                break;
            default:
                throw new System.ArgumentException($"{value} is not a
                primary color. Choose from: red, green, blue.");
        }
    }
}
```

In the `Main` method, add the following code:

```
sam.FavoriteIceCream = "Chocolate Fudge";
WriteLine($"Sam's favorite ice-cream flavor is {sam.FavoriteIceCream}.");
sam.FavoritePrimaryColor = "Red";
WriteLine($"Sam's favorite primary color is {sam.FavoritePrimaryColor}.");
```

Run the application and view the output:

```
Sam's favorite ice-cream flavor is Chocolate Fudge.
Sam's favorite primary color is Red.
```

If you try to set the color to any value other than red, green, or blue, then the code will throw an exception. The calling code could then use a `try` statement to display the error message.

Good Practice

Use properties instead of fields when you want to validate what value can be stored, when you want to data bind in XAML (we will cover this in Chapter 12, *Building Windows Apps Using XAML and Fluent Design*), and when you want to read and write to fields without using methods. You can read more about encapsulation of fields using properties at the following link:

https://www.microsoft.com/net/tutorials/csharp/getting-started/encapsulation-oop

Defining indexers

Indexers allow the calling code to use the array syntax to access a property. For example, the `string` type defines an **indexer** so that the calling code can access individual characters in the string individually. We will define an indexer to simplify access to the children of a person.

In the `Person2.cs` file, add the following code to define an indexer to get and set a child using the index (position) of the child:

```
// indexers
public Person this[int index]
{
    get
    {
        return Children[index];
    }
```

```
   set
   {
      Children[index] = value;
   }
}
```

 You can overload indexers so that different types can be used to call them. For example, as well as passing an `int` value, you could also pass a `string` value.

In the `Main` method, add the following code. After adding to the children, we will access the first and second child using the longer `Children` field and the shorter indexer syntax:

```
sam.Children.Add(new Person { Name = "Charlie" });
sam.Children.Add(new Person { Name = "Ella" });
WriteLine($"Sam's first child is {sam.Children[0].Name}");
WriteLine($"Sam's second child is {sam.Children[1].Name}");
WriteLine($"Sam's first child is {sam[0].Name}");
WriteLine($"Sam's second child is {sam[1].Name}");
```

Run the application and view the output:

```
Sam's first child is Charlie
Sam's second child is Ella
Sam's first child is Charlie
Sam's second child is Ella
```

 Good Practice
Only use indexers if it makes sense to use the square bracket/array syntax. As you can see from the preceding example, indexers rarely add much value.

Summary

In this chapter, you learned about making your own types using OOP. You learned about some of the different categories of members that a type can have, including fields to store data and methods to perform actions. You used OOP concepts, such as aggregation and encapsulation, and explored some of the new language syntax features in C# 7.0 and 7.1.

In the next chapter, you will take these concepts further by defining delegates and events, implementing interfaces, and inheriting from existing classes.

4

Implementing Interfaces and Inheriting Classes

This chapter is about deriving new types from existing ones using **object-oriented programming (OOP)**. You will learn about defining operators and C# 7 local functions for performing simple actions, delegates and events for exchanging messages between types, implementing interfaces for common functionality, inheriting from a base class to create a derived class to reuse functionality, overriding a type member, using polymorphism, creating extension methods, and casting between classes in an inheritance hierarchy.

This chapter covers the following topics:

- Setting up a class library and console application
- Simplifying methods with operators
- Defining local functions
- Raising and handling events
- Implementing interfaces
- Making types more reusable with generics
- Managing memory with reference and value types
- Inheriting from classes
- Casting within inheritance hierarchies
- Inheriting and extending .NET types

Setting up a class library and console application

We will start by defining a solution with two projects like the one created in Chapter 3, *Building Your Own Types with Object-Oriented Programming*. If you completed all the exercises in that chapter, then you can open it and continue with it. Otherwise, follow the instructions for your preferred development tool given here.

Using Visual Studio 2017

In Visual Studio 2017, press *Ctrl + Shift + N* or go to **File** | **New** | **Project...**.

In the **New Project** dialog, in the **Installed** list, expand **Visual C#**, and select **.NET Standard**. In the center list, select **Class Library (.NET Standard)**, type **Name** as PacktLibrary, change **Location** to C:\Code, type **Solution name** as Chapter06, and then click on **OK**.

In **Solution Explorer**, right-click on the file named Class1.cs and choose **Rename**. Type the name as Person. Modify the contents like this:

```
namespace Packt.CS7
{
    public class Person
    {
    }
}
```

Add a new console application project named PeopleApp.

In the solution's properties, set the startup project to be the PeopleApp project.

In **Solution Explorer**, in the PeopleApp project, right-click on **Dependencies** and choose **Add Reference...**.

In the **Reference Manager - PeopleApp** dialog box, in the list on the left-hand side, choose **Projects**, select the PacktLibrary assembly, and then click on **OK**.

Using Visual Studio Code

Create a folder named Chapter06 with two subfolders named PacktLibrary and PeopleApp, as shown in this hierarchy:

- Chapter06
    - PacktLibrary
    - PeopleApp

Start Visual Studio Code and open the Chapter06 folder.

In **Integrated Terminal**, enter the following commands:

```
cd PacktLibrary
dotnet new classlib
cd ..
cd PeopleApp
dotnet new console
```

In the **EXPLORER** pane, in the PacktLibrary project, rename the file named Class1.cs to Person.cs.

Modify the class file contents, as shown in the following code:

```
namespace Packt.CS7
{
    public class Person
    {
    }
}
```

In the **EXPLORER** pane, expand the folder named PeopleApp and click on the file named PeopleApp.csproj.

Add a project reference to PacktLibrary, as shown in the following markup:

```
<Project Sdk="Microsoft.NET.Sdk">
  <PropertyGroup>
    <OutputType>Exe</OutputType>
    <TargetFramework>netcoreapp2.0</TargetFramework>
  </PropertyGroup>

  <ItemGroup>
```

```
    <ProjectReference Include="..\PacktLibrary\PacktLibrary.csproj" />
  </ItemGroup>

</Project>
```

In **Integrated Terminal**, note that you are in the `PeopleApp` folder, enter the `dotnet build` command, and note the output indicating that both projects have been built successfully, as shown in the following screenshot:

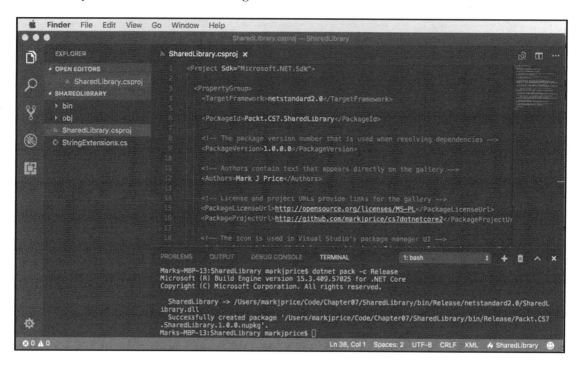

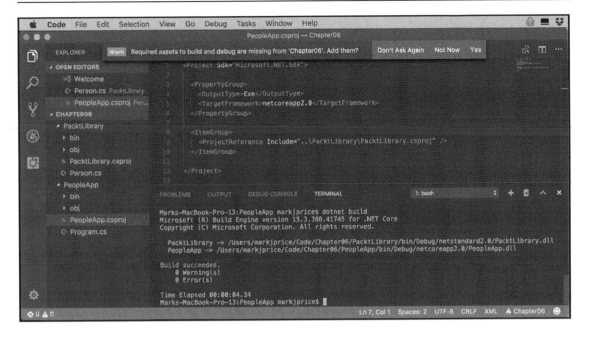

If prompted, click on **Yes** to add required assets.

Defining the classes

In either Visual Studio 2017 or Visual Studio Code, add statements to the Person class, as shown in the following code:

```
using System; using System.Collections.Generic; using static
System.Console; namespace Packt.CS7 { public partial class Person { //
fields public string Name; public DateTime DateOfBirth; public List<Person>
Children = new List<Person>(); // methods public void WriteToConsole() {
WriteLine($"{Name} was born on {DateOfBirth:dddd, d MMMM yyyy}"); } } }
```

Simplifying methods with operators

We might want two instances of a person to be able to procreate. We can implement this by writing methods. Instance methods are actions an object does to itself; static methods are actions the type does. Which you choose depends on what makes sense for the action.

Good Practice
Having both the static and instance methods to perform similar actions often makes sense. For example, `string` has both a `Compare` static method and a `CompareTo` instance method. This makes the functionality more visible to programmers using the type.

Implementing some functionality with a method

Add two methods to the `Person` class that will allow two `Person` objects to procreate, as shown in the following code:

```
// methods to "multiply"
public static Person Procreate(Person p1, Person p2)
{
    var baby = new Person
    {
        Name = $"Baby of {p1.Name} and {p2.Name}"
    };
    p1.Children.Add(baby);
    p2.Children.Add(baby);
    return baby;
}

public Person ProcreateWith(Person partner)
{
    return Procreate(this, partner);
}
```

Note the following:

- In the `static` method named `Procreate`, the `Person` objects to procreate are passed as parameters named p1 and p2
- A new `Person` class named `baby` is created with a name made of a combination of the two people who have procreated
- The `baby` object is added to the `Children` collection of both parents and then returned
- In the instance method named `ProcreateWith`, the `Person` object to procreate with is passed as a parameter named `partner`, and it along with `this` are passed to the static `Procreate` method

Good Practice

A method that creates a new object, or modified an existing object, should return that object so that the caller can see the results.

In the `PeopleApp` project, at the top of the `Program.cs` file, import the namespace for our class and statically import the `Console` type, as shown in the following code:

```
using System;
using Packt.CS7;
using static System.Console;
```

In the `Main` method, create three people and have them procreate, as shown in the following code:

```
var harry = new Person { Name = "Harry" };
var mary = new Person { Name = "Mary" };
var jill = new Person { Name = "Jill" };

// call instance method
var baby1 = mary.ProcreateWith(harry);

// call static method
var baby2 = Person.Procreate(harry, jill);

WriteLine($"{mary.Name} has {mary.Children.Count} children.");
WriteLine($"{harry.Name} has {harry.Children.Count} children.");
WriteLine($"{jill.Name} has {jill.Children.Count} children.");
WriteLine($"{mary.Name}'s first child is named
\"{mary.Children[0].Name}\".");
```

Run the console application and view the output:

```
Mary has 1 children.
Harry has 2 children.
Jill has 1 children.
Mary's first child is named "Baby of Harry and Mary".
```

Implementing some functionality with an operator

The `System.String` class has a static method named `Concat` that concatenates two `string` values, as shown in the following code:

```
string s1 = "Hello ";
string s2 = "World!";
string s3 = string.Concat(s1, s2);
WriteLine(s3); // => Hello World!
```

Calling a method like `Concat` works, but it might be more natural for a programmer to use the + symbol to *add* two `string` values together, as shown in the following code:

```
string s1 = "Hello ";
string s2 = "World!";
string s3 = s1 + s2;
WriteLine(s3); // => Hello World!
```

A well-known phrase is *Go forth and multiply*, meaning to procreate. So let's write code so that the * (multiply) symbol will allow two `Person` objects to procreate.

We do this by defining a `static` operator for a symbol like *. The syntax is rather like a method, because in effect, an operator is a method, but using a symbol instead of a method name.

 The list of symbols that your types can use as operators are listed at this link:
https://docs.microsoft.com/en-us/dotnet/csharp/programming-guide/statements-expressions-operators/overloadable-operators

In the `PacktLibrary` project, in the `Person` class, create a `static` operator for the * symbol, as shown in the following code:

```
// operator to "multiply"
public static Person operator *(Person p1, Person p2)
{
    return Person.Procreate(p1, p2);
}
```

Good Practice

Unlike methods, operators do not appear in IntelliSense lists for a type. For every operator you define, make a method as well, because it may not be obvious to a programmer that the operator is available. The implementation of the operator can then call the method, reusing the code you have written. A second reason for providing a method is that operators can be slower than method calls. If performance is a priority, then a programmer can call your method at the cost of readability.

In the `Main` method, after calling the static `Procreate` method, use the `*` operator to make another baby, as shown in the following highlighted code:

```
// call static method
var baby2 = Person.Procreate(harry, jill);
// call an operator
var baby3 = harry * mary;
```

Run the application and view the output:

```
Mary has 2 children.
Harry has 3 children.
Jill has 1 children.
Mary's first child is named "Baby of Harry and Mary".
```

Defining local functions

A language feature introduced in C# 7 is the ability to define a local function. Local functions are the method equivalent to local variables. In other words, they are methods that are only visible and callable from within the containing method in which they have been defined. In other languages, they are sometimes called **nested** or **inner** functions.

We will use a local function to implement a factorial calculation.

Add the following code to the `Person` class:

```
// method with a local function
public static int Factorial(int number)
{
    if (number < 0)
    {
        throw new ArgumentException(
            $"{nameof(number)} cannot be less than zero.");
    }
    return localFactorial(number);

    int localFactorial(int localNumber)
    {
        if (localNumber < 1) return 1;
        return localNumber * localFactorial(localNumber - 1);
    }
}
```

 Local functions can be defined anywhere inside a method: the top, the bottom, or even somewhere in the middle!

In the `Program.cs` file, in the `Main` method, add the following statement:

```
WriteLine($"5! is {Person.Factorial(5)}");
```

Run the console application and view the output:

```
5! is 120
```

Raising and handling events

Methods are often described as *actions that an object can do*. For example, a `List` class can add an item to itself or clear itself.

Events are often described as *actions that happen to an object*. For example, in a user interface, `Button` has a `Click` event, click being something that happens to a button.

Another way of thinking of events is that they provide a way of exchanging messages between two objects.

Calling methods using delegates

You have already seen the most common way to call or execute a method: use the **dot** syntax to access the method using its name. For example, `Console.WriteLine` tells the `Console` type to write out the message to the console window or Terminal.

The other way to call or execute a method is to use a **delegate**. If you have used languages that support function pointers, then think of a delegate as being a type-safe method pointer. In other words, a delegate is the memory address of a method that matches the same signature as the delegate so that it can be safely called.

For example, imagine there is a method that must have a `string` datatype passed as its only parameter and it returns an `int` datatype:

```
public int MethodIWantToCall(string input)
{
    return input.Length; // it doesn't matter what this does
}
```

I can call this method directly like this:

```
int answer = p1.MethodIWantToCall("Frog");
```

Alternatively, I can define a delegate with a matching signature to call the method indirectly. Notice that the names of the parameters do not have to match. Only the types of parameters and return values must match:

```
delegate int DelegateWithMatchingSignature(string s);
```

Now, I can create an instance of the delegate, point it at the method, and finally, call the delegate (which calls the method!), as shown here:

```
var d = new DelegateWithMatchingSignature(p1.MethodIWantToCall);
int answer2 = d("Frog");
```

You are probably thinking, "What's the point of that?" Well, it provides flexibility.

We could use delegates to create a queue of methods that need to be called in order. Delegates have built-in support for asynchronous operations that run on a different thread for better performance. Most importantly, delegates allow us to create events.

Delegates and events are one of the most advanced features of C# and can take a few attempts to understand, so don't worry if you feel lost!

Defining events

Microsoft has two predefined delegates for use as events. They look like this:

```
public delegate void EventHandler(object sender, EventArgs e);
public delegate void EventHandler<TEventArgs>(object sender, TEventArgs e);
```

Good Practice
When you want to define an event in your own type, you should use one of these two predefined delegates.

Add the following code to the `Person` class. The code defines an event named `Shout`. It also defines a field to store `AngerLevel` and a method named `Poke`. Each time a person is poked, their anger level increments. Once their anger level reaches three, they raise the `Shout` event, but only if the event delegate is pointing at a method defined somewhere else in code, that is, not null:

```
// event
public event EventHandler Shout;

// field
public int AngerLevel;

// method
public void Poke()
{
    AngerLevel++;
    if (AngerLevel >= 3)
    {
        // if something is listening...
        if (Shout != null)
        {
            // ...then raise the event
            Shout(this, EventArgs.Empty);
```

```
        }
    }
}
```

 Checking if an object is null before calling one of its methods is very common. C# allows these statements to be simplified like this:
`Shout?.Invoke(this, EventArgs.Empty);`

Using Visual Studio 2017

In Visual Studio 2017, in the `Main` method, start typing the following code to assign an event handler:

```
harry.Shout +=
```

Notice the IntelliSense that appears when you enter the += operator, as shown in the following screenshot:

Press *Tab*. You will see a preview of what Visual Studio 2017 would like to do for you.

Press *Enter* to accept the name of the method.

Visual Studio 2017 inserts a method that correctly matches the signature of the event delegate. This method will be called when the event is raised.

Scroll down to find the method Visual Studio 2017 created for you, and delete the statement that throws `NotImplementedException`.

Using Visual Studio Code

In Visual Studio Code, you must write the method and assign its name yourself. The name can be anything, but `Harry_Shout` is sensible.

In the `Program` class, add a method, as shown in the following code:

```
private static void Harry_Shout(object sender, System.EventArgs e)
{
}
```

In the `Main` method, add the following statement to assign the method to the event:

```
harry.Shout += Harry_Shout;
```

Using Visual Studio 2017 or Visual Studio Code

Add statements to the `Harry_Shout` method to get a reference to the `Person` object and output some information about them, as shown in the following code:

```
private static void Harry_Shout(object sender, EventArgs e)
{
    Person p = (Person)sender;
    WriteLine($"{p.Name} is this angry: {p.AngerLevel}.");
}
```

Back in the `Main` method, add the following statements to call the `Poke` method four times, after assigning the method to the `Shout` event:

```
harry.Shout += Harry_Shout;
harry.Poke();
harry.Poke();
harry.Poke();
harry.Poke();
```

Run the application and view the output. Note that Harry only gets angry enough to shout once he's been poked at least three times:

```
Harry is this angry: 3.
Harry is this angry: 4.
```

> You can define your own custom `EventArgs`-derived types so that you can pass additional information into an event handler method. You can read more at the following link:
> https://docs.microsoft.com/en-us/dotnet/standard/events/how-to-raise-and-consume-events

Implementing interfaces

Interfaces are a way of connecting different types together to make new things. Think of them like the studs on top of LEGO™ bricks that allow them to "stick" together, or electrical standards for plugs and sockets.

If a type implements an interface, then it is making a promise to the rest of .NET that it supports a certain feature.

Common interfaces

Here are some common interfaces that your types might want to implement:

Interface	Method(s)	Description
`IComparable`	`CompareTo` (other)	This defines a comparison method that a type implements to order or sort its instances.
`IComparer`	`Compare` (first, second)	This defines a comparison method that a secondary type implements to order or sort instances of a primary type.
`IDisposable`	`Dispose ()`	This defines a disposal method to release unmanaged resources more efficiently than waiting for a finalizer.
`IFormattable`	`ToString` (format, culture)	This defines a culture-aware method to format the value of an object into a string representation.
`IFormatter`	`Serialize` (stream, object), `Deserialize` (stream)	This defines methods to convert an object to and from a stream of bytes for storage or transfer.
`IFormatProvider`	`GetFormat` (Type)	This defines a method to format inputs based on a language and region.

Comparing objects when sorting

One of the most common interfaces that you will want to implement is `IComparable`. It allows arrays and collections of your type to be sorted.

Attempting to sort objects without a method to compare

Add the following code to the `Main` method, which creates an array of the `Person` instances, outputs the array, attempts to sort it, and then outputs the sorted array:

```
Person[] people =
{
    new Person { Name = "Simon" },
    new Person { Name = "Jenny" },
    new Person { Name = "Adam" },
    new Person { Name = "Richard" }
};

WriteLine("Initial list of people:");
foreach (var person in people)
{
    WriteLine($"{person.Name}");
}

WriteLine("Use Person's IComparable implementation to sort:");
Array.Sort(people);
foreach (var person in people)
{
    WriteLine($"{person.Name}");
}
```

Run the application, and you will see this runtime error:

```
Unhandled Exception: System.InvalidOperationException: Failed to compare
two elements in the array. ---> System.ArgumentException: At least one
object must implement IComparable.
```

As the error explains, to fix the problem, our type must implement `IComparable`.

Defining a method to compare

In the `PacktLibrary` project, in the `Person` class, after the class name, add a colon and enter `IComparable<Person>`, as shown in the following code:

```
public partial class Person : IComparable<Person>
```

Visual Studio 2017 and Visual Studio Code will draw a red squiggle under the new code to warn you that you have not yet implemented the method you have promised to.

Visual Studio 2017 and Visual Studio Code can write the skeleton implementation for you if you click on the light bulb and choose the **Implement interface** option, as shown in the following screenshot:

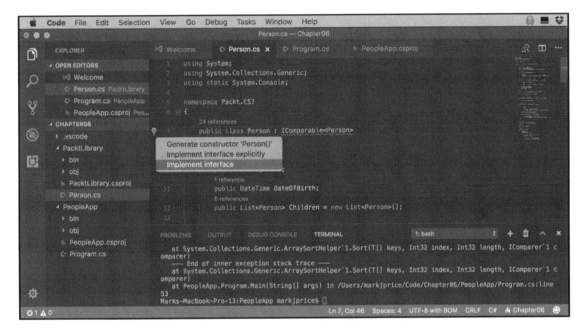

Interfaces can be implemented implicitly and explicitly. Implicit implementations are simpler. Explicit implementations are only necessary if a type must have multiple methods with the same name. For example, both `IGamePlayer` and `IKeyHolder` might have a method called `Lose`. In a type that must implement both interfaces, only one implementation of `Lose` can be the implicit method. The other `Lose` method would have to be implemented, and called, explicitly. You can read more at the following link:

https://docs.microsoft.com/en-us/dotnet/csharp/programming-guide/interfaces/explicit-interface-implementation

Scroll down to find the method that was written for you and delete the statement that throws the `NotImplementedException` error. Add a statement to call the `CompareTo` method of the `Name` field, which uses the `string` type's implementation of `CompareTo`, as shown in the following code:

```
public int CompareTo(Person other)
{
    return Name.CompareTo(other.Name);
}
```

We have chosen to compare two `Person` instances by comparing their `Name` fields. People will, therefore, be sorted alphabetically by their name.

Run the application. This time, it works:

```
Initial list of people:
Simon
Jenny
Adam
Richard
Use Person's IComparable implementation to sort:
Adam
Jenny
Richard
Simon
```

Defining a separate comparer

Sometimes, you won't have access to the source code for a type, and it might not implement the `IComparable` interface. Luckily, there is another way to sort instances of a type. You can create a secondary type that implements a slightly different interface, named `IComparer`.

In the `PacktLibrary` project, add a new class named `PersonComparer` that implements the `IComparer` interface, as shown in the following block of code. It will compare two people by comparing the length of their `Name` field, or if the names are the same length, then by comparing the names alphabetically:

```
using System.Collections.Generic;

namespace Packt.CS7
{
    public class PersonComparer : IComparer<Person>
    {
        public int Compare(Person x, Person y)
        {
            // Compare the Name lengths...
            int temp = x.Name.Length.CompareTo(y.Name.Length);

            /// ...if they are equal...
            if (temp == 0)
            {
                // ...then sort by the Names...
                return x.Name.CompareTo(y.Name);
            }
            else
            {
                // ...otherwise sort by the lengths.
                return temp;
            }
        }
    }
}
```

In `PeopleApp`, in the `Program` class, in the `Main` method, add the following code:

```
WriteLine("Use PersonComparer's IComparer implementation to sort:");
Array.Sort(people, new PersonComparer());
foreach (var person in people)
{
    WriteLine($"{person.Name}");
}
```

Run the application and view the output.

This time, when we sort the people array, we explicitly ask the sorting algorithm to use the PersonComparer type instead, so that the people are sorted with the shortest names first, and when the lengths of two or more names are equal, to sort them alphabetically:

```
Use Person's IComparable implementation to sort:
Adam
Jenny
Richard
Simon
Use PersonComparer's IComparer implementation to sort:
Adam
Jenny
Simon
Richard
```

Good Practice

If anyone would want to sort an array or collection of instances of your type, then implement the IComparable interface.

Making types more reusable with generics

In 2005, with C# and .NET Framework 2.0, Microsoft introduced a feature named **generics** that enables your types to be more reusable, by allowing a programmer to pass types as parameters similar to how you can pass objects as parameters.

Making a generic type

First, let's see an example of a non-generic type, so that you can understand the problem that generics is designed to solve.

In the PacktLibrary project, add a new class named Thing, as shown in the following code, and note the following:

- Thing has a field named Data of the object type
- Thing has a method named Process that accepts an input parameter of the string type, and returns a string value

If we wanted the `Thing` type to be flexible in .NET Framework 1.0, we would have to use the `object` type for the field.

```csharp
using System;

namespace Packt.CS7
{
    public class Thing
    {
        public object Data = default(object);

        public string Process(string input)
        {
            if (Data == input)
            {
                return Data.ToString() + Data.ToString();
            }
            else
            {
                return Data.ToString();
            }
        }
    }
}
```

In the `PeopleApp` project, add some statements to the end of `Main`, as shown in the following code:

```csharp
var t = new Thing();
t.Data = 42;
WriteLine($"Thing: {t.Process("42")}");
```

Run the console application and view the output, and note the warning:

```
Thing.cs(11,17): warning CS0252: Possible unintended reference comparison;
to get a value comparison, cast the left hand side to type 'string'
[/Users/markjprice/Code/Chapter06/PacktLibrary/PacktLibrary.csproj]
```

`Thing` is currently flexible, because any type can be set for the `Data` field. But there is no type checking, so inside the `Process`, method we cannot safely do much beyond calling `ToString`.

In the `PacktLibrary` project, add a new class named `GenericThing`, as shown in the following code:

```
using System;

namespace Packt.CS7
{
    public class GenericThing<T> where T : IComparable, IFormattable
    {
        public T Data = default(T);

        public string Process(string input)
        {
            if (Data.ToString().CompareTo(input) == 0)
            {
                return Data.ToString() + Data.ToString();
            }
            else
            {
                return Data.ToString();
            }
        }
    }
}
```

Note the following:

- `GenericThing` has a generic type parameter named `T`, that can be any type that implements `IComparable` and `IFormattable`, so it must have methods named `CompareTo` and `ToString`. By convention, use the type parameter name `T` if there is only one type parameter
- `GenericThing` has a field named `Data` of the `T` type
- `GenericThing` has a method named `Process` that accepts an input parameter of the `string` type, and returns a value of the `string` type

In the `PeopleApp` project, add some statements to the end of `Main`, as shown in the following code, and note the following:

- When instantiating an instance of a generic type, the developer must pass a type parameter. In this example, we pass `int` as the type, so wherever `T` appears in the `GenericThing` class, it is replaced with `int`.

- When setting the `Data` field, we must use an `int` value, like 42:

```
var gt = new GenericThing<int>();
gt.Data = 42;
WriteLine($"GenericThing: {gt.Process("42")}");
```

Run the console application and view the output, and note the logic of the `Process` method correctly works for `GenericThing`, but not `Thing`:

```
Thing: 42
GenericThing: 4242
```

Making a generic method

Generics can be used for methods, even inside a non-generic type.

In `PacktLibrary`, add a new class named `Squarer`, with a generic method named `Square`, as shown in the following code:

```
using System;
using System.Threading;

namespace Packt.CS7
{
    public static class Squarer
    {
        public static double Square<T>(T input)
        where T : IConvertible
        {
            double d = input.ToDouble(
            Thread.CurrentThread.CurrentCulture);
            return d * d;
        }
    }
}
```

Note the following:

- The static `Squarer` class is non-generic.
- The static `Square` method is generic, and its type parameter `T` must implement `IConvertible`, so we know it has a `ToDouble` method. `T` is used as the type for the `input` parameter.

- `ToDouble` requires a parameter that implements `IFormatProvider` for understanding the format of numbers for a language and region. We can pass the `CurrentCulture` property of the current thread to specify the language and region used by your computer. You will learn about cultures in Chapter 6, *Using Common .NET Standard Types*.
- The return value is the input value multiplied by itself.

In `PeopleApp`, in the `Program` class, at the bottom of the `Main` method, add the following code. Note that when calling a generic method, you can specify the type parameter to make it clearer, although the compiler can usually work it out without you telling it the type:

```
string number1 = "4";
WriteLine($"{number1} squared is {Squarer.Square<string>(number1)}");

byte number2 = 3;
WriteLine($"{number2} squared is {Squarer.Square<byte>(number2)}");
```

Run the console application and view the output:

```
4 squared is 16
3 squared is 9
```

Managing memory with reference and value types

There are two categories of memory: **stack** memory and **heap** memory. Stack memory is fast but limited, and heap memory is slow but plentiful.

There are two C# keywords that you can use to create object types: `class` and `struct`. Both can have the same members. The difference between the two is how memory is allocated.

When you define a type using class, you are defining a reference type. This means that the memory for the object itself is allocated on the heap, and only the memory address of the object (and a little overhead) is stored on the stack.

When you define a type using `struct`, you are defining a value type. This means that the memory for the object itself is allocated on the stack.

If a `struct` uses types that are not of the `struct` type for any of its fields, then those fields will be stored on the heap!

These are the most common `struct` types in .NET Core:

- **Numbers**: `byte`, `sbyte`, `short`, `ushort`, `int`, `uint`, `long`, `ulong`, `float`, `double`, and `decimal`
- **Miscellaneous**: `char` and `bool`
- **System.Drawing**: `Color`, `Point`, and `Rectangle`

Almost all the other types in .NET Core are the `class` types, including `string`.

 You cannot inherit from `struct`.

Defining a struct type

Add a class file named `DisplacementVector.cs` to the `PacktLibrary` project.

 There isn't an item template in Visual Studio 2017 for `struct`, so you must use `class` and then change it manually.

Modify the file, as shown in the following code, and note the following:

- The type is a `struct` value type instead of a `class` reference type
- It has two fields of type `int`, named `X` and `Y`
- It has a constructor for setting initial values for `X` and `Y`
- It has an operator for adding two instances together that returns a new instance with `X` added to `X`, and `Y` added to `Y`

```
namespace Packt.CS7
{
    public struct DisplacementVector
    {
        public int X;
        public int Y;
```

```
public DisplacementVector(int initialX, int initialY)
{
    X = initialX;
    Y = initialY;
}

public static DisplacementVector operator
    +(DisplacementVector vector1, DisplacementVector vector2)
{
    return new DisplacementVector(
      vector1.X + vector2.X,vector1.Y + vector2.Y);
}
    }
}
```

In the `PeopleApp` project, in the `Program` class, in the `Main` method, add the following code to create two new instances of `DisplacementVector`, add them together, and output the result:

```
var dv1 = new DisplacementVector(3, 5);
var dv2 = new DisplacementVector(-2, 7);
var dv3 = dv1 + dv2;
WriteLine($"({dv1.X}, {dv1.Y}) + ({dv2.X}, {dv2.Y}) = ({dv3.X},{dv3.Y})");
```

Run the application and view the output:

```
(3, 5) + (-2, 7) = (1, 12)
```

Good Practice

If all the fields in your type use 16 bytes or less of stack memory, your type only uses the `struct` types for its fields, and you will never want to derive from your type, then Microsoft recommends that you use a `struct` type. If your type uses more than 16 bytes of stack memory, or if it uses class types for its fields, or if you might want to inherit from it, then use `class`.

Releasing unmanaged resources

In the previous chapter, we saw that constructors can be used to initialize fields and that a type may have multiple constructors.

Imagine that a constructor allocates an unmanaged resource, that is, anything that is not controlled by .NET. The unmanaged resource must be manually released because .NET cannot do it for us.

For this topic, I will show some code examples, but you do not need to create them in your current project.

Each type can have a single **finalizer** (aka destructor) that will be called by the CLR when the resources need to be released. A finalizer has the same name as a constructor, that is, the type name, but it is prefixed with a tilde (~), as shown in the following example:

```
public class Animal
{
    public Animal()
    {
        // allocate an unmanaged resource
    }
    ~Animal() // Finalizer aka destructor
    {
        // deallocate the unmanaged resource
    }
}
```

Do not confuse a finalizer (aka **destructor**) with a **deconstructor**. A destructor releases resources, that is, it destroys an object. A deconstructor returns an object split up into its constituent parts and uses the new C# 7 deconstruction syntax.

This is the minimum you should do in this scenario. The problem with just providing a finalizer is that the .NET garbage collector requires two garbage collections to completely release the allocated resources for this type.

Though optional, it is recommended to also provide a method to allow a developer who uses your type to explicitly release resources so that the garbage collector can then release the object in a single collection.

There is a standard mechanism to do this in .NET by implementing the `IDisposable` interface, as shown in the following example:

```
public class Animal : IDisposable
{
    public Animal()
    {
        // allocate unmanaged resource
    }

    ~Animal() // Finalizer
    {
        if(disposed) return;
        Dispose(false);
    }

    bool disposed = false; // have resources been released?

    public void Dispose()
    {
        Dispose(true);
        GC.SuppressFinalize(this);
    }

    protected virtual void Dispose(bool disposing)
    {
        if (disposed) return;
        // deallocate the *unmanaged* resource
        // ...
        if (disposing)
        {
            // deallocate any other *managed* resources
            // ...
        }
        disposed = true;
    }
}
```

There are two `Dispose` methods. The `public` method will be called by a developer using your type. The `Dispose` method with a `bool` parameter is used internally to implement the deallocation of resources, both unmanaged and managed. When the public `Dispose` method is called, both unmanaged and managed resources need to be deallocated, but when the finalizer runs, only unmanaged resources need to be deallocated.

Also, note the call to GC.SuppressFinalize(this) is what notifies the garbage collector that it no longer needs to run the finalizer, and removes the need for a second collection.

Ensuring that dispose is called

When someone uses a type that implements IDisposable, they can ensure that the public Dispose method is called with the using statement, as shown in the following code:

```
using(Animal a = new Animal())
{
    // code that uses the Animal instance
}
```

The compiler converts your code into something like the following, which guarantees that even if an exception occurs, the Dispose method will still be called:

```
Animal a = new Animal();
try
{
    // code that uses the Animal instance
}
finally
{
    if (a != null) a.Dispose();
}
```

> You will see practical examples of releasing unmanaged resources with IDisposable, the using statements, and the try...finally blocks in Chapter 7, *Working with Files, Streams, and Serialization*.

Inheriting from classes

The Person type we created earlier is implicitly derived (inherited) from System.Object. Now, we will create a new class that inherits from Person.

Add a new class named Employee.cs to the PacktLibrary project.

Modify its code as shown in the following code:

```
using System;

namespace Packt.CS7
{
    public class Employee : Person
    {
    }
}
```

Add statements to the Main method to create an instance of the Employee class:

```
Employee e1 = new Employee
{
    Name = "John Jones",
    DateOfBirth = new DateTime(1990, 7, 28)
};
e1.WriteToConsole();
```

Run the console application and view the output:

John Jones was born on Saturday, 28 July 1990

Note that the Employee class has inherited all the members of Person.

Extending classes

Now, we will add some employee-specific members to extend the class.

In the Employee class, add the following code to define two properties:

```
public string EmployeeCode { get; set; }
public DateTime HireDate { get; set; }
```

Back in the Main method, add the following code:

```
e1.EmployeeCode = "JJ001";
e1.HireDate = new DateTime(2014, 11, 23);
WriteLine($"{e1.Name} was hired on {e1.HireDate:dd/MM/yy}");
```

Run the console application and view the output:

```
John Jones was hired on 23/11/14
```

Hiding members

So far, the `WriteToConsole` method is being inherited from `Person`, and it only outputs the employee's name and date of birth. We might want to change what this method does for an employee.

In the `Employee` class, add the following highlighted code to redefine the `WriteToConsole` method:

 Note that you will need to statically import `System.Console`.

```
using System;
using static System.Console;

namespace Packt.CS7
{
    public class Employee : Person
    {
        public string EmployeeCode { get; set; }
        public DateTime HireDate { get; set; }

        public void WriteToConsole()
        {
            WriteLine($"{Name}'s birth date is {DateOfBirth:dd/MM/yy} and hire
date was {HireDate:dd/MM/yy}");
        }
    }
}
```

Run the application and view the output:

```
John Jones's birth date is 28/07/90 and hire date was 01/01/01
John Jones was hired on 23/11/14
```

Both Visual Studio 2017 and Visual Studio Code warn you that your method now hides the method with the same name that you inherited from the Person class by drawing a green squiggle under the method name, as shown in the following screenshot:

```
2 references
public class Employee : Person
{
    1 reference
    public strin    'Employee.WriteToConsole()' hides inherited member 'Person.WriteToC
    3 references    onsole()'. Use the new keyword if hiding was intended. [Ch07_PacktL
    public DateT    ibrary]

    1 reference     void Employee.WriteToConsole()
    public void WriteToConsole()
    {
        WriteLine($"{Name}'s birth date is {DateOfBirth:dd/MM/yy} and hire date was {H:
    }
}
```

You can remove this warning by applying the new keyword to the method, to indicate that you are deliberately replacing the old method, as shown in the following code:

```
public new void WriteToConsole()
```

Overriding members

Rather than hiding a method, it is usually better to override it. You can only override members if the base class chooses to allow overriding, by applying the virtual keyword.

In the Main method, add the following statement:

```
WriteLine(e1.ToString());
```

Run the application. The ToString method is inherited from System.Object. The implementation outputs the namespace and type name, as follows:

```
Packt.CS7.Employee
```

Let's override this behavior for the Person class.

Make this change to the `Person` class, not the `Employee` class.

Using Visual Studio 2017

In Visual Studio 2017, open the `Person.cs` file, and at the bottom (but inside the class brackets), type the keyword `override` and enter a space after the word. You will see that Visual Studio shows a list of methods that have been marked as `virtual` so that they can be overridden, as shown in the following screenshot:

Use the arrow keys on your keyboard to choose `ToString` and then press *Enter*.

Using Visual Studio 2017 or Visual Studio Code

In Visual Studio 2017, add a `return` statement to the method, or in Visual Studio Code, write the whole method, as shown in the following code:

```
// overridden methods
public override string ToString()
{
    return $"{Name} is a {base.ToString()}";
}
```

Run the console application and view the output. Now, when the `ToString` method is called, it outputs the person's name, as well as the base classes implementation of `ToString`, as shown in the following output:

```
John Jones is a Packt.CS7.Employee
```

Good Practice
Many real-world APIs, for example, Microsoft's Entity Framework Core, Castle's DynamicProxy, and Episerver's content models, require the properties that you define in your classes to be marked as `virtual`. Unless you have a good reason, mark your method and property members as `virtual`.

Preventing inheritance and overriding

You can prevent someone from inheriting from your class by applying the `sealed` keyword to its definition. No one can inherit from Scrooge McDuck:

```
public sealed class ScroogeMcDuck
{
}
```

An example of `sealed` in the real world is the `string` class. Microsoft has implemented some extreme optimizations inside the `string` class that could be negatively affected by your inheritance; so, Microsoft prevents that.

You can prevent someone from overriding a method in your class by applying the `sealed` keyword to the method. No one can change the way Lady Gaga sings:

```
public class LadyGaga
{
    public sealed void Sing()
    {
    }
}
```

Polymorphism

You have now seen two ways to change the behavior of an inherited method. We can hide it using `new` (known as **non polymorphic inheritance**), or we can override it (**polymorphic inheritance**).

Both ways can call the base class using the `base` keyword, so what is the difference?

It all depends on the type of the variable holding a reference to the object. For example, a variable of the `Person` type can hold a reference to a `Person` class, *or any type that derives* from `Person`.

In the `Employee` class, add the following code:

```
public override string ToString()
{
    return $"{Name}'s code is {EmployeeCode}";
}
```

In the `Main` method, write the following code:

```
Employee aliceInEmployee = new Employee { Name = "Alice", EmployeeCode =
"AA123" };
Person aliceInPerson = aliceInEmployee;
aliceInEmployee.WriteToConsole();
aliceInPerson.WriteToConsole();
WriteLine(aliceInEmployee.ToString());
WriteLine(aliceInPerson.ToString());
```

Run the console application and view the output:

```
Alice's birth date is 01/01/01 and hire date was 01/01/01
Alice was born on Monday, 1 January 0001
Alice's code is AA123
Alice's code is AA123
```

Note that when a method is hidden with `new`, the compiler is not smart enough to know that the object is an employee, so it calls the `WriteToConsole` method in `Person`.

When a method is overridden with `virtual` and `override`, the compiler is smart enough to know that although the variable is declared as a `Person` class, the object itself is an `Employee` class and, therefore, the `Employee` implementation of `ToString` is called.

The access modifiers and the affect they have is summarized in the following table:

Variable type	Access modifier	Method executed	In class
Person		WriteToConsole	Person
Employee	new	WriteToConsole	Employee
Person	virtual	ToString	Employee
Employee	override	ToString	Employee

Polymorphism is literally academic to most programmers. If you get the concept, that's fine; but, if not, I suggest that you don't worry about it. Some people like to make others feel inferior by saying understanding polymorphism is important, but IMHO it's not. You can have a successful career with C# and never need to be able to explain polymorphism, just as a racing car driver doesn't need to be able to explain the engineering behind fuel injection.

Casting within inheritance hierarchies

Casting is subtly different from converting between types.

Implicit casting

In the previous example, you saw how an instance of a derived type can be stored in a variable of its base type (or its base's base type, and so on). When we do this, it is called **implicit casting**.

Explicit casting

Going the other way is an explicit cast, and you must use parentheses to do it.

In the `Main` method, add the following code:

```
Employee e2 = aliceInPerson;
```

Visual Studio 2017 and Visual Studio Code display a red squiggle and a compile error in the **Error List** and **Problems** windows, as shown in the following screenshot:

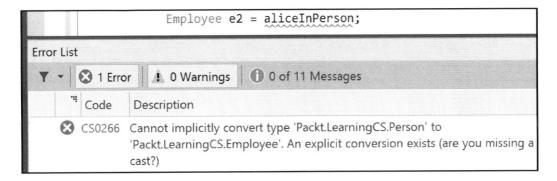

Change the code as follows:

```
Employee e2 = (Employee)aliceInPerson;
```

Handling casting exceptions

The compiler is now happy; *but*, because `aliceInPerson` might be a different derived type, like `Student` instead of `Employee`, we need to be careful. This statement might throw an `InvalidCastException` error.

We can handle this by writing a `try` statement, but there is a better way. We can check the current type of the object using the `is` keyword.

Wrap the explicit cast statement in an `if` statement, as follows:

```
if (aliceInPerson is Employee)
{
    WriteLine($"{nameof(aliceInPerson)} IS an Employee");
    Employee e2 = (Employee)aliceInPerson;
    // do something with e2
}
```

Run the console application and view the output:

```
aliceInPerson IS an Employee
```

Alternatively, you can use the `as` keyword to cast. Instead of throwing an exception, the `as` keyword returns `null` if the type cannot be cast.

Add the following statements to the end of the `Main` method:

```
Employee e3 = aliceInPerson as Employee;
if (e3 != null)
{
    WriteLine($"{nameof(aliceInPerson)} AS an Employee");
    // do something with e3
}
```

Since accessing a `null` variable can throw a `NullReferenceException` error, you should always check for `null` before using the result.

Run the console application and view the output:

```
aliceInPerson AS an Employee
```

Good Practice
Use the `is` and `as` keywords to avoid throwing exceptions when casting between derived types.

Inheriting and extending .NET types

.NET has prebuilt class libraries containing hundreds of thousands of types. Rather than creating your own completely new types, you can often start by inheriting from one of Microsoft's.

Inheriting from an exception

In the `PacktLibrary` project, add a new class named `PersonException`, as shown in the following code:

```
using System;

namespace Packt.CS7
{
    public class PersonException : Exception
    {
        public PersonException() : base() { }
        public PersonException(string message) : base(message) { }
```

```
    public PersonException(string message, Exception innerException) :
    base(message, innerException) { }
  }
}
```

 Unlike ordinary methods, constructors are not inherited, so we must explicitly declare and explicitly call the base constructor implementations in System.Exception to make them available to programmers who might want to use those constructors in our custom exception.

In the Person class, add the following method:

```
public void TimeTravel(DateTime when)
{
    if (when <= DateOfBirth)
    {
        throw new PersonException("If you travel back in time to a
        date earlier than your own birth then the universe will
        explode!");
    }
    else
    {
        WriteLine($"Welcome to {when:yyyy}!");
    }
}
```

In the Main method, add the following statements to test what happens when we try to time travel too far back:

```
try
{
    e1.TimeTravel(new DateTime(1999, 12, 31));
    e1.TimeTravel(new DateTime(1950, 12, 25));
}
catch (PersonException ex)
{
    WriteLine(ex.Message);
}
```

Run the console application and view the output:

Welcome to 1999!
If you travel back in time to a date earlier than your own birth then the universe will explode!

Good Practice
When defining your own exceptions, give them the same three constructors.

Extending types when you can't inherit

Earlier, we saw how the `sealed` modifier can be used to prevent inheritance.

Microsoft has applied the `sealed` keyword to the `System.String` class so that no one can inherit and potentially break the behavior of strings.

Can we still add new methods to strings? Yes, if we use a language feature named **extension methods**, which was introduced with C# 3.

Using static methods to reuse functionality

Since the first version of C#, we could create the `static` methods to reuse functionality, such as the ability to validate that a string contains an email address.

In the `PacktLibrary` project, add a new class named `StringExtensions.cs`, as shown in the following code, and note the following:

- The class imports a namespace for handling regular expressions
- The `IsValidEmail` static method uses the `Regex` type to check for matches against a simple email pattern that looks for valid characters before and after the @ symbol

You will learn about regular expressions in Chapter 6, *Using Common .NET Standard Types*.

```
using System.Text.RegularExpressions;

namespace Packt.CS7
{
    public class StringExtensions
    {
        public static bool IsValidEmail(string input)
        {
            // use simple regular expression to check
```

```
            // that the input string is a valid email
            return Regex.IsMatch(input, @"[a-zA-Z0-9\.-_]+@[a-zA-Z0-9\.-_]+");
        }
    }
}
```

Add the following statements to the bottom of the `Main` method to validate two examples of email addresses:

```
string email1 = "pamela@test.com";
string email2 = "ian&test.com";

WriteLine($"{email1} is a valid e-mail address:
{StringExtensions.IsValidEmail(email1)}.");
WriteLine($"{email2} is a valid e-mail address:
{StringExtensions.IsValidEmail(email2)}.");
```

Run the application and view the output:

```
pamela@test.com is a valid e-mail address: True.
ian&test.com is a valid e-mail address: False.
```

This works, but extension methods can reduce the amount of code we must type and simplify the usage of this function.

Using extension methods to reuse functionality

In the `StringExtensions` class, add the `static` modifier before the class, and add the `this` modifier before the `string` type, as highlighted in the following code:

```
public static class StringExtensions
{
    public static bool IsValidEmail(this string input)
    {
```

These two changes inform the compiler that it should treat the method as a method that extends the `string` type.

Back in the `Program` class, add some new statements to use the extension method for strings:

```
WriteLine($"{email1} is a valid e-mail address:{email1.IsValidEmail()}.");
WriteLine($"{email2} is a valid e-mail address:{email2.IsValidEmail()}.");
```

Note the subtle change in the syntax. The `IsValidEmail` method now appears to be an instance member of the `string` type, as shown in the following screenshot:

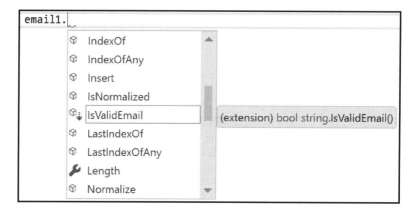

 Extension methods cannot replace or override existing instance methods, so you cannot, for example, redefine the `Insert` method of a `string` variable. The extension method will appear as an overload, but the instance method will be called in preference to the extension method with the same name and signature.

Summary

In this chapter, you learned about delegates and events, implementing interfaces, generics, and deriving types using inheritance and OOP. You also learned about base and derived classes, how to override a type member, use polymorphism, and cast between types.

In the next part, you will learn about .NET Core 2.1 and .NET Standard 2.0, and the types that they provide you with to implement common functionality such as file handling, database access, encryption, and multitasking.

5
Understanding and Packaging .NET Standard Types

This chapter is about .NET Core 2.0 and how it implements the types that are defined in .NET Standard 2.0. You will learn how C# keywords are related to .NET types, and about the relationship between namespaces and assemblies. You will learn how to package and publish your .NET Core apps and libraries for use cross-platform, how to use existing .NET Framework libraries in .NET Standard libraries, and the possibility of porting .NET Framework code bases to .NET Core.

This chapter covers the following topics:

- Understanding assemblies and namespaces
- Sharing code cross-platform with .NET Standard class libraries
- Understanding NuGet packages
- Publishing your applications for deployment
- Packaging your libraries for NuGet distribution
- Porting from .NET Framework to .NET Core

Understanding assemblies and namespaces

.NET Core is made up of several pieces, which are as follows:

- **Language compilers**: These turn your source code (written with languages such as C#, F#, and Visual Basic) into **intermediate language (IL)** code stored in assemblies (applications and class libraries). C# 6 introduced a completely rewritten compiler known as Roslyn.
- **Common Language Runtime (CoreCLR)**: The runtime loads assemblies, compiles the IL code stored in them into native code instructions for your computer's CPU, and executes the code within an environment that manages resources such as threads and memory.
- **Base Class Libraries (BCL) and NuGet packages (CoreFX)**: These are prebuilt assemblies of types for performing common tasks when building applications. You can use them to quickly build anything you want, rather like combining LEGO™ pieces. .NET Core 2.0 is based on .NET Standard 2.0, which is a superset of all previous versions of .NET Standard, and lifts .NET Core up to parity with the modern parts of .NET Framework and Xamarin.

Base Class Libraries and CoreFX

.NET Framework's BCL and .NET Core's CoreFX are libraries of prebuilt code that are divided into assemblies and namespaces that make it easier to manage the tens of thousands of types available. It is important to understand the difference between an assembly and a namespace.

Assemblies, NuGet packages, and platforms

An **assembly** is where a type is stored in the filesystem. Assemblies are a mechanism for deploying code. For example, the `System.Data.dll` assembly contains types for managing data. To use types in other assemblies, they must be referenced.

Assemblies are often distributed as **NuGet packages**, which can contain multiple assemblies and other resources. You will also hear the talk about **metapackages** and **platforms**, which are combinations of NuGet packages.

Namespaces

A **namespace** is the address of a type. Namespaces are a mechanism to uniquely identify a type by requiring a full address rather than just a short name.

In the real world, *Bob* of *34 Sycamore Street* is different from *Bob* of *12 Willow Drive*.

In .NET Core, the `IActionFilter` interface of the `System.Web.Mvc` namespace is different from the `IActionFilter` interface of the `System.Web.Http.Filters` namespace.

Understanding dependent assemblies

If an assembly is compiled as a **class library** (it provides types for other assemblies to use), then it has the file extension `.dll` (**dynamic link library**) and it cannot be executed standalone. It must be executed by the `dotnet run` command.

If an assembly is compiled as an **application**, then it has the file extension `.exe` (executable) and can be executed standalone.

Any assembly (both EXE applications and DLL class libraries) can reference one or more DLL class library assemblies as dependencies, but you cannot have circular references, so assembly *B* cannot reference assembly *A*, if assembly *A* already references assembly *B*. Visual Studio will warn you if you attempt to add a dependency reference that would cause a circular reference.

Good Practice

Circular references are often a warning sign of poor code design. If you are sure that you need a circular reference, then use an interface to solve it, as explained in the Stack Overflow answer at the following link: `https://stackoverflow.com/questions/6928387/how-to-solve-circular-reference`

Every application created for .NET Core has a dependency reference to the **Microsoft .NET Core App platform**. This special platform contains thousands of types in NuGet packages that almost all applications would need, such as the `int` and `string` variables.

Using Visual Studio 2017

In Visual Studio 2017, press *Ctrl + Shift + N* or navigate to **File | New | Project....**

In the **New Project** dialog, in the **Installed** list, expand **Visual C#** and select **.NET Core**. In the list at the center, select **Console App (.NET Core)**, type the name `Assemblies`, change the location to `C:\Code`, type the solution name `Chapter07`, and then click on **OK**.

In **Solution Explorer**, right-click **Assemblies** project, and choose **Edit Assemblies.csproj**.

Using Visual Studio Code

In Visual Studio Code, use **Integrated Terminal** to create a folder named `Chapter07` with a subfolder named `Assemblies`.

Use `dotnet new console` to create a console application.

Open `Assemblies.csproj`.

Using Visual Studio 2017 and Visual Studio Code

When using .NET Core, you reference the dependency assemblies, NuGet packages, and platforms that your application needs in a project file.

 The original project file for .NET Core 1.0 was a JSON format file named `project.json`. The *newer* format for .NET Core 1.1 and later is an XML file with the `.csproj` extension. I say *newer*, because it is actually an older format that has been used since the beginning of .NET in 2002. Microsoft changed their mind after the release of .NET Core 1.0!

`Assemblies.csproj` is a typical project file for a .NET Core application, as shown in the following markup:

```
<Project Sdk="Microsoft.NET.Sdk">

  <PropertyGroup>
  <OutputType>Exe</OutputType>
  <TargetFramework>netcoreapp2.0</TargetFramework>
  </PropertyGroup>

</Project>
```

Relating assemblies and namespaces

To understand the relationship between assemblies and namespaces, we will use a tool available in Visual Studio 2017. If you are using Visual Studio Code, just look at the screenshots.

Browsing assemblies with Visual Studio 2017

Using Visual Studio 2017, navigate to **View** | **Object Browser**, or press *Ctrl + W, J*, and you will see that your solution has dependencies on assemblies such as System.Console, used in all the coding exercises so far, as shown in the following screenshot:

Object Browser can be used to learn about the assemblies and namespaces that .NET Core uses to logically and physically group types together.

For types that are only used in some scenarios, for example, the `Console` type is only used in console applications, not in web applications or mobile apps, there is an assembly for just that one type and its supporting types. The `System.Console.dll` assembly is located in the filesystem, as shown in the following screenshot:

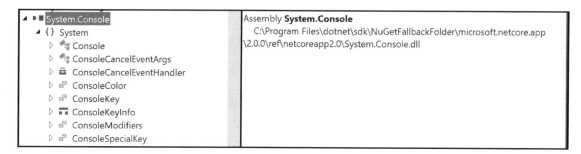

The `System.Console.dll` assembly only contains eight types, all of them in the `System` namespace, and all to support the `Console` type, as shown in the following screenshot:

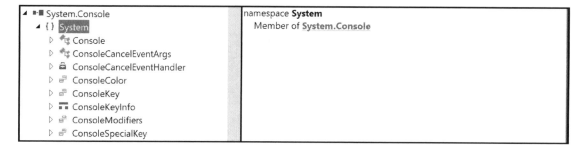

By default, **Object Browser** shows types grouped by assembly, that is, the file that *contains* the namespaces and types in the filesystem. Sometimes, it is more useful to ignore the *physical* location of a type and focus on its *logical* grouping, that is, its namespace.

In its toolbar, click on **Object Browser Settings** (the last button that looks like a gear icon), and select **View Namespaces**, as shown in the following screenshot:

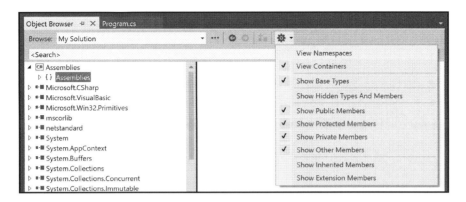

Now, **Object Browser** shows types grouped by their namespace, and when a namespace is selected, for example System, it shows a list of the assemblies that have types in that namespace, as shown in the following screenshot:

Most common .NET Core types are in the `System.Runtime.dll` assembly. You can see the relationship between some assemblies and the namespaces that they supply types for, and note that there is not always a one-to-one mapping between assemblies and namespaces, as shown in the following table:

Assembly	Example namespaces	Example types
`System.Runtime.dll`	`System, System.Collections,` `System.Collections.Generics`	`Int32, String,` `List<T>`
`System.Console.dll`	`System`	`Console`
`System.Threading.dll`	`System.Threading`	`Interlocked,` `Monitor, Mutex`
`System.Xml.XDocument.dll`	`System.Xml.Linq`	`XDocument,` `XElement, XNode`

Using Visual Studio 2017 or Visual Studio Code

In either Visual Studio 2017 or Visual Studio Code, inside the `Main` method, enter the following code:

```
var doc = new XDocument();
```

The `XDocument` type is not recognized because we have not told the compiler what the namespace of the type is. Although this project already has a reference to the assembly that contains the type, we also need to either prefix the type name with its namespace or to import the namespace.

Importing a namespace

Click inside the `XDocument` class name. Visual Studio 2017 and Visual Studio Code both display a light bulb, showing that it recognizes the type and can automatically fix the problem for you.

Click on the light bulb, or in Windows, press *Ctrl* + . (dot), or in macOS, press *Cmd* + . (dot).

Visual Studio 2017 shows an explanation of your choices, and a preview of its suggested changes, as shown in the following screenshot:

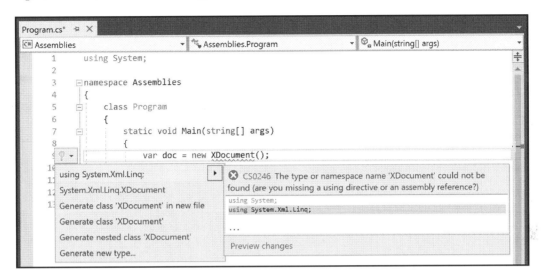

Visual Studio Code has no explanation and preview, but it does have almost the same choices, as shown in the following screenshot:

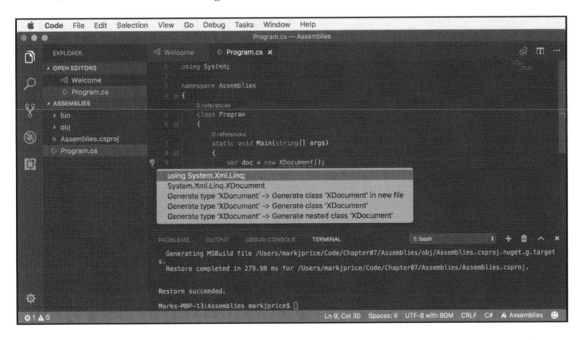

Select using System.Xml.Linq; from the menu. This will *import the namespace* by adding a using statement to the top of the file.

Once a namespace is imported at the top of a code file, then all the types within the namespace are available for use in that code file by just typing their name.

Relating C# keywords to .NET types

One of the common questions I get from new C# programmers is, *What is the difference between* string *with a lowercase and* String *with an uppercase?*

The short answer is easy: none.

The long answer is that all C# type keywords are aliases for a .NET type in a class library assembly.

When you use the string keyword, the compiler turns it into a System.String type. When you use the int type, the compiler turns it into a System.Int32 type. You can even see this if you hover your mouse over an int type, as shown in the following screenshot:

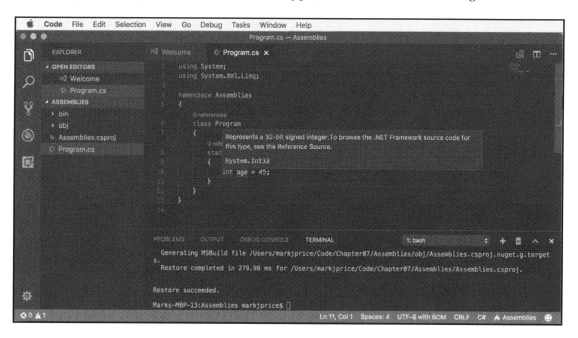

Good Practice
Use the C# keyword instead of the actual type because the keywords do not need the namespace imported.

The following table shows the 16 C# type keywords and their actual .NET types:

Keyword	.NET type	Keyword	.NET type
string	System.String	char	System.Char
sbyte	System.SByte	byte	System.Byte
short	System.Int16	ushort	System.UInt16
int	System.Int32	uint	System.UInt32
long	System.Int64	ulong	System.UInt64
float	System.Single	double	System.Double
decimal	System.Decimal	bool	System.Boolean
object	System.Object	dynamic	System.Dynamic.DynamicObject

Other .NET programming language compilers can do the same thing. For example, the Visual Basic .NET language has a type named Integer that is its alias for System.Int32.

Sharing code cross-platform with .NET Standard 2.0 class libraries

Before .NET Standard 2.0, there was **Portable Class Libraries (PCL)**. With PCLs, you can create a library of code and explicitly specify which platforms you want the library to support, such as Xamarin, Silverlight, and Windows 8. Your library can then use the intersection of APIs that are supported by the specified platforms.

Microsoft realized that this is unsustainable, so they have been working on .NET Standard 2.0—a single API that all future .NET platforms will support. There are older versions of .NET Standard, but they are not supported by multiple .NET platforms.

.NET Standard 2.0 is similar to HTML5 in that they are both standards that a platform should support. Just as Google's Chrome browser and Microsoft's Edge browser implement HTML5 standard, so .NET Core and Xamarin implement .NET Standard 2.0.

If you want to create a library of types that will work across .NET Framework (on Windows), .NET Core (on Windows, macOS, and Linux), and Xamarin (on iOS, Android, and Windows Mobile), you can do so most easily with .NET Standard 2.0.

The following table summarizes versions of .NET Standard, and which platforms they support:

Platform	1.1	1.2	1.3	1.4	1.5	1.6	2.0
.NET Core	→	→	→	→	→	1.0, 1.1	2.0
.NET Framework	4.5	4.5.1	4.6	→	→	→	4.6.1
Xamarin/Mono	→	→	→	→	→	4.6	5.4
UWP	→	→	→	10	→	→	6.0

Creating a .NET Standard 2.0 class library

We will create a class library using .NET Standard 2.0 so that it can be used cross-platform on Windows, macOS, and Linux.

Using Visual Studio 2017

Start Microsoft Visual Studio 2017.

In Visual Studio, press *Ctrl + Shift + N* or go to **File** | **Add** | **New Project...**.

In the **New Project** dialog, in the **Installed** list, expand **Visual C#**, and then select **.NET Standard**. In the list at the center, select **Class Library (.NET Standard)**, type the name `SharedLibrary`, and then click on **OK**, as shown in the following screenshot:

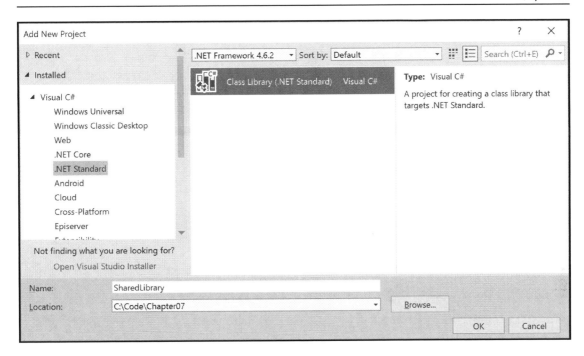

In **Solution Explorer**, right-click on the **SharedLibrary** project, and choose **Edit SharedLibrary.csproj**.

A **Class Library (.NET Standard)** project will target version 2.0 by default, as shown in the following markup:

```
<Project Sdk="Microsoft.NET.Sdk"> <PropertyGroup>
<TargetFramework>netstandard2.0</TargetFramework> </PropertyGroup>
</Project>
```

Using Visual Studio Code

In the `Code/Chapter07` folder, create a subfolder named `SharedLibrary`.

In Visual Studio Code, open the `SharedLibrary` folder.

In Visual Studio Code, navigate to **View | Integrated Terminal**, and then enter the following command:

```
dotnet new classlib
```

Click on `SharedLibrary.csproj` and note that a class library generated by the `dotnet` CLI targets version 2.0 by default, as shown in the following markup:

```
<Project Sdk="Microsoft.NET.Sdk">

  <PropertyGroup>
    <TargetFramework>netstandard2.0</TargetFramework>
  </PropertyGroup>

</Project>
```

Understanding NuGet packages

.NET Core is split into a set of packages, distributed using a Microsoft-defined package management technology named NuGet. Each of these packages represents a single assembly of the same name. For example, the `System.Collections` package contains the `System.Collections.dll` assembly.

The following are the benefits of packages:

- Packages can ship on their own schedule
- Packages can be tested independently of other packages
- Packages can support different OSes and CPUs
- Packages can have dependencies specific to only one library
- Apps are smaller because unreferenced packages aren't part of the distribution

The following table lists some of the more important packages:

Package	Important types
System.Runtime	Object, String, Int32, Array
System.Collections	List<T>, Dictionary<TKey, TValue>
System.Net.Http	HttpClient, HttpResponseMessage
System.IO.FileSystem	File, Directory
System.Reflection	Assembly, TypeInfo, MethodInfo

Understanding metapackages

Metapackages describe a set of packages that are used together. Metapackages are referenced just like any other NuGet package. By referencing a metapackage, you have, in effect, added a reference to each of its dependent packages.

Older versions of Visual Studio 2017 nicely showed the relationship between metapackages, packages, and assemblies, as shown in the following screenshot:

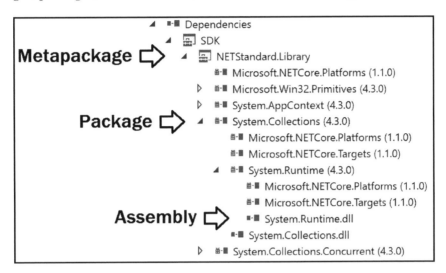

 Metapackages are often just referred to as packages in Microsoft's documentation, as you are about to see.

The following list contains links to some common metapackages and packages, including an official list of their dependencies:

- https://www.nuget.org/packages/Microsoft.NETCore.App
- https://www.nuget.org/packages/NETStandard.Library
- https://www.nuget.org/packages/Microsoft.NETCore.Runtime.CoreCLR
- https://www.nuget.org/packages/System.IO
- https://www.nuget.org/packages/System.Collections
- https://www.nuget.org/packages/System.Runtime

If you were to go to the link for the `Microsoft.NETCore.App` metapackage, you would see information about the metapackage, including how to install it, dependencies, version history, and how many downloads it has had, as shown in the following screenshot:

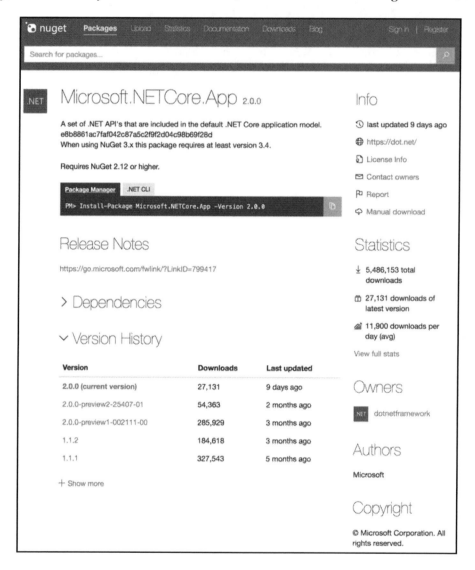

If you were to expand **Dependencies**, you would see the list of dependencies for the metapackage, as shown in the following screenshot:

.NETCoreApp 2.0

Microsoft.NETCore.DotNetHostPolicy (>= 2.0.0)
Microsoft.NETCore.Platforms (>= 2.0.0)
NETStandard.Library (>= 2.0.0)

 `Microsoft.NETCore.App` version 2.0.0 has a dependency on `NETStandard.Library` version 2.0.0.

Understanding frameworks

There is a two-way relationship between frameworks and packages. Packages define the APIs, frameworks group packages. A framework without any packages would not define any APIs.

 If you have a strong understanding of interfaces and types that implement them, you might find the following URL useful for grasping how packages and their APIs relate to frameworks such as the various .NET Standard versions:
https://gist.github.com/davidfowl/8939f305567e1755412d6dc0b8baf1b7

.NET Core packages each support a set of frameworks. For example, the `System.IO.FileSystem` package supports the following frameworks, as shown in the following screenshot:

- .NETStandard, version 1.3
- .NETFramework, version 4.6
- Six Xamarin platforms (for example, Xamarin.iOS 1.0)

Good Practice
Choose `NETStandard.Library` if you are creating a class library that is intended to be referenced by multiple platforms, such as .NET Framework and Xamarin, as well as .NET Core.

Fixing dependencies

To consistently restore packages and write reliable code, it's important that you fix your dependencies. Fixing dependencies means you are using the same family of packages released for a specific version of .NET Core, for example, 1.0.

To fix dependencies, every package should have a single version with no additional qualifiers. Additional qualifiers include release candidates (`rc4`) and wildcards (`*`). Wildcards allow future versions to be automatically referenced and used because they always represent the most recent release. But wildcards are therefore dangerous, because it could result in the restoration of future incompatible packages that break your code.

The following dependencies are NOT fixed and should be avoided:

```
<PackageReference Include="System.Net.Http" Version="4.1.0-*" />
<PackageReference Include="Microsoft.NETCore.App" Version="1.0.0-
rc4-00454-00" />
```

Good Practice
Microsoft guarantees that if you fixed your dependencies to what ships with a specific version of .NET Core, for example, 2.0, those packages will all work together. Always fix your dependencies.

Publishing your applications for deployment

There are two ways to publish and deploy a .NET Core application:

- Framework-dependent
- Self-contained

If you choose to deploy your application and its dependencies, but not .NET Core itself, then you rely on .NET Core already being on the target computer. This works well for web applications deployed to a server because .NET Core and lots of other web applications are likely already on the server.

Sometimes, you want to be able to give someone a USB stick containing your application and know that it can execute on their computer. You want to perform a self-contained deployment. The size of the deployment files will be larger, but you will know that it will work.

Creating a console application to publish

Add a new console application project named `DotNetCoreEverywhere`.

Modify the code to look like this:

```
using static System.Console;

namespace DotNetCoreEverywhere
{
    class Program
    {
        static void Main(string[] args)
        {
            WriteLine("I can run everywhere!");
        }
    }
}
```

Open `DotNetCoreEverywhere.csproj`, and add the runtime identifiers to target four operating systems, inside the `<PropertyGroup>` element, as shown in the following markup:

```
<Project Sdk="Microsoft.NET.Sdk">

  <PropertyGroup>
    <OutputType>Exe</OutputType>
    <TargetFramework>netcoreapp2.0</TargetFramework>
    <RuntimeIdentifiers>
      win10-x64;osx.10.12-x64;rhel.7-x64;ubuntu.14.04-x64
    </RuntimeIdentifiers>
  </PropertyGroup>

</Project>
```

The `win10-x64` RID value means Windows 10 or Windows Server 2016. The `osx.10.12-x64` RID value means macOS Sierra. You can find the full list of currently supported **Runtime IDentifier (RID)** values at the following link:
`https://docs.microsoft.com/en-us/dotnet/articles/core/rid-catalog`

Publishing with Visual Studio 2017 on Windows

In Visual Studio 2017, right-click on **DotNetCoreEverywhere**, and choose **Publish...**, then select **Folder**, and then click on **Publish**, as shown in the following screenshot:

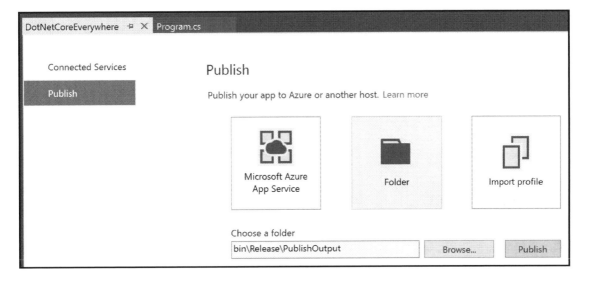

By default, you have now published the Windows 10 64-bit version, as shown in the following screenshot:

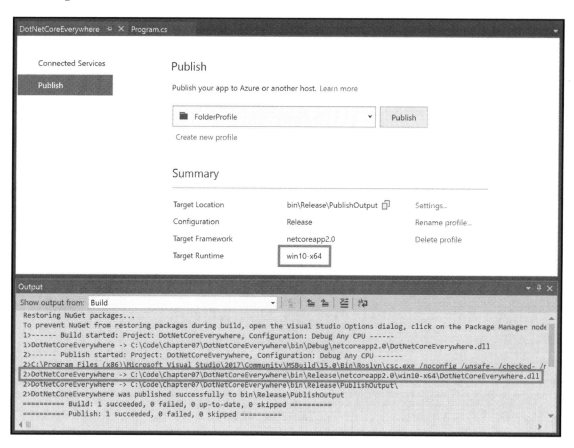

Click on **Settings...**, and change **Target Runtime** to **osx.10.12-x64**, as shown in the following screenshot, and then click on **Save**:

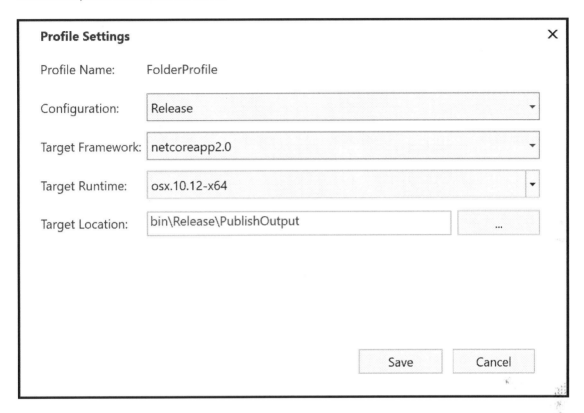

Next, click on **Publish**.

In **Solution Explorer**, show all files, expand **bin**, **Release**, **netcoreapp2.0**, **osx.10.12-x64**, and **win10-x64**, as shown in the following screenshot, and note the application files:

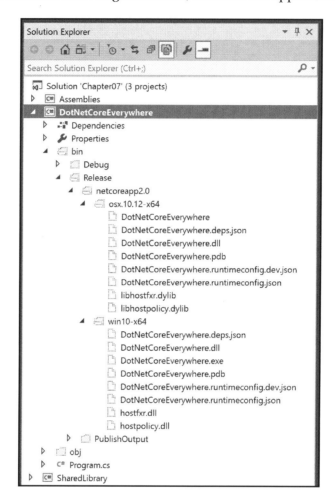

Publishing with Visual Studio Code on macOS

In Visual Studio Code, in **Integrated Terminal**, enter the following command to build the release version of the console application for Windows 10:

```
dotnet publish -c Release -r win10-x64
```

Microsoft Build Engine will compile and publish the console application, as shown in the following screenshot:

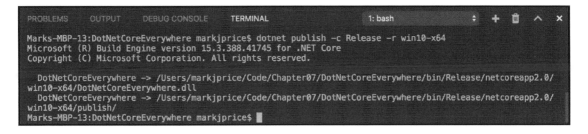

In **Integrated Terminal**, enter the following commands to build release versions for macOS, **Red Hat Enterprise Linux** (**RHEL**), and Ubuntu Linux:

```
dotnet publish -c Release -r osx.10.12-x64
dotnet publish -c Release -r rhel.7-x64
dotnet publish -c Release -r ubuntu.14.04-x64
```

Open a macOS **Finder** window, navigate to
`DotNetCoreEverywhere\bin\Release\netcoreapp2.0`, and note the output folders for the four operating systems and the files, including a Windows executable named
`DotNetCoreEverywhere.exe`, as shown in the following screenshot:

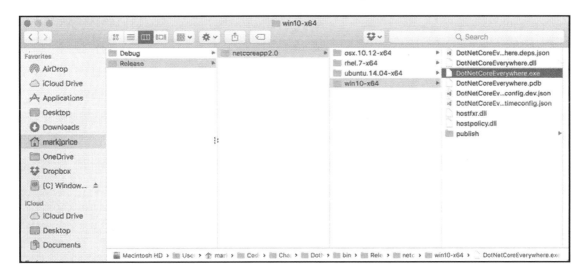

If you copy any of those folders to the appropriate operating system, the console application will run because it is a self-contained deployable .NET Core application.

Packaging your libraries for NuGet distribution

When you install .NET Core SDK, it includes the **command-line interface (CLI)** named `dotnet`.

Understanding dotnet commands

The `dotnet` command-line interface has commands that work on the current folder to create a new project using templates, some of which are listed here:

- `dotnet new console`: This creates a new console application project
- `dotnet new classlib`: This creates a new assembly library project
- `dotnet new web`: This creates a new empty ASP.NET Core project
- `dotnet new mvc`: This creates a new ASP.NET Core MVC project
- `dotnet new razor`: This creates a new ASP.NET Core MVC project with support for Razor Pages
- `dotnet new angular`: This creates a new ASP.NET Core MVC project with support for an Angular Single Page Application as the frontend
- `dotnet new react`: This creates a new ASP.NET Core MVC project with support for an React **Single Page Application (SPA)** as the frontend
- `dotnet new webapi`: This creates a new ASP.NET Core Web API project

You can install additional templates from the following link:
`https://github.com/dotnet/templating/wiki/Available-templates-for-dotnet-new`
You can define your own project templates, as explained in the official documentation for the `dotnet new` command at the following link:
`https://docs.microsoft.com/en-us/dotnet/core/tools/dotnet-new?tabs=netcore2x`

Enter the `dotnet new -l` command to list your currently installed templates, as shown in the following screenshot:

```
● ● ●                          ⬆ markjprice — -bash — 104×39
[Marks-MBP-13:~ markjprice$ dotnet new -l
Getting ready...
Usage: new [options]

Options:
  -h, --help          Displays help for this command.
  -l, --list          Lists templates containing the specified name. If no name is specified, lists all
templates.
  -n, --name          The name for the output being created. If no name is specified, the name of the cu
rrent directory is used.
  -o, --output        Location to place the generated output.
  -i, --install       Installs a source or a template pack.
  -u, --uninstall     Uninstalls a source or a template pack.
  --type              Filters templates based on available types. Predefined values are "project", "item
" or "other".
  --force             Forces content to be generated even if it would change existing files.
  -lang, --language   Specifies the language of the template to create.


Templates                                      Short Name      Language      Tags
----------------------------------------------------------------------------------------------------
Console Application                            console         [C#], F#, VB  Common/Console
Class library                                  classlib        [C#], F#, VB  Common/Library
Unit Test Project                              mstest          [C#], F#, VB  Test/MSTest
xUnit Test Project                             xunit           [C#], F#, VB  Test/xUnit
ASP.NET Core Empty                             web             [C#], F#      Web/Empty
ASP.NET Core Web App (Model-View-Controller)   mvc             [C#], F#      Web/MVC
ASP.NET Core Web App                           razor           [C#]          Web/MVC/Razor Pages
ASP.NET Core with Angular                      angular         [C#]          Web/MVC/SPA
ASP.NET Core with React.js                     react           [C#]          Web/MVC/SPA
ASP.NET Core with React.js and Redux           reactredux      [C#]          Web/MVC/SPA
ASP.NET Core Web API                           webapi          [C#], F#      Web/WebAPI
global.json file                               globaljson                    Config
Nuget Config                                   nugetconfig                   Config
Web Config                                     webconfig                     Config
Solution File                                  sln                           Solution
Razor Page                                     page                          Web/ASP.NET
MVC ViewImports                                viewimports                   Web/ASP.NET
MVC ViewStart                                  viewstart                     Web/ASP.NET
```

The `dotnet` CLI has the following commands that work on the project in the current folder, to manage the project:

- `dotnet restore`: This downloads dependencies for the project
- `dotnet build`: This compiles the project
- `dotnet test`: This runs unit tests on the project
- `dotnet run`: This runs the project
- `dotnet migrate`: This migrates a .NET Core project created with the preview CLI tools to the current CLI tool MS Build format
- `dotnet pack`: This creates a NuGet package for the project

- `dotnet publish`: This compiles and publishes the project, either with dependencies or as a self-contained application
- `add`: This adds a reference to a package to the project
- `remove`: This removes a reference to a package from the project
- `list`: This lists the package references for the project

Adding a package reference

Let's say that you want to add a package created by a third-party developer, for example, Newtonsoft.Json, a popular package for working with the **JavaScript Object Notation (JSON)** serialization format.

Using Visual Studio Code

In Visual Studio Code, open the `Chapter07/Assemblies` folder that you created earlier, and then enter the following command in **Integrated Terminal**:

```
dotnet add package newtonsoft.json
```

Visual Studio Code outputs information about adding the reference, as shown in the following output:

```
info : Adding PackageReference for package 'newtonsoft.json' into project
'/Users/markjprice/Code/Chapter07/Assemblies/Assemblies.csproj'.
log : Restoring packages for
/Users/markjprice/Code/Chapter07/Assemblies/Assemblies.csproj...
info : GET
https://api.nuget.org/v3-flatcontainer/newtonsoft.json/index.json
info : OK https://api.nuget.org/v3-flatcontainer/newtonsoft.json/index.json
485ms
info : GET
https://api.nuget.org/v3-flatcontainer/newtonsoft.json/10.0.3/newtonsoft.js
on.10.0.3.nupkg
info : OK
https://api.nuget.org/v3-flatcontainer/newtonsoft.json/10.0.3/newtonsoft.js
on.10.0.3.nupkg 602ms
log : Installing Newtonsoft.Json 10.0.3.
info : Package 'newtonsoft.json' is compatible with all the specified
frameworks in project
'/Users/markjprice/Code/Chapter07/Assemblies/Assemblies.csproj'.
info : PackageReference for package 'newtonsoft.json' version '10.0.3'
added to file
'/Users/markjprice/Code/Chapter07/Assemblies/Assemblies.csproj'.
```

Open `Assemblies.csproj`, and you will see the package reference has been added, as shown in the following markup:

```
<Project Sdk="Microsoft.NET.Sdk">
  <PropertyGroup>
    <OutputType>Exe</OutputType>
    <TargetFramework>netcoreapp2.0</TargetFramework>
  </PropertyGroup>
  <ItemGroup>
    <PackageReference Include="newtonsoft.json" Version="10.0.3" />
  </ItemGroup>
</Project>
```

Using Visual Studio 2017

In Visual Studio 2017, right-click on a project in **Solution Explorer**, and select **Manage NuGet Packages...**, and then use **NuGet Package Manager** to search for the **Newtonsoft.Json** package, as shown in the following screenshot:

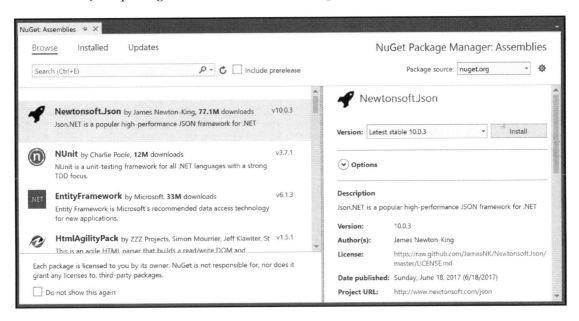

Click on **Install**, and accept the license agreement.

Right-click on the **Assemblies** project, select **Edit Assemblies.csproj**, and note the change to the file, as shown earlier for Visual Studio Code.

In Visual Studio 2017, you can navigate to **Tools | NuGet Package Manager | Package Manager Console** to use a command line for installing, updating, and removing package references, in a similar way to Visual Studio Code's **Integrated Terminal**.

Packaging a library for NuGet

Now, let's package the `SharedLibrary` project that you created earlier.

In the `SharedLibrary` project, rename `Class1.cs` to `StringExtensions.cs`, and modify its contents, as shown in the following code:

```
using System.Text.RegularExpressions;

namespace Packt.CS7
{
    public static class StringExtensions
    {
        public static bool IsValidXmlTag(this string input)
        {
            return Regex.IsMatch(input,
              @"^<([a-z]+)([^<]+)*(?:>(.*)<\/\1>|\s+\/>)$");
        }

        public static bool IsValidPassword(this string input)
        {
            // minimum of eight valid characters
            return Regex.IsMatch(input, "^[a-zA-Z0-9_-]{8,}$");
        }

        public static bool IsValidHex(this string input)
        {
            // three or six valid hex number characters
            return Regex.IsMatch(input,
              "^#?([a-fA-F0-9]{3}|[a-fA-F0-9]{6})$");
        }
    }
}
```

These extension methods use regular expressions to validate the `string` value. You will learn how to write regular expressions in `Chapter 6`, *Using Common .NET Standard Types*.

Edit `SharedLibrary.csproj`, and modify its contents, as shown in the following markup, and note the following:

- `PackageId` must be globally unique, so you must use a different value if you want to publish this NuGet package to the `https://www.nuget.org/` public feed for others to reference and download
- All the other elements are self-explanatory:

```
<Project Sdk="Microsoft.NET.Sdk">

<PropertyGroup>
  <TargetFramework>netstandard2.0</TargetFramework>
  <GeneratePackageOnBuild>true</GeneratePackageOnBuild>
  <PackageId>Packt.CS7.SharedLibrary</PackageId>
  <PackageVersion>1.0.0.0</PackageVersion>
  <Authors>Mark J Price</Authors>
  <PackageLicenseUrl>
    http://opensource.org/licenses/MS-PL
  </PackageLicenseUrl>
  <PackageProjectUrl>
    http://github.com/markjprice/cs7dotnetcore2
  </PackageProjectUrl>
  <PackageIconUrl>
    http://github.com/markjprice/cs7dotnetcore2/nuget.png
  </PackageIconUrl>
  <PackageRequireLicenseAcceptance>true</PackageRequireLicenseAcceptance>
  <PackageReleaseNotes>
    Example shared library packaged for NuGet.
  </PackageReleaseNotes>
  <Description>
    Three extension methods to validate a string value.
  </Description>
  <Copyright>
    Copyright ©2017 Packt Publishing Limited
  </Copyright>
  <PackageTags>string extension packt cs7</PackageTags>
</PropertyGroup>

</Project>
```

In Visual Studio 2017, right-click on the **SharedLibrary** project, and select **Pack**.

In Visual Studio Code, in **Integrated Terminal**, enter a command to generate a NuGet package, as shown here:

```
dotnet pack -c Release
```

Visual Studio 2017 and Visual Studio Code display output indicating success, as shown in the following screenshot:

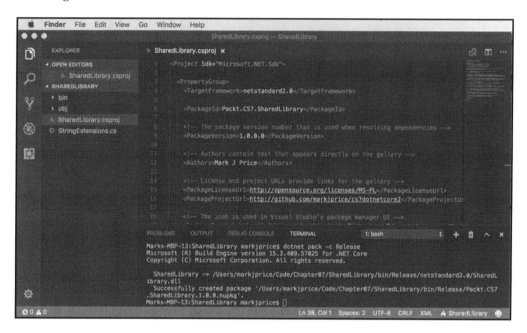

Start your favorite browser and navigate to the following link:
https://www.nuget.org/packages/manage/upload

 You will need to register with https://www.nuget.org/ if you want to upload a NuGet package for other developers to reference as a dependency package.

Click on **Browse...** and select the `.nupkg` file that was created by the `pack` command, as shown in the following screenshot:

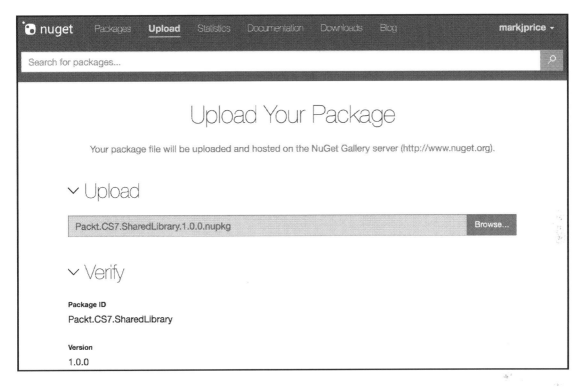

Verify that the information you entered in the `SharedLibrary.csproj` file has been correctly filled in, and then click on **Submit**.

After a few seconds, you will see a success message and you will see your package has been uploaded, as shown in the following screenshot:

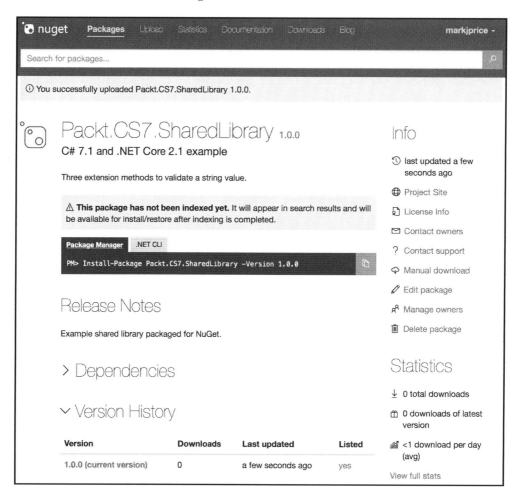

Testing your package

You will now test your uploaded package by referencing it in the Assemblies project.

Using Visual Studio Code

In Visual Studio Code, open the `Assemblies` project, and modify the project file to reference your package, as shown in the following markup:

```xml
<Project Sdk="Microsoft.NET.Sdk">
  <PropertyGroup>
    <OutputType>Exe</OutputType>
    <TargetFramework>netcoreapp2.0</TargetFramework>
  </PropertyGroup>
  <ItemGroup>
    <PackageReference Include="newtonsoft.json" Version="10.0.3" />
    <PackageReference Include="packt.cs7.sharedlibrary" Version="1.0.0" />
  </ItemGroup>
</Project>
```

Using Visual Studio 2017

In Visual Studio 2017, use **NuGet Package Manager** to search for the package and install it, as shown in the following screenshot:

Using Visual Studio 2017 and Visual Studio Code

Edit `Program.cs` to import the `Packt.CS7` namespace, and in the `Main` method, prompt the user to enter some string values, and then validate them using the extension methods in the package, as shown in the following code:

```
using static System.Console;
using Packt.CS7;

namespace Assemblies
{
    class Program
    {
        static void Main(string[] args)
        {
            Write("Enter a valid color value in hex: ");
            string hex = ReadLine();
            WriteLine($"Is {hex} a valid color value:
            {hex.IsValidHex()}");

            Write("Enter a valid XML tag: ");
            string xmlTag = ReadLine();
            WriteLine($"Is {xmlTag} a valid XML tag:
            {xmlTag.IsValidXmlTag()}");

            Write("Enter a valid password: ");
            string password = ReadLine();
            WriteLine($"Is {password} a valid password:
            {password.IsValidPassword()}");
        }
    }
}
```

Run the console application and view the output:

```
Enter a valid color value in hex: 00ffc8
Is 00ffc8 a valid color value: True
Enter a valid XML tag: <h1 class="<" />
Is <h1 class="<" /> a valid XML tag: False
Enter a valid password: secretsauce
Is secretsauce a valid password: True
```

Porting from .NET Framework to .NET Core

If you are an existing .NET Framework developer, then you may have existing applications that you are wondering if you should port to .NET Core. You should consider if porting is the right choice for your code. Sometimes, the best choice is not to port.

Could you port?

.NET Core has great support for the following types of applications:

- **ASP.NET Core MVC** web applications
- **ASP.NET Core Web API** web services (REST/HTTP)
- **Universal Windows Platform** (**UWP**) applications
- **Console** applications

.NET Core does not support the following types of applications:

- **ASP.NET Web Forms** web applications
- **Windows Forms** desktop applications
- **Windows Presentation Foundation** (**WPF**) desktop applications
- **Silverlight** applications

Luckily, WPF and Silverlight applications use a dialect of XAML, which is like the XAML dialect used by UWP and Xamarin.Forms.

Should you port?

Even if you *could* port, *should* you? What benefits do you gain? Some common benefits include the following:

- **Deployment to Linux or Docker**: These OSes are lightweight and cost-effective as web application and web service platforms, especially when compared to Windows Server

- **Removal of dependency on IIS and System.Web.dll**: Even if you continue to deploy to Windows Server, ASP.NET Core can be hosted on lightweight, higher performance Kestrel (or other) web servers
- **Command-line tools**: These include those tools that developers and administrators use to automate their tasks are written as console applications. The ability to run a single tool cross-platform is very useful.

Differences between .NET Framework and .NET Core

There are three key differences, as shown in the following table:

.NET Core	.NET Framework
Distributed as NuGet packages, so each application can be deployed with its own app-local copy of the version of .NET Core that it needs.	Distributed as a system-wide, shared set of assemblies (literally, in the **Global Assembly Cache (GAC)**).
Split into small, layered components, so a minimal deployment can be performed.	Single, monolithic deployment.
Removes older technologies, such as Windows Forms and Web Forms, and noncross-platform features, such as AppDomains, .NET Remoting, and binary serialization.	Retains some older technologies such as Windows Forms, WPF, and ASP.NET Web Forms.

Understanding the .NET Portability Analyzer

Microsoft has a useful tool that you can run against your existing applications to generate a report for porting. You can watch a demonstration of the tool at the following link:

```
https://channel9.msdn.com/Blogs/Seth-Juarez/A-Brief-Look-at-the-NET-Portability
-Analyzer
```

Using non-.NET Standard libraries

70% of existing NuGet packages can be used with .NET Core 2.0, even if they are not compiled for .NET Standard 2.0.
To search for useful NuGet packages, follow this link:
`https://www.nuget.org/packages`

For example, there is a package of custom collections for handling matrices created by Dialect Software LLC, documented at the following link:
`https://www.nuget.org/packages/DialectSoftware.Collections.Matrix/`

The package was last updated in 2013, as shown in the following screenshot:

2013 was long before .NET Core existed, so this package was built for .NET Framework. As long as an assembly package like this only uses APIs available in .NET Standard 2.0, it can be used in a .NET Core 2.0 project.

Open `Assemblies.csproj,` and add `<PackageReference>` for Dialect Software's package, as shown in the following markup:

```
<PackageReference Include="dialectsoftware.collections.matrix"
Version="1.0.0" />
```

Open `Program.cs,` add statements to import the `DialectSoftware.Collections` and `DialectSoftware.Collections.Generics` namespaces, and add statements to create instances of `Axis` and `Matrix<T>`, populate them with values, and output them, as shown in the following code:

```
var x = new Axis("x", 0, 10, 1);
var y = new Axis("y", 0, 4, 1);

var matrix = new Matrix<long>(new[] { x, y });
int i = 0;
for (; i < matrix.Axes[0].Points.Length; i++)
{
    matrix.Axes[0].Points[i].Label = "x" + i.ToString();
}
```

```
i = 0;
for (; i < matrix.Axes[1].Points.Length; i++)
{
    matrix.Axes[1].Points[i].Label = "y" + i.ToString();
}

foreach (long[] c in matrix)
{
    matrix[c] = c[0] + c[1];
}

foreach (long[] c in matrix)
{
    WriteLine("{0},{1} ({2},{3}) = {4}", matrix.Axes[0].Points[c[0]].Label,
        matrix.Axes[1].Points[c[1]].Label, c[0], c[1], matrix[c]);
}
```

Run the console application, view the output, and note the warning message:

```
/Users/markjprice/Code/Chapter07/Assemblies/Assemblies.csproj : warning
NU1701: Package 'DialectSoftware.Collections.Matrix 1.0.0' was restored
using '.NETFramework,Version=v4.6.1' instead of the project target
framework '.NETCoreApp,Version=v2.0'. This package may not be fully
compatible with your project.
x0,y0 (0,0) = 0
x0,y1 (0,1) = 1
x0,y2 (0,2) = 2
x0,y3 (0,3) = 3
...and so on.
```

Summary

In this chapter, you explored the relationship between assemblies and namespaces, we discussed options for porting existing .NET Framework code bases, published your apps and libraries, and deployed your code cross-platform.

In the next chapter, you will learn about some common .NET Standard 2.0 types that are included with .NET Core 2.0.

6
Using Common .NET Standard Types

This chapter is about some common .NET Standard 2.0 types that are included with .NET Core 2.0. This includes types for manipulating numbers, text, collections, network access, reflection, attributes, drawing images, and internationalization.

This chapter covers the following topics:

- Working with numbers
- Working with text
- Working with collections
- Working with network resources
- Working with types and attributes
- Internationalizing your code

Working with numbers

One of the most common types of data are numbers. The most common types in .NET Standard 2.0 for working with numbers are shown in the following table:

Namespace	Example type(s)	Description
System	SByte, Int16, Int32, Int64	Integers, that is, positive and negative whole numbers.
System	Byte, UInt16, UInt32, UInt64	Cardinals, that is, positive whole numbers.
System	Single, Double	Reals, that is, floating point numbers.
System	Decimal	Accurate reals, that is, for use in science, engineering, or financial scenarios.

System .Numerics	BigInteger, Complex, Quaternion	Arbitrarily large integers, complex numbers, and quaternion numbers.

You can read more at the following link:

https://docs.microsoft.com/en-us/dotnet/standard/numerics

Create a new console application named WorkingWithNumbers in a solution named Chapter08.

Working with big integers

The largest whole number that can be stored in .NET Standard types that have a C# alias is about eighteen and a half quintillion, stored in an unsigned long.

In Program.cs, add a statement to import System.Numerics, as shown in the following code:

```
using System.Numerics;
```

In Main, add statements to output the largest value of ulong, and a number with 30 digits using BigInteger, as shown in the following code:

```
var largestLong = ulong.MaxValue;
WriteLine($"{largestLong,40:N0}");

var atomsInTheUniverse =
BigInteger.Parse("1234567890123456789012345678901234567890");
WriteLine($"{atomsInTheUniverse,40:N0}");
```

 The , 40 in the format code means right-align forty characters, so both numbers are lined up to the right hand edge.

Run the console application and view the output:

```
           18,446,744,073,709,551,615
123,456,789,012,345,678,901,234,567,890
```

Working with complex numbers

A complex number can be expressed as $a + bi$, where a and b are real numbers, and i is the imaginary unit, where $i2 = -1$. If the real part is zero it is a pure imaginary number. If the imaginary part is zero, it is a real number. Complex numbers have practical applications in many **STEM** (**science**, **technology**, **engineering**, **mathematics**) fields of study.

Complex numbers are added by separately adding the real and imaginary parts of the summands; consider this:

$(a + bi) + (c + di) = (a + c) + (b + d)i$

In `Main`, add statements to add two complex numbers, as shown in the following code:

```
var c1 = new Complex(4, 2);
var c2 = new Complex(3, 7);
var c3 = c1 + c2;
WriteLine($"{c1} added to {c2} is {c3}");
```

Run the console application and view the output:

```
(4, 2) added to (3, 7) is (7, 9)
```

Quarterions are a number system that extend complex numbers. They form a four-dimensional associative normed division algebra over the real numbers, and therefore also a domain.

Huh? Yes, I know. I don't understand that either. Don't worry, we're not going to write any code using them! Suffice to say, they are good at describing spatial rotations, so video game engines use them, as do many computer simulations and flight control systems.

Working with text

One of the other most common types of data for variables is text. The most common types in .NET Standard 2.0 for working with text are shown in the following table:

Namespace	Example types	Description
System	Char	Storage for a single text character
System	String	Storage for multiple text characters
System.Text	StringBuilder	Efficiently manipulates strings
System.Text.RegularExpressions	Regex	Efficiently pattern-matches strings

Getting the length of a string

Add a new console application project named WorkingWithText.

In Visual Studio 2017, set the solution's startup project to be the current selection.

Sometimes, you need to find out the length of a piece of text stored in a string class.

In Main, add statements to define a variable to store the name of the city London, and then output its name and length, as shown in the following code:

```
string city = "London";
WriteLine($"{city} is {city.Length} characters long.");
```

Getting the characters of a string

A string class uses an array of char internally to store the text. It also has an indexer, which means that we can use the array syntax to read its characters.

Add the following statement, and then run the console application:

```
WriteLine($"First char is {city[0]} and third is {city[2]}.");
```

Splitting a string

Sometimes, you need to split some text wherever there is a character, such as a comma.

Add more lines of code to define a single string with comma-separated city names. You can use the `Split` method and specify a character that you want to treat as the separator. An array of strings is then created that you can enumerate using a `foreach` statement:

```
string cities = "Paris,Berlin,Madrid,New York";
string[] citiesArray = cities.Split(',');
foreach (string item in citiesArray)
{
    WriteLine(item);
}
```

Getting part of a string

Sometimes, you need to get part of some text. For example, if you had a person's full name stored in a string with a space character between the first and last name, then you could find the position of the space and extract the first name and last name as two parts, like this:

```
string fullname = "Alan Jones";
int indexOfTheSpace = fullname.IndexOf(' ');
string firstname = fullname.Substring(0, indexOfTheSpace);
string lastname = fullname.Substring(indexOfTheSpace + 1);
WriteLine($"{lastname}, {firstname}");
```

 If the format of the initial full name was different, for example, `Lastname, Firstname`, then the code would be slightly different. As an optional exercise, try writing some statements that would change the input `Jones, Alan` into `Alan Jones`.

Checking a string for content

Sometimes, you need to check whether a piece of text starts or ends with some characters or contains some characters:

```
string company = "Microsoft";
bool startsWithM = company.StartsWith("M");
bool containsN = company.Contains("N");
WriteLine($"Starts with M: {startsWithM}, contains an N:{containsN}");
```

Other string members

Here are some other `string` members:

Member	Description
`Trim`, `TrimStart`, and `TrimEnd`	These trim whitespaces from the beginning and/or end of the string.
`ToUpper` and `ToLower`	These convert the string into uppercase or lowercase.
`Insert` and `Remove`	These insert or remove some text in the `string` variable.
`Replace`	This replaces some text.
`string.Concat`	This concatenates two `string` variables. The + operator calls this method when used between `string` variables.
`string.Join`	This concatenates one or more `string` variables with a character in between each one.
`string.IsNullOrEmpty`	This checks whether a `string` variable is `null` or empty (`""`).
`string.IsNullOrWhitespace`	This checks whether a `string` variable is `null` or whitespace, that is, a mix of any number of horizontal and vertical spacing characters, for example, tab, space, carriage return, line feed, and so on.
`string.Empty`	This can be used instead of allocating memory each time you use a literal `string` value using an empty pair of double quotes (`""`).
`string.Format`	An older, alternative method to output formatted strings, that uses positioned instead of named parameters.

Note that some of the preceding methods are **static** methods. This means that the method can only be called from the type, not from a variable instance.

For example, if I want to take an array of `string` values and combine them back together into a single `string` variable with separators, I can use the `Join` method like this:

```
string recombined = string.Join(" => ", citiesArray);
WriteLine(recombined);
```

If I want to use positioned parameters instead of interpolated `string` formatting syntax, I can use the `Format` method like this:

```
string fruit = "Apples";
decimal price = 0.39M;
DateTime when = DateTime.Today;

WriteLine($"{fruit} cost {price:C} on {when:dddd}s.");

WriteLine(string.Format("{0} cost {1:C} on {2:dddd}s.",
fruit, price, when));
```

 Positioned parameters start counting at zero. Sometimes they can be more easily formatted in code compared to `string` interpolation syntax, as you can see in the previous code example.

If you run the console application and view the output, it should look like this:

```
London is 6 characters long.
First char is L and third is n.
Paris
Berlin
Madrid
New York
Jones, Alan
Starts with M: True, contains an N: False
Paris => Berlin => Madrid => New York
Apples cost £0.39 on Mondays.
Apples cost £0.39 on Mondays.
```

Building strings efficiently

You can concatenate two strings to make a new `string` variable using the `String.Concat` method or simply using the + operator. But both of these choices are bad practice, because .NET must create a completely new `string` variable in memory. This might not be noticeable if you are only adding two `string` values, but if you concatenate inside a loop with many iterations, it can have a significant negative impact on performance and memory use.

In Chapter 8, *Improving Performance and Scalability Using Multitasking,* you will learn how to concatenate the string variables efficiently using the StringBuilder type.

Pattern matching with regular expressions

Regular expressions are useful for validating input from the user. They are very powerful and can get very complicated. Almost all programming languages have support for regular expressions and use a common set of special characters to define them.

Add a new console application project named WorkingWithRegularExpressions.

At the top of the file, import the following namespaces:

```
using System.Text.RegularExpressions;
using static System.Console;
```

In the Main method, add the following statements:

```
Write("Enter your age: ");
string input = ReadLine();
var ageChecker = new Regex(@"\d");
if (ageChecker.IsMatch(input))
{
    WriteLine("Thank you!");
}
else
{
    WriteLine($"This is not a valid age: {input}");
}
```

Good Practice

The @ character in front of string switches off the ability to use escape characters in string. Escape characters are prefixed with a backslash (\). For example, \t means a tab and \n means a new line. When writing regular expressions, we need to disable this feature. To paraphrase the television show *The West Wing,* "Let backslash be backslash."

Run the console application and view the output.

If you enter a whole number for the age, you will see `Thank you!`

```
Enter your age: 34
Thank you!
```

If you enter `carrots`, you will see the error message:

```
Enter your age: carrots
This is not a valid age: carrots
```

However, if you enter `bob30smith`, you will see `Thank you!`

```
Enter your age: bob30smith
Thank you!
```

The regular expression we used is \d, which means one digit. However, it does not specify what can be entered *before* and *after* the one digit. This regular expression could be described in English as "Enter any characters you want as long as you enter at least one digit character."

Change the regular expression to ^\d$, like this:

```
var ageChecker = new Regex(@"^\d$");
```

Rerun the application. Now, it rejects anything except a single digit.

We want to allow one or more digits. To do this, we add a + (plus) after the \d expression to modify the meaning to *one or more*. Change the regular expression to look like this:

```
var ageChecker = new Regex(@"^\d+$");
```

Run the application and see how the regular expression now only allows positive whole numbers of any length.

The syntax of a regular expression

Here are some common symbols that you can use in regular expressions:

Symbol	Meaning	Symbol	Meaning
`^`	Start of input	`$`	End of input
`\d`	A single digit	`\D`	A single NON-digit
`\w`	Whitespace	`\W`	NON-whitespace
`[A-Za-z0-9]`	Range(s) of characters	`\^`	`^` (caret) character
`[aeiou]`	Set of characters	`[^aeiou]`	NOT in a set of characters
`.`	A single character	`\.`	. (dot) character

Here are some quantifiers that affect the previous symbol in a regular expression:

Symbol	Meaning	Symbol	Meaning
`+`	One or more	`?`	One or none
`{3}`	Exactly three	`{3,5}`	Three to five
`{3,}`	Three or more	`{,3}`	Up to three

Examples of regular expressions

Here are some example regular expressions:

Expression	Meaning
`\d`	A single digit somewhere in the input
`a`	The a character somewhere in the input
`Bob`	The word Bob somewhere in the input
`^Bob`	The word Bob at the start of the input
`Bob$`	The word Bob at the end of the input
`^\d{2}$`	Exactly two digits
`^[0-9]{2}$`	Exactly two digits
`^[A-Z]{4,}$`	At least four uppercase letters only
`^[A-Za-z]{4,}$`	At least four upper or lowercase letters only
`^[A-Z]{2}\d{3}$`	Two uppercase letters and three digits only
`^d.g$`	The letter d, then any character, and then the letter g, so it would match both dig and dog or any single character between the d and g

`^d\.g$`	The letter d, then a dot (.), and then the letter g, so it would match d.g only

Good Practice

Use regular expressions to validate input from the user. The same regular expressions can be reused in other languages such as JavaScript.

Working with collections

Another of the most common types of data are collections. If you need to store multiple values in a variable, then you can use a collection.

A **collection** is a data structure in memory that can manage multiple items in different ways, although all collections have some shared functionality.

The most common types in .NET Standard 2.0 for working with collections are shown in the following table:

Namespace	Example type(s)	Description
`System .Collections`	`IEnumerable, IEnumerable<T>`	Interfaces and base classes used by collections.
`System .Collections .Generic`	`List<T>, Dictionary<T>, Queue<T>, Stack<T>`	Introduced in C# 2.0 with .NET Framework 2.0. These collections allow you to specify the type you want to store using a generic type parameter (which is safer, faster, and more efficient).
`System .Collections .Concurrent`	`BlockingCollection, ConcurrentDictionary, ConcurrentQueue`	These collections are safe to use in multithreaded scenarios.
`System .Collections .Immutable`	`ImmutableArray, ImmutableDictionary, ImmutableList, ImmutableQueue`	Designed for scenarios where the contents of the collection should never change.

You can read more at the following link:

```
https://docs.microsoft.com/en-us/dotnet/standard/collections
```

Common features of all collections

All collections implement the `ICollection` interface; this means that they must have a `Count` property to tell you how many items are in it.

For example, if we had a collection named `passengers`, we could do this:

```
int howMany = passengers.Count;
```

All collections implement the `IEnumerable` interface, which means that they must have a `GetEnumerator` method that returns an object that implements `IEnumerator`; this means that they must have a `MoveNext` method and a `Value` property so that they can be iterated using the `foreach` statement.

For example, to perform an action on all the items in the passengers' collection, we can do this:

```
foreach (var passenger in passengers)
{
    // do something with each passenger
}
```

To understand collections, it can be useful to see the most common interfaces that collections implement, as shown in the following diagram:

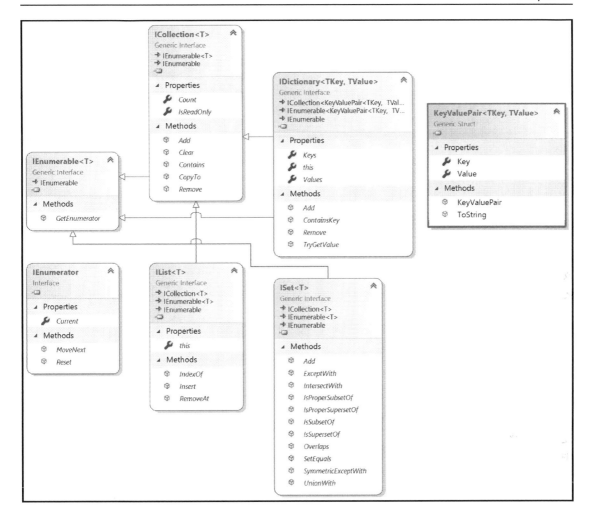

Lists, that is, a type that implements `IList`, are *ordered collections*, this means that they implement `ICollection`; so they must have a `Count` property and an `Add` method to put an item at the end of the collection, and also an `Insert` method to put an item in the list at a specified position, and `RemoveAt` to remove an item at a specified position.

Understanding collections

There are several different collection categories: lists, dictionaries, stacks, queues, sets, and many other more specialized collections.

Lists

Lists are a good choice when you want to manually control the order of items in a collection. Each item in a list has a unique index (or position) that is automatically assigned. Items can be any type (although they should all be the same type) and items can be duplicated. Indexes are `int` types and start from 0, so the first item in a list is at index 0, as shown in the following table:

Index	Item
0	London
1	Paris
2	London
3	Sydney

If a new item (for example, **Santiago**) is inserted between **London** and **Sydney**, then the index of **Sydney** is automatically incremented. Therefore, you must be aware that an item's index can change after inserting or removing items, as shown in the following table:

Index	Item
0	London
1	Paris
2	London
3	Santiago
4	Sydney

Dictionaries

Dictionaries are a good choice when each value (or item) has a unique subvalue (or a made-up value) that can be used as a key to quickly find the value in the collection later. The key must be unique. If you are storing a list of people, you can use a government-issued identity number as the key.

Think of the key as being like an index entry in a real-world dictionary. It allows you to quickly find the definition of a word because the words (for example, keys) are kept sorted, and if we know we're looking for the definition of *Manatee*, we would jump to the middle of the dictionary to start looking, because the letter M is in the middle of the alphabet. Dictionaries in programming are similarly smart when looking something up.

Both the key and the value can be any type. This example uses strings for both:

Key	Value
BSA	Bob Smith
MW	Max Williams
BSB	Bob Smith
AM	Amir Mohammed

Stacks

Stacks are a good choice when you want to implement the **last-in, first-out (LIFO)** behavior. With a stack, you can only directly access the one item at the top of the stack, although you can enumerate to read through the whole stack of items. You cannot, for example, access the second item in a stack.

For example, word processors use a stack to remember the sequence of actions you have recently performed, and then when you press *Ctrl + Z*, it will undo the last action in the stack, and then the next last action, and so on.

Queues

Queues are a good choice when you want to implement the **first-in, first-out (FIFO)** behavior. With a queue, you can only directly access the one item at the front of the queue, although you can enumerate to read through the whole queue of items. You cannot, for example, access the second item in a queue.

For example, background processes use a queue to process work items in the order that they arrive, just like people standing in line at the post office.

Sets

Sets are a good choice when you want to perform set operations between two collections. For example, you may have two collections of city names, and you want to know which names appear in both sets (known as the **intersect** between the sets).

Working with lists

Add a new console application project named `WorkingWithLists`.

At the top of the file, import the following namespaces:

```
using System;
using System.Collections.Generic;
using static System.Console;
```

In the `Main` method, type the following code that illustrates some of the common ways of working with lists:

```
var cities = new List<string>();
cities.Add("London");
cities.Add("Paris");
cities.Add("Milan");
WriteLine("Initial list");
foreach (string city in cities)
{
   WriteLine($"  {city}");
}
WriteLine($"The first city is {cities[0]}.");
WriteLine($"The last city is {cities[cities.Count - 1]}.");
cities.Insert(0, "Sydney");
WriteLine("After inserting Sydney at index 0");
foreach (string city in cities)
{
   WriteLine($"  {city}");
}
cities.RemoveAt(1);
cities.Remove("Milan");
WriteLine("After removing two cities");
foreach (string city in cities)
{
   WriteLine($"  {city}");
}
```

Run the console application to see the output:

```
Initial list
  London
  Paris
  Milan
The first city is London.
The last city is Milan.
After inserting Sydney at index 0
  Sydney
```

```
        London
        Paris
        Milan
After removing two cities
        Sydney
        Paris
```

Working with dictionaries

Add a new console application project named `WorkingWithDictionaries`.

Import the same namespaces as before.

In the `Main` method, type the following code that illustrates some of the common ways of working with dictionaries:

```
var keywords = new Dictionary<string, string>();
keywords.Add("int", "32-bit integer data type");
keywords.Add("long", "64-bit integer data type");
keywords.Add("float", "Single precision floating point number");
WriteLine("Keywords and their definitions");
foreach (KeyValuePair<string, string> item in keywords)
{
    WriteLine($"  {item.Key}: {item.Value}");
}
WriteLine($"The definition of long is {keywords["long"]}");
```

Run the application to view the output:

```
Keywords and their definitions
    int: 32-bit integer data type
    long: 64-bit integer data type
    float: Single precision floating point number
The definition of long is 64-bit integer data type
```

Sorting collections

A `List<T>` class can be sorted by calling its `Sort` method (but remember that the indexes of each item will change).

> Sorting a list of strings or other built-in types works automatically, but if you create a collection of your own type, then that type must implement an interface named `IComparable`. You learned how to do this in `Chapter 4`, *Implementing Interfaces and Inheriting Classes*.

A `Dictionary<T>`, `Stack<T>`, or `Queue<T>` collection cannot be sorted because you wouldn't usually want that functionality; for example, you would never sort a queue of guests checking into a hotel. But sometimes, you might want to sort a dictionary or a set.

The differences between these sorted collections are often subtle, but can have an impact on the memory requirements and performance of your application, so it is worth putting effort into picking the most appropriate option for your requirements.

Some common sorted collections are shown in the following table:

Collection	Description
`SortedDictionary<TKey, TValue>`	This represents a collection of key/value pairs that are sorted on the key
`SortedList<TKey, TValue>`	This represents a collection of key/value pairs that are sorted by key, based on the associated `IComparer<T>` implementation
`SortedSet<T>`	This represents a collection of objects that is maintained in a sorted order

Using specialized collections

There are a few other collections for special situations:

Collection	Description
`System.Collections.BitArray`	This manages a compact array of bit values, which are represented as Booleans, where `true` indicates that the bit is on (1) and `false` indicates the bit is off (0)
`System.Collections.Generics.LinkedList<T>`	This represents a doubly linked list where every item has a reference to its previous and next items

Using immutable collections

Sometimes you need to make a collection immutable, meaning that its members cannot change; that is, you cannot add or remove them.

If you import the `System.Collections.Immutable` namespace, then any collection that implements `IEnumerable<T>` is given six extension methods to convert it into an immutable list, dictionary, hashset, and so on.

Open the `WorkingWithLists` project, import the `System.Collections.Immutable` namespace, and add the following statements to the end of the `Main` method, as shown in the following code:

```
var immutableCities = cities.ToImmutableList();

var newList = immutableCities.Add("Rio");

Write("Immutable cities:");
foreach (string city in immutableCities)
{
    Write($" {city}");
}
WriteLine();

Write("New cities:");
foreach (string city in newList)
{
    Write($" {city}");
}
WriteLine();
```

Run the console application, view the output, and note that the immutable list of cities does not get modified when you call the `Add` method on it; instead it returns a new list with the newly added city:

```
After removing two cities
   Sydney
   Paris
Immutable cities: Sydney Paris
New cities: Sydney Paris Rio
```

Working with network resources

Sometimes you will need to work with network resources. The most common types in .NET Standard for working with network resources are shown in the following table:

Namespace	Example type(s)	Description
`System.Net`	`Dns, Uri, Cookie, WebClient, IPAddress`	These are for working with DNS servers, URIs, IP addresses, and so on
`System.Net`	`FtpStatusCode, FtpWebRequest, FtpWebResponse`	These are for working with FTP servers
`System.Net`	`HttpStatusCode, HttpWebRequest, HttpWebResponse`	These are for working with HTTP servers, that is, websites
`System.Net.Mail`	`Attachment, MailAddress, MailMessage, SmtpClient`	These are for working with SMTP servers, that is, sending email messages
`System.Net.NetworkInformation`	`IPStatus, NetworkChange, Ping, TcpStatistics`	These are for working with low-level network protocols

Working with URIs, DNS, and IP addresses

Add a new console application project named `WorkingWithNetworkResources`.

At the top of the file, import the following namespaces:

```
using System;
using System.Net;
using static System.Console;
```

In the `Main` method, enter statements to prompt the user to enter a website address, and then use the `Uri` type to break it down into its parts, including scheme (HTTP, FTP, and so on), port number, and host, as shown in the following code:

```
Write("Enter a valid web address: ");
string url = ReadLine();
if (string.IsNullOrWhiteSpace(url))
{
    url = "http://world.episerver.com/cms/?q=pagetype";
}

var uri = new Uri(url);

WriteLine($"Scheme: {uri.Scheme}");
WriteLine($"Port: {uri.Port}");
WriteLine($"Host: {uri.Host}");
```

Chapter 6

```
WriteLine($"Path: {uri.AbsolutePath}");
WriteLine($"Query: {uri.Query}");
```

Run the console application, enter a valid website address, press *Enter*, and view the output:

```
Enter a valid web address:
Scheme: http
Port: 80
Host: world.episerver.com
Path: /cms/
Query: ?q=pagetype
```

Add the following statements to `Main` to get the IP address for the entered website, as shown in the following code:

```
IPHostEntry entry = Dns.GetHostEntry(uri.Host);
WriteLine($"{entry.HostName} has the following IP addresses:");
foreach (IPAddress address in entry.AddressList)
{
    WriteLine($" {address}");
}
```

Run the console application, enter a valid website address, press *Enter*, and view the output:

```
world.episerver.com has the following IP addresses: 217.114.90.249
```

Pinging a server

In `Program.cs`, add a statement to import `System.Net.NetworkInformation`, as shown in the following code:

```
using System.Net.NetworkInformation;
```

Add the following statements to `Main` to get the IP addresses for the entered website, as shown in the following code:

```
var ping = new Ping();
PingReply reply = ping.Send(uri.Host);
WriteLine($"{uri.Host} was pinged, and replied: {reply.Status}.");
if (reply.Status == IPStatus.Success)
{
```

```
    WriteLine($"Reply from {reply.Address} took
    {reply.RoundtripTime:N0}ms");
}
```

Run the console application, press *Enter*, view the output, and note that Episerver's developer site does not respond to ping requests (this is often done to avoid DDoS attacks):

world.episerver.com was pinged, and replied: TimedOut.

Run the console application again, and enter http://google.com, as shown in the following output:

```
Enter a valid web address: http://google.com
Scheme: http
Port: 80
Host: google.com
Path: /
Query:
google.com has the following IP addresses:
  216.58.206.78
  2a00:1450:4009:804::200e
google.com was pinged, and replied: Success.
Reply from 216.58.206.78 took 9ms
```

Working with types and attributes

Reflection is a programming feature that allows code to understand and manipulate itself. An assembly is made up of up to four parts:

- **Assembly metadata and manifest**: Name, assembly and file version, referenced assemblies, and so on
- **Type metadata**: Information about the types, their members, and so on
- **IL code**: Implementation of methods, properties, constructors, and so on
- **Embedded Resources (optional)**: Images, strings, JavaScript, and so on

Metadata comprises of items of information about your code. Metadata is applied to your code using attributes. Attributes can be applied at multiple levels: to assemblies, to types, and to their members, as shown in the following code:

```
// an assembly-level attribute
[assembly: AssemblyTitle("Working with Reflection")]

[Serializable] // a type-level attribute
```

```
public class Person
// a member-level attribute
[Obsolete("Deprecated: use Run instead.")]
public void Walk()
{
    // ...
}
```

Versioning of assemblies

Version numbers in .NET are a combination of three numbers, with two optional additions. If you follow the rules of semantic versioning:

- **Major**: Breaking changes
- **Minor**: Non-breaking changes, including new features and bug fixes
- **Patch**: Non-breaking bug fixes

Optionally, a version can include these:

- **Prerelease**: Unsupported preview releases
- **Build number**: Nightly builds

Good Practice
Follow the rules of semantic versioning, as described at the following link: http://semver.org

Reading assembly metadata

Add a new console application project named `WorkingWithReflection`.

At the top of the file, import the following types and namespaces:

```
using static System.Console;
using System;
using System.Reflection;
```

In the `Main` method, enter statements to get the console apps assembly, output its name and location, and get all assembly-level attributes and output their types, as shown in the following code:

```
WriteLine("Assembly metadata:");
```

```
Assembly assembly = Assembly.GetEntryAssembly();

WriteLine($" Full name: {assembly.FullName}");
WriteLine($" Location: {assembly.Location}");

var attributes = assembly.GetCustomAttributes();

WriteLine($" Attributes:");
foreach (Attribute a in attributes)
{
    WriteLine($"   {a.GetType()}");
}
```

Run the console application and view the output:

```
Assembly metadata:
  Full name: WorkingWithReflection, Version=1.0.0.0, Culture=neutral,
PublicKeyToken=null
  Location:
/Users/markjprice/Code/Chapter08/WorkingWithReflection/bin/Debug/netcoreapp
2.0/WorkingWithReflection.dll
  Attributes:
    System.Runtime.CompilerServices.CompilationRelaxationsAttribute
    System.Runtime.CompilerServices.RuntimeCompatibilityAttribute
    System.Diagnostics.DebuggableAttribute
    System.Runtime.Versioning.TargetFrameworkAttribute
    System.Reflection.AssemblyCompanyAttribute
    System.Reflection.AssemblyConfigurationAttribute
    System.Reflection.AssemblyDescriptionAttribute
    System.Reflection.AssemblyFileVersionAttribute
    System.Reflection.AssemblyInformationalVersionAttribute
    System.Reflection.AssemblyProductAttribute
    System.Reflection.AssemblyTitleAttribute
```

Now that we know some of the attributes decorating the assembly, we can ask for them specifically.

Add statements to the end of the `Main` method to get the `AssemblyInformationalVersionAttribute` and `AssemblyCompanyAttribute` classes, as shown in the following code:

```
var version =
assembly.GetCustomAttribute<AssemblyInformationalVersionAttribute>();
WriteLine($" Version: {version.InformationalVersion}");

var company = assembly.GetCustomAttribute<AssemblyCompanyAttribute>();
WriteLine($" Company: {company.Company}");
```

Run the console application and view the output:

```
Version: 1.0.0
Company: WorkingWithReflection
```

Hmm, let's explicitly set this information. The .NET Framework way to set these values is to add attributes in the C# source code file, as shown in the following code:

```
[assembly: AssemblyCompany("Packt Publishing")]
[assembly: AssemblyInformationalVersion("1.0.0")]
```

Roslyn compiler sets these attributes automatically, so we can't use the old way. Instead, they can be set in the project file.

Modify `WorkingWithReflection.csproj`, as shown in the following example:

```
<Project Sdk="Microsoft.NET.Sdk">

  <PropertyGroup>
    <OutputType>Exe</OutputType>
    <TargetFramework>netcoreapp2.0</TargetFramework>
    <Version>1.3.0</Version>
    <Company>Packt Publishing</Company>
  </PropertyGroup>

</Project>
```

Run the console application and view the output:

```
Version: 1.3.0
Company: Packt Publishing
```

Creating custom attributes

You can define your own attributes by inheriting from the `Attribute` class.

Add a class named `CoderAttribute`, as shown in the following code:

```
using System;

[AttributeUsage(AttributeTargets.Class | AttributeTargets.Method,
                AllowMultiple = true)]
public class CoderAttribute : Attribute
{
    public string Coder { get; set; }
    public DateTime LastModified { get; set; }
```

```
    public CoderAttribute(string coder, string lastModified)
    {
       Coder = coder;
       LastModified = DateTime.Parse(lastModified);
    }
}
```

In `Program`, add a method named `DoStuff`, and decorate it with the `Coder` attribute, as shown in the following code:

```
[Coder("Mark Price", "22 August 2017")]
[Coder("Johnni Rasmussen", "13 September 2017")]
public static void DoStuff()
{

}
```

In `Program.cs`, import `System.Linq`, as shown in the following code:

```
using System.Linq;
```

In `Main`, add code to get the types, enumerate their members, read any `Coder` attributes on those members, and output the information, as shown in the following code:

```
WriteLine($"Types:");
Type[] types = assembly.GetTypes();

foreach (Type type in types)
{
    WriteLine($" Name: {type.FullName}");

    MemberInfo[] members = type.GetMembers();

    foreach (MemberInfo member in members)
    {
        WriteLine($" {member.MemberType}: {member.Name}
        ({member.DeclaringType.Name})");

        var coders = member.GetCustomAttributes<CoderAttribute>()
        .OrderByDescending(c => c.LastModified);
        foreach (CoderAttribute coder in coders)
        {
            WriteLine($" Modified by {coder.Coder} on
            {coder.LastModified.ToShortDateString()}");
        }
    }
}
```

Run the console application and view the output:

```
Types:
  Name: CoderAttribute
    Method: get_Coder (CoderAttribute)
    Method: set_Coder (CoderAttribute)
    Method: get_LastModified (CoderAttribute)
    Method: set_LastModified (CoderAttribute)
    Method: Equals (Attribute)
    Method: GetHashCode (Attribute)
    Method: get_TypeId (Attribute)
    Method: Match (Attribute)
    Method: IsDefaultAttribute (Attribute)
    Method: ToString (Object)
    Method: GetType (Object)
    Constructor: .ctor (CoderAttribute)
    Property: Coder (CoderAttribute)
    Property: LastModified (CoderAttribute)
    Property: TypeId (Attribute)
  Name: WorkingWithReflection.Program
    Method: DoStuff (Program)
      Modified by Johnni Rasmussen on 13/09/2017
      Modified by Mark Price on 22/08/2017
    Method: ToString (Object)
    Method: Equals (Object)
    Method: GetHashCode (Object)
    Method: GetType (Object)
    Constructor: .ctor (Program)
  Name: WorkingWithReflection.Program+<>c
    Method: ToString (Object)
    Method: Equals (Object)
    Method: GetHashCode (Object)
    Method: GetType (Object)
    Constructor: .ctor (<>c)
    Field: <>9 (<>c)
    Field: <>9__0_0 (<>c)
```

Doing more with reflection

This is just a taster of what can be achieved with reflection. We only used reflection to read metadata from our code. Reflection can also do the following:

- Dynamically load assemblies that are not currently referenced
- Dynamically execute code
- Dynamically generate new code and assemblies

Internationalizing your code

Internationalization is the process of enabling your code to run correctly all over the world. It has two parts: **globalization** and **localization**.

Globalization is about writing your code to accommodate multiple language and region combinations. The combination of a language and a region is known as a culture. It is important for your code to know both the language and region because the date and currency formats are different in Quebec and Paris, despite them both using the French language.

There are **International Organization for Standardization (ISO)** codes for all culture combinations. For example, in the code da-DK, da indicates the Danish language and DK indicates the Denmark region, or in the code fr-CA, fr indicates the French language and CA indicates the Canadian region.

ISO is not an acronym. ISO is a reference to the Greek word **isos** (which means *equal*).

Localization is about customizing the user interface to support a language, for example, changing the label of a button to be **Close** (en) or **Fermer** (fr). Since localization is more about the language, it doesn't always need to know about the region, although ironically enough, standardization (en-US) and standardisation (en-GB) suggest otherwise.

Internationalization is a huge topic on which several thousand-page books have been written. In this section, you will get a brief introduction to the basics using the CultureInfo type in the System.Globalization namespace.

Globalizing an application

Add a new console application project named `Internationalization`.

At the top of the file, import the following types and namespaces:

```
using static System.Console;
using System;
using System.Globalization;
```

In the `Main` method, enter the following statements:

```
CultureInfo globalization = CultureInfo.CurrentCulture;
CultureInfo localization = CultureInfo.CurrentUICulture;
WriteLine($"The current globalization culture is
{globalization.Name}: {globalization.DisplayName}");
WriteLine($"The current localization culture is
{localization.Name}: {localization.DisplayName}");
WriteLine();
WriteLine("en-US: English (United States)");
WriteLine("da-DK: Danish (Denmark)");
WriteLine("fr-CA: French (Canada)");
Write("Enter an ISO culture code: ");
string newculture = ReadLine();
if (!string.IsNullOrEmpty(newculture))
{
    var ci = new CultureInfo(newculture);
    CultureInfo.CurrentCulture = ci;
    CultureInfo.CurrentUICulture = ci;
}
Write("Enter your name: ");
string name = ReadLine();
Write("Enter your date of birth: ");
string dob = ReadLine();
Write("Enter your salary: ");
string salary = ReadLine();
DateTime date = DateTime.Parse(dob);
int minutes = (int)DateTime.Today.Subtract(date).TotalMinutes;
decimal earns = decimal.Parse(salary);
WriteLine($"{name} was born on a {date:dddd} and is {minutes:N0}
minutes old and earns {earns:C}.");
```

When you run an application, it automatically sets its thread to use the culture of the operating system. I am running my code in London, UK, so the thread is already set to English (United Kingdom).

The code prompts the user to enter an alternative ISO code. This allows your applications to replace the default culture at runtime.

The application then uses standard format codes to output the day of the week, dddd; the number of minutes with thousand separators, N0; and the salary with the currency symbol, C. These adapt automatically, based on the thread's culture.

Run the console application and view the output. Enter en-GB for the ISO code and then enter some sample data. You will need to enter a date in a format valid for British English:

```
Enter an ISO culture code: en-GB
Enter your name: Alice
Enter your date of birth: 30/3/1967
Enter your salary: 23500
Alice was born on a Thursday, is 25,469,280 minutes old and earns
£23,500.00.
```

Rerun the application and try a different culture, such as Danish in Denmark (da-DK):

```
Enter an ISO culture code: da-DK
Enter your name: Mikkel
Enter your date of birth: 12/3/1980
Enter your salary: 34000
Mikkel was born on a onsdag, is 18.656.640 minutes old and earns kr.
34.000,00.
```

Good Practice

Consider whether your application needs to be internationalized and plan for that before you start coding! Write down all the pieces of text in the user interface that will need to be localized. Think about all the data that will need to be globalized (date formats, number formats, and sorting text behavior).

Summary

In this chapter, you explored some choices for types to store and manipulate text, which collections to use for storing multiple items, and how to internationalize your code.

In the next chapter, we will manage files and streams, encode and decode text, and perform serialization.

7
Working with Files, Streams, and Serialization

This chapter is about reading and writing to files and streams, text encoding, and serialization.

This chapter will cover the following topics:

- Managing the filesystem
- Reading and writing with streams
- Encoding text
- Serializing object graphs

Managing the filesystem

Your applications will often need to perform input and output with files and directories in different environments. The `System` and `System.IO` namespaces contain classes for this purpose.

Handling cross-platform environments and filesystems

In Visual Studio 2017, press *Ctrl + Shift + N* or choose **File | New | Project...**.

In the **New Project** dialog, in the **Installed** list, select **.NET Core**. In the center list, select **Console App (.NET Core)**, type **Name** as WorkingWithFileSystems, change the location to C:\Code, type the solution name as Chapter09, and then click on **OK**.

In Visual Studio Code, in **Integrated Terminal**, make a new directory named Chapter09 and a subdirectory named WorkingWithFileSystems. Open the folder and enter the dotnet new console command.

At the top of the Program.cs file, add the following import statements. Note that we will statically import the Directory, Path, and Environment types to simplify our code:

```
using static System.Console;
using System.IO;
using static System.IO.Directory;
using static System.IO.Path;
using static System.Environment;
```

The paths are different for Windows, macOS, and Linux, so we will start by exploring how .NET Core handles this.

Create a static OutputFileSystemInfo method, and write statements to the following:

- Output the path and directory separation characters
- Output the path of the current directory
- Output some special paths for system files, temporary files, and documents

```
static void OutputFileSystemInfo()
{
    WriteLine($"Path.PathSeparator: {PathSeparator}");
    WriteLine($"Path.DirectorySeparatorChar: {DirectorySeparatorChar}");
    WriteLine($"Directory.GetCurrentDirectory(): {GetCurrentDirectory()}");
    WriteLine($"Environment.CurrentDirectory: {CurrentDirectory}");
    WriteLine($"Environment.SystemDirectory: {SystemDirectory}");
    WriteLine($"Path.GetTempPath(): {GetTempPath()}");
    WriteLine($"GetFolderPath(SpecialFolder):");
    WriteLine($" System: {GetFolderPath(SpecialFolder.System)}");
    WriteLine($" ApplicationData:
    {GetFolderPath(SpecialFolder.ApplicationData)}");
    WriteLine($" MyDocuments: {GetFolderPath(SpecialFolder.MyDocuments)}");
    WriteLine($" Personal: {GetFolderPath(SpecialFolder.Personal)}");
```

```
}
```

The `Environment` type has many other useful members, including the `GetEnvironmentVariables` method and the `OSVersion` and `ProcessorCount` properties.

In the `Main` method, call `OutputFileSystemInfo`, as shown in the following code:

```
static void Main(string[] args)
{
    OutputFileSystemInfo();
}
```

Using Windows 10

Run the console application and view the output, as shown in the following screenshot:

```
C:\WINDOWS\system32\cmd.exe                              —    □    ×
Path.PathSeparator:                   ;
Path.DirectorySeparatorChar:          \
Directory.GetCurrentDirectory(): C:\Code\Chapter09\WorkingWithFileSystem
Environment.CurrentDirectory:    C:\Code\Chapter09\WorkingWithFileSystem
Environment.SystemDirectory:     C:\WINDOWS\system32
Path.GetTempPath():              C:\Users\markj\AppData\Local\Temp\
GetFolderPath(SpecialFolder):
  System:                        C:\WINDOWS\system32
  ApplicationData:               C:\Users\markj\AppData\Roaming
  MyDocuments:                   \\Mac\Home\Documents
  Personal:                      \\Mac\Home\Documents
Press any key to continue . . .
```

Windows uses a backslash for the directory separator character.

Using macOS

Run the console application and view the output, as shown in the following screenshot:

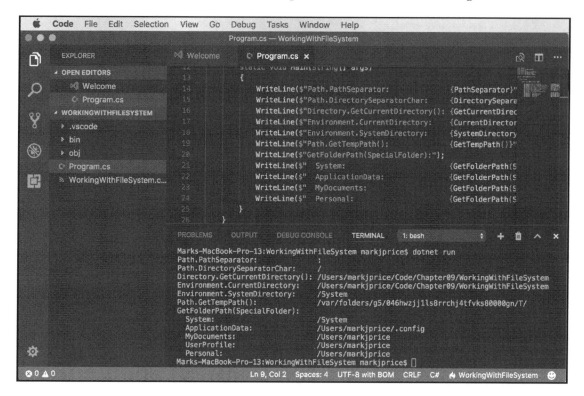

 macOS uses a forward slash for the directory separator character.

Managing drives

To manage drives, use `DriveInfo`, which has a static method that returns information about all the drives connected to your computer. Each drive has a drive type.

`DriveInfo` and `DriveType` are shown in the following diagram:

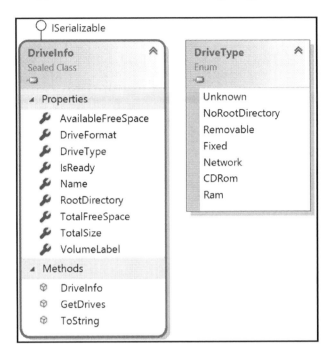

Create a `WorkWithDrives` method, and write statements to get all the drives and output their name, type, size, available free space, and format, but only if the drive is ready, as shown in the following code:

```
static void WorkWithDrives()
{
    WriteLine($"|----------------------------------|------------|
---------|--------------------|--------------------|");
    WriteLine($"| Name | Type | Format | Size | Free space |");
    WriteLine($"|----------------------------------|------------|
---------|--------------------|--------------------|");

    foreach (DriveInfo drive in DriveInfo.GetDrives())
    {
        if (drive.IsReady)
        {
            WriteLine($"| {drive.Name,-30} |
            {drive.DriveType,-10} | {drive.DriveFormat, -7} |
            {drive.TotalSize,18:N0} |
            {drive.AvailableFreeSpace,18:N0} |");
        }
```

```
        else
        {
            WriteLine($"| {drive.Name,-30} | {drive.DriveType,-10} |");
        }
    }
    WriteLine($"|-------------------------------|------------|
    ---------|--------------------|--------------------|");
}
```

Good Practice
Check that a drive is ready before reading properties such as `TotalSize` or you will see an exception thrown with removable drives.

In `Main`, comment out the previous method call, and add a call to `WorkWithDrives`, as shown in the following code:

```
static void Main(string[] args)
{
    // OutputFileSystemInfo();

    WorkWithDrives();
}
```

Run the console application and view the output, as shown in the following screenshot:

Name	Type	Format	Size	Free space
/	Fixed	hfs	498,954,403,840	135,917,678,592
/dev	Ram	devfs	191,488	0
/net	Network	autofs	0	0
/home	Network	autofs	0	0
/Volumes/LaCie	Fixed	hfs	4,000,443,056,128	3,775,136,669,696
/Volumes/[C] Windows 10.hidden	Network	smbfs	136,844,406,784	43,311,140,864

Managing directories

To manage directories, use the `Directory`, `Path` and `Environment` static classes, as shown in the following diagram:

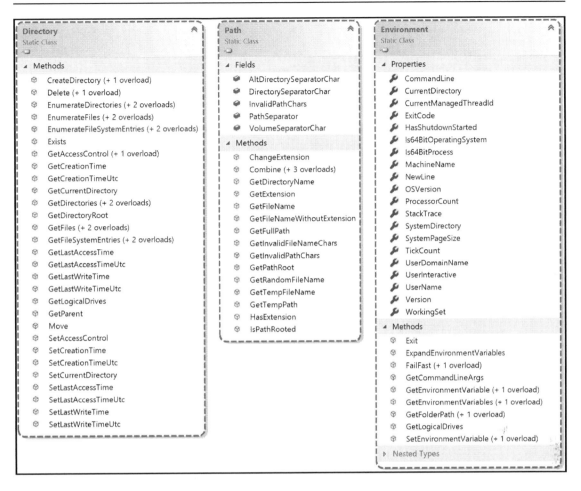

When constructing custom paths, you must be careful to write your code so that it makes no assumptions about platform, for example, what to use for the directory separator character.

Create a `WorkWithDirectories` method, and write statements to do the following:

- Define a custom path under the user's home directory by creating an array of strings for the directory names, and then properly combining them with the `Path` type's `Combine` method
- Check for the existence of the custom directory path

- Create, and then delete the directory, including files and subdirectories within it:

```
static void WorkWithDirectories()
{
    // define a custom directory path
    string userFolder = GetFolderPath(SpecialFolder.Personal);

    var customFolder = new string[]
    { userFolder, "Code", "Chapter09", "NewFolder" };
    string dir = Combine(customFolder);

    WriteLine($"Working with: {dir}");

    // check if it exists
    WriteLine($"Does it exist? {Exists(dir)}");

    // create directory
    WriteLine("Creating it...");
    CreateDirectory(dir);
    WriteLine($"Does it exist? {Exists(dir)}");

    Write("Confirm the directory exists, and then press ENTER: ");
    ReadLine();

    // delete directory
    WriteLine("Deleting it...");
    Delete(dir, recursive: true);
    WriteLine($"Does it exist? {Exists(dir)}");
}
```

In the `Main` method, comment out the previous method call, and add a call to `WorkWithDirectories`, as shown in the following code:

```
static void Main(string[] args)
{
    // OutputFileSystemInfo();
    // WorkWithDrives();

    WorkWithDirectories();
}
```

Run the console application and view the output, and use your favorite file management tool to confirm that the directory has been created before pressing *Enter* to delete it:

```
Working with: /Users/markjprice/Code/Chapter09/NewFolder
Does it exist? False
Creating it...
Does it exist? True
Confirm the directory exists, and then press ENTER:
Deleting it...
Does it exist? False
```

Managing files

When working with files, you could statically import the `File` type, just as we did for the `Directory` type, but, for the next example, we will not, because it has some of the same methods as the `Directory` type and they would conflict. The `File` type has a short enough name not to matter in this case.

Create a `WorkWithFiles` method, and write statements to do the following:

- Check for the existence of a file
- Create a text file
- Write a line of text to the file
- Copy the file to a backup
- Delete the original file
- Read the backup file's contents

```
static void WorkWithFiles()
{
    // define a custom directory path
    string userFolder = GetFolderPath(SpecialFolder.Personal);

    var customFolder = new string[]
    { userFolder, "Code", "Chapter09", "OutputFiles" };

    string dir = Combine(customFolder);
    CreateDirectory(dir);

    // define file paths
    string textFile = Combine(dir, "Dummy.txt");
    string backupFile = Combine(dir, "Dummy.bak");

    WriteLine($"Working with: {textFile}");
```

```
// check if a file exists
WriteLine($"Does it exist? {File.Exists(textFile)}");

// create a new text file and write a line to it
StreamWriter textWriter = File.CreateText(textFile);
textWriter.WriteLine("Hello, C#!");
textWriter.Close(); // close file and release resources

WriteLine($"Does it exist? {File.Exists(textFile)}");

// copy the file, and overwrite if it already exists
File.Copy(
    sourceFileName: textFile,
    destFileName: backupFile,
    overwrite: true);

WriteLine($"Does {backupFile} exist? {File.Exists(backupFile)}");

Write("Confirm the files exist, and then press ENTER: ");
ReadLine();

// delete file
File.Delete(textFile);

WriteLine($"Does it exist? {File.Exists(textFile)}");

// read from the text file backup
WriteLine($"Reading contents of {backupFile}:");
StreamReader textReader = File.OpenText(backupFile);
WriteLine(textReader.ReadToEnd());
textReader.Close();
}
```

 In .NET Standard 2.0, you can use either the `Close` or `Dispose` method when you are finished working with `StreamReader` or `StreamWriter`. In .NET Core 1.x, you could only use `Dispose`, because Microsoft had over-simplified the API.

In `Main`, comment out the previous method call, and add a call to `WorkWithFiles`.

Run the console application and view the output:

```
Working with: /Users/markjprice/Code/Chapter09/OutputFiles/Dummy.txt
Does it exist? False
Does it exist? True
Does /Users/markjprice/Code/Chapter09/OutputFiles/Dummy.bak exist? True
Confirm the files exist, and then press ENTER:
Does it exist? False
Reading contents of /Users/markjprice/Code/Chapter09/OutputFiles/Dummy.bak:
Hello, C#!
```

Managing paths

Sometimes, you need to work with parts of a path, for example, you might want to extract just the folder name, the file name, or the extension. Sometimes, you need to generate temporary folders and file names. You can do this with the Path class.

Add the following statements to the end of the WorkWithFiles method:

```
WriteLine($"File Name: {GetFileName(textFile)}");
WriteLine($"File Name without Extension:
{GetFileNameWithoutExtension(textFile)}");
WriteLine($"File Extension: {GetExtension(textFile)}");
WriteLine($"Random File Name: {GetRandomFileName()}");
WriteLine($"Temporary File Name: {GetTempFileName()}");
```

Run the console application and view the output:

```
File Name: Dummy.txt
File Name without Extension: Dummy
File Extension: .txt
Random File Name: u45w1zki.co3
Temporary File Name:
/var/folders/tz/xx0y_wld5sx0nv0fjtq4tnpc0000gn/T/tmpyqrepP.
tmp
```

 GetTempFileName creates a zero-byte file and returns its name, ready for you to use. GetRandomFileName just returns a filename; it doesn't create the file.

Getting file information

To get more information about a file or directory, for example, its size or when it was last accessed, you can create an instance of the `FileInfo` or `DirectoryInfo` class, as shown in the following diagram:

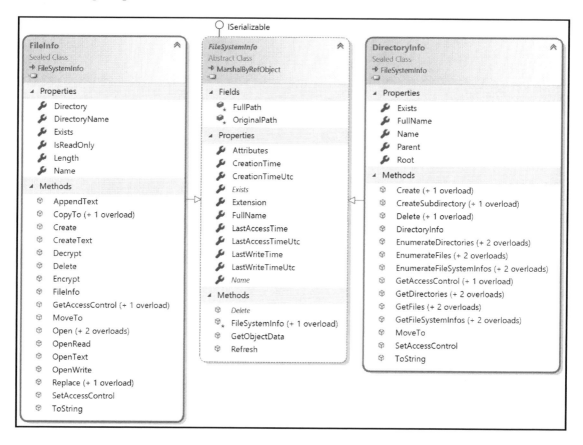

 `FileInfo` and `DirectoryInfo` both inherit from `FileSystemInfo`, so they both have members such as `LastAccessTime` and `Delete`.

Add the following statements to the end of the `WorkWithFiles` method:

```
var info = new FileInfo(backupFile);
WriteLine($"{backupFile}:");
WriteLine($"  Contains {info.Length} bytes");
WriteLine($"  Last accessed {info.LastAccessTime}");
WriteLine($"  Has readonly set to {info.IsReadOnly}");
```

Run the console application and view the output:

```
/Users/markjprice/Code/Chapter09/OutputFiles/Dummy.bak:
  Contains 11 bytes
  Last accessed 26/08/2017 09:08:26
  Has readonly set to False
```

Controlling files

When working with files, you often need to control options. To do this, use the `File.Open` method because it has overloads to specify additional options using the `enum` values as shown in the following diagram:

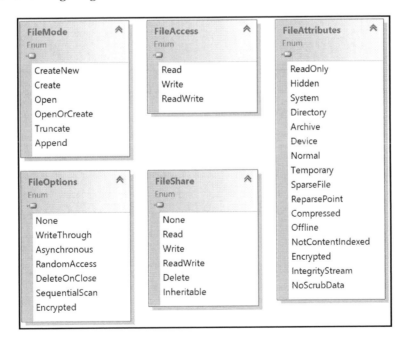

The `enum` types are as follows:

- `FileMode`: This controls what you want to do with the file
- `FileAccess`: This controls what level of access you need
- `FileShare`: This controls locks on the file to allow other processes the specified level of access
- `FileOptions`: This is for advanced options
- `FileAttributes`: This is for a `FileSystemInfo`-derived type, use this `enum` type to check its `Attributes` property

You might want to open a file and read from it, and allow other processes to read it too, as shown in the following code:

```
FileStream file = File.Open(pathToFile, FileMode.Open, FileAccess.Read,
FileShare.Read);
```

You might want to check a file or directory's attributes, as shown in the following code:

```
var info = new FileInfo(backupFile);
WriteLine($"Compressed?
{info.Attributes.HasFlag(FileAttributes.Compressed)}");
```

Reading and writing with streams

A **stream** is a sequence of bytes that can be read from and written to. Although files can be processed rather like arrays, with random access provided by knowing the position of a byte within the file, it can be useful to process files as a stream in which the bytes can be accessed in sequential order.

Streams can also be used to process terminal input and output and networking resources such as sockets and ports that do not provide random access and cannot seek to a position. So you can write code to process some arbitrary bytes without knowing or caring where it comes from. Your code simply reads or writes to a stream, and another piece of code handles where the bytes are actually stored.

There is an abstract class named `Stream` that represents a stream. There are many classes that inherit from this base class, so they all work the same way, as shown in the following class diagram:

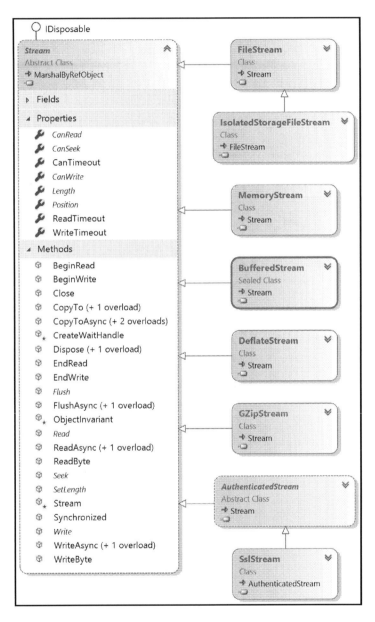

All streams implement `Disposable`, so they have a `Dispose` method to release unmanaged resources.

In the following table are some of the common members of the `Stream` class:

Member	Description
`CanRead`, `CanWrite`	This determines whether you can read from and write to the stream
`Length`, `Position`	This determines the total number of bytes and the current position within the stream
`Dispose()`	This closes the stream and releases its resources
`Flush()`	If the stream has a buffer, then it is cleared and written to the underlying stream
`Read()`, `ReadAsync()`	This reads a specified number of bytes from the stream into a byte array and advances the position
`ReadByte()`	This reads the next byte from the stream and advances the position
`Seek()`	This moves the position to the specified position (if `CanSeek` is true)
`Write()`, `WriteAsync()`	This writes the contents of a byte array into the stream
`WriteByte()`	This writes a byte to the stream

Storage streams represent a location where the bytes will be stored.

Namespace	Class	Description
`System.IO`	`FileStream`	Bytes stored in the filesystem
`System.IO`	`MemoryStream`	Bytes stored in memory in the current process
`System.Net.Sockets`	`NetworkStream`	Bytes stored at a network location

Function streams can only be "plugged onto" other streams to add functionality.

Namespace	Class	Description
`System.Security.Cryptography`	`CryptoStream`	This encrypts and decrypts the stream
`System.IO.Compression`	`GZipStream, DeflateStream`	This compresses and decompresses the stream
`System.Net.Security`	`AuthenticatedStream`	This sends credentials across the stream

Although there will be occasions where you need to work with streams at a low level, most often, you can plug helper classes into the chain to make things easier, as shown in the following diagram:

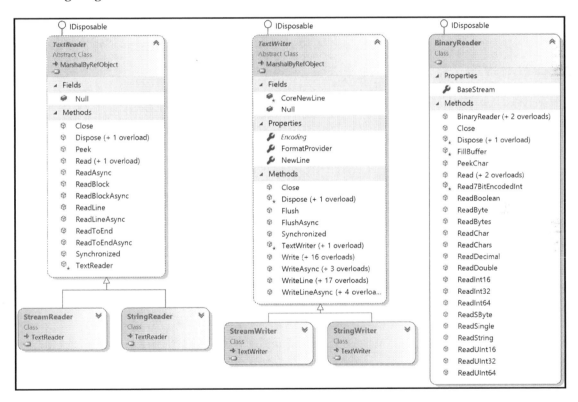

All the helper types for streams implement `Disposable`, so they have a `Dispose` method to release unmanaged resources.

Here are some helper classes to handle common scenarios:

Namespace	Class	Description
`System.IO`	`StreamReader`	This reads from streams as text
`System.IO`	`StreamWriter`	This writes to streams as text
`System.IO`	`BinaryReader`	This reads from streams as .NET types
`System.IO`	`BinaryWriter`	This writes to streams as .NET types
`System.Xml`	`XmlReader`	This reads from streams as XML
`System.Xml`	`XmlWriter`	This writes to streams as XML

Writing to text and XML streams

Add a new console application project named `WorkingWithStreams`.

In Visual Studio 2017, set the solution's start-up project to be the current selection.

Writing to text streams

Import the `System.IO` and `System.Xml` namespaces, and statically import the `System.Console`, `System.Environment` and `System.IO.Path` types.

Define an array of Viper pilot call signs, and create a `WorkWithText` method that enumerates the call signs, writing each one into a text file, as shown in the following code:

```
// define an array of Viper pilot call signs
static string[] callsigns = new string[] { "Husker", "Starbuck",
"Apollo", "Boomer", "Bulldog", "Athena", "Helo", "Racetrack" };

static void WorkWithText()
{
   // define a file to write to
   string textFile = Combine(CurrentDirectory, "streams.txt");

   // create a text file and return a helper writer
   StreamWriter text = File.CreateText(textFile);

   // enumerate the strings, writing each one
   // to the stream on a separate line
```

```
      foreach (string item in callsigns)
      {
          text.WriteLine(item);
      }
      text.Close(); // release resources

      // output the contents of the file to the Console
      WriteLine($"{textFile} contains
      {new FileInfo(textFile).Length} bytes.");
      WriteLine(File.ReadAllText(textFile));
}
```

In `Main`, call the `WorkWithText` method, as shown in the following code:

```
static void Main(string[] args)
{
    WorkWithText();
}
```

Run the console application and view the output:

```
/Users/markjprice/Code/Chapter09/WorkingWithStreams/streams.txt contains 60
bytes.
Husker
Starbuck
Apollo
Boomer
Bulldog
Athena
Helo
Racetrack
```

Open the file that was created and check that it contains the list of call signs.

Writing to XML streams

Create a `WorkWithXml` method that enumerates the call signs, writing each one into an XML file, as shown in the following code:

```
static void WorkWithXml()
{
    // define a file to write to
    string xmlFile = Combine(CurrentDirectory, "streams.xml");

    // create a file streams
    FileStream xmlFileStream = File.Create(xmlFile);

    // wrap the file stream in an XML writer helper
    // and automatically indent nested elements
    XmlWriter xml = XmlWriter.Create(xmlFileStream,
    new XmlWriterSettings { Indent = true });

    // write the XML declaration
    xml.WriteStartDocument();

    // write a root element
    xml.WriteStartElement("callsigns");

    // enumerate the strings writing each one to the stream
    foreach (string item in callsigns)
    {
        xml.WriteElementString("callsign", item);
    }

    // write the close root element
    xml.WriteEndElement();

    // close helper and stream
    xml.Close();
    xmlFileStream.Close();

    // output all the contents of the file to the Console
    WriteLine($"{xmlFile} contains {new FileInfo(xmlFile).Length} bytes.");
    WriteLine(File.ReadAllText(xmlFile));
}
```

In `Main`, comment the previous method call, and add a call to the `WorkWithXml` method.

Run the console application and view the output:

```
/Users/markjprice/Code/Chapter09/WorkingWithStreams/streams.xml contains
310 bytes.
<?xml version="1.0" encoding="utf-8"?>
<callsigns>
  <callsign>Husker</callsign>
  <callsign>Starbuck</callsign>
  <callsign>Apollo</callsign>
  <callsign>Boomer</callsign>
  <callsign>Bulldog</callsign>
  <callsign>Athena</callsign>
  <callsign>Helo</callsign>
  <callsign>Racetrack</callsign>
</callsigns>
```

Disposing of file resources

When you open a file to read or write to it, you are using resources outside of .NET. These are called unmanaged resources and must be disposed of when you are done working with them. To guarantee that they are disposed of, we can call the Dispose method inside of a finally block.

Implementing disposal with try statement

Modify the WorkWithXml method, as shown highlighted in the following code:

```
static void WorkWithXml()
{
    FileStream xmlFileStream = null;
    XmlWriter xml = null;
    try
    {
        // define a file to write to
        string xmlFile = Combine(CurrentDirectory, "streams.xml");

        // create a file stream
        xmlFileStream = File.Create(xmlFile);

        // wrap the file stream in an XML writer helper
        // and automatically indent nested elements
        xml = XmlWriter.Create(xmlFileStream,
        new XmlWriterSettings { Indent = true });
```

```
    // write the XML declaration
    xml.WriteStartDocument();

    // write a root element
    xml.WriteStartElement("callsigns");

    // enumerate the strings writing each one to the stream
    foreach (string item in callsigns)
    {
        xml.WriteElementString("callsign", item);
    }

    // write the close root element
    xml.WriteEndElement();

    // close helper and stream
    xml.Close();
    xmlFileStream.Close();

    // output all the contents of the file to the Console
    WriteLine($"{xmlFile} contains
    {new FileInfo(xmlFile).Length} bytes.");
    WriteLine(File.ReadAllText(xmlFile));
}
catch(Exception ex)
{
    // if the path doesn't exist the exception will be caught
    WriteLine($"{ex.GetType()} says {ex.Message}");
}
finally
{
    if (xml != null)
    {
        xml.Dispose();
        WriteLine("The XML writer's unmanaged resources have been
disposed.");
    }
    if (xmlFileStream != null)
    {
        xmlFileStream.Dispose();
        WriteLine("The file stream's unmanaged resources have been
disposed.");
    }
}
}
```

Run the console application and view the extra output:

```
The XML writer's unmanaged resources have been disposed.
The file stream's unmanaged resources have been disposed.
```

Good Practice
Before calling `Dispose`, check that the object is not `null`.

Simplifying disposal with the using statement

If you don't need to catch any exceptions, then you can simplify the code that needs to check for a non-null object and then call its `Dispose` method by using the `using` statement.

Confusingly, there are two uses for the `using` statement: importing a namespace, and generating a `finally` statement that disposes of an object.

The compiler changes your code into a full `try` and `finally` statement, but without a `catch` statement. You can use nested `try` statements; so, if you do want to catch any exceptions, you can, as shown in the following code example:

```
using (FileStream file2 = File.OpenWrite(Path.Combine(path, "file2.txt")))
{
    using (StreamWriter writer2 = new StreamWriter(file2))
    {
        try
        {
            writer2.WriteLine("Welcome, .NET Core!");
        }
        catch(Exception ex)
        {
            WriteLine($"{ex.GetType()} says {ex.Message}");
        }
    } // automatically calls Dispose if the object is not null
} // automatically calls Dispose if the object is not null
```

Many types, including `FileStream` and `StreamWriter` mentioned earlier, provide a `Close` method as well as a `Dispose` method. In .NET Standard 2.0, you can use either because they do the same thing, by literally calling each other. In .NET Core 1.1, Microsoft had over-simplified the API, so you had to use `Dispose`.

Compressing streams

XML is relatively verbose, so it takes up more space in bytes than plain text. We can squeeze the XML using a common compression algorithm known as **GZIP**.

Import the following namespace:

```
using System.IO.Compression;
```

Add a `WorkWithCompression` method, as shown in the following code:

```
static void WorkWithCompression()
{
    // compress the XML output
    string gzipFilePath = Combine(CurrentDirectory, "streams.gzip");

    FileStream gzipFile = File.Create(gzipFilePath);
    using (GZipStream compressor =
    new GZipStream(gzipFile, CompressionMode.Compress))
    {
        using (XmlWriter xmlGzip = XmlWriter.Create(compressor))
        {
            xmlGzip.WriteStartDocument();
            xmlGzip.WriteStartElement("callsigns");
            foreach (string item in callsigns)
            {
                xmlGzip.WriteElementString("callsign", item);
            }
        }
    }
    } // also closes the underlying stream

    // output all the contents of the compressed file to the Console
    WriteLine($"{gzipFilePath} contains
    {new FileInfo(gzipFilePath).Length} bytes.");
    WriteLine(File.ReadAllText(gzipFilePath));

    // read a compressed file
    WriteLine("Reading the compressed XML file:");
    gzipFile = File.Open(gzipFilePath, FileMode.Open);
```

```
using (GZipStream decompressor = new GZipStream(gzipFile,
CompressionMode.Decompress))
{
    using (XmlReader reader = XmlReader.Create(decompressor))
    {
        while (reader.Read())
        {
            // check if we are currently on an element node named callsign
            if ((reader.NodeType == XmlNodeType.Element) && (reader.Name ==
            "callsign"))
            {
                reader.Read(); // move to the Text node inside the element
                WriteLine($"{reader.Value}"); // read its value
            }
        }
    }
}
```

In `Main`, leave the call to `WorkWithXml`, and add a call to `WorkWithCompression`, as shown in the following code:

```
static void Main(string[] args)
{
    // WorkWithText();
    WorkWithXml();
    WorkWithCompression();
}
```

Run the console application and compare the sizes of the XML file and the compressed XML file. It is less than half the size of the same XML without compression, as shown in the following edited output:

```
/Users/markjprice/Code/Chapter09/WorkingWithStreams/streams.xml contains
310 bytes.
/Users/markjprice/Code/Chapter09/WorkingWithStreams/streams.gzip contains
150 bytes.
```

Encoding text

Text characters can be represented in different ways. For example, the alphabet can be encoded using Morse code into a series of dots and dashes for transmission over a telegraph line.

In a similar way, text inside a computer is stored as bits (ones and zeros). .NET uses a standard called **Unicode** to encode text internally. Sometimes, you will need to move text outside .NET for use by systems that do not use Unicode or use a variation of Unicode.

The following table lists some alternative text encodings commonly used by computers:

Encoding	Description
ASCII	This encodes a limited range of characters using the lower seven bits of a byte
UTF-8	This represents each Unicode code point as a sequence of one to four bytes
UTF-16	This represents each Unicode code point as a sequence of one or two 16-bit integers
ANSI/ISO encodings	This provides support for a variety of code pages that are used to support a specific language or group of languages

Encoding strings as byte arrays

Add a new console application project named `WorkingWithEncodings`.

Import the `System.Text` namespace, statically import `Console`, and add the following statements to the `Main` method. The code encodes a string using the chosen encoding, loops through each byte, and then decodes back into a string and outputs it:

```
WriteLine("Encodings");
WriteLine("[1] ASCII");
WriteLine("[2] UTF-7");
WriteLine("[3] UTF-8");
WriteLine("[4] UTF-16 (Unicode)");
WriteLine("[5] UTF-32");
WriteLine("[any other key] Default");

// choose an encoding
Write("Press a number to choose an encoding: ");
ConsoleKey number = ReadKey(false).Key;
WriteLine();
WriteLine();

Encoding encoder;
switch (number)
{
    case ConsoleKey.D1:
      encoder = Encoding.ASCII;
      break;
    case ConsoleKey.D2:
      encoder = Encoding.UTF7;
      break;
    case ConsoleKey.D3:
```

```
      encoder = Encoding.UTF8;
      break;
    case ConsoleKey.D4:
      encoder = Encoding.Unicode;
      break;
    case ConsoleKey.D5:
      encoder = Encoding.UTF32;
      break;
    default:
      encoder = Encoding.Default;
      break;
}

// define a string to encode
string message = "A pint of milk is £1.99";

// encode the string into a byte array
byte[] encoded = encoder.GetBytes(message);

// check how many bytes the encoding needed
WriteLine($"{encoder.GetType().Name} uses {encoded.Length}
bytes.");

// enumerate each byte
WriteLine($"Byte   Hex   Char");
foreach (byte b in encoded)
{
    WriteLine($"{b,4} {b.ToString("X"),4} {(char)b,5}");
}

// decode the byte array back into a string and display it
string decoded = encoder.GetString(encoded);
WriteLine(decoded);
```

 .NET Core 1.0 and 1.1 did not support Encoding.Default, so you had to use GetEncoding(0) instead.

Run the application and press 1 to choose ASCII. Notice that when outputting the bytes, the pound sign (£) cannot be represented in ASCII, so it uses a question mark (?) instead:

```
Encodings
[1] ASCII
[2] UTF-7
[3] UTF-8
[4] UTF-16 (Unicode)
[5] UTF-32
[any other key] Default
Press a number to choose an encoding: 1
ASCIIEncoding uses 23 bytes.
Byte   Hex   Char
  65    41     A
  32    20
 112    70     p
 105    69     i
 110    6E     n
 116    74     t
  32    20
 111    6F     o
 102    66     f
  32    20
 109    6D     m
 105    69     i
 108    6C     l
 107    6B     k
  32    20
 105    69     i
 115    73     s
  32    20
  63    3F     ?
  49    31     1
  46    2E     .
  57    39     9
  57    39     9
A pint of milk is ?1.99
```

Rerun the application and press 3 to choose UTF-8. Notice that, UTF-8 requires one extra byte (24 bytes instead of 23 bytes), but it can store the £ sign:

```
UTF8Encoding uses 24 bytes.
Byte   Hex   Char
  65    41     A
  32    20
 112    70     p
 105    69     i
 110    6E     n
```

```
116    74    t
 32    20
111    6F    o
102    66    f
 32    20
109    6D    m
105    69    i
108    6C    l
107    6B    k
 32    20
105    69    i
115    73    s
 32    20
194    C2    Â
163    A3    £
 49    31    1
 46    2E    .
 57    39    9
 57    39    9
A pint of milk is £1.99
```

Rerun the application and press 4 to choose Unicode (UTF-16). Notice that UTF-16 requires two bytes for every character, and it can store the £ sign:

```
UnicodeEncoding uses 46 bytes.
```

Encoding and decoding text in files

When using stream helper classes, such as StreamReader and StreamWriter, you can specify the encoding you want to use. As you write to the helper, the strings will automatically be encoded, and as you read from the helper, the bytes will be automatically decoded.

This is how you can specify the encoding, as shown in the following code:

```
var reader = new StreamReader(stream, Encoding.UTF7);
var writer = new StreamWriter(stream, Encoding.UTF7);
```

Good Practice

Often, you won't have the choice of which encoding to use, because you will be generating a file for use by another system. However, if you do, pick one that uses the least number of bytes, but can store every character you need.

Serializing object graphs

Serialization is the process of converting a live object into a sequence of bytes using a specified format. **Deserialization** is the reverse process.

There are dozens of formats you can choose, but the two most common ones are **eXtensible Markup Language (XML)** and **JavaScript Object Notation (JSON)**.

Good Practice

JSON is more compact and is best for web and mobile applications. XML is more verbose, but is better supported in older systems.

.NET Standard has multiple classes that will serialize to and from XML and JSON. We will start by looking at `XmlSerializer` and `JsonSerializer`.

Serializing with XML

Add a new console application project named `WorkingWithSerialization`.

To show a common example, we will define a custom class to store information about a person and then create an object graph using a list of `Person` instances with nesting.

Add a class named `Person` with the following definition. Notice that the `Salary` property is protected, meaning it is only accessible to itself and derived classes. To populate the salary, the class has a constructor with a single parameter to set the initial salary:

```
using System;
using System.Collections.Generic;

namespace Packt.CS7
{
    public class Person
    {
        public Person(decimal initialSalary)
        {
```

```
            Salary = initialSalary;
        }
        public string FirstName { get; set; }
        public string LastName { get; set; }
        public DateTime DateOfBirth { get; set; }
        public HashSet<Person> Children { get; set; }
        protected decimal Salary { get; set; }
    }
}
```

Back in `Program.cs`, import the following namespaces:

```
using System;                       // DateTime
using System.Collections.Generic;   // List<T>, HashSet<T>
using System.Xml.Serialization;     // XmlSerializer
using System.IO;                    // FileStream
using Packt.CS7;                    // Person
using static System.Console;
using static System.Environment;
using static System.IO.Path;
```

Add the following statements to the `Main` method:

```
// create an object graph
var people = new List<Person>
{
    new Person(30000M) { FirstName = "Alice", LastName = "Smith",
    DateOfBirth = new DateTime(1974, 3, 14) },
    new Person(40000M) { FirstName = "Bob", LastName = "Jones",
    DateOfBirth = new DateTime(1969, 11, 23) },
    new Person(20000M) { FirstName = "Charlie", LastName = "Rose",
    DateOfBirth = new DateTime(1964, 5, 4),
    Children = new HashSet<Person>
    { new Person(0M) { FirstName = "Sally", LastName = "Rose",
      DateOfBirth = new DateTime(1990, 7, 12) } } }
};

// create a file to write to
string path = Combine(CurrentDirectory, "people.xml");

FileStream stream = File.Create(path);

// create an object that will format as List of Persons as XML
var xs = new XmlSerializer(typeof(List<Person>));

// serialize the object graph to the stream
xs.Serialize(stream, people);
```

```
    // you must close the stream to release the file lock
    stream.Close();

    WriteLine($"Written {new FileInfo(path).Length} bytes of XML to
    {path}");
    WriteLine();

    // Display the serialized object graph
    WriteLine(File.ReadAllText(path));
```

Run the console application, view the output, and note that an exception is thrown:

```
Unhandled Exception: System.InvalidOperationException:
Packt.CS7.Person cannot be serialized because it does not
have a parameterless constructor.
```

Back in the `Person.cs` file, add the following statement to define a parameter-less constructor. Note that the constructor does not need to do anything, but it must exist so that the `XmlSerializer` can call it to instantiate new `Person` instances during the deserialization process:

```
public Person() { }
```

Rerun the console application and view the output.

Note that the object graph is serialized as XML and the `Salary` property is not included:

```
Written 754 bytes of XML to
/Users/markjprice/Code/Chapter09/WorkingWithSerialization/people.xml
<?xml version="1.0"?>
<ArrayOfPerson xmlns:xsi="http://www.w3.org/2001/XMLSchema-instance"
  xmlns:xsd="http://www.w3.org/2001/XMLSchema">
  <Person>
    <FirstName>Alice</FirstName>
    <LastName>Smith</LastName>
    <DateOfBirth>1974-03-14T00:00:00</DateOfBirth>
  </Person>
  <Person>
    <FirstName>Bob</FirstName>
    <LastName>Jones</LastName>
    <DateOfBirth>1969-11-23T00:00:00</DateOfBirth>
  </Person>
  <Person>
    <FirstName>Charlie</FirstName>
    <LastName>Rose</LastName>
    <DateOfBirth>1964-05-04T00:00:00</DateOfBirth>
    <Children>
      <Person>
```

```
    <FirstName>Sally</FirstName>
    <LastName>Rose</LastName>
    <DateOfBirth>1990-07-12T00:00:00</DateOfBirth>
  </Person>
 </Children>
</Person>
</ArrayOfPerson>
```

We could make the XML more efficient using attributes instead of elements for some fields.

In the `Person.cs` file, import the `System.Xml.Serialization` namespace and decorate all the properties, except `Children`, with the `[XmlAttribute]` attribute, setting a short name, as shown in the following code:

```
[XmlAttribute("fname")]
public string FirstName { get; set; }
[XmlAttribute("lname")]
public string LastName { get; set; }
[XmlAttribute("dob")]
public DateTime DateOfBirth { get; set; }
```

Rerun the application and notice that the XML is now more efficient:

```
Written 464 bytes of XML to C:\Code\Ch10_People.xml
<?xml version="1.0"?>
  <ArrayOfPerson xmlns:xsi="http://www.w3.org/2001/XMLSchema-instance"
    xmlns:xsd="http://www.w3.org/2001/XMLSchema">
    <Person fname="Alice" lname="Smith" dob="1974-03-14T00:00:00" />
    <Person fname="Bob" lname="Jones" dob="1969-11-23T00:00:00" />
    <Person fname="Charlie" lname="Rose" dob="1964-05-04T00:00:00">
     <Children>
        <Person fname="Sally" lname="Rose" dob="1990-07-12T00:00:00" />
     </Children>
    </Person>
  </ArrayOfPerson>
```

The size of the file has been reduced from 754 to 464 bytes, a space saving of 38%.

Deserializing with XML

Add the following statements to the end of the `Main` method:

```
FileStream xmlLoad = File.Open(path, FileMode.Open);
// deserialize and cast the object graph into a List of Person
var loadedPeople = (List<Person>)xs.Deserialize(xmlLoad);

foreach (var item in loadedPeople)
{
    WriteLine($"{item.LastName} has {item.Children.Count}
    children.");
}
xmlLoad.Close();
```

Rerun the application and notice that the people are loaded successfully from the XML file:

```
Smith has 0 children.
Jones has 0 children.
Rose has 1 children.
```

Customizing the XML

There are many other attributes that can be used to control the XML generated. Refer to the references at the end of this chapter for more information.

Good Practice

When using `XmlSerializer`, remember that only the `public` fields and properties are included, and the type must have a parameter-less constructor. You can customize the output with attributes.

Serializing with JSON

The best library for working with JSON serialization format is **Newtonsoft.Json**.

In Visual Studio 2017, in **Solution Explorer**, in the **WorkingWithSerialization** project, right-click on **Dependencies** and choose **Manage NuGet Packages....** Search for `Newtonsoft.Json`, select the found item, and then click on **Install**.

In Visual Studio Code, edit the `WorkingWithSerialization.csproj` file to add a package reference for the latest version of `Newtonsoft.Json`, as shown in the following markup:

```
<Project Sdk="Microsoft.NET.Sdk">

  <PropertyGroup>
    <OutputType>Exe</OutputType>
    <TargetFramework>netcoreapp2.0</TargetFramework>
  </PropertyGroup>

  <ItemGroup>
    <PackageReference Include="Newtonsoft.Json" Version="10.0.3" />
  </ItemGroup>

</Project>
```

Good Practice
Search for NuGet packages on Microsoft's NuGet feed to discover the latest supported version, as shown at the following link:
https://www.nuget.org/packages/Newtonsoft.Json/

Import the following namespace at the top of the `Program.cs` file:

```
using Newtonsoft.Json;
```

Add the following statements to the end of the `Main` method:

```
// create a file to write to
string jsonPath = Combine(CurrentDirectory, "people.json");

StreamWriter jsonStream = File.CreateText(jsonPath);

// create an object that will format as JSON
var jss = new JsonSerializer();

// serialize the object graph into a string
jss.Serialize(jsonStream, people);
jsonStream.Close(); // release the file lock

WriteLine();
WriteLine($"Written {new FileInfo(jsonPath).Length} bytes of
JSON to: {jsonPath}");

// Display the serialized object graph
WriteLine(File.ReadAllText(jsonPath));
```

Rerun the application and notice that JSON requires less than half the number of bytes compared to XML with elements. It's even smaller than the XML file which uses attributes, as shown in the following output:

```
Written 368 bytes of JSON to:
/Users/markjprice/Code/Chapter09/WorkingWithSerialization/people.json
[{"FirstName":"Alice","LastName":"Smith","DateOfBirth":"\/Date(132451200000
)\/","Children":null},{"FirstName":"Bob","LastName":"Jones","DateOfBirth":"
\/Date(-3369600000)\/","Children":null},{"FirstName":"Charlie","LastName":"
Rose","DateOfBirth":"\/Date(-178678800000)\/","Children":[{"FirstName":"Sal
ly","LastName":"Rose","DateOfBirth":"\/Date(647737200000)\/","Children":nul
l}]}]
```

> **Good Practice**
> Use JSON to minimize the size of serialized object graphs. JSON is also a good choice when sending object graphs to web applications and mobile applications because JSON is the native serialization format for JavaScript.

Serializing with other formats

There are many other formats available as NuGet packages that you can use for serialization. A commonly used pair are: `DataContractSerializer` (for XML) and `DataContractJsonSerializer` (for JSON), which are both in the `System.Runtime.Serialization` namespace.

Summary

In this chapter, you learned how to read from and write to text files and XML files, how to compress and decompress files, how to encode and decode text, and how to serialize an object into JSON and XML (and deserialize it back again).

8
Improving Performance and Scalability Using Multitasking

This chapter is about allowing multiple actions to occur at the same time to improve performance, scalability, and user productivity.

In this chapter, we will cover the following topics:

- Monitoring performance and resource usage
- Understanding processes, threads, and tasks
- Running tasks asynchronously
- Synchronizing access to shared resources
- Understanding `async` and `await`

Monitoring performance and resource usage

Before we can improve the performance of some code, we need to be able to monitor its speed and efficiency to record a baseline we can start measuring from.

Evaluating the efficiency of types

What is the best type to use for a scenario? To answer this question, we need to carefully consider what we mean by best. We should consider the following factors:

- **Functionality**: This can be decided by checking whether the type provides the features you need
- **Memory size**: This can be decided by the number of bytes of memory the type takes up
- **Performance**: This can be decided by how fast the type is
- **Future needs**: This depends on the changes in requirements and maintainability

There will be scenarios, such as storing numbers, where multiple types have the same functionality, so we will need to consider the memory and performance to make a choice.

If we need to store millions of numbers, then the best type to use would be the one that requires the least number of bytes of memory. If we only need to store a few numbers, but we need to perform lots of calculations on them, then the best type to use would be the one that runs fastest on a CPU.

You have seen the use of the `sizeof()` function to show the number of bytes a single instance of a type uses in memory. When we are storing lots of values in more complex data structures, such as arrays and lists, then we need a better way of measuring memory usage.

You can read lots of advice online and in books, but the only way to know for sure what the best type would be for your code is to compare the types yourself. In the next section, you will learn how to write the code to monitor the actual memory requirements and the actual performance when using different types.

Today a `short` variable might be the best choice, but it might be a better choice to use an `int` variable even though it takes twice as much space in memory, because we might need a wider range of values to be stored in the future.

There is another metric we should consider: maintenance. This is a measure of how much effort another programmer would have to put in to understand and modify your code. If you use a nonobvious type choice, it might confuse the programmer who comes along later and needs to fix a bug or add a feature. There are analyzing tools that will generate a report that shows how easily maintainable your code is.

Monitoring performance and memory use

The `System.Diagnostics` namespace has lots of useful types for monitoring your code. The first one we will look at is the `Stopwatch` type.

Using Visual Studio 2017

In Visual Studio 2017, press *Ctrl* + *Shift* + *N* or navigate to **File | New | Project...**.

In the **New Project** dialog, in the **Installed** list, expand **Visual C#**, and select **.NET Standard**. In the list at the center, select **Class Library (.NET Standard)**, type the name `MonitoringLib`, change the location to `C:\Code`, type the solution name as `Chapter13`, and then click on **OK**. Rename `Class1.cs` to `Recorder.cs`.

In Visual Studio 2017, add a new console application project named `MonitoringApp`.

Set your solution's startup project as the current selection.

In **Solution Explorer**, in the `MonitoringApp` project, right-click on **Dependencies** and choose **Add Reference...**, select the `MonitoringLib` project, and then click on **OK**.

Using Visual Studio Code

In Visual Studio Code, in the `Code` folder, create a folder named `Chapter13`, with two subfolders named `MonitoringLib` and `MonitoringApp`.

In Visual Studio Code, open the folder named `MonitoringLib`.

In **Integrated Terminal**, enter the following command:

```
dotnet new classlib
```

Open the folder named `MonitoringApp`.

In **Integrated Terminal**, enter the following command:

```
dotnet new console
```

Open the folder named `Chapter13`.

In the **EXPLORER** window, expand `MonitoringLib` and rename the `Class1.cs` file as `Recorder.cs`.

In the `MonitoringApp` project folder, open the file named `MonitoringApp.csproj`, and add a package reference to the `MonitoringLib` library, as shown highlighted in the following markup:

```
<Project Sdk="Microsoft.NET.Sdk">

  <PropertyGroup>
    <OutputType>Exe</OutputType>
    <TargetFramework>netcoreapp2.0</TargetFramework>
  </PropertyGroup>

  <ItemGroup>
    <ProjectReference Include="..\MonitoringLib\MonitoringLib.csproj"
    />
  </ItemGroup>

</Project>
```

In **Integrated Terminal**, enter the following commands:

```
cd MonitoringApp
dotnet build
```

Creating the Recorder class

In both Visual Studio 2017 and Visual Studio Code, open the `Recorder.cs` file and change its contents to look like this:

```
using System;
using System.Diagnostics;
using static System.Console;
using static System.Diagnostics.Process;

namespace Packt.CS7
{
    public static class Recorder
    {
        static Stopwatch timer = new Stopwatch();
        static long bytesPhysicalBefore = 0;
        static long bytesVirtualBefore = 0;

        public static void Start()
        {
```

```
            GC.Collect();
            GC.WaitForPendingFinalizers();
            GC.Collect();
            bytesPhysicalBefore = GetCurrentProcess().WorkingSet64;
            bytesVirtualBefore = GetCurrentProcess().VirtualMemorySize64;
            timer.Restart();
        }

        public static void Stop()
        {
            timer.Stop();
            long bytesPhysicalAfter = GetCurrentProcess().WorkingSet64;
            long bytesVirtualAfter = GetCurrentProcess().VirtualMemorySize64;
            WriteLine("Stopped recording.");
            WriteLine($"{bytesPhysicalAfter - bytesPhysicalBefore:N0}
            physical bytes used.");
            WriteLine($"{bytesVirtualAfter - bytesVirtualBefore:N0}
            virtual bytes used.");
            WriteLine($"{timer.Elapsed} time span ellapsed.");
            WriteLine($"{timer.ElapsedMilliseconds:N0}
            total milliseconds ellapsed.");
        }
    }
}
```

 The Start method of the Recorder class uses the **garbage collector (GC)** type to ensure that all the currently allocated memory is collected before recording the amount of used memory. This is an advanced technique that you should almost never use in production code.

In the Program class, in the Main method, write statements to start and stop the Recorder while generating an array of ten thousand integers, as shown in the following code:

```
using System.Linq;
using Packt.CS7;
using static System.Console;

namespace MonitoringApp
{
    class Program
    {
        static void Main(string[] args)
        {
            Write("Press ENTER to start the timer: ");
            ReadLine();
            Recorder.Start();
            int[] largeArrayOfInts = Enumerable.Range(1, 10000).ToArray();
```

```
            Write("Press ENTER to stop the timer: ");
            ReadLine();
            Recorder.Stop();
            ReadLine();
        }
    }
}
```

You have created a class named `Recorder` with two methods to start and stop recording the time and memory used by any code you run. The `Main` method starts recording when the user presses *Enter*, creates an array of ten thousand `int` variables, and then stops recording when the user presses *Enter* again.

The `Stopwatch` type has some useful members, as shown in the following table:

Member	Description
The `Restart` method	This resets the elapsed time to zero and then starts the stopwatch
The `Stop` method	This stops the stopwatch
The `Elapsed` property	This is the elapsed time stored as a `TimeSpan` format (*hours:minutes:seconds*)
The `ElapsedMilliseconds` property	This is the elapsed time in milliseconds stored as a long integer

The `Process` type has some useful members, as shown in the following table:

Member	Description
`VirtualMemorySize64`	This displays the amount of virtual memory, in bytes, allocated for the process
`WorkingSet64`	This displays the amount of physical memory, in bytes, allocated for the process

Run the console application without the debugger attached. The application will start recording the time and memory used when you press *Enter*, and then stop recording when you press *Enter* again. Wait for a few seconds between pressing *Enter* twice, as you can see that I did with the following output:

```
Press ENTER to start the timer:
Press ENTER to stop the timer:
Stopped recording.
942,080 physical bytes used.
0 virtual bytes used.
00:00:03.1166037 time span ellapsed.
3,116 total milliseconds ellapsed.
```

Measuring the efficiency of processing strings

Now that you've seen how the `Stopwatch` and `Process` types can be used to monitor your code, we will use them to evaluate the best way to process string variables.

Comment out the previous code in the `Main` method by wrapping it in `/* */`.

Add the following code to the `Main` method. It creates an array of fifty thousand `int` variables and then concatenates them with commas for separators using a `string` and `StringBuilder` class:

```
int[] numbers = Enumerable.Range(1, 50000).ToArray();
Recorder.Start();
WriteLine("Using string");
string s = "";
for (int i = 0; i < numbers.Length; i++)
{
    s += numbers[i] + ", ";
}
Recorder.Stop();
Recorder.Start();
WriteLine("Using StringBuilder");
var builder = new System.Text.StringBuilder();
for (int i = 0; i < numbers.Length; i++)
{
    builder.Append(numbers[i]);
    builder.Append(", ");
}
Recorder.Stop();
ReadLine();
```

Run the console application and view the output:

```
Using string
Stopped recording.
12,447,744 physical bytes used.
1,347,584 virtual bytes used.
00:00:03.4700170 time span ellapsed.
3,470 total milliseconds ellapsed.

Using StringBuilder
Stopped recording.
12,288 physical bytes used.
0 virtual bytes used.
00:00:00.0051490 time span ellapsed.
5 total milliseconds ellapsed.
```

We can summarize the results as follows:

- The `string` class used about 12.5 MB of memory and took 3.5 seconds
- The `StringBuilder` class used 12.3 KB of memory and took 5 milliseconds

In this scenario, `StringBuilder` is about seven hundred times faster and about one thousand times more memory efficient when concatenating text!

Good Practice

Avoid using the `String.Concat` method or the + operator inside loops. Avoid using C# $ string interpolation inside loops. It uses less physical memory but twice as much virtual memory, and it takes more than 30 seconds! Instead, use `StringBuilder`.

Now that you've learned how to measure performance and resource efficiency of your code, let's learn about processes, threads, and tasks.

Understanding processes, threads, and tasks

A **process**, for example, each of the console applications we have created, has resources allocated to it like memory and threads. A **thread** executes your code, statement by statement. By default, each process only has one thread, and this can cause problems when we need to do more than one **task** at the same time.

Threads are also responsible for keeping track of things like the currently authenticated user and any internationalization rules that should be followed for the current language and region.

Windows and most other modern operating systems use preemptive multitasking, which simulates the parallel execution of tasks. It divides the processor time among the threads, allocating a *time slice* to each thread one after another. The current thread is suspended when its time slice finishes. The processor allows another thread to run for a time slice.

When Windows switches from one thread to another, it saves the context of the thread and reloads the previously saved context of the next thread in the thread queue. This takes time and resources.

Threads have a `Priority` property and a `ThreadState` property, and there is a `ThreadPool` class for managing a pool of background worker threads, as shown in the following diagram:

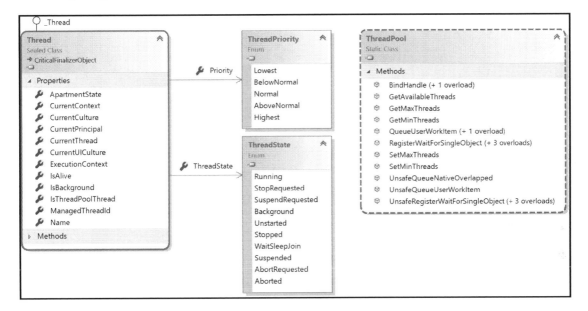

Threads may have to compete for, and wait for access to, shared resources, such as variables, files, and database objects.

Depending on the task, doubling the number of threads (workers) to perform a task does not halve the number of seconds the task will take. In fact, it can *increase* the duration of the task, as pointed out by the following tweet:

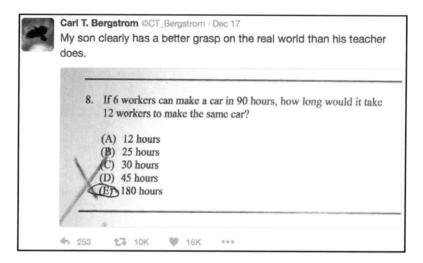

Carl T. Bergstrom @CT_Bergstrom · Dec 17
My son clearly has a better grasp on the real world than his teacher does.

8. If 6 workers can make a car in 90 hours, how long would it take 12 workers to make the same car?

(A) 12 hours
(B) 25 hours
(C) 30 hours
(D) 45 hours
(E) 180 hours

Good Practice
Never assume that more threads (workers) will improve performance. Run performance tests on a baseline code implementation *without* multiple threads, and then again on a code implementation *with* multiple threads. Run performance tests in a staging environment that is as close as possible to the production environment.

Running tasks asynchronously

First, we will write a simple console application that needs to execute three methods, and execute them synchronously (one after the other).

Running multiple actions synchronously

In Visual Studio 2017, press *Ctrl + Shift + N* or go to **File** | **Add** | **New Project...**.

In the **New Project** dialog, in the **Installed** list, expand **Visual C#**, and select **.NET Core**. In the center list, select **Console App (.NET Core)**, type the name as `WorkingWithTasks`, change the location to `C:\Code`, type the solution name as `Chapter13`, and then click on **OK**.

In Visual Studio Code, create a directory named `Chapter13` with a subfolder named `WorkingWithTasks`, and open the `WorkingWithTasks` folder. In **Integrated Terminal**, execute the command: `dotnet new console`.

In both Visual Studio 2017 and Visual Studio Code, ensure that the following namespaces have been imported:

```
using System;
using System.Threading;
using System.Threading.Tasks;
using System.Diagnostics;
using static System.Console;
```

There will be three methods that need to be executed: the first takes 3 seconds, the second takes 2 seconds, and the third takes 1 second. To simulate that work, we can use the `Thread` class to tell the current thread to go to sleep for a specified number of milliseconds.

Inside the `Program` class, add the following code:

```
static void MethodA()
{
    WriteLine("Starting Method A...");
    Thread.Sleep(3000); // simulate three seconds of work
    WriteLine("Finished Method A.");
}

static void MethodB()
{
    WriteLine("Starting Method B...");
    Thread.Sleep(2000); // simulate two seconds of work
    WriteLine("Finished Method B.");
}

static void MethodC()
{
    WriteLine("Starting Method C...");
    Thread.Sleep(1000); // simulate one second of work
    WriteLine("Finished Method C.");
}
```

In the `Main` method, add the following statements:

```
static void Main(string[] args)
{
    var timer = Stopwatch.StartNew();

    WriteLine("Running methods synchronously on one thread.");
```

```
MethodA();
MethodB();
MethodC();

WriteLine($"{timer.ElapsedMilliseconds:#,##0}ms elapsed.");

WriteLine("Press ENTER to end.");
ReadLine();
}
```

 The calls to `WriteLine` and `ReadLine` at the end of the `Main` method prompting the user to press *Enter* are only necessary when using Visual Studio 2017 with the debugger attached, because Visual Studio 2017 will automatically terminate the application at the end of `Main`! By calling `ReadLine`, the console application stays running until the user presses *Enter*. For Visual Studio Code, you can leave out those two statements.

Run the console application and view the output, and note that as there is only one thread, the total time required is just over 6 seconds:

```
Running methods synchronously on one thread.
Starting Method A...
Finished Method A.
Starting Method B...
Finished Method B.
Starting Method C...
Finished Method C.
6,047ms elapsed.
Press ENTER to end.
```

Running multiple actions asynchronously using tasks

The `Thread` class has been available since the first version of C# and can be used to create new threads and manage them, but it can be tricky to work with directly.

C# 4 introduced the `Task` class, which is a wrapper around a thread that enables easier creating and management. Creating multiple threads wrapped in tasks will allow our code to execute asynchronously (at the same time).

Each `Task` has a `Status` property and a `CreationOptions` property, has a `ContinueWith` method that can be customized with the `TaskContinuationOptions` enum, and can be managed with the `TaskFactory` class, as shown in the following diagram:

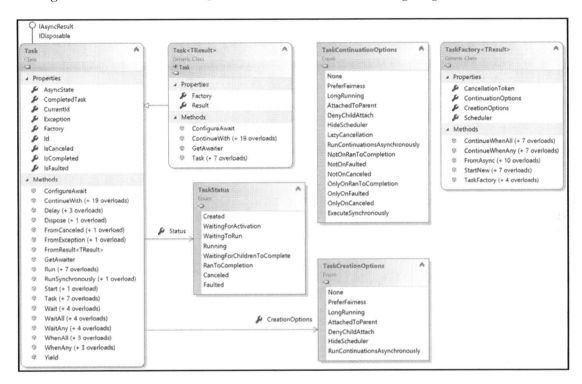

We will look at three ways to start the methods using `Task` instances. Each has a slightly different syntax, but they all define a `Task` and start it.

Comment out the calls to the three methods and the associated console message, and then add the new statements, as shown highlighted in the following code:

```
static void Main(string[] args)
{
    var timer = Stopwatch.StartNew();
    //WriteLine("Running methods synchronously on one thread.");
    //MethodA();
    //MethodB();
    //MethodC();
    WriteLine("Running methods asynchronously on multiple threads.");
    Task taskA = new Task(MethodA);
    taskA.Start();
    Task taskB = Task.Factory.StartNew(MethodB);
```

```
Task taskC = Task.Run(new Action(MethodC));
WriteLine($"{timer.ElapsedMilliseconds:#,##0}ms elapsed.");
WriteLine("Press ENTER to end.");
ReadLine();
}
```

Run the console application and view the output, and note the elapsed milliseconds will depend on the performance of your CPU, so you are likely to see a different value than shown in the following example output:

```
Running methods asynchronously on multiple threads.
Starting Method A...
Starting Method B...
Starting Method C...
23ms elapsed.
Press ENTER to end.
Finished Method C.
Finished Method B.
Finished Method A.
```

Note the elapsed time is output almost immediately, because each of the three methods are now being executed by three *new* threads. The *original* thread continues executing until it reaches the ReadLine call at the end of the Main method.

Meanwhile, the three new threads execute their code simultaneously, and they start in any order. MethodC will usually finish first, because it takes only 1 second, then MethodB, and finally MethodA, because it takes 3 seconds.

However, the actual CPU used has a big effect on the results. It is the CPU that allocates time slices to each process to allow them to execute their threads. You have no control over when the methods run.

Waiting for tasks

Sometimes, you need to wait for a task to complete before continuing. To do this, you can use the Wait method on a Task instance, or the WaitAll or WaitAny static methods on an array of tasks, as described in the following table:

Method	Description
t.Wait()	This waits for the task instance named t to complete execution
Task.WaitAny(Task[])	This waits for any of the tasks in the array to complete execution
Task.WaitAll(Task[])	This waits for all the tasks in the array to complete execution

Add the following statements to the `Main` method immediately after creating the three tasks and before outputting the elapsed time. This will combine references to the three tasks into an array and pass them to the `WaitAll` method. Now, the original thread will pause on that statement, waiting for all three tasks to finish before outputting the elapsed time:

```
Task[] tasks = { taskA, taskB, taskC };
Task.WaitAll(tasks);
```

Rerun the console application and view the output:

```
Running methods asynchronously on multiple threads.
Starting Method A...
Starting Method B...
Starting Method C...
Finished Method C.
Finished Method B.
Finished Method A.
3,024 milliseconds elapsed.
Press ENTER to end.
```

Notice that the total time is now slightly more than the time to run the longest method. If all three tasks can be performed at the same time, then this will be all we need to do.

However, often a task is dependent on the output from another task. To handle this scenario, we need to define **continuation tasks**.

Continuing with another task

Add the following methods to the `Program` class:

```
static decimal CallWebService()
{
    WriteLine("Starting call to web service...");
    Thread.Sleep((new Random()).Next(2000, 4000));
    WriteLine("Finished call to web service.");
    return 89.99M;
}

static string CallStoredProcedure(decimal amount)
{
    WriteLine("Starting call to stored procedure...");
    Thread.Sleep((new Random()).Next(2000, 4000));
    WriteLine("Finished call to stored procedure.");
    return $"12 products cost more than {amount:C}.";
}
```

These methods simulate a call to a web service that returns a monetary amount that then needs to be used to retrieve how many products cost more than that amount in a database. The result returned from the first method needs to be fed into the input of the second method.

 I used the Random class to wait for a random interval of between 2 and 4 seconds for each method call to simulate the work.

Inside the Main method, comment out the previous tasks by wrapping them in multiline comment characters /* */.

Then, add the following statements before the existing statement that outputs the total time elapsed and then calls ReadLine to wait for the user to press *Enter:*

```
WriteLine("Passing the result of one task as an input into another.");

var taskCallWebServiceAndThenStoredProcedure =
Task.Factory.StartNew(CallWebService).
ContinueWith(previousTask => CallStoredProcedure(previousTask.Result));

WriteLine($"{taskCallWebServiceAndThenStoredProcedure.Result}");
```

Run the console application and view the output:

```
Passing the result of one task as an input into another.
Starting call to web service...
Finished call to web service.
Starting call to stored procedure...
Finished call to stored procedure.
12 products cost more than £89.99.
5,971 milliseconds elapsed.
Press ENTER to end.
```

Nested and child tasks

Add a new console application project named NestedAndChildTasks.

In Visual Studio 2017, in the solution's **Properties**, remember to change **Startup Project** to **Current selection**.

Ensure the following namespaces have been imported:

```
using System;
using System.Threading;
using System.Threading.Tasks;
using System.Diagnostics;
using static System.Console;
```

Inside the Main method, add the following statements:

```
var outer = Task.Factory.StartNew(() =>
{
    WriteLine("Outer task starting...");
    var inner = Task.Factory.StartNew(() =>
    {
        WriteLine("Inner task starting...");
        Thread.Sleep(2000);
        WriteLine("Inner task finished.");
    });
});
outer.Wait();
WriteLine("Outer task finished.");
WriteLine("Press ENTER to end.");
ReadLine();
```

Run the console application and view the output:

```
Outer task starting...
Outer task finished.
Inner task starting...
Inner task finished.
Press ENTER to end.
```

Note that, although we wait for the outer task to finish, its inner task does not have to finish as well. To link the two tasks, we must use a special option.

Modify the existing code that defines the inner task to add a TaskCreationOption value of AttachedToParent:

```
var inner = Task.Factory.StartNew(() =>
{
    WriteLine("Inner task starting...");
    Thread.Sleep(2000);
    WriteLine("Inner task finished.");
}, TaskCreationOptions.AttachedToParent);
```

Rerun the console application and view the output. Note that the inner task must finish before the outer task can:

```
Outer task starting...
Inner task starting...
Inner task finished.
Outer task finished.
Press ENTER to end.
```

Synchronizing access to shared resources

When you have multiple threads executing at the same time, there is a possibility that two or more threads may access the same variable or another resource at the same time and cause a problem.

For this reason, you should carefully consider how to make your code *thread safe*.

The simplest mechanism for implementing thread safety is to use an object variable as a *flag* or *traffic light* to indicate when a shared resource has an exclusive lock applied.

 In William Golding's *Lord of the Flies*, Piggy and Ralph spot a conch shell and use it to call a meeting. The boys impose a "rule of the conch" on themselves, deciding that no one can speak unless he's holding the conch. I like to name the object variable I use the "conch." When a thread has the conch, no other thread can access the shared resource(s) represented by that conch.

We will explore some types that can be used to synchronize access to resources, as shown in the following diagram:

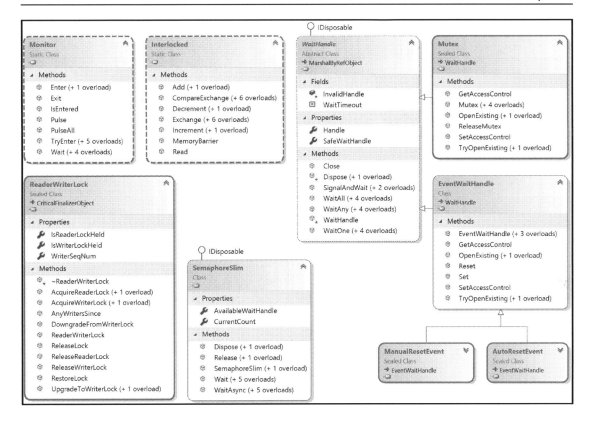

Accessing a resource from multiple threads

Add a new console application project named `SynchronizingResourceAccess`.

Ensure that the following namespaces have been imported:

```
using System;
using System.Threading;
using System.Threading.Tasks;
using System.Diagnostics;
using static System.Console;
```

Inside the `Program` class, add the following statements to do the following:

- Declare and instantiate an object to generate random wait times
- Declare a `string` variable to store a message (this is the shared resource)
- Declare two methods that add a letter, A or B, to the shared `string` five times in a loop, and wait for a random interval of up to 2 seconds for each iteration
- A `Main` method that executes both methods on separate threads using a pair of tasks and waits for them to complete before outputting the elapsed milliseconds it took

```
static Random r = new Random();
static string Message; // a shared resource

static void MethodA()
{
    for (int i = 0; i < 5; i++)
    {
        Thread.Sleep(r.Next(2000));
        Message += "A";
        Write(".");
    }
}

static void MethodB()
{
    for (int i = 0; i < 5; i++)
    {
        Thread.Sleep(r.Next(2000));
        Message += "B";
        Write(".");
    }
}

static void Main(string[] args)
{
    WriteLine("Please wait for the tasks to complete.");
    Stopwatch watch = Stopwatch.StartNew();

    Task a = Task.Factory.StartNew(MethodA);
    Task b = Task.Factory.StartNew(MethodB);

    Task.WaitAll(new Task[] { a, b });
```

```
    WriteLine();
    WriteLine($"Results: {Message}.");
    WriteLine($"{watch.ElapsedMilliseconds:#,##0} elapsed
    milliseconds.");
}
```

Run the console application and view the output:

```
Please wait for the tasks to complete.
..........
Results: BABBABBAAA.
6,099 elapsed milliseconds.
```

Note that the results show that both threads were modifying the message concurrently. In an actual application, this could be a problem. We can prevent concurrent access by applying a mutually exclusive lock.

Applying a mutually exclusive lock to a resource

In the `Program` class, define an object variable instance to act as a *conch*:

```
static object conch = new object();
```

In both `MethodA` and `MethodB`, add a `lock` statement around the `for` statement:

```
lock (conch)
{
    for (int i = 0; i < 5; i++)
    {
        Thread.Sleep(r.Next(2000));
        Message += "A";
        Write(".");
    }
}
```

Rerun the console application and view the output:

```
Please wait for the tasks to complete.
..........
Results: AAAAABBBBB.
9,751 elapsed milliseconds.
```

Although the time elapsed was longer, only one method at a time could access the shared resource. Once a method has finished its work on the shared resource, then the conch gets released, and the other method has a chance to do its work.

 Either `MethodA` or `MethodB` could start first.

Understanding the lock statement

You might wonder how the `lock` statement works when it *locks* an object variable. The compiler changes this:

```
lock (conch)
{
    // access shared resource
}
```

The preceding code block is changed into this:

```
try
{
    Monitor.Enter(conch);
    // access shared resource
}
finally
{
    Monitor.Exit(conch);
}
```

Knowing how the `lock` statement works internally is important, because using the `lock` statement can cause a deadlock.

Deadlocks occur when there are two or more shared resources (and therefore conches) and the following sequence of events happens:

- Thread X locks conch A
- Thread Y locks conch B
- Thread X attempts to lock conch B but is blocked because thread Y already has it
- Thread Y attempts to lock conch A but is blocked because thread X already has it

A proven way to prevent deadlocks is to specify a timeout when attempting to get a lock. To do this, you must manually use the `Monitor` class instead of using the `lock` statement.

Modify your code to replace the `lock` statements with code that tries to enter the conch with a timeout like this:

```
try
{
    Monitor.TryEnter(conch, TimeSpan.FromSeconds(15));
    for (int i = 0; i < 5; i++)
    {
        Thread.Sleep(r.Next(2000));
        Message += "A";
        Write(".");
    }
}
finally
{
    Monitor.Exit(conch);
}
```

Rerun the console application and view the output. It should return the same results as before, but is better code because it will avoid potential deadlocks.

Good Practice
Never use the `lock` keyword. Always use the `Monitor.TryEnter` method instead, in combination with a `try` statement, so that you can supply a timeout and avoid a potential deadlock scenario.

Making operations atomic

Look at the following increment operation:

```
int x = 3;
x++; // is this an atomic CPU operation?
```

Atomic: This is from Greek *atomos*, *undividable*.

It is not atomic! Incrementing an integer requires the following three CPU operations:

1. Load a value from an instance variable into a register.
2. Increment the value.
3. Store the value in the instance variable.

A thread could be preempted after executing the first two steps. A second thread could then execute all three steps. When the first thread resumes execution, it will overwrite the value in the variable, and the effect of the increment or decrement performed by the second thread will be lost!

There is a type named `Interlocked` that can perform atomic actions on value types, such as integers and floats.

Declare another shared resource that will count how many operations have occurred:

```
static int Counter; // another shared resource
```

In both methods, inside the `for` statement, after modifying `string`, add the following statement to safely increment the counter:

```
Interlocked.Increment(ref Counter);
```

After outputting the elapsed time, output the counter:

```
WriteLine($"{Counter} string modifications.");
```

Rerun the console application and view the output:

```
10 string modifications.
```

Applying other types of synchronization

`Monitor` and `Interlocked` are mutually exclusive locks that are simple and effective, but sometimes, you need more advanced options to synchronize access to shared resources:

Type	Description
`ReaderWriterLock` and `ReaderWriterLockSlim` (recommended)	These allow multiple threads to be in **read mode**, one thread to be in the **write mode** with exclusive ownership of the lock, and one thread that has read access to be in the **upgradeable read mode**, from which the thread can upgrade to the write mode without having to relinquish its read access to the resource
`Mutex`	Like `Monitor`, this provides exclusive access to a shared resource, except it is used for **inter-process** synchronization
`Semaphore` and `SemaphoreSlim`	These limit the number of threads that can access a resource or pool of resources concurrently by defining **slots**
`AutoResetEvent` and `ManualResetEvent`	Event wait handles allow threads to synchronize activities by **signaling** each other and by waiting for each other's signals

Understanding async and await

C# 5 introduced two keywords to simplify working with the `Task` type. They are especially useful for the following:

- Implementing multitasking for a **graphical user interface (GUI)**
- Improving the scalability of web applications and web services

In Chapter 10, *Building Web Sites Using ASP.NET Core MVC*, and in Chapter 11, *Building Web Services and Applications Using ASP.NET Core*, we will explore how the `async` and `await` keywords can improve scalability in websites, web services, and web applications.

In Chapter 12, *Building Windows Apps Using XAML and Fluent Design*, and in Chapter 13, *Building Mobile Apps Using XAML and Xamarin.Forms*, we will explore how the async and await keywords can implement multitasking with a GUI running on Universal Windows Platform and Xamarin.

For now, let's learn the theory of why these two C# keywords were introduced, and then later you will see them used in practice.

Improving responsiveness for console apps

One of the limitations with console applications is that you can only use the await keyword inside methods that are marked as async..., and C# 7 and earlier do not allow the Main method to be marked as async!

Luckily, a new feature in C# 7.1 is support for async on Main.

Create a new console app named AsyncConsole.

Import the System.Net.Http and System.Threading.Tasks namespaces, and statically import System.Console, as shown in the following code:

```
using System.Net.Http;
using System.Threading.Tasks;
using static System.Console;
```

Add statements to the Main method to create an HttpClient instance, make a request for Apple's home page, and output how many bytes it has, as shown in the following code:

```
var client = new HttpClient();
HttpResponseMessage response = await
client.GetAsync("http://www.apple.com/");
WriteLine($"Apple's home page has
{response.Content.Headers.ContentLength:N0} bytes.");
```

Build the project, and note the error message, as shown in the following output:

```
Program.cs(12,44): error CS4033: The 'await' operator can only be used
within an async method. Consider marking this method with the 'async'
modifier and changing its return type to 'Task'.
[/Users/markjprice/Code/Chapter13/AsyncConsole/AsyncConsole.csproj]
```

Add the `async` keyword to the `Main` method, change its return type to `Task`, build the project, and note the error message, as shown in the following output:

```
Program.cs(10,22): error CS8107: Feature 'async main' is not available in
C# 7. Please use language version 7.1 or greater.
[/Users/markjprice/Code/Chapter13/AsyncConsole/AsyncConsole.csproj]
CSC : error CS5001: Program does not contain a static 'Main' method
suitable for an entry point
[/Users/markjprice/Code/Chapter13/AsyncConsole/AsyncConsole.csproj]
```

Modify `AsyncConsole.csproj` to specify C# 7.1, as shown highlighted in the following markup:

```
<Project Sdk="Microsoft.NET.Sdk">

  <PropertyGroup>
    <OutputType>Exe</OutputType>
    <TargetFramework>netcoreapp2.0</TargetFramework>
    <LangVersion>7.1</LangVersion>
  </PropertyGroup>

</Project>
```

Build the project, and note that it now builds successfully.

Run the console application and view the output:

```
Apple's home page has 42,740 bytes.
```

Improving responsiveness for GUI apps

So far we have only built console applications. Life for a programmer gets more complicated when building web applications, web services, and apps with GUIs such as UWP and mobile apps.

One reason for this is that for a GUI app, there is a special thread: the **user interface (UI)** thread.

There are two rules for working in GUIs:

- Do not perform long-running tasks on the UI thread
- Do not access UI elements on any thread except the UI thread

To handle these rules, programmers used to have to write complex code to ensure that long-running tasks were executed by a nonUI thread, but once complete, the results of the task were safely passed to the UI thread to present to the user. It could quickly get messy!

Luckily, with C# 5 and later, you have the use of `async` and `await`. They allow you to continue to write your code as if it is synchronous, which keeps your code clean and easy to understand, but underneath, the C# compiler creates a complex state machine and keeps track of running threads. It's kind of magical!

Improving scalability for web applications and web services

The `async` and `await` keywords can also be applied on the server side when building websites, applications, and services. From the client application's point of view, nothing changes (or they might even notice a small increase in the time for a request to return). So, from a single client's point of view, the use of `async` and `await` to implement multitasking on the server side makes their experience worse!

On the server side, additional, cheaper worker threads are created to wait for long-running tasks to finish so that expensive IO threads can handle other client's requests instead of being blocked. This improves the overall scalability of a web application or service. More clients can be supported simultaneously.

Common types that support multitasking

Here are some common types that have asynchronous methods that you can await:

Type	Methods
DbContext\<T\>	AddAsync, AddRangeAsync, FindAsync, and SaveChangesAsync
DbSet\<T\>	AddAsync, AddRangeAsync, ForEachAsync, SumAsync, ToListAsync, ToDictionaryAsync, AverageAsync, and CountAsync
HttpClient	GetAsync, PostAsync, PutAsync, DeleteAsync, and SendAsync
StreamReader	ReadAsync, ReadLineAsync, and ReadToEndAsync
StreamWriter	WriteAsync, WriteLineAsync, and FlushAsync

Good Practice
Any time you see a method that ends in the suffix `Async`, check to see whether it returns `Task` or `Task<T>`. If it does, then you should use it instead of the synchronous non `Async` suffixed method. Remember to call it using `await` and decorate your method with `async`.

Await in catch blocks

In C# 5, it was only possible to use the `await` keyword in a `try` exception handling block, but not in a `catch` block. In C# 6 or later, it is now possible to use `await` in both the `try` and `catch` blocks.

Summary

In this chapter, you learned how to define and start a task, how to wait for one or more tasks to finish, and how to control task completion order. You also learned how to synchronize access to shared resources, and the theory behind `async` and `await`.

In the next part, you will learn how to create applications for the App Models supported by .NET Core, such as web applications, web services, and Universal Windows Platform apps, and App Models, such as Xamarin, that are supported by .NET Standard.

Building Web Sites Using ASP.NET Core Razor Pages

9

This chapter is about building websites with a modern HTTP architecture on the server side using Microsoft ASP.NET Core. You will learn about building simple websites using the new ASP.NET Core 2.0 Razor Pages feature.

This chapter will cover the following topics:

- Understanding web development
- Understanding ASP.NET Core
- Exploring Razor Pages
- Using Entity Framework Core with ASP.NET Core

Understanding web development

Developing for the web is developing with HTTP.

Understanding HTTP

To communicate with a web server, the client, aka **user agent**, makes calls over the network using a protocol known as **Hypertext Transfer Protocol (HTTP)**. HTTP is the technical underpinning of the *web*. So, when we talk about web applications or web services, we mean that they use HTTP to communicate between a client (often a web browser) and a server.

A client makes an HTTP request for a resource, such as a page identified by a **Uniform Resource Locator** (URL), and the server sends back an HTTP response, as shown in the following diagram:

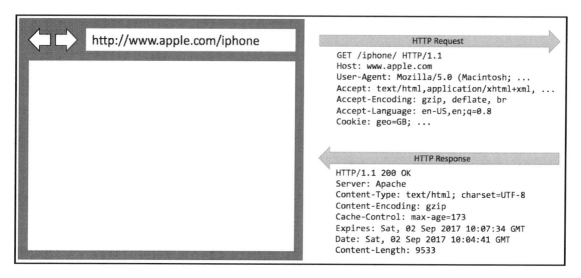

You can use Google Chrome and other browsers to record requests and responses.

Good Practice

Google Chrome is available on more operating systems than any other browser, and it has powerful, built-in developer tools, so it is a good first choice of browser. Always test your web application with Chrome and at least two other browsers, for example, **Firefox** and either **Microsoft Edge** for Windows 10 or **Safari** for macOS.

Start **Google Chrome**. To show developer tools in Chrome, do the following:

- On macOS, press *Alt + Cmd + I*
- On Windows, press *F12* or *Ctrl + Shift + I*

Click on the **Network** tab. Chrome should immediately start recording the network traffic between your browser and any web servers, as shown in the following screenshot:

In Chrome's address box, enter the following URL:
```
https://www.asp.net/get-started
```

In the **Developer tools** window, in the list of recorded requests, click on the first entry, as shown in the following screenshot:

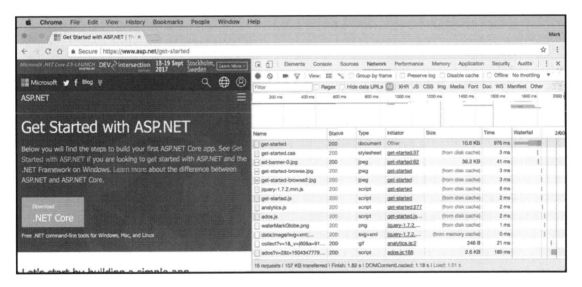

On the right-hand side, click on the **Headers** tab, and you will see details about the request and the response, as shown in the following screenshot:

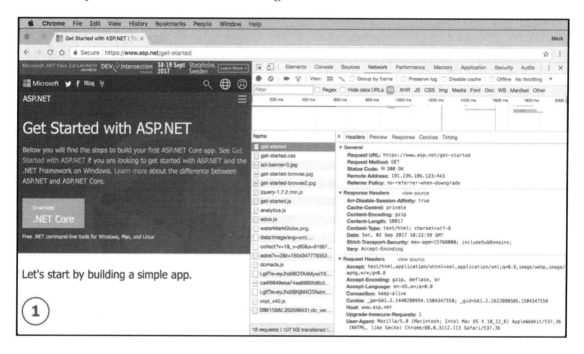

Note the following aspects:

- **Request Method** is GET. Other methods that HTTP defines include POST, PUT, DELETE, HEAD, and PATCH.
- **Status Code** is 200 OK. This means that the server found the resource that the browser requested. Other status codes include 404 Missing.
- **Request Headers** include **Accept**, which lists what formats the browser accepts. In this case, the browser is saying it understands HTML, XHTML, XML, and others.
- **Accept-Encoding** header means the browser has told the server that it understands the GZIP and DEFLATE compression algorithms.
- The browser has also told the server which human languages it would prefer: US English and then any dialect of English (with a quality value of 0.8).
- I must have been to this site before because a Google Analytics cookie, named _ga, is being sent to the server so that it can track me.
- The server has sent back the response compressed using the GZIP algorithm because it knows that the client can decompress that format.

Client-side web development

When building web applications, a developer needs to know more than just C# and .NET Core. On the client (that is, in the web browser), you will use a combination of the following components:

- **HTML5**: This is used for the content and structure of a web page
- **CSS3**: This is used for the styles applied to elements on the web page
- **JavaScript**: This is used for the procedural actions of the web page

Although HTML5, CSS3, and JavaScript are the fundamental components of frontend web development, there are many libraries that can make frontend web development more productive, including the following:

- **Bootstrap:** This is a CSS3 library for implementing responsive design in web pages. Optionally, it can use jQuery to add some advanced dynamic features.
- **jQuery**: This is a popular JavaScript library.
- **TypeScript**: This is a language created by Microsoft and embraced by Google, that adds C# type features to the JavaScript language. TypeScript files (`*.ts`) can be compiled into JavaScript files (`*.js`) during the build process.
- **Angular**: This is a popular library for building **single page applications** (**SPAs**) using TypeScript.
- **React:** This is another popular library for building SPAs.
- **Redux:** This is a library for managing state.

As part of the build and deploy process, you will likely use a combination of these technologies:

- **Node.js**: This is a server-side JavaScript library.
- **NPM**: This is the **Node Package Manager**, and has become the de facto package manager for JavaScript and many other web development modules.
- **Bower**: This is a client-side package manager for the web.
- **Gulp**: This is a toolkit for automating painful or time-consuming tasks.
- **Webpack**: This is a popular module bundler, a tool for compiling, transforming, and bundling application source code.

This book is about C# and .NET Core, so we will cover some of the basics of frontend web development, but for more detail, try *HTML5 Web Application Development By Example* at: `https://www.packtpub.com/web-development/html5-web-application-development-example-beginners-guide`, and *ASP.NET Core and Angular 2* at: `https://www.packtpub.com/application-development/aspnet-core-and-angular-2`

To make it easier to work with HTML5, CSS3, and JavaScript, both Visual Studio 2017 and Visual Studio Code have extensions such as the ones listed here:

- Mads Kristensen's extensions for Visual Studio:
  `https://marketplace.visualstudio.com/search?term=publisher%3A%22Mads%20Kristensen%22&target=VS&sortBy=Relevance`
- HTML Programming in VS Code:
  `https://code.visualstudio.com/Docs/languages/html`
- Microsoft's Visual Studio Code extensions:
  `https://marketplace.visualstudio.com/search?term=publisher%3A%22Microsoft%22&target=VSCode&sortBy=Relevance`

Mads Kristensen wrote one of the most popular extensions for web development with Visual Studio 2010, and later named it *Web Essentials*. It has now been broken up into smaller extensions that can be individually installed.

Understanding ASP.NET Core

Microsoft ASP.NET Core is part of a history of Microsoft technologies used to build web applications and services that have evolved over the years:

- **Active Server Pages** (ASP) was released in 1996, and was Microsoft's first attempt at a platform for dynamic server-side execution of web application code. ASP files are written in the VBScript language.
- **ASP.NET Web Forms** was released in 2002 with the .NET Framework, and is designed to enable nonweb developers, such as those familiar with Visual Basic, to quickly create web applications by dragging and dropping visual components and writing event-driven code in Visual Basic or C#. Web Forms can only be hosted on Windows, but it is still used today in products such as Microsoft SharePoint. It should be avoided for new web projects in favor of ASP.NET Core.

- **Windows Communication Foundation (WCF)** was released in 2006, and enables developers to build SOAP and REST services. SOAP is powerful but complex, so it should be avoided unless you need advanced features, such as distributed transactions and complex messaging topologies.
- **ASP.NET MVC** was released in 2009, and is designed to cleanly separate the concerns of web developers between the *models* that temporarily store the data, the *views* that present the data using various formats in the UI, and the *controllers* that fetch the model and pass it to a view. This separation enables improved reuse and unit testing.
- **ASP.NET Web API** was released in 2012, and enables developers to create HTTP aka REST services that are simpler and more scalable than SOAP services.
- **ASP.NET SignalR** was released in 2013, and enables real-time communication in web applications by abstracting underlying technologies and techniques, such as *Web Sockets* and *Long Polling*.
- **ASP.NET Core** was released in 2016 and combines MVC, Web API, and SignalR, running on .NET Core. Therefore, it can execute cross-platform. ASP.NET Core 2.0 adds many templates to get you started with both server-side coding with .NET Core, and client-side coding with Angular or React or other frontend technologies.

Good Practice
Choose ASP.NET Core to develop web applications and services because it includes web-related technologies that are modern and cross-platform.

ASP.NET Core is .NET Standard 2.0-compliant so it can execute on .NET Framework 4.6.1 or later (Windows only) as well as .NET Core 2.0 or later (cross-platform).

Classic ASP.NET versus modern ASP.NET Core

ASP.NET celebrates its 15th birthday in 2017. It's a teenager!

Until now, it has been built on top of a large assembly in the .NET Framework named `System.Web.dll`. Over the years, this assembly has accumulated a lot of features, many of which are not suitable for modern cross-platform development.

ASP.NET Core is a major redesign of ASP.NET. It removes the dependency on the `System.Web.dll` assembly and is composed of modular lightweight packages, just like the rest of .NET Core.

You can develop and run ASP.NET Core applications cross-platform on Windows, macOS, and Linux. Microsoft has even created a cross-platform, super performant web server named **Kestrel**. The entire stack is open source, and it is designed to integrate with a variety of client-side tools and frameworks, including Bower, Gulp, Grunt, Angular, jQuery, and Bootstrap.

Creating an ASP.NET Core project with Visual Studio 2017

In Visual Studio 2017, press *Ctrl + Shift + N* or go to **File** | **New** | **Project....**

In the **New Project** dialog, in the **Installed** list, expand **Visual C#**, and select **.NET Core**. In the center list, select **ASP.NET Core Web Application**, type the name as `NorthwindWeb`, type the location as `C:\Code`, type the solution name as `Part3`, and then click on **OK**.

In the **New ASP.NET Core Web Application - NorthwindWeb** dialog, select **.NET Core**, select **ASP.NET Core 2.0**, and select the **Empty** template. The **Enable Docker Support** box should be left unchecked. Click on **OK**, as shown in the following screenshot:

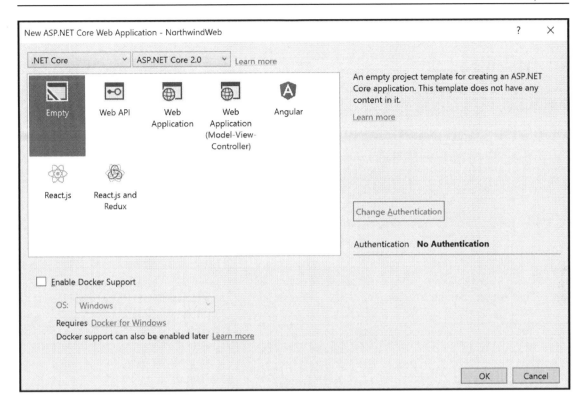

Creating an ASP.NET Core project with Visual Studio Code

Create a folder named Part3 with a subfolder named NorthwindWeb.

In Visual Studio Code, open the NorthwindWeb folder. In **Integrated Terminal**, enter the following command to create an ASP.NET Core Empty website:

```
dotnet new web
```

Reviewing the ASP.NET Core Empty project template

In both Visual Studio 2017 and Visual Studio Code, edit `NorthwindWeb.csproj`, and note the following:

- The target framework is .NET Core 2.0.
- When published, the contents of the folder name `wwwroot\` will be included.
- A single package reference named `Microsoft.AspNetCore.All`. In older versions of ASP.NET Core, you would need to include lots of references. With ASP.NET Core 2.0 and later, you can use this special reference:

```
<Project Sdk="Microsoft.NET.Sdk.Web">

  <PropertyGroup>
    <TargetFramework>netcoreapp2.0</TargetFramework>
  </PropertyGroup>

  <ItemGroup>
    <Folder Include="wwwroot\" />
  </ItemGroup>

  <ItemGroup>
    <PackageReference
      Include="Microsoft.AspNetCore.All" Version="2.0.0" />
  </ItemGroup>

</Project>
```

> `Microsoft.AspNetCore.All` is a metapackage that includes all ASP.NET Core packages, all **Entity Framework Core** (**EF Core**) packages, and all dependencies of ASP.NET Core and EF Core. Read more about the .NET Core Runtime Package Store at the following link:
> https://docs.microsoft.com/en-us/dotnet/core/deploying/runtime-store

Open `Program.cs`, and note the following:

- It is like a console application, with a static `Main` method
- The `WebHost` specifies a startup class. This is used to configure the website:

```
public class Program
{
    public static void Main(string[] args)
    {
        BuildWebHost(args).Run();
    }

    public static IWebHost BuildWebHost(string[] args) =>
        WebHost.CreateDefaultBuilder(args)
        .UseStartup<Startup>()
        .Build();
}
```

 You can see exactly what the `CreateDefaultBuilder` method does at the following link:
https://github.com/aspnet/MetaPackages/blob/dev/src/Microsoft.AspNetCore/WebHost.cs

Open `Startup.cs`, and note the following:

- The `ConfigureServices` method is used to add services to the host container
- The `Configure` method is used to configure the HTTP request pipeline. The method currently does two things: when developing, any unhandled exceptions will be shown in the browser window for the developer to see its details, and it runs, waits for requests, and responds to all requests by returning the plain text, `Hello World!`:

```
public class Startup
{
    public void ConfigureServices(IServiceCollection services)
    {
    }

    public void Configure(
    IApplicationBuilder app, IHostingEnvironment env)
    {
        if (env.IsDevelopment())
        {
            app.UseDeveloperExceptionPage();
        }
```

```
        app.Run(async (context) =>
        {
            await context.Response.WriteAsync("Hello World!");
        });
    }
}
```

Testing the empty website

In Visual Studio 2017, press *Ctrl + F5*, or go to **Debug** | **Start Without Debugging**.

In Visual Studio Code, in **Integrated Terminal**, enter the dotnet run command.

With Visual Studio 2017, a browser will run and make a request for the website, as shown in the following screenshot:

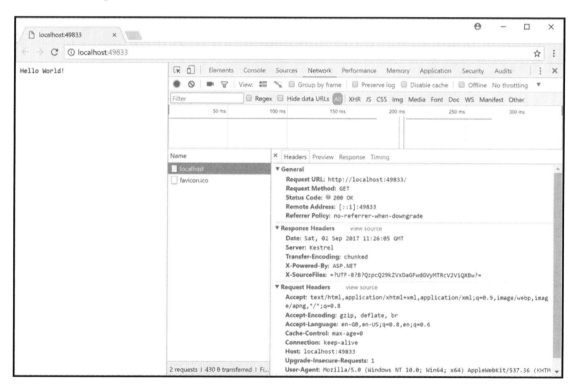

In Visual Studio 2017, go to **View** | **Output**, choose to show output from the **ASP.NET Core Web Server**, and note the requests being handled, as shown in the following screenshot:

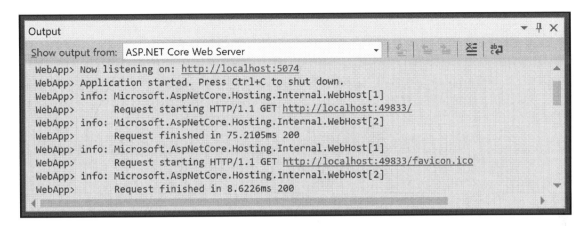

In Visual Studio Code, note the messages in **Integrated Terminal**, as shown in the following output:

```
Hosting environment: Production
Content root path: /Users/markjprice/Code/Chapter14/WebApp
Now listening on: http://localhost:5000
Application started. Press Ctrl+C to shut down.
```

With Visual Studio Code, you must run a browser manually.

Start Chrome, enter the address: `http://localhost:5000/`, and note that you get the same response as shown in the previous screenshots for Visual Studio 2017.

In Visual Studio Code, press *Ctrl + C* to stop the web server. Remember to do this whenever you have finished testing a website.

Close your browser.

Enabling static files

A website that only ever returns a single plain text message isn't very useful! At a minimum, it ought to return static HTML pages, CSS stylesheets the web pages use, and any other static resources such as images and videos.

In both Visual Studio 2017 and Visual Studio Code, add a new file to the `wwwroot` folder named `index.html`, and modify its content to link to CDN-hosted Bootstrap, and use modern good practices such as setting the viewport, as shown in the following markup:

 Make sure that you put the `index.html` file in the `wwwroot` folder!

```
<!DOCTYPE html>
<html lang="en">
<head>
  <meta charset="utf-8" />
  <meta name="viewport" content=
   "width=device-width, initial-scale=1, shrink-to-fit=no" />
  <link rel="stylesheet"
href="https://maxcdn.bootstrapcdn.com/bootstrap/4.0.0-beta/css/bootstrap.mi
n.css"
    integrity="sha384-
/Y6pD6FV/Vv2HJnA6t+vslU6fwYXjCFtcEpHbNJ0lyAFsXTsjBbfaDjzALeQsN6M"
    crossorigin="anonymous" />
  <title>Welcome ASP.NET Core!</title>
</head>
<body>
   <div class="container">
     <div class="jumbotron">
       <h1 class="display-3">Welcome to Northwind!</h1>
       <p class="lead">We supply products to our customers.</p>
       <hr />
       <p>Our customers include restaurants, hotels, and cruise lines.</p>
       <p>
       <a class="btn btn-primary"
         href="https://www.asp.net/">Learn more</a>
     </p>
     </div>
   </div>
</body>
</html>
```

 To understand the Bootstrap classes that I have used to style the page, read the documentation at this link:
`https://getbootstrap.com/docs/4.0/components/jumbotron/`

If you were to start the website, and enter /index.html in the address box, the website would continue to return the plain text Hello World!.

To enable the website to return static files such as index.html, we must explicitly configure those features.

In Startup.cs, in the Configure method, comment the statements that return the Hello World! response, and add a statement to enable static files, as shown in the following code:

```
public void Configure(
    IApplicationBuilder app, IHostingEnvironment env)
{
    if (env.IsDevelopment())
    {
        app.UseDeveloperExceptionPage();
    }

    // app.Run(async (context) =>
    // {
    //     await context.Response.WriteAsync("Hello World!");
    // });

    app.UseStaticFiles();
}
```

Start the website, and note the 404 error for the website, as shown in the following screenshot:

With Visual Studio Code, you must manually start the browser and enter this:
http://localhost:5000

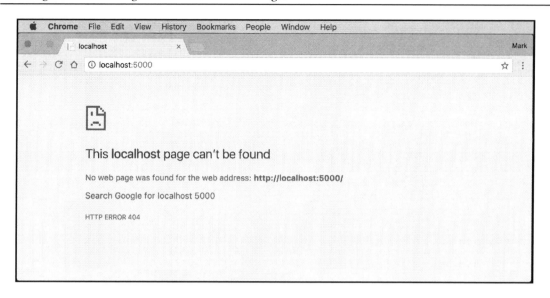

In the address box, enter /index.html, and note that the index.html web page is found and returned, as shown in the following screenshot:

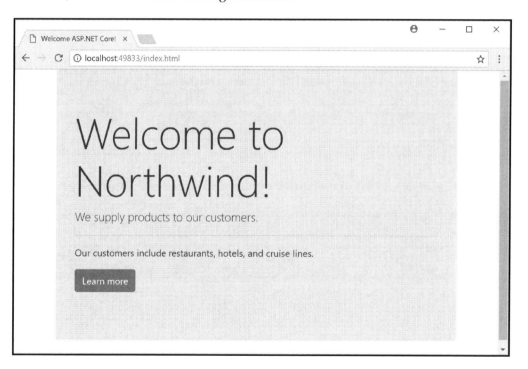

Enabling default files

If the `index.html` file was returned as the default response for the website instead of having to enter its filename, it would be better.

In `Startup.cs`, add a statement to the `Configure` method to enable default files, as shown in the following code:

```
app.UseDefaultFiles(); // index.html, default.html, and so on
```

> The call to `UseDefaultFiles` must be before the call to `UseStaticFiles`, or it won't work!

Start the website, and note that the `index.html` file is now returned immediately because it is the default web page for this website.

If all web pages are static, that is, they only get changed manually by a web editor, then our website programming work is complete. But, almost all websites need dynamic content. For example, a web page that is generated at runtime by executing code. The easiest way to do that is to use a new feature of ASP.NET Core named **Razor Pages**.

Exploring Razor Pages

Razor Pages allow a developer to easily mix HTML markup with C# code statements. That is why they use the `.cshtml` file extension. The Razor syntax is indicated by the @ symbol.

In the `NorthwindWeb` project, create a folder named `Pages`.

> ASP.NET Core runtime looks for Razor Pages in the `Pages` folder by default.

Move the `index.html` file into the `Pages` folder, and rename the file extension from `.html` to `.cshtml`.

Enabling Razor Pages

To enable Razor Pages, we must add and enable a service named MVC, because Razor Pages is a part of MVC.

In `Startup.cs`, in the `ConfigureServices` method, add statements to add MVC, as shown in the following code:

```
public void ConfigureServices(IServiceCollection services)
{
    services.AddMvc();
}
```

In `Startup.cs`, in the `Configure` method, after the existing statements to use default files and static files, add a statement to use MVC, as shown in the following code:

```
app.UseDefaultFiles(); // index.html, default.html, and so on
app.UseStaticFiles();
app.UseMvc(); // includes Razor Pages
```

Defining a Razor Page

Razor Pages can be described as follows:

- They require the `@page` directive at the top of the file
- They can have a `@functions` section that defines these:
  - Properties for storing data values, just like a class
  - Methods named `OnGet`, `OnPost`, `OnDelete`, and so on, that execute when HTTP requests are made such as `GET`, `POST`, and `DELETE`

Modify `index.cshtml`, by adding C# statements to the top of the file to define this file as a Razor Page with `@page`, and define a property to store the current day name, and a method to set it that executes when a HTTP GET request is made for the page, as shown in the following code:

```
@page
@functions {
  public string DayName { get; set; }
  public void OnGet()
  {
    Model.DayName = DateTime.Now.ToString("dddd");
  }
```

```
}
```

Modify `index.cshtml` to output the day name inside one of the paragraphs, as shown in the following markup:

```
<p>It's @Model.DayName! Our customers include restaurants, hotels, and
cruise lines.</p>
```

Start the website, and note the current day name is output on the page, as shown in the following screenshot:

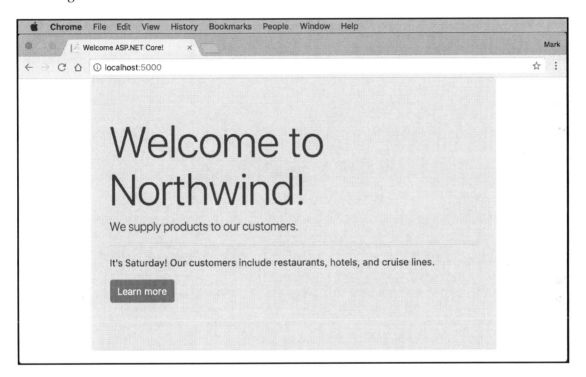

Using shared layouts with Razor Pages

Most websites have more than one page. If every page had to contain all of the boilerplate markup that is currently in `index.cshtml`, that would become a pain to manage. So, ASP.NET Core has **layouts**.

Setting a shared layout

To use layouts, we must first create a specially named file to set a default layout for all Razor Pages (and all MVC views). The name of this file must be `_ViewStart.cshtml`.

In Visual Studio 2017, in the `Pages` folder, add a new **MVC View Start Page** item, as shown in the following screenshot:

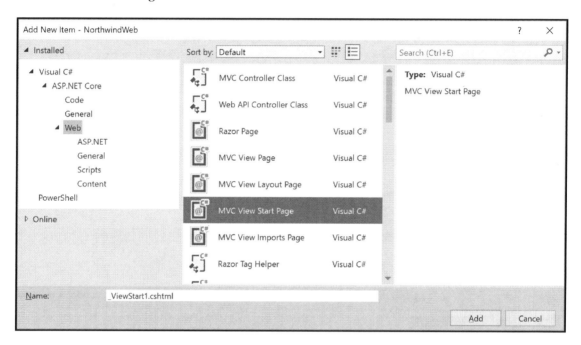

In Visual Studio Code, in the `Pages` folder, create a file named `_ViewStart.cshtml`, and modify its content, as shown in the following markup:

```
@{
    Layout = "_Layout";
}
```

Defining a shared layout

To use layouts, we must next create a Razor `.cshtml` file to define the default layout for all Razor Pages (and all MVC views). The name of this file can be anything, but `_Layout.cshtml` is good practice, so that is the name that you previously set in the `_ViewStart.cshtml` file.

In Visual Studio 2017, in the `Pages` folder, add a new **MVC View Layout Page** item.

In Visual Studio Code, in the `Pages` folder, create a file named `_Layout.cshtml`.

In both Visual Studio 2017 and Visual Studio Code, modify the content of `_Layout.cshtml`, as shown in the following markup (it is similar to `index.cshtml`, so you can copy and paste it from there):

```
<!DOCTYPE html>
<html lang="en">
<head>
<meta charset="utf-8" />
<meta name="viewport" content=
  "width=device-width, initial-scale=1, shrink-to-fit=no" />
  <link rel="stylesheet"
href="https://maxcdn.bootstrapcdn.com/bootstrap/4.0.0-beta/css/bootstrap.mi
n.css"
    integrity="sha384-
/Y6pD6FV/Vv2HJnA6t+vslU6fwYXjCFtcEpHbNJ0lyAFsXTsjBbfaDjzALeQsN6M"
    crossorigin="anonymous" />
  <title>@ViewData["Title"]</title>
</head>
<body>
  <div class="container">
    @RenderBody()
    <hr />
    <footer>
      <p>Copyright &copy; 2017 - @ViewData["Title"]</p>
    </footer>
  </div>
  <script src="https://code.jquery.com/jquery-3.2.1.slim.min.js"
    integrity="sha384-
KJ3o2DKtIkvYIK3UENzmM7KCkRr/rE9/Qpg6aAZGJwFDMVNA/GpGFF93hXpG5KkN"
    crossorigin="anonymous"></script>
  <script
src="https://cdnjs.cloudflare.com/ajax/libs/popper.js/1.11.0/umd/popper.min
.js"
    integrity="sha384-
b/U6ypiBEHpOf/4+1nzFpr53nxSS+GLCkfwBdFNTxtclqqenISfwAzpKaMNFNmj4"
    crossorigin="anonymous"></script>
  <script
src="https://maxcdn.bootstrapcdn.com/bootstrap/4.0.0-beta/js/bootstrap.min.
js"
    integrity="sha384-
h0AbiXch4ZDo7tp9hKZ4TsHbi047NrKGLO3SEJAg45jXxnGIfYzk4Si90RDIqNm1"
    crossorigin="anonymous"></script>
```

```
    @RenderSection("Scripts", required: false)
  </body>
  </html>
```

 The layout we will use for all of the pages on the site is similar to that originally used in index.cshtml, but with some scripts at the bottom to implement some dynamic features of Bootstrap that we will use later.

Modify index.cshtml, remove all HTML markup except `<div class="jumbotron">` and its contents, add a statement to the OnGet method to store a page title in the ViewData dictionary, and modify the button to navigate to a suppliers page (which we will create in the next topic), as shown in the following markup:

```
@page
@functions {
  public string DayName { get; set; }

  public void OnGet()
  {
     ViewData["Title"] = "Northwind Web Site";
     Model.DayName = DateTime.Now.ToString("dddd");
  }
}
<div class="jumbotron">
  <h1 class="display-3">Welcome to Northwind!</h1>
  <p class="lead">We supply products to our customers.</p>
  <hr />
  <p>
     It's @Model.DayName! Our customers include restaurants,
     hotels, and cruise lines.
  </p>
  <p>
    <a class="btn btn-primary" href="suppliers">
       Learn more about our suppliers
    </a>
  </p>
</div>
```

ViewData is a dictionary that uses the string values for its keys. It is handy for passing values between Razor Pages and a shared layout without needing to define a property on the model as we did for DayName. Note that ViewData["Title"] is set in the Razor Page, and read in the shared layout.

Start the website, and note that it has similar behavior as before.

 When using Visual Studio Code, remember to stop the web server with *Ctrl* + *C* and then restart with dotnet run to see changes.

Using code-behind files with Razor Pages

Sometimes, it is better to separate the HTML markup from the data and executable code, so Razor Pages allows **code-behind** class files.

In Visual Studio 2017, right-click on the **Pages** folder, select **Add | New Item....** In the **Add New Item** dialog, select **Razor Page**, change the name to Suppliers.cshtml, and click on **Add**.

In Visual Studio Code, add two files to the Pages folder named Suppliers.cshtml and Suppliers.cshtml.cs.

Modify the contents of Suppliers.cshtml.cs, as shown in the following code, and note the following:

- SuppliersModel inherits from PageModel, so it has members such as ViewData
- SuppliersModel defines a property for storing a collection of string values
- When a HTTP GET request is made for this Razor Page, the Suppliers property is populated with some example supplier names:

```
using Microsoft.AspNetCore.Mvc.RazorPages;
using System.Collections.Generic;

namespace NorthwindWeb.Pages
{
    public class SuppliersModel : PageModel
    {
        public IEnumerable<string> Suppliers { get; set; }
```

```
        public void OnGet()
        {
            ViewData["Title"] = "Northwind Web Site - Suppliers";
            Suppliers = new[]
            { "Alpha Co", "Beta Limited", "Gamma Corp" };
        }
    }
}
```

 In this example, we are focusing on learning about code-behind files. In the next topic, we will load the list of suppliers from a database, but for now, we will simulate that with a hard-coded array of the string values.

Modify the contents of Suppliers.cshtml, as shown in the following code, and note the following:

- The model for this Razor Page is set to SuppliersModel
- The page outputs an HTML table with Bootstrap styles
- The data rows in the table are generated by looping through the Suppliers property of Model

```
@page
@model NorthwindWeb.Pages.SuppliersModel
<div class="row">
  <h1 class="display-2">Suppliers</h1>
  <table class="table">
     <thead class="thead-inverse">
        <tr><th>Company Name</th></tr>
     </thead>
        <tbody>
           @foreach(string name in Model.Suppliers)
           {
              <tr><td>@name</td></tr>
           }
        </tbody>
  </table>
</div>
```

Start the website, click on the button to learn more about suppliers, and note the table of suppliers, as shown in the following screenshot:

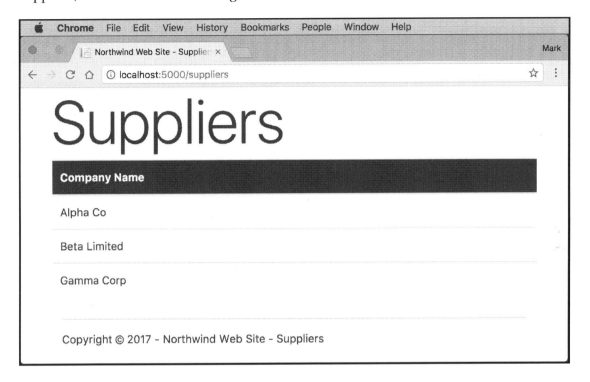

Using Entity Framework Core with ASP.NET Core

Entity Framework Core 2.0 is included with ASP.NET Core 2.0, so it is a natural way to get real data into a website.

Creating Entity models for Northwind

Creating entity data models in separate class libraries that are .NET Standard 2.0-compatible so that they can be reused in other types of projects is good practice.

Creating a class library for the Northwind entity classes

In Visual Studio 2017, choose **File | Add | New Project...**.

In the **Add New Project** dialog, in the **Installed** list, expand **Visual C#**, and select **.NET Standard**. In the center list, select **Class Library (.NET Standard)**, type the name as NorthwindEntitiesLib, type the location as C:\Code\Part3, and then click on **OK**, as shown in the following screenshot:

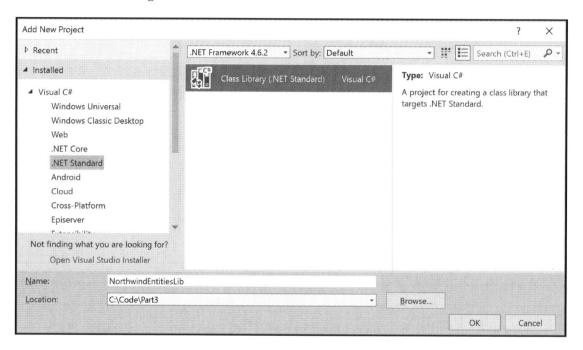

In Visual Studio Code, in the Part3 folder, create a folder named NorthwindEntitiesLib, and open it with Visual Studio Code.

In the **Integrated Terminal,** enter the command: dotnet new classlib.

In Visual Studio Code, open the Part3 folder, and in the **Integrated Terminal**, enter the command: cd NorthwindWeb.

Defining the entity classes

In both Visual Studio 2017 and Visual Studio Code, add the following class files to the NorthwindEntitiesLib project: Category.cs, Customer.cs, Employee.cs, Order.cs, OrderDetail.cs, Product.cs, Shipper.cs, and Supplier.cs.

Category.cs should look like this:

```
using System.Collections.Generic;

namespace Packt.CS7
{
    public class Category
    {
        public int CategoryID { get; set; }
        public string CategoryName { get; set; }
        public string Description { get; set; }
        public ICollection<Product> Products { get; set; }
    }
}
```

Customer.cs should look like this:

```
using System.Collections.Generic;

namespace Packt.CS7
{
    public class Customer
    {
        public string CustomerID { get; set; }
        public string CompanyName { get; set; }
        public string ContactName { get; set; }
        public string ContactTitle { get; set; }
        public string Address { get; set; }
        public string City { get; set; }
        public string Region { get; set; }
        public string PostalCode { get; set; }
        public string Country { get; set; }
        public string Phone { get; set; }
        public string Fax { get; set; }
        public ICollection<Order> Orders { get; set; }
    }
}
```

`Employee.cs` should look like this:

```
using System;
using System.Collections.Generic;

namespace Packt.CS7
{
    public class Employee
    {
        public int EmployeeID { get; set; }
        public string LastName { get; set; }
        public string FirstName { get; set; }
        public string Title { get; set; }
        public string TitleOfCourtesy { get; set; }
        public DateTime? BirthDate { get; set; }
        public DateTime? HireDate { get; set; }
        public string Address { get; set; }
        public string City { get; set; }
        public string Region { get; set; }
        public string PostalCode { get; set; }
        public string Country { get; set; }
        public string HomePhone { get; set; }
        public string Extension { get; set; }
        public string Notes { get; set; }
        public int ReportsTo { get; set; }
        public Employee Manager { get; set; }
        public ICollection<Order> Orders { get; set; }
    }
}
```

`Order.cs` should look like this:

```
using System;
using System.Collections.Generic;

namespace Packt.CS7
{
    public class Order
    {
        public int OrderID { get; set; }
        public string CustomerID { get; set; }
        public Customer Customer { get; set; }
        public int EmployeeID { get; set; }
        public Employee Employee { get; set; }
        public DateTime? OrderDate { get; set; }
        public DateTime? RequiredDate { get; set; }
        public DateTime? ShippedDate { get; set; }
        public int ShipVia { get; set; }
```

```
    public Shipper Shipper { get; set; }
    public decimal? Freight { get; set; } = 0;
    public ICollection<OrderDetail> OrderDetails { get; set; }
  }
}
```

`OrderDetail.cs` **should look like this:**

```
namespace Packt.CS7
{
  public class OrderDetail
  {
    public int OrderID { get; set; }
    public Order Order { get; set; }
    public int ProductID { get; set; }
    public Product Product { get; set; }
    public decimal UnitPrice { get; set; } = 0;
    public short Quantity { get; set; } = 1;
    public double Discount { get; set; } = 0;
  }
}
```

`Product.cs` **should look like this:**

```
namespace Packt.CS7
{
  public class Product
  {
    public int ProductID { get; set; }
    public string ProductName { get; set; }
    public int? SupplierID { get; set; }
    public Supplier Supplier { get; set; }
    public int? CategoryID { get; set; }
    public Category Category { get; set; }
    public string QuantityPerUnit { get; set; }
    public decimal? UnitPrice { get; set; } = 0;
    public short? UnitsInStock { get; set; } = 0;
    public short? UnitsOnOrder { get; set; } = 0;
    public short? ReorderLevel { get; set; } = 0;
    public bool Discontinued { get; set; } = false;
  }
}
```

`Shipper.cs` should look like this:

```
using System.Collections.Generic;

namespace Packt.CS7
{
    public class Shipper
    {
        public int ShipperID { get; set; }
        public string ShipperName { get; set; }
        public string Phone { get; set; }
        public ICollection<Order> Orders { get; set; }
    }
}
```

`Supplier.cs` should look like this:

```
using System.Collections.Generic;

namespace Packt.CS7
{
    public class Supplier
    {
        public int SupplierID { get; set; }
        public string CompanyName { get; set; }
        public string ContactName { get; set; }
        public string ContactTitle { get; set; }
        public string Address { get; set; }
        public string City { get; set; }
        public string Region { get; set; }
        public string PostalCode { get; set; }
        public string Country { get; set; }
        public string Phone { get; set; }
        public string Fax { get; set; }
        public string HomePage { get; set; }
        public ICollection<Product> Products { get; set; }
    }
}
```

Good Practice

You should create a separate class library project for your entity data models that does not have a dependency on anything except .NET Standard 2.0. This allows easier sharing between backend servers and frontend clients.

Creating a class library for Northwind database context

With Visual Studio 2017, you will use the EF Core data provider for SQL Server.

With Visual Studio Code, you will use the EF Core data provider for SQLite.

Using Visual Studio 2017

In Visual Studio 2017, go to **File** | **Add** | **New Project…**.

In the **Add New Project** dialog, in the **Installed** list, expand **Visual C#**, and select **.NET Standard**. In the center list, select **Class Library (.NET Standard)**, type the name as `NorthwindContextLib`, type the location as `C:\Code\Part3`, and then click on **OK**.

In the **NorthwindContextLib** project, right-click on **Dependencies**, and select **Add Reference…**.

In the **Reference Manager - NorthwindContextLib** dialog, select **NorthwindEntitiesLib**, and click on **OK**, as shown in the following screenshot:

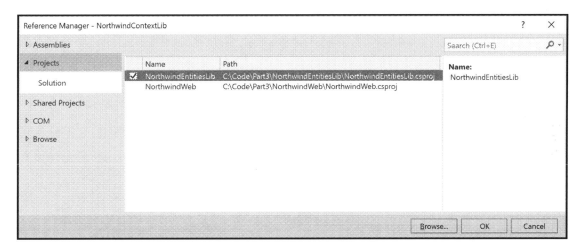

In the **NorthwindContextLib** project, right-click on **Dependencies**, and select **Manage NuGet Packages…**.

In **NuGet Package Manager: NorthwindContextLib**, select **Browse**, search for and install w, and click on **OK**.

Using Visual Studio Code

In Visual Studio Code, in the `Part3` folder, create a folder named `NorthwindContextLib`, and open it with Visual Studio Code.

In **Integrated Terminal**, enter the command: `dotnet new classlib`.

In Visual Studio Code, modify `NorthwindContextLib.csproj` to add a reference to the `NorthwindEntitiesLib` project, and the Entity Framework Core 2.0 package for SQLite, as shown in the following markup:

```
<Project Sdk="Microsoft.NET.Sdk">

  <PropertyGroup>
    <TargetFramework>netstandard2.0</TargetFramework>
  </PropertyGroup>

  <ItemGroup>
    <ProjectReference
      Include="..\NorthwindEntitiesLib\NorthwindEntitiesLib.csproj" />
    <PackageReference
      Include="Microsoft.EntityFrameworkCore.SQLite" Version="2.0.0" />
  </ItemGroup>

</Project>
```

In Visual Studio Code, open the `Part3` folder, and in **Integrated Terminal**, enter the command: `cd NorthwindWeb`.

Defining the database context class

In both Visual Studio 2017 and Visual Studio Code, in the `NorthwindContextLib` project, rename the `Class1.cs` class file as `Northwind.cs`.

`Northwind.cs` should look like this:

```
using Microsoft.EntityFrameworkCore;

namespace Packt.CS7
{
  public class Northwind : DbContext
  {
    public DbSet<Category> Categories { get; set; }
    public DbSet<Customer> Customers { get; set; }
    public DbSet<Employee> Employees { get; set; }
    public DbSet<Order> Orders { get; set; }
```

```
public DbSet<OrderDetail> OrderDetails { get; set; }
public DbSet<Product> Products { get; set; }
public DbSet<Shipper> Shippers { get; set; }
public DbSet<Supplier> Suppliers { get; set; }

public Northwind(DbContextOptions options)
    : base(options) { }

protected override void OnModelCreating(ModelBuilder modelBuilder)
{
   base.OnModelCreating(modelBuilder);

   modelBuilder.Entity<Category>()
     .Property(c => c.CategoryName)
     .IsRequired()
     .HasMaxLength(15);

   // define a one-to-many relationship
   modelBuilder.Entity<Category>()
     .HasMany(c => c.Products)
     .WithOne(p => p.Category);

   modelBuilder.Entity<Customer>()
     .Property(c => c.CustomerID)
     .IsRequired()
     .HasMaxLength(5);

   modelBuilder.Entity<Customer>()
     .Property(c => c.CompanyName)
     .IsRequired()
     .HasMaxLength(40);

   modelBuilder.Entity<Customer>()
     .Property(c => c.ContactName)
     .HasMaxLength(30);

   modelBuilder.Entity<Customer>()
     .Property(c => c.Country)
     .HasMaxLength(15);

   modelBuilder.Entity<Employee>()
     .Property(c => c.LastName)
     .IsRequired()
     .HasMaxLength(20);

   modelBuilder.Entity<Employee>()
     .Property(c => c.FirstName)
     .IsRequired()
```

```
        .HasMaxLength(10);

    modelBuilder.Entity<Employee>()
      .Property(c => c.Country)
      .HasMaxLength(15);

    modelBuilder.Entity<Product>()
      .Property(c => c.ProductName)
      .IsRequired()
      .HasMaxLength(40);

    modelBuilder.Entity<Product>()
      .HasOne(p => p.Category)
      .WithMany(c => c.Products);

    modelBuilder.Entity<Product>()
      .HasOne(p => p.Supplier)
      .WithMany(s => s.Products);

    modelBuilder.Entity<OrderDetail>()
      .ToTable("Order Details");

    // define multi-column primary key
    // for Order Details table
    modelBuilder.Entity<OrderDetail>()
      .HasKey(od => new { od.OrderID, od.ProductID });

    modelBuilder.Entity<Supplier>()
      .Property(c => c.CompanyName)
      .IsRequired()
      .HasMaxLength(40);

    modelBuilder.Entity<Supplier>()
      .HasMany(s => s.Products)
      .WithOne(p => p.Supplier);
  }
 }
}
```

 We will set the database connection string in the ASP.NET Core startup so that it does not need to be done in the Northwind class, but the class derived from DbContext must have a constructor with a DbContextOptions parameter.

Configure Entity Framework Core as a service

Services such as the Entity Framework Core, that are needed by ASP.NET Core, must be registered as a service during startup.

In Visual Studio 2017, in **NorthwindWeb** project, right-click on **Dependencies**, and add a reference to the `NorthwindContextLib` project.

In Visual Studio Code, in the `NorthwindWeb` project, modify `NorthwindWeb.csproj`, and add a reference to the `NorthwindContextLib` project, as shown in the following markup:

```
<Project Sdk="Microsoft.NET.Sdk.Web">

  <PropertyGroup>
    <TargetFramework>netcoreapp2.0</TargetFramework>
  </PropertyGroup>

  <ItemGroup>
    <Folder Include="wwwroot\" />
  </ItemGroup>

  <ItemGroup>
    <PackageReference Include="Microsoft.AspNetCore.All" Version="2.0.0" />
    <ProjectReference
        Include="..\NorthwindContextLib\NorthwindContextLib.csproj" />
  </ItemGroup>

</Project>
```

In both Visual Studio 2017 and Visual Studio Code, open the `Startup.cs` file, and import the `Microsoft.EntityFrameworkCore` and `Packt.CS7` namespaces, as shown in the following code:

```
using Microsoft.EntityFrameworkCore;
using Packt.CS7;
```

Add the following statement to the `ConfigureServices` method.

For SQL Server LocalDB, use this statement:

```
services.AddDbContext<Northwind>(options => options.UseSqlServer(
"Server=(localdb)\\mssqllocaldb;Database=Northwind;
Trusted_Connection=True;MultipleActiveResultSets=true"));
```

For SQLite, use this one:

```
services.AddDbContext<Northwind>(options => options.UseSqlite("Data
Source=../Northwind.db"));
```

In the `NorthwindWeb` project, in the `Pages` folder, open `Suppliers.cshtml.cs`, and import the `Packt.CS7` and `System.Linq` namespaces, as shown in the following code:

```
using System.Linq;
using Packt.CS7;
```

In the `SuppliersModel` class, add a private field and a constructor to get the `Northwind` database context, as shown in the following code:

```
private Northwind db;

public SuppliersModel(Northwind injectedContext)
{
    db = injectedContext;
}
```

In the `OnGet` method, modify the statements to use `Northwind` to get the names of suppliers, as shown in the following code:

```
public void OnGet()
{
    ViewData["Title"] = "Northwind Web Site - Suppliers";

    Suppliers = db.Suppliers.Select(s => s.CompanyName).ToArray();
}
```

Start the website, and note that the supplier table now loads from the database, as shown in the following screenshot:

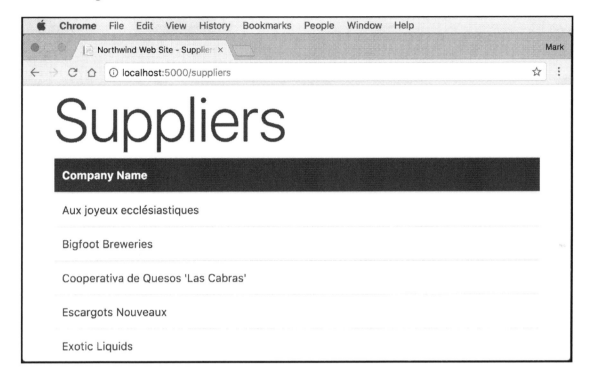

Manipulating data

Let's add the functionality to insert a new supplier.

Open `Suppliers.cshtml.cs`, and import the following namespace:

```
using Microsoft.AspNetCore.Mvc;
```

In the `SuppliersModel` class, add a property to store a supplier, and a method named `OnPost` that adds the supplier if its model is valid, as shown in the following code:

```
[BindProperty]
public Supplier Supplier { get; set; }

public IActionResult OnPost()
{
  if (ModelState.IsValid)
```

```
    {
        db.Suppliers.Add(Supplier);
        db.SaveChanges();
        return RedirectToPage("/suppliers");
    }
    return Page();
}
```

Open `Suppliers.cshtml`, and add tag helpers, as shown in the following markup:

```
@addTagHelper *, Microsoft.AspNetCore.Mvc.TagHelpers
```

At the bottom of the `.cshtml` file, add a form to insert a new supplier, and use the `asp-for` tag helper to connect the `CompanyName` property of the `Supplier` class to the input box, as shown in the following markup:

```
<div class="row">
  <p>Enter a name for a new supplier:</p>
  <form method="POST">
    <div><input asp-for="Supplier.CompanyName" /></div>
    <input type="submit" />
  </form>
</div>
```

Start the website, click on **Learn more about our suppliers**, scroll down to the form to add a new supplier, enter `Bob's Burgers`, and click on **Submit**:

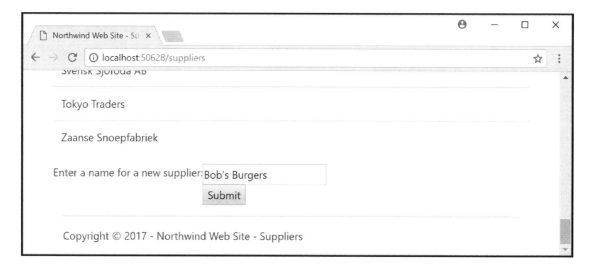

If you were to set a breakpoint inside the OnPost method and add a watch expression for the Supplier property, you would see that its properties have been populated automatically, as shown here:

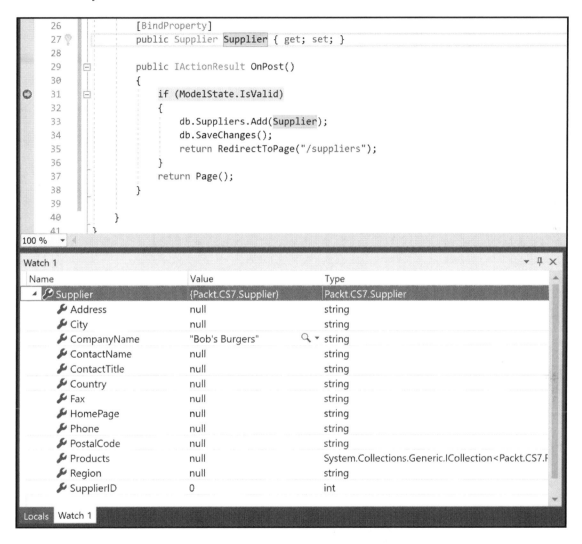

After clicking on **Submit**, you will be redirected back to the **Suppliers** list, as shown in the following screenshot:

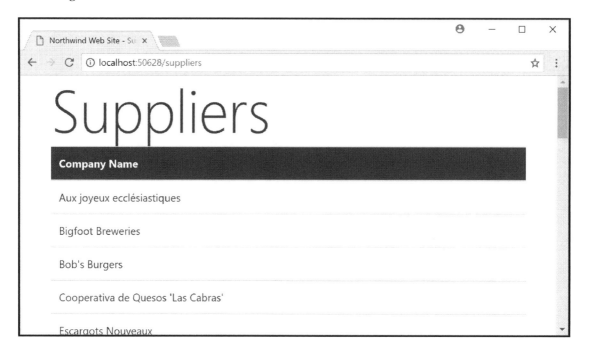

Summary

In this chapter, you learned how to build a simple website that returns static files, and used ASP.NET Core Razor Pages and Entity Framework Core to create web pages dynamically generated from a database.

In the next chapter, you will learn how to build more complex websites using ASP.NET Core MVC, which separates concerns into models, views, and controllers.

10
Building Web Sites Using ASP.NET Core MVC

This chapter is about building websites with a modern HTTP architecture on the server-side using Microsoft ASP.NET Core MVC, including the startup configuration, authentication, authorization, routes, models, views, and controllers that make up ASP.NET Core MVC.

This chapter will cover the following topics:

- Setting up an ASP.NET Core MVC website
- Understanding an ASP.NET Core MVC website

Setting up an ASP.NET Core MVC website

ASP.NET Core Razor Pages are great for simple websites. For more complex websites, it would be better to have a more formal structure to manage that complexity.

This is where the Model-View-Controller design pattern is useful. It uses technologies similar to Razor Pages, but allows a cleaner separation between concerns, as shown in the following list:

- **Models**: A folder that contains classes that represent the data used in the websites.
- **Views**: A folder that contains Razor files, that is, the `.cshtml` files, that convert models into HTML pages.

- **Controllers**: A folder that contains classes that execute code when an HTTP request arrives. The code usually creates a model and passes it to a view.

The best way to understand MVC is to see a working example.

Creating an ASP.NET Core MVC website

Visual Studio 2017 has a graphical way to create an MVC website and Visual Studio Code has a command-line way. It's worth looking at both to see the similarities and differences.

Using Visual Studio 2017

In Visual Studio 2017, open the `Part3` solution, and press *Ctrl + Shift + N* or go to **File | Add | New Project....**

In the **Add New Project** dialog, in the **Installed** list, expand **Visual C#**, and select **.NET Core**. In the center list, select **ASP.NET Core Web Application**, type the name as `NorthwindMvc`, and then click on **OK**.

In the **New ASP.NET Core Web Application - NorthwindMvc** dialog, select **.NET Core**, select **ASP.NET Core 2.0**, and select the **Web Application (Model-View-Controller)** template.

Click on **Change Authentication**, select **Individual User Accounts**, select **Store user accounts in-app**, and click on **OK**, as shown in the following screenshot:

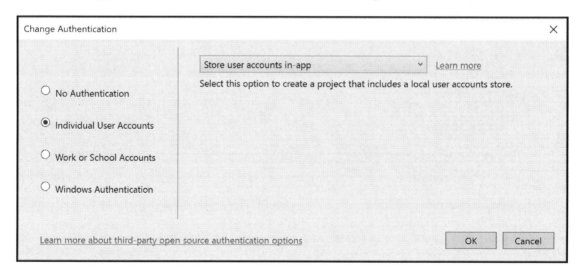

In the **New ASP.NET Core Web Application - NorthwindMvc** dialog, leave the **Enable Docker Support** box unchecked, and then click on **OK**, as shown in the following screenshot:

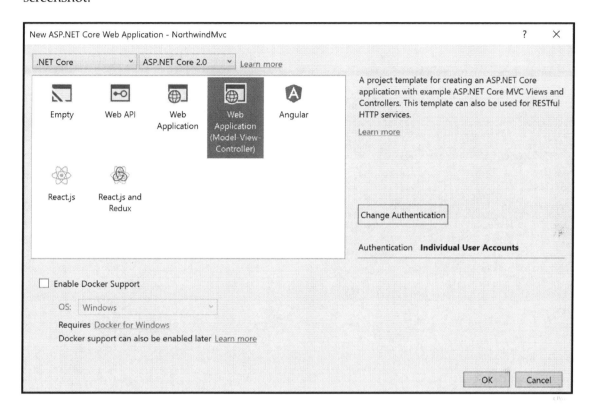

Using Visual Studio Code

In the folder named `Part3`, create a folder named `NorthwindMvc`.

In Visual Studio Code, open the `NorthwindMvc` folder.

In the **Integrated Terminal**, enter the following command to create an ASP.NET Core MVC application with a database for authenticating and authorizing users:

```
dotnet new mvc --auth Individual
```

The MVC project template uses **Bower** to manage client-side packages, for example, Bootstrap and jQuery. Bower are not installed with Visual Studio Code by default, so we need to install it now.

In Visual Studio Code, go to **View** | **Extensions** or press *Shift + Cmd + X.*

Search for `bower` to find the most popular Bower extension, and click on **Install**, as shown in the following screenshot:

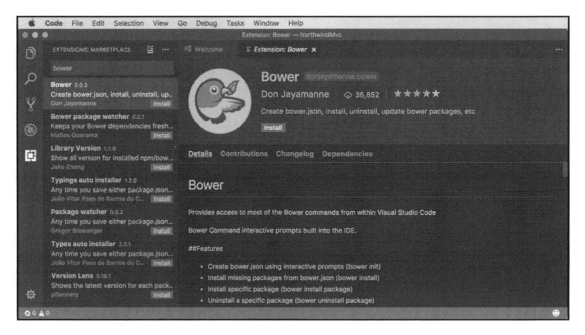

Once Bower has installed, click on **Reload**, and then **Reload Window** to reload Visual Studio Code.

Navigate to **View** | **Command Palette...**, or press *Shift + Cmd + P.*

Enter the `Bower` command, and then choose **Bower Install** to restore client-side packages such as Bootstrap, as shown in the following screenshot:

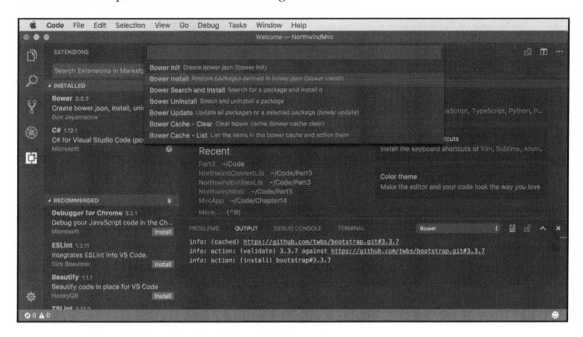

Navigate to **View** | **Explorer...**, or press *Shift + Cmd + E*.

Expand `wwwroot` and note that the `lib` folder has been created with four subfolders for the packages that are specified in the `bower.json` file, as shown in the following code:

```
{
    "name": "webapplication",
    "private": true,
    "dependencies": {
      "bootstrap": "3.3.7",
      "jquery": "2.2.0",
      "jquery-validation": "1.14.0",
      "jquery-validation-unobtrusive": "3.2.6"
    }
}
```

Reviewing the ASP.NET Core MVC project template

In Visual Studio 2017, look at the **Solution Explorer**. In Visual Studio Code, look at the **EXPLORER** pane, as shown in the following screenshot:

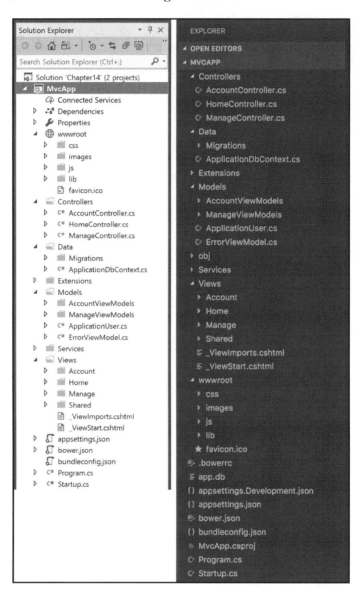

Note the following:

- `wwwroot`: This folder contains static content, such as CSS for styles, images, JavaScript, and a `favicon.ico` file.
- `Data`: This folder contains Entity Framework Core classes used by the **ASP.NET Identity** system to provide authentication and authorization.
- `Dependencies` (*Visual Studio 2017 only*): This folder contains a graphical representation of `NuGet` for modern package management. The actual NuGet references are in `MvcApp.csproj`. In Visual Studio 2017, you can edit the project manually by right-clicking on the project and choosing **Edit MvcApp.csproj**.
- `NorthwindMvc.csproj` (*Visual Studio Code only*): This file contains a list of NuGet packages that your project requires.
- `.vscode/launch.json` (*Visual Studio Code only*) and `Properties/launchSettings.json` (*Visual Studio 2017 only*): These files configure options for starting the web application from inside your development environment.
- `Controllers`: This folder contains C# classes that have methods (known as actions) that fetch a *model* and pass it to a *view*.
- `Models`: This folder contains C# classes that represent all of the data required to respond to an HTTP request.
- `Views`: This folder contains the `.cshtml` Razor files that combine HTML and C# code to enable the dynamic generation of an HTML response.
- `Services`: This folder contains C# interfaces and classes for integrating with external services, such as sending email messages.
- `Extensions`: This folder contains extension methods for the project.
- `appsettings.json`: This file contains settings that your web application can load at runtime, for example, the database connection string for the ASP.NET Identity system.
- `bower.json`: This file contains client-side packages that combine resources such as jQuery and Bootstrap.

- `Program.cs`: This file is a console application that contains the `Main` entry point that performs initial configuration, compilation, and executes the web application. It can call the `UseStartup<T>()` method to specify another class that can perform additional configuration.
- `Startup.cs`: This optional file performs additional configuration of the services, for example, ASP.NET Identity for authentication, SQLite for data storage, and so on, and routes for your application.

Performing database migrations

Before we test the web application, we need to ensure that the database migrations have been executed to create the tables used by ASP.NET Identity, an authentication and authorization system.

Using Visual Studio 2017

Open the `appsettings.json` file and note the database connection string. It will look something like this:

```
Server=(localdb)\\mssqllocaldb;Database=aspnet-NorthwindMvcApp-584f323f-
a60e-4933-9845-f67225753337;
Trusted_Connection=True;MultipleActiveResultSets=true
```

When the database migrations execute, it will create a database with the preceding name in Microsoft SQL Server LocalDB.

From the Windows Start menu, start **Developer Command Prompt for VS 2017**.

Change to the project directory and execute the database migrations by entering the following commands:

```
cd C:\Code\Part3\NorthwindMvc
dotnet ef database update
```

You should see output, as shown in the following screenshot:

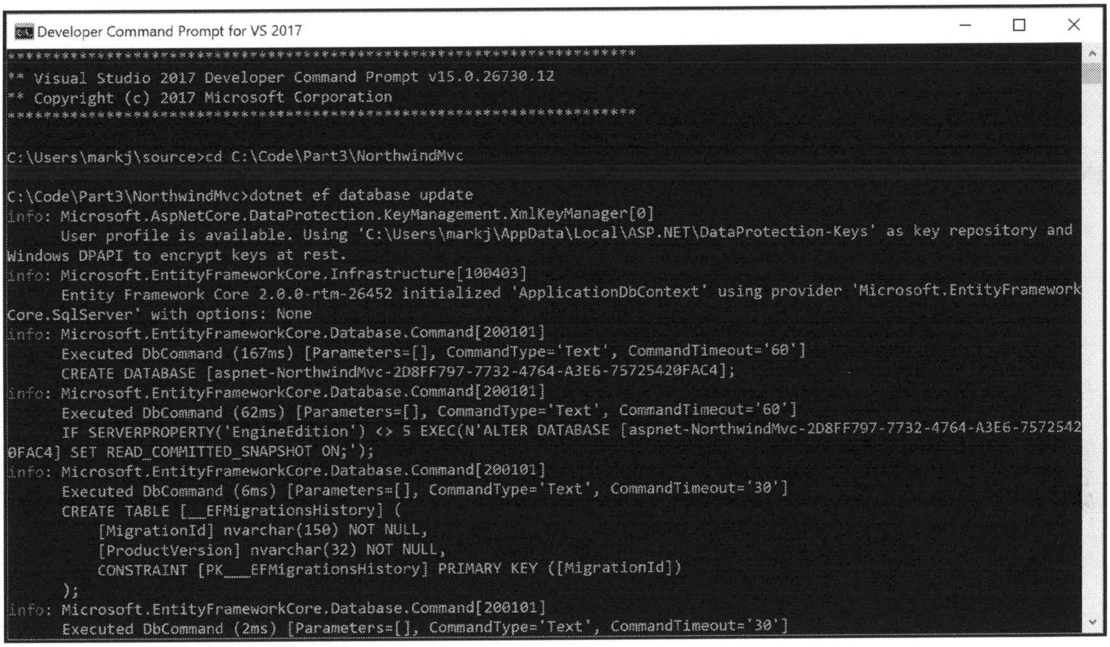

Close the **Developer Command Prompt for VS 2017** window.

Using Visual Studio Code

Open the `appsettings.json` file and note the database connection string. It will be something like this:

```
Data Source=app.db
```

When the database migrations execute, it will create a database with the preceding name in the current folder using SQLite.

In the **Integrated Terminal**, enter the following command to execute the database migrations:

```
dotnet ef database update
```

In the **EXPLORER** pane, note that the SQLite database named `app.db` has been created.

If you installed an SQLite tool such as **SQLiteStudio**, then you can open the database and see the tables that the ASP.NET Identity system uses to register users and roles, as shown in the following screenshot:

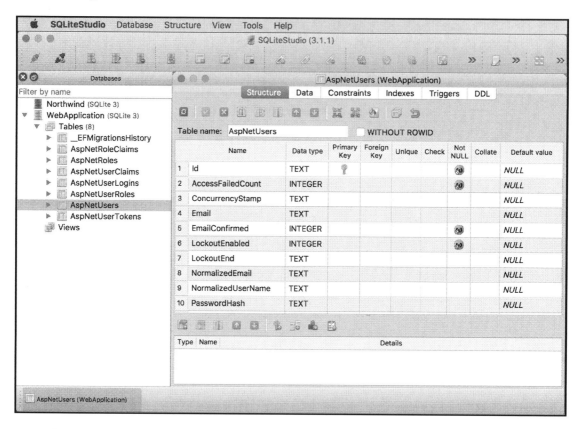

Testing the ASP.NET MVC website

In both Visual Studio 2017 and Visual Studio Code, start the website.

With Visual Studio 2017, a web browser will start automatically. With Visual Studio Code, you must start your browser manually and enter the following address:
`http://localhost:5000/`
For Visual Studio 2017, if you are prompted to trust the self-signed certificate that IIS Express has generated for SSL, click on **Yes**.

Note that your ASP.NET Core application is hosted in a cross-platform web server named **Kestrel** (when using Visual Studio 2017, it is integrated with IIS Express) using a random port number for local testing. Also note that the ASP.NET Core MVC project is a site with half a dozen pages, including **Home**, **About**, **Contact**, **Register**, and **Log in**, as shown in the following screenshot:

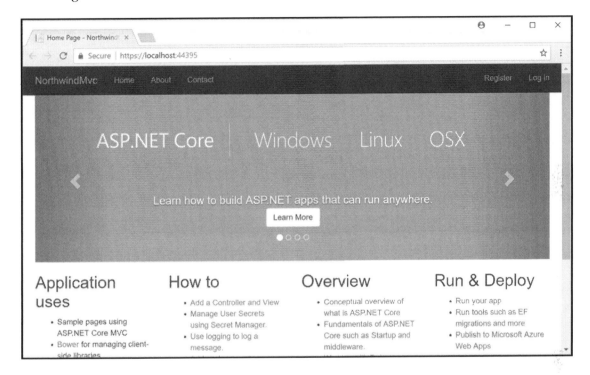

Click on the **Register** link and then complete the form to create a new account in the database that was created by the migration, as shown in the following screenshot:

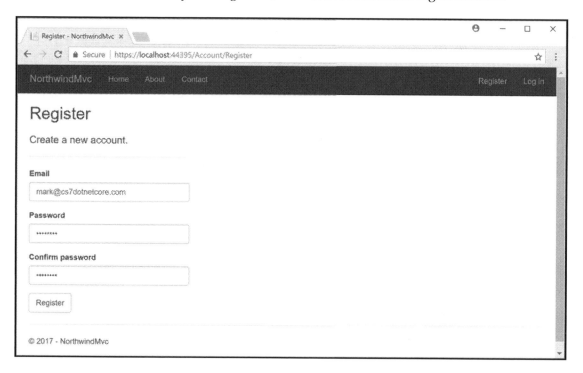

Note that if you enter a password that is not strong enough, there is built-in validation.

Click on **Register**, and note that you are now registered and logged in, as shown in the following screenshot:

Close Chrome.

In Visual Studio Code, in **Integrated Terminal**, press *Ctrl + C* to stop the console application and shut down the Kestrel web server that is hosting your ASP.NET Core website.

Reviewing authentication with ASP.NET Identity

In Visual Studio 2017, go to **View** | **Server Explorer**.

Right-click on **Data Connections**, and select **Add Connection....**

In the **Add Connection** dialog, enter a **Server name** of (localdb)\mssqllocaldb, and select the **aspnet-NorthwindMvc-GUID** database from the drop-down list, as shown in the following screenshot:

In **Server Explorer**, expand **Tables**, right-click on the **AspNetUsers** table, select **Show Table Data**, and note the row that was added to the database when you completed the register form:

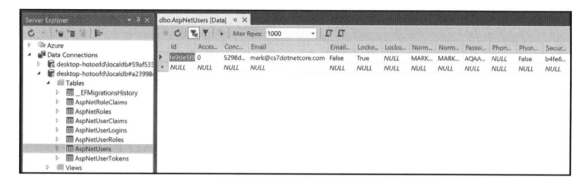

Good Practice
The ASP.NET Core web application project follows good practice by storing a hash of the password instead of the password itself. The ASP.NET Core Identity system can be extended to support two-factor authentication.

Close the table, and in **Server Explorer**, right-click on the database connection, and select **Close Connection**.

Understanding an ASP.NET Core MVC website

Let's walk through the parts that make up a modern ASP.NET Core MVC application.

ASP.NET Core startup

Open the `Startup.cs` file.

Note that the `ConfigureServices` method adds support for MVC along with other frameworks and services such as ASP.NET Identity, as shown in the following code:

```
public void ConfigureServices(IServiceCollection services)
{
    services.AddDbContext<ApplicationDbContext>(options =>
     options.UseSqlServer(Configuration
     .GetConnectionString("DefaultConnection")));

    services.AddIdentity<ApplicationUser, IdentityRole>()
     .AddEntityFrameworkStores<ApplicationDbContext>()
     .AddDefaultTokenProviders();

    // Add application services.
    services.AddTransient<IEmailSender, EmailSender>();

    services.AddMvc();
}
```

Next, we have the `Configure` method, as shown in the following code:

```
public void Configure(IApplicationBuilder app, IHostingEnvironment env)
{
    if (env.IsDevelopment())
    {
        app.UseDeveloperExceptionPage();
        app.UseDatabaseErrorPage();
    }
    else
    {
        app.UseExceptionHandler("/Home/Error");
    }

    app.UseStaticFiles();

    app.UseAuthentication();

    app.UseMvc(routes =>
    {
        routes.MapRoute(
          name: "default",
          template: "{controller=Home}/{action=Index}/{id?}");
    });
}
```

Note the following:

- If the website is running in the development environment, then these two things happen:
    - When an exception is thrown, a rich error page showing source code is displayed.
    - Also, a database error page is enabled.
- If the website is running in a production environment, the visitor will be redirected to /Home/Error.
- Static files are enabled to allow CSS, JavaScript, and so on, to be served from the filesystem.
- ASP.NET Identity is enabled for authentication and authorization.
- The most important statement here is the one that calls UseMvc and maps a default route. This route is very flexible, because it will map to almost any incoming URL, as you will see in the next section.

Understanding the default route

The default route looks at any URL entered by the user in the address bar and matches it to extract the name of a controller, the name of an action, and an optional id value (the ? symbol makes it optional). If the user hasn't entered these names, it uses defaults of Home for the controller and Index for the action (the = assignment sets a default for a named segment).

Contents in curly-brackets { } are called **segments**, and they are like a named parameter of a method. The value of these segments can be any string.

The responsibility of a route is to discover the name of a controller and an action.

The following table contains example URLs and how MVC would work out the names:

URL	Controller	Action	ID
/	Home	Index	
/Muppet	Muppet	Index	
/Muppet/Kermit	Muppet	Kermit	
/Muppet/Kermit/Green	Muppet	Kermit	Green
/Products	Products	Index	
/Products/Detail	Products	Detail	
/Products/Detail/3	Products	Detail	3

Note that if the user does not supply a name, then the defaults, Home and Index, are used as specified when the route was registered. You could change these defaults if you wanted.

Understanding ASP.NET Core MVC controllers

From the route and an incoming URL, ASP.NET Core MVC knows the name of the controller and action, so it will look for a class that implements an interface named IController. To simplify the requirements, Microsoft supplies a class named Controller that your classes can inherit from.

The responsibilities of a controller are as follows:

- To extract parameters from the HTTP request
- To use the parameters to fetch the correct model and pass it to the correct view client as an HTTP response
- To return the results from the view to the client as an HTTP response

Expand the Controllers folder and double-click on the file named HomeController.cs:

```
public class HomeController : Controller
{
    public IActionResult Index()
    {
        return View();
    }

    public IActionResult About()
    {
        ViewData["Message"] = "Your application description page.";
        return View();
    }

    public IActionResult Contact()
    {
        ViewData["Message"] = "Your contact page.";
        return View();
    }

    public IActionResult Error()
    {
        return View(new ErrorViewModel {
          RequestId = Activity.Current?.Id ??
          HttpContext.TraceIdentifier });
    }
}
```

```
}
```

 If the user enters / or /Home, then it is the equivalent of /Home/Index because those were the defaults.

Note the following:

- None of the action methods use a model
- Two of the action methods use the dictionary named ViewData to store a string item named Message that can then be read inside a view
- All of the action methods call a method named View() and return the results as an IActionResult interface to the client

Understanding ASP.NET Core MVC models

In ASP.NET Core MVC, the model represents the data required for a request. For example, an HTTP GET request for http://www.example.com/products/details/3 might mean that the browser is asking for the details of product number 3.

The controller would need to use the ID value 3 to retrieve the record for that product and pass it to a view that can then turn the model into HTML for display in the browser.

Configuring an EF Core entity data model

We will reference the Entity Framework Core entity data model for the Northwind database that you created in the previous chapter.

In Visual Studio 2017, in the **NorthwindMvc** project, right-click on **Dependencies**, and select **Add Reference...**. Select **NorthwindContextLib**, and click on **OK**.

In Visual Studio Code, in the NorthwindMvc project, modify NorthwindMvc.csproj, and add a project reference to NorthwindContextLib.

In both Visual Studio 2017 and Visual Studio Code, modify `Startup.cs`, to add the following statement to the `ConfigureServices` method.

For SQL Server LocalDB, add this statement:

```
services.AddDbContext<Packt.CS7.Northwind>(options =>
  options.UseSqlServer("Server=(localdb)\\mssqllocaldb;" +
  "Database=Northwind;Trusted_Connection=True;" +
  "MultipleActiveResultSets=true"));
```

For SQLite, add this one:

```
services.AddDbContext<Packt.CS7.Northwind>(options =>
  options.UseSqlite("Data Source=../Northwind.db"));
```

Creating view models for requests

Imagine that when a user comes to our website, we want to show them a carousel of categories, a list of products, and a count of the number of visitors we have had this month. All of the data that we want to show in response to a request is the MVC model, sometimes called a **view model**, because it is a *model* that is passed to a *view*.

Add a class to the `Models` folder and name it `HomeIndexViewModel`.

Modify the class definition, as shown in the following code:

```
using System.Collections.Generic;

namespace Packt.CS7
{
    public class HomeIndexViewModel
    {
        public int VisitorCount;
        public IList<Category> Categories { get; set; }
        public IList<Product> Products { get; set; }
    }
}
```

Fetch the model in the controller

Open the `HomeController` class.

Import the `Packt.CS7` namespace.

Add a field to store a reference to a `Northwind` instance, and initialize it in a constructor, as shown in the following code:

```
private Northwind db;

public HomeController(Northwind injectedContext)
{
    db = injectedContext;
}
```

Modify the contents of the `Index` action method, as shown in the following code:

```
var model = new HomeIndexViewModel
{
    VisitorCount = (new Random()).Next(1, 1001),
    Categories   = db.Categories.ToList(),
    Products = db.Products.ToList()
};
return View(model); // pass model to view
```

We have simulated a visitor count using the `Random` class to generate a number between 1 and 1000.

Understanding ASP.NET Core MVC views

The responsibility of a view is to transform a model into HTML or other formats. There are multiple **view engines** that can be used to do this. The default view engine for ASP.NET MVC 3 and later is called **Razor**, and it uses the @ symbol to indicate server-side code execution.

The new Razor Pages feature in ASP.NET Core 2.0 uses the same view engine and so can use the same Razor syntax.

Rendering the Home controller's views

Expand the `Views` folder, and then expand the `Home` folder. Note the three files with the `.cshtml` file extension.

> The `.cshtml` file extension means that this is a file that mixes C# and HTML.

When the `View()` method is called in a controller's action method, ASP.NET Core MVC looks in the `Views` folder for a subfolder with the same name as the current controller, that is, `Home`. It then looks for a file with the same name as the current action, that is, `Index`, `About`, or `Contact`.

In the `Index.cshtml` file, note the block of C# code wrapped in `@{ }`. This will execute first and can be used to store data that needs to be passed into a shared layout file:

```
@{
    ViewData["Title"] = "Home Page";
}
```

Note the static HTML content in several `<div>` elements that uses Bootstrap for styling.

Good Practice
As well as defining your own styles, base your styles on a common library, such as Bootstrap, that implements responsive design. To learn more about CSS3 and responsive design, read the book *Responsive Web Design with HTML5 and CSS3 - Second Edition* by *Packt Publishing* at the following link:
https://www.packtpub.com/web-development/responsive-web-design-html5-and-css3-second-edition

Sharing layouts between views

Just as with Razor Pages, there is a file named `_ViewStart.cshtml` that gets executed by the `View()` method. It is used to set defaults that apply to all views.

For example, it sets the `Layout` property of all views to a shared layout file:

```
@{
    Layout = "_Layout";
}
```

In the `Shared` folder, open the `_Layout.cshtml` file. Note that the title is being read from the `ViewData` dictionary that was set earlier in the `Index.cshtml` view.

Note the rendering of common styles to support Bootstrap and the two sections. During *development*, the fully commented and nicely formatted versions of CSS files will be used. For *staging* and *release*, the minified versions will be used:

```
<environment include="Development">
  <link rel="stylesheet" href="~/lib/bootstrap/dist/css/bootstrap.css" />
  <link rel="stylesheet" href="~/css/site.css" />
</environment>
<environment exclude="Development">
  <link rel="stylesheet" href="https://ajax.aspnetcdn.com/ajax/
    bootstrap/3.3.5/css/bootstrap.min.css"
    asp-fallback-href="~/lib/bootstrap/dist/css/bootstrap.min.css"
    asp-fallback-test-class="sr-only"
    asp-fallback-test-property="position"
    asp-fallback-test-value="absolute" />
  <link rel="stylesheet" href="~/css/site.min.css"
    asp-append-version="true" />
</environment>
```

 Here, ~ means the `wwwroot` folder.

Note the rendering of hyperlinks to allow users to click between pages using the navigation bar at the top of every page. The <a> elements use *tag helper* attributes to specify the controller name and action name that will execute when the link is clicked on:

```
<div class="navbar-collapse collapse">
  <ul class="nav navbar-nav">
    <li><a asp-controller="Home" asp-action="Index">Home</a></li>
    <li><a asp-controller="Home" asp-action="About">About</a></li>
    <li><a asp-controller="Home" asp-action="Contact">Contact</a></li>
  </ul>
</div>
```

Note the rendering of the body:

```
@RenderBody()
```

Note the rendering of script blocks at the bottom of the page so that it doesn't slow down the display of the page:

```
<environment include="Development">
  <script src="~/lib/jquery/dist/jquery.js"></script>
  <script src="~/lib/bootstrap/dist/js/bootstrap.js"></script>
  <script src="~/js/site.js" asp-append-version="true"></script>
</environment>
<environment exclude="Development">
  <script src="https://ajax.aspnetcdn.com/ajax/jquery/jquery-2.1.4.min.js"
    asp-fallback-src="~/lib/jquery/dist/jquery.min.js"
    asp-fallback-test="window.jQuery">
  </script>
  <script
src="https://ajax.aspnetcdn.com/ajax/bootstrap/3.3.5/bootstrap.min.js"
    asp-fallback-src="~/lib/bootstrap/dist/js/bootstrap.min.js"
    asp-fallback-test="window.jQuery && window.jQuery.fn &&
    window.jQuery.fn.modal">
  </script>
    <script src="~/js/site.min.js" asp-append-version="true">
  </script>
</environment>
```

You can add your own script blocks into an optional defined section named `scripts`:

```
@RenderSection("scripts", required: false)
```

Defining custom styles

In the `wwwroot\css` folder, open the `site.css` file.

Add a new style that will apply to an element with the `newspaper` ID, like this:

```
#newspaper {
  column-count: 3;
}
```

In Visual Studio Code, you will need to add the style to `site.min.css` too. Usually, you would have a build step to minify your `site.css` into a `site.min.css`, but for now, just do it manually.

Defining a typed view

To improve the IntelliSense when writing a view, you can define the type the view can expect using a `@model` directive at the top.

In the `Views\Home` folder, open `Index.cshtml` view, and add a statement to set the model type to use the `HomeIndexViewModel` as the first line of the file, as shown in the following code:

```
@model Packt.CS7.HomeIndexViewModel
```

Now, whenever we type `Model` in this view, the IntelliSense will know the correct type and will provide IntelliSense.

To declare the type for the model, use `@model` (with lowercase `m`).

To interact with the model, use `@Model` (with uppercase `M`).

In `Index.cshtml`, modify the carousel `<div>` element, delete all of the other `<div>` elements, and replace them with the new markup to output products as an unordered list, as shown in the following markup:

```
@model Packt.CS7.HomeIndexViewModel
@{
    ViewData["Title"] = "Home Page";
}
<div id="myCarousel" class="carousel slide" data-ride="carousel"
 data-interval="6000">
    <ol class="carousel-indicators">
      @for (int c = 0; c < Model.Categories.Count; c++)
      {
          if (c == 0)
          {
              <li data-target="#myCarousel" data-slide-to="@c"
               class="active"></li>
          }
          else
          {
              <li data-target="#myCarousel" data-slide-to="@c"></li>
          }
      }
    </ol>
    <div class="carousel-inner" role="listbox">
      @for (int c = 0; c < Model.Categories.Count; c++)
      {
          if (c == 0)
          {
              <div class="item active">
                <img src="~/images/category@
                 (Model.Categories[c].CategoryID).jpeg"
                 alt="@Model.Categories[c].CategoryName"
                 class="img-responsive" />
                <div class="carousel-caption" role="option">
                  <p>
                    @Model.Categories[c].Description
                    <a class="btn btn-default" href="/category/
                     @Model.Categories[c].CategoryID">
                        @Model.Categories[c].CategoryName
                    </a>
                  </p>
                </div>
              </div>
          }
          else
          {
              <div class="item">
```

```
                    <img src="~/images/category@
                      (Model.Categories[c].CategoryID).jpeg"
                      alt="@Model.Categories[c].CategoryName"
                      class="img-responsive" />
                      <div class="carousel-caption" role="option">
                        <p>
                          @Model.Categories[c].Description
                          <a class="btn btn-default" href="/category/
                           @Model.Categories[c].CategoryID">
                              @Model.Categories[c].CategoryName
                          </a>
                        </p>
                      </div>
                  </div>
              }
          }
      </div>
      <a class="left carousel-control" href="#myCarousel" role="button"
       data-slide="prev">
        <span class="glyphicon glyphicon-chevron-left"
         aria-hidden="true"></span>
        <span class="sr-only">Previous</span>
      </a>
      <a class="right carousel-control" href="#myCarousel" role="button"
       data-slide="next">
        <span class="glyphicon glyphicon-chevron-right"
         aria-hidden="true">
        </span>
        <span class="sr-only">Next</span>
      </a>
  </div>
  <div class="row">
    <div class="col-md-12">
      <h1>Northwind</h1>
      <p class="lead">
        We have had @Model.VisitorCount
        visitors this month.
      </p>
      <h2>Products</h2>
      <div id="newspaper">
        <ul>
          @foreach (var item in @Model.Products)
          {
            <li>
              <a asp-controller="Home"
                asp-action="ProductDetail"
                asp-route-id="@item.ProductID">
                @item.ProductName costs
```

```
            @item.UnitPrice.Value.ToString("C")
          </a>
        </li>
      }
    </ul>
  </div>
  </div>
</div>
```

Note how easy it is to mix static HTML elements such as <ul> and <li> with C# code to output the list of product names.

Note the <div> element with the id attribute of newspaper. This will use the custom style that we defined earlier, so all of the content in that element will display in three columns.

In the wwwroot folder, in the images folder, add eight image files named category1.jpeg, category2.jpeg, and so on, up to category8.jpeg.

 You can download images from the Github repository for this book at the following link:
https://github.com/markjprice/cs7dotnetcore2/tree/master/Assets
To find suitable images for the eight categories, I searched on a site that has free stock photos for commercial use with no attribution required, at the following link:
https://www.pexels.com

In Visual Studio 2017, press *Ctrl + F5*.

In Visual Studio Code, enter the dotnet run command, and then run Chrome and navigate to http://localhost:5000/.

The home page will have a rotating carousel showing categories, and a list of products in three columns, as shown in the following screenshot:

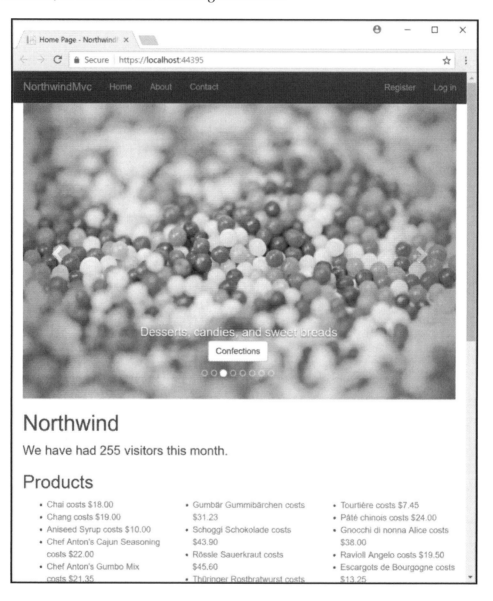

At the moment, clicking on any of the product links gives a 404 error, as shown in the following screenshot:

Now that you've seen the basics of how models, views, and controllers work together to provide a web application, let's look at some common scenarios, such as passing parameters, so that we can see the details of a product.

Passing parameters using a route value

Back in the HomeController class, add an action method named ProductDetail, as shown in the following code:

```
public IActionResult ProductDetail(int? id)
{
    if (!id.HasValue)
    {
        return NotFound("You must pass a product ID in the route, for
        example, /Home/ProductDetail/21");
    }
    var model = db.Products.SingleOrDefault(p => p.ProductID == id);
    if (model == null)
    {
        return NotFound($"A product with the ID of {id} was not found.");
```

```
    }
    return View(model); // pass model to view
}
```

Note the following:

- This method uses a feature of ASP.NET Core called **model binding** to automatically match the `id` passed in the route to the parameter named `id` in the method
- Inside the method, we check to see whether `id` is null, and if so, it returns a `404` status code and message
- Otherwise, we can connect to the database and try to retrieve a product using the `id` variable
- If we find a product, we pass it to a view; otherwise, we return a different `404` status code and message

 Model binders are very powerful, and the default one does a lot for you. For advanced scenarios, you can create your own by implementing the `IModelBinder` interface, but that is beyond the scope of this book.

Now, we need to create a view for this request.

In Visual Studio 2017, inside the `Views` folder, right-click on **Home** and choose **Add | New Item....** Choose **MVC View Page** and name it `ProductDetail.cshtml`.

In Visual Studio Code, inside the `Views/Home` folder, add a new file named `ProductDetail.cshtml`.

Modify the contents, as shown in the following markup:

```
@model Packt.CS7.Product
@{
    ViewData["Title"] = "Product Detail - " + Model.ProductName;
}
<h2>Product Detail</h2>
<hr />
<div>
  <dl class="dl-horizontal">
    <dt>Product ID</dt>
    <dd>@Model.ProductID</dd>
    <dt>Product Name</dt>
    <dd>@Model.ProductName</dd>
```

```
        <dt>Category ID</dt>
        <dd>@Model.CategoryID</dd>
        <dt>Unit Price</dt>
        <dd>@Model.UnitPrice.Value.ToString("C")</dd>
        <dt>Units In Stock</dt>
        <dd>@Model.UnitsInStock</dd>
    </dl>
</div>
```

Run the web application, and when the home page appears with the list of products, click on one of them, for example, the second product, **Chang**. The result should look as shown in the following screenshot:

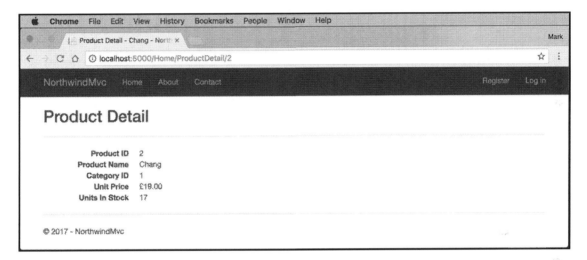

Passing parameters using a query string

In the `HomeController` class, import the `Microsoft.EntityFrameworkCore` namespace. We need this to add the `Include` extension method so that we can include related entities.

Add a new action method, as shown in the following code:

```
public IActionResult ProductsThatCostMoreThan(decimal? price)
{
    if (!price.HasValue)
    {
        return NotFound("You must pass a product price in the query
        string, for example, /Home/ProductsThatCostMoreThan?price=50");
    }
    var model = db.Products.Include(p => p.Category).Include(
```

```
      p => p.Supplier).Where(p => p.UnitPrice > price).ToArray();
      if (model.Count() == 0)
      {
          return NotFound($"No products cost more than {price:C}.");
      }
      ViewData["MaxPrice"] = price.Value.ToString("C");
      return View(model); // pass model to view
  }
```

Inside the `Views/Home` folder, add a new file named
`ProductsThatCostMoreThan.cshtml`.

Modify the contents, as shown in the following code:

```
@model IEnumerable<Packt.CS7.Product>
@{
    ViewData["Title"] =
      "Products That Cost More Than " + ViewData["MaxPrice"];
}
<h2>Products That Cost More Than @ViewData["MaxPrice"]</h2>
<table class="table">
  <tr>
    <th>Category Name</th>
    <th>Supplier's Company Name</th>
    <th>Product Name</th>
    <th>Unit Price</th>
    <th>Units In Stock</th>
  </tr>
  @foreach (var item in Model)
  {
    <tr>
      <td>
        @Html.DisplayFor(modelItem => item.Category.CategoryName)
      </td>
      <td>
        @Html.DisplayFor(modelItem => item.Supplier.CompanyName)
      </td>
      <td>
        @Html.DisplayFor(modelItem => item.ProductName)
      </td>
      <td>
        @Html.DisplayFor(modelItem => item.UnitPrice)
      </td>
      <td>
        @Html.DisplayFor(modelItem => item.UnitsInStock)
      </td>
```

```
      </tr>
    }
  </table>
```

In the `Views/Home` folder, open `Index.cshtml`, and add the following `form` element near the bottom of the file, but above the `Products` heading and its listing of products. This will provide a form for the user to enter a price. The user can then click on a `submit` button to call the action method that shows only products that cost more than the entered price:

```
<form asp-action="ProductsThatCostMoreThan" method="get">
  <input name="price" placeholder="Enter a product price" />
  <input type="submit" />
</form>
```

Run the web application, and on the home page, scroll down and enter a price in the form, for example, 50, and then click on **Submit**, as shown in the following screenshot:

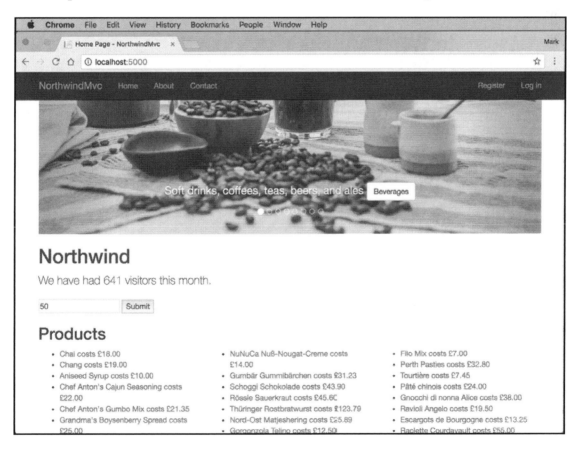

You will see a table of the products that cost more than the price that you entered, as shown in the following screenshot:

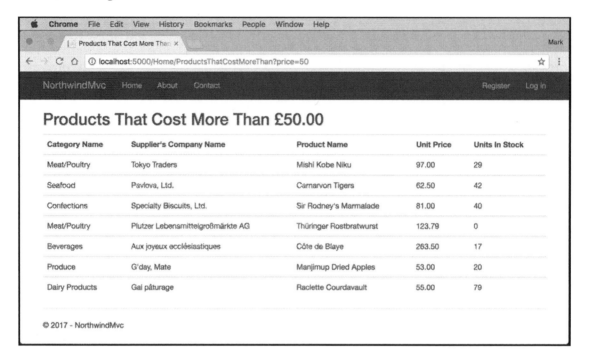

Summary

In this chapter, you learned how to build more complex websites using ASP.NET Core MVC.

In the next chapter, you will learn how to build web applications using backend web services built with ASP.NET Core Web API, and using frontend technologies including Angular and React.

11

Building Web Services and Applications Using ASP.NET Core

This chapter is about learning how to build web applications using a combination of backend web services using ASP.NET Core Web API and frontend **Single Page Applications (SPAs)** with Angular or React.

In this chapter, we will cover the following topics:

- Building web services using ASP.NET Core Web API
- Documenting and testing web services using Swagger
- Building SPAs using Angular
- Using other project templates

Building web services using ASP.NET Core Web API

Although HTTP was originally designed to request and respond with HTML and other resources for humans to look at, it is also good for building services. Roy Fielding stated in his doctoral dissertation, describing the **Representational State Transfer (REST)** architectural style, that the HTTP standard defines the following:

- URLs to uniquely identify resources
- Methods to perform common tasks, such as GET, POST, PUT, and DELETE
- The ability to negotiate media formats, such as XML and JSON

Web services are services that use the HTTP communication standard, so they are sometimes called HTTP or RESTful services.

Understanding ASP.NET Core controllers

To allow the easy creation of web services, ASP.NET Core has combined what used to be two types of controller.

In earlier versions of ASP.NET, you would derive web services from `ApiController` to create a Web API service and then register API routes in the same route table that MVC uses.

With ASP.NET Core, you use the same `Controller` base class as you used with MVC, except the routes are configured on the controller itself, using attributes, rather than in the route table.

Creating an ASP.NET Core Web API project

We will build a web service that provides a way to work with data in the `Northwind` database using ASP.NET Core so that the data can be used on any platform that can make HTTP requests and receive HTTP responses.

Using Visual Studio 2017

In Visual Studio 2017, open the `Part3` solution, and press *Ctrl* + *Shift* + *N* or go to **File** | **Add** | **New Project....**

In the **Add New Project** dialog, in the **Installed** list, expand **Visual C#**, and select **.NET Core**. In the center list, select **ASP.NET Core Web Application**, type the name as `NorthwindService`, and then click on **OK**.

In the **New ASP.NET Core Web Application - NorthwindService** dialog, select **.NET Core**, select **ASP.NET Core 2.0**, and then select the **Web API** template. Make sure that **No Authentication** is selected, with no Docker support. Click on **OK**.

Using Visual Studio Code

In the folder named `Part3`, create a folder named `NorthwindService`.

In Visual Studio Code, open the `NorthwindService` folder.

In **Integrated Terminal**, enter the following command to create a new ASP.NET Core Web API project:

```
dotnet new webapi
```

Using Visual Studio 2017 and Visual Studio Code

In the `Controllers` folder, open `ValuesController.cs`, and note the following:

- The `[Route]` attribute registers the `/api/values` relative URL for clients to use to make HTTP requests that will be handled by this controller. The `/api/` base route followed by a controller name is a convention to differentiate between MVC and Web API. You do not have to use it. If you use `[controller]` as shown, it uses the characters before `Controller` in the class name, or you can simply enter a different name without the brackets.
- The `[HttpGet]` attribute registers the `Get` method to respond to HTTP GET requests, and it returns an array of `string` values.
- The `[HttpGet]` attribute with a parameter registers the `Get` method with an `id` parameter to respond to HTTP GET requests that include a parameter value in the route.

- The [HttpPost], [HttpPut], and [HttpDelete] attributes register three other methods to respond to the equivalent HTTP methods, but currently do nothing:

```csharp
using System.Collections.Generic;
using Microsoft.AspNetCore.Mvc;

namespace NorthwindService.Controllers
{
    [Route("api/[controller]")]
    public class ValuesController : Controller
    {
        // GET api/values
        [HttpGet]
        public IEnumerable<string> Get()
        {
            return new string[] { "value1", "value2" };
        }

        // GET api/values/5
        [HttpGet("{id}")]
        public string Get(int id)
        {
            return "value";
        }

        // POST api/values
        [HttpPost]
        public void Post([FromBody]string value)
        {
        }

        // PUT api/values/5
        [HttpPut("{id}")]
        public void Put(int id, [FromBody]string value)
        {
        }

        // DELETE api/values/5
        [HttpDelete("{id}")]
        public void Delete(int id)
        {
        }
    }
}
```

If you have used older versions of ASP.NET Web API for .NET Framework, then you know that you could create C# methods that begin with any HTTP method (GET, POST, PUT, and so on), and the controller would automatically execute the correct one. In ASP.NET Core, this doesn't happen anymore because we are not inheriting from ApiController. So, you must apply an attribute such as [HttpGet] to explicitly map HTTP methods to C# methods. Although this requires more code, it allows us to use any name we like for the controller's methods.

Modify the second Get method to return a message telling the client what id value they sent, as shown in the following code:

```
// GET api/values/5
[HttpGet("{id}")]
public string Get(int id)
{
    return $"You sent me the id: {id}";
}
```

Start the website.

In Visual Studio 2017, press *Ctrl* + *F5*.

In Visual Studio Code, enter dotnet run, and then start Chrome. Navigate to http:/localhost:5000/api/values.

In Chrome, show the **Developer tools**, and press *F5* to refresh.

The Web API service should return a JSON document, as shown in the following screenshot:

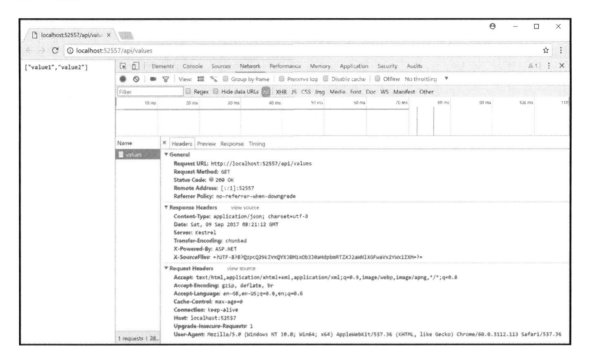

In Visual Studio 2017, you do not need to enter the `/api/values` relative URL because the project's **Debug** properties have been configured to do that for you, as shown in the following screenshot:

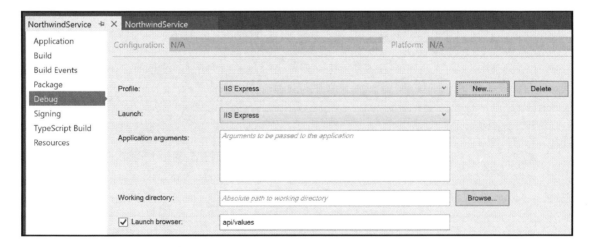

Navigate to `http:/localhost:5000/api/values/42`, and note the response, as shown in the following screenshot:

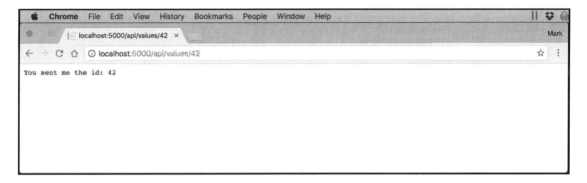

Close Google Chrome.

In Visual Studio Code, in **Integrated Terminal**, press *Ctrl* + *C* to stop the console application and shut down the Kestrel web server that is hosting your ASP.NET Core web service.

Creating a web service for the Northwind database

Unlike controllers for MVC, controllers for Web API do not call Razor views to return HTML responses for humans to see in browsers. Instead, they use **content negotiation** with the client application that made the HTTP request to return data in formats such as XML, JSON, or X-WWW-FORMURLENCODED in the HTTP response.

The client application must then deserialize the data from the negotiated format. The most commonly used format for modern web services is **JavaScript Object Notation (JSON)** because it is compact and works natively with JavaScript in a browser.

We will reference the Entity Framework Core entity data model for the Northwind database that you created in `Chapter 9`, *Building Web Sites Using ASP.NET Core Razor Pages*.

Using Visual Studio 2017

In Visual Studio 2017, in the **NorthwindService** project, right-click on **Dependencies**, and select **Add Reference...**. Select **NorthwindContextLib**, and click on **OK**.

Using Visual Studio Code

In Visual Studio Code, in the **NorthwindService** project, open `NorthwindService.csproj`, and add a project reference to `NorthwindContextLib`, as shown in the following markup:

```
<ItemGroup>
  <PackageReference Include="Microsoft.AspNetCore.All" Version="2.0.0" />
  <ProjectReference
    Include="..\NorthwindContextLib\NorthwindContextLib.csproj" />
</ItemGroup>
```

Using Visual Studio 2017 and Visual Studio Code

In both Visual Studio 2017 and Visual Studio Code, modify `Startup.cs`, import the `Microsoft.EntityFrameworkCore` and `Packt.CS7` namespaces, and add the following statement to the `ConfigureServices` method before the call to `AddMvc`.

For SQL Server LocalDB, add this statement:

```
services.AddDbContext<Northwind>(options => options.UseSqlServer(
"Server=(localdb)\\mssqllocaldb;Database=Northwind;Trusted_Connection=True;
MultipleActiveResultSets=true"));
```

For SQLite, add this one:

```
services.AddDbContext<Northwind>(options =>
options.UseSqlite("Data Source=../Northwind.db"));
```

Creating data repositories for entities

Defining and implementing a data repository to provide CRUD operations is good practice:

- C for Create
- R for Retrieve (or Read)
- U for Update
- D for Delete

We will create a data repository for the `Customers` table in `Northwind`. We will follow modern good practice and make the repository API asynchronous.

In the `NorthwindService` project, create a `Repositories` folder.

Add two class files to the `Repositories` folder named `ICustomerRepository.cs` and `CustomerRepository.cs`.

`ICustomerRepository` should look like this:

```
using Packt.CS7;
using System.Collections.Generic;
using System.Threading.Tasks;

namespace NorthwindService.Repositories
{
    public interface ICustomerRepository
    {
        Task<Customer> CreateAsync(Customer c);

        Task<IEnumerable<Customer>> RetrieveAllAsync();

        Task<Customer> RetrieveAsync(string id);

        Task<Customer> UpdateAsync(string id, Customer c);

        Task<bool> DeleteAsync(string id);
    }
}
```

`CustomerRepository` should look like this:

```
using Microsoft.EntityFrameworkCore.ChangeTracking;
using Packt.CS7;
using System.Collections.Generic;
using System.Collections.Concurrent;
using System.Linq;
using System.Threading.Tasks;

namespace NorthwindService.Repositories
{
    public class CustomerRepository : ICustomerRepository
    {
        // cache the customers in a thread-safe dictionary
        // to improve performance
        private static ConcurrentDictionary<string, Customer> customersCache;

        private Northwind db;

        public CustomerRepository(Northwind db)
        {
            this.db = db;
```

```
      // pre-load customers from database as a normal
      // Dictionary with CustomerID is the key,
      // then convert to a thread-safe ConcurrentDictionary
      if (customersCache == null)
      {
         customersCache = new ConcurrentDictionary<string, Customer>(
         db.Customers.ToDictionary(c => c.CustomerID));
      }
   }

   public async Task<Customer> CreateAsync(Customer c)
   {
      // normalize CustomerID into uppercase
      c.CustomerID = c.CustomerID.ToUpper();

      // add to database using EF Core
      EntityEntry<Customer> added = await db.Customers.AddAsync(c);

      int affected = await db.SaveChangesAsync();

      if (affected == 1)
      {
         // if the customer is new, add it to cache, else
         // call UpdateCache method
         return customersCache.AddOrUpdate(c.CustomerID, c,
         UpdateCache);
      }
      else
      {
         return null;
      }
   }

   public async Task<IEnumerable<Customer>> RetrieveAllAsync()
   {
      // for performance, get from cache
      return await Task.Run<IEnumerable<Customer>>(
      () => customersCache.Values);
   }

   public async Task<Customer> RetrieveAsync(string id)
   {
      return await Task.Run(() =>
      {
         // for performance, get from cache
         id = id.ToUpper();
         Customer c;
         customersCache.TryGetValue(id, out c);
```

```
      return c;
   });
}

private Customer UpdateCache(string id, Customer c)
{
   Customer old;
   if (customersCache.TryGetValue(id, out old))
   {
      if (customersCache.TryUpdate(id, c, old))
      {
         return c;
      }
   }
   return null;
}

public async Task<Customer> UpdateAsync(string id, Customer c)
{
   return await Task.Run(() =>
   {
      // normalize customer ID
      id = id.ToUpper();
      c.CustomerID = c.CustomerID.ToUpper();

      // update in database
      db.Customers.Update(c);
      int affected = db.SaveChanges();

      if (affected == 1)
      {
         // update in cache
         return Task.Run(() => UpdateCache(id, c));
      }
      return null;
   });
}

public async Task<bool> DeleteAsync(string id)
{
   return await Task.Run(() =>
   {
      id = id.ToUpper();

      // remove from database
      Customer c = db.Customers.Find(id);
      db.Customers.Remove(c);
      int affected = db.SaveChanges();
```

```
                    if (affected == 1)
                    {
                       // remove from cache
                       return Task.Run(() => customersCache.TryRemove(id, out c));
                    }
                    else
                    {
                       return null;
                    }
                });
            }
        }
    }
```

Configuring and registering the customers repository

Open the `Startup.cs` file, and import the following namespace:

```
using NorthwindService.Repositories;
```

Add the following statement to the bottom of the `ConfigureServices` method that will register the `CustomerRepository` for use at runtime by ASP.NET Core, as shown in the following code:

```
services.AddScoped<ICustomerRepository, CustomerRepository>();
```

Creating the Web API controller

In the `Controllers` folder, add a new class named `CustomersController.cs`.

 We could delete the `ValuesController.cs` file, but it is good to have a simple Web API controller with minimal dependencies in a service for testing purposes.

In the `CustomersController` class, add the following code, and note the following:

- The controller class registers a route that starts with `api` and includes the name of the controller, that is, `api/customers`.
- The constructor uses dependency injection to get the registered repository for customers.
- There are five methods to perform CRUD operations on customers—two `GET` methods (all customers or one customer), `POST` (create), `PUT` (update), and `DELETE`.
- `GetCustomers` can have a `string` parameter passed with a country name. If it is missing, all customers are returned. If it is present, it is used to filter customers by country.
- `GetCustomer` has a route explicitly named `GetCustomer` so that it can be used to generate a URL after inserting a new customer:

```
using Microsoft.AspNetCore.Mvc;
using Packt.CS7;
using NorthwindService.Repositories;
using System.Collections.Generic;
using System.Linq;
using System.Threading.Tasks;

namespace NorthwindService.Controllers
{
    // base address: api/customers
    [Route("api/[controller]")]
    public class CustomersController : Controller
    {
        private ICustomerRepository repo;

        // constructor injects registered repository
        public CustomersController(ICustomerRepository repo)
        {
            this.repo = repo;
        }

        // GET: api/customers
        // GET: api/customers/?country=[country]
        [HttpGet]
        public async Task<IEnumerable<Customer>> GetCustomers(string country)
        {
            if (string.IsNullOrWhiteSpace(country))
            {
                return await repo.RetrieveAllAsync();
            }
```

```
      else
      {
         return (await repo.RetrieveAllAsync())
         .Where(customer => customer.Country == country);
      }
   }

   // GET: api/customers/[id]
   [HttpGet("{id}", Name = "GetCustomer")]
   public async Task<IActionResult> GetCustomer(string id)
   {
      Customer c = await repo.RetrieveAsync(id);
      if (c == null)
      {
         return NotFound(); // 404 Resource not found
      }
      return new ObjectResult(c); // 200 OK
   }

   // POST: api/customers
   // BODY: Customer (JSON, XML)
   [HttpPost]
   public async Task<IActionResult> Create([FromBody] Customer c)
   {
      if (c == null)
      {
         return BadRequest(); // 400 Bad request
      }
      Customer added = await repo.CreateAsync(c);
      return CreatedAtRoute("GetCustomer", // use named route
      new { id = added.CustomerID.ToLower() }, c); // 201 Created
   }

   // PUT: api/customers/[id]
   // BODY: Customer (JSON, XML)
   [HttpPut("{id}")]
   public async Task<IActionResult> Update(string id, [FromBody]
   Customer c)
   {
      id = id.ToUpper();
      c.CustomerID = c.CustomerID.ToUpper();

      if (c == null || c.CustomerID != id)
      {
         return BadRequest(); // 400 Bad request
      }

      var existing = await repo.RetrieveAsync(id);
```

```
            if (existing == null)
            {
                return NotFound(); // 404 Resource not found
            }

            await repo.UpdateAsync(id, c);
            return new NoContentResult(); // 204 No content
        }

        // DELETE: api/customers/[id]
        [HttpDelete("{id}")]
        public async Task<IActionResult> Delete(string id)
        {
            var existing = await repo.RetrieveAsync(id);
            if (existing == null)
            {
                return NotFound(); // 404 Resource not found
            }

            bool deleted = await repo.DeleteAsync(id);

            if (deleted)
            {
                return new NoContentResult(); // 204 No content
            }
            else
            {
                return BadRequest();
            }
        }
    }
}
```

Documenting and testing web services using Swagger

You can easily test a web service by making GET requests, using a browser.

Testing GET requests with any browser

Start the web service.

In Chrome, in the address bar, enter the following URL:

```
http://localhost:5000/api/customers
```

You should see a JSON document returned, containing all the 91 customers in the `Northwind` database, as shown in the following screenshot:

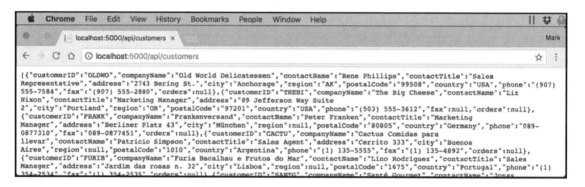

In the address bar, enter the following URL:

```
http://localhost:5000/api/customers/alfki
```

You should see a JSON document returned containing only the customer named **Alfreds Futterkiste**, as shown in the following screenshot:

In the address bar, enter the following URL:

```
http://localhost:5000/api/customers/?country=Germany
```

You should see a JSON document returned, containing the customers in Germany, as shown in the following screenshot:

But how can we test the other HTTP methods, such as POST, PUT, and DELETE? And how can we document our web service so it's easy for anyone to understand how to interact with it?

Testing POST, PUT, and DELETE requests with Swagger

Swagger is the world's most popular technology for documenting and testing HTTP APIs.

The most important part of Swagger is the **OpenAPI Specification** that defines a REST-style contract for your API, *detailing all of its resources and operations in a human and machine readable format for easy development, discovery, and integration.*

For us, another useful feature is Swagger UI, because it automatically generates documentation for your API with built-in visual testing capabilities.

Read more about Swagger at the following link:
`https://swagger.io`

Installing a Swagger package

To use Swagger, we must install a Swagger implementation package. The most popular for ASP.NET Core is named Swashbuckle.

Using Visual Studio 2017

In **Solution Explorer**, in **NorthwindService**, right-click on **Dependencies**, and select **Manage NuGet Packages....**

Select **Browse**, and enter `Swashbuckle.AspNetCore` in the search box, and click on **Install**, as shown in the following screenshot:

Using Visual Studio Code

Edit `NorthwindService.csproj`, and add a package reference for `Swashbuckle.AspNetCore`, as shown highlighted in the following markup:

```
<ItemGroup>
  <PackageReference Include="Microsoft.AspNetCore.All" Version="2.0.0" />
  <ProjectReference
  Include="..\NorthwindContextLib\NorthwindContextLib.csproj" />
  <PackageReference Include="Swashbuckle.AspNetCore" Version="1.0.0" />
</ItemGroup>
```

Using Visual Studio 2017 and Visual Studio Code

Open Startup.cs, and import the Swashbuckle's Swagger namespace, as shown in the following code:

```
using Swashbuckle.AspNetCore.Swagger;
```

In the ConfigureServices method, add a statement to add Swagger support with documentation for the Northwind service, as shown in the following code:

```
// Register the Swagger generator, and define a Swagger document
//for Northwind service
services.AddSwaggerGen(c =>
{
    c.SwaggerDoc("v1", new Info { Title = "Northwind Service API",
    Version = "v1" });
});
```

In the Configure method, add a statement to use Swagger and Swagger UI, and define an endpoint for the OpenAPI specification JSON document, as shown in the following code:

```
app.UseSwagger();

app.UseSwaggerUI(c =>
{
    c.SwaggerEndpoint("/swagger/v1/swagger.json",
    "Northwind Service API V1");
});
```

Testing GET requests with Swagger UI

Start the website, and navigate to /swagger/; note that both the **Customers** and **Values** controllers have been discovered and documented, as shown in the following screenshot:

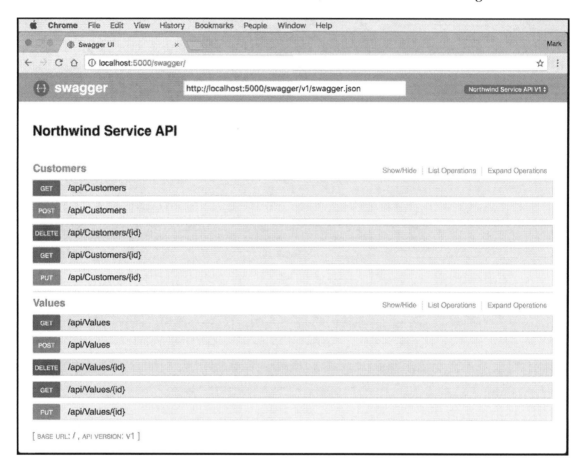

Click on **GET /api/Customers/{id}**, and note the required parameter for the ID of a customer, as shown in the following screenshot:

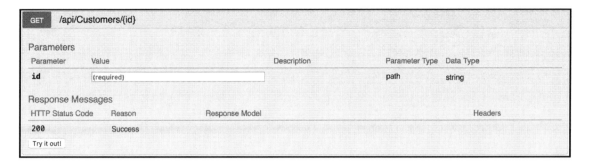

Enter an ID of ALFKI, select **Try it out!**, and note the **Request URL**, **Response Body**, **Response Code**, and **Response Headers**, as shown in the following screenshot:

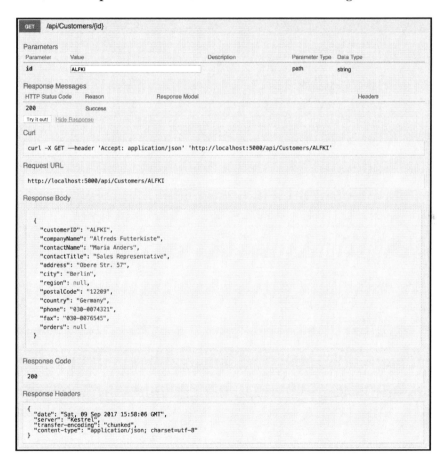

Testing POST requests with Swagger UI

Click on **POST /api/Customers**.

Click on the body of the **Example Value** to copy it to the **c** parameter value box, and modify the JSON to define a new customer, as shown in the following JSON and screenshot:

```
{
    "customerID": "SUPER",
    "companyName": "Super Company",
    "contactName": "Rasmus Ibensen",
    "contactTitle": "Sales Leader",
    "address": "Rotterslef 23",
    "city": "Billund",
    "region": null,
    "postalCode": "4371",
    "country": "Denmark",
    "phone": "31 21 43 21",
    "fax": "31 21 43 22",
    "orders": null
}
```

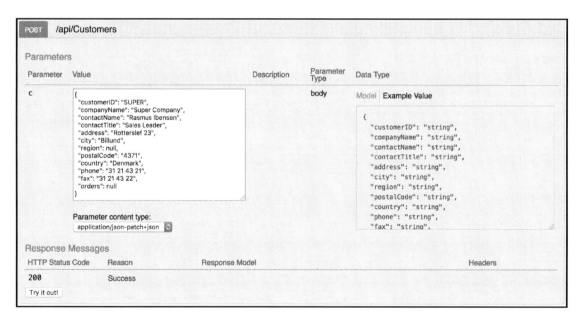

Click on **Try it out!**, and note the **Request URL**, **Response Body**, **Response Code**, and **Response Headers**, as shown in the following screenshot:

Request URL

```
http://localhost:5000/api/Customers
```

Response Body

```
{
    "customerID": "SUPER",
    "companyName": "Super Company",
    "contactName": "Rasmus Ibensen",
    "contactTitle": "Sales Leader",
    "address": "Rotterslef 23",
    "city": "Billund",
    "region": null,
    "postalCode": "4371",
    "country": "Denmark",
    "phone": "31 21 43 21",
    "fax": "31 21 43 22",
    "orders": null
}
```

Response Code

```
201
```

Response Headers

```
{
    "location": "http://localhost:5000/api/Customers/super",
    "date": "Sat, 09 Sep 2017 16:10:19 GMT",
    "server": "Kestrel",
    "transfer-encoding": "chunked",
    "content-type": "application/json; charset=utf-8"
}
```

 A response code of 201 means the customer was created successfully.

Click on the **GET /api/Customers** method, enter `Denmark` for the **country** parameter, and click on **Try it out!**, to confirm that the new customer was added to the database, as shown in the following screenshot:

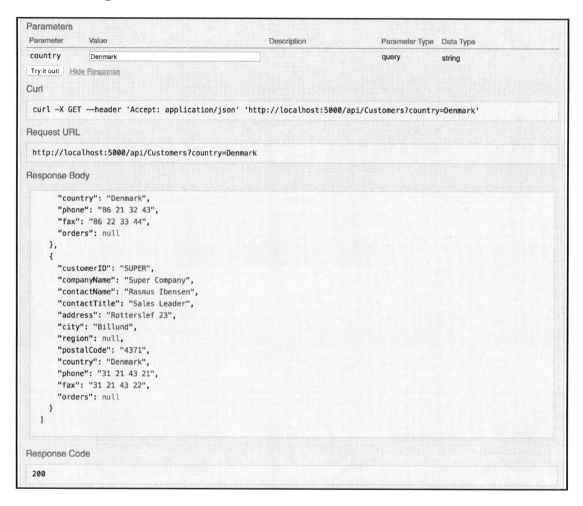

Click on **DELETE /api/Customers/{id}**, enter `super` for the ID, click on **Try it out!**, and note that the Response Code is `204`, indicating it was successfully deleted, as shown in the following screenshot:

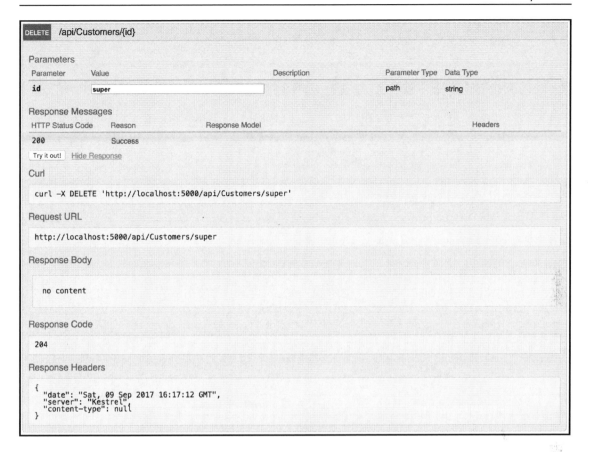

Click on **Try it out!** again, and note that the **Response Code** is 404, indicating the customer does not exist any more.

Use the GET methods to confirm that the new customer has been deleted from the database.

I will leave testing updates using PUT, to the reader.

Close Chrome.

In **Integrated Terminal**, press *Ctrl* + *C* to stop the console application and shut down the Kestrel web server that is hosting your ASP.NET Core web service.

You are now ready to build a web application that calls the web service.

Building SPAs using Angular

Angular is a popular frontend framework for building web and mobile applications. It uses TypeScript, a Microsoft-created, strongly-typed language that compiles into JavaScript.

Understanding the Angular project template

ASP.NET Core has a project template specifically for Angular. Let's see what it includes.

Using Visual Studio 2017

In Visual Studio 2017, open the Part3 solution, and press *Ctrl + Shift + N* or go to **File | Add | New Project....**

In the **Add New Project** dialog, in the **Installed** list, expand **Visual C#**, and select **.NET Core**. In the center list, select **ASP.NET Core Web Application**, type the name as ExploreAngular, and then click on **OK**.

In the **New ASP.NET Core Web Application - ExploreAngular** dialog; select **.NET Core**, **ASP.NET Core 2.0**, and the **Angular** template; and click on **OK**.

Using Visual Studio Code

In the folder named Part3, create a folder named ExploreAngular.

In Visual Studio Code, open the ExploreAngular folder.

In **Integrated Terminal**, enter the following commands to create a new ASP.NET Core Web API project, and then use Node Package Manager to install dependent packages:

```
dotnet new angular
npm install
```

On the first build, NuGet and NPM will download all package dependencies, which can take some time. Annoyingly, the tooling gives no feedback about what's happening, so you might think it's broken!

Using Visual Studio 2017 and Visual Studio Code

Start the website, as shown in the following screenshot:

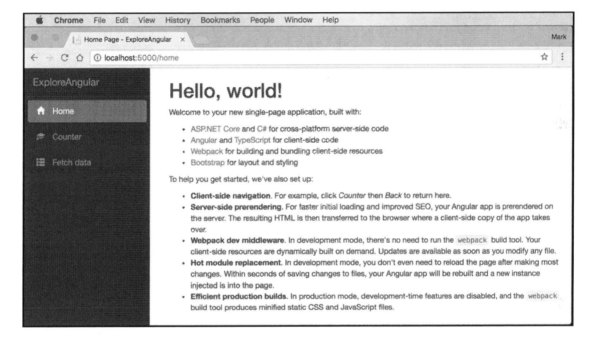

Click on **Fetch data**, as shown in the following screenshot:

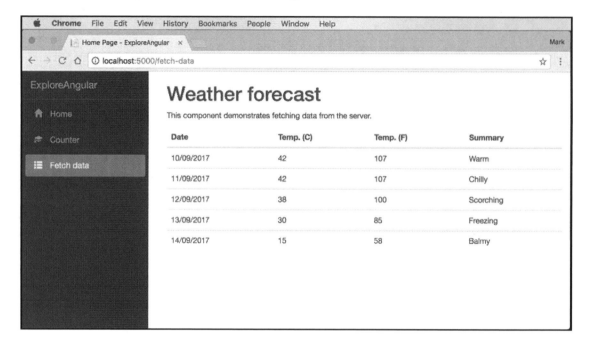

Close Chrome, and let's see how this works.

Open `Startup.cs`, and note that it is mostly similar to the MVC project template, except that it also does the following:

- It uses Webpack middleware to support hot module replacement, meaning that if a developer makes a change to an Angular module while a website is running, that module's changes can be immediately pushed to the client and used
- It adds a fallback route if the SPA fails to show the `Home` controller's `Index` view

In the `Controllers` folder, open `HomeController.cs`, and note that the `Index` method does nothing special.

In the `Views` folder, in the `Home` folder, open `Index.cshtml`, and note the `<app>` element that references the `ClientApp/dist/main-server` folder that contains server-side code, and the `<script>` element that references the `dist` folder's `main-client.js` file that contains client-side code, as shown in the following markup:

```
@{
    ViewData["Title"] = "Home Page";
}

<app asp-prerender-module="ClientApp/dist/main-server">Loading...</app>

<script src="~/dist/vendor.js" asp-append-version="true"></script>
@section scripts {
 <script src="~/dist/main-client.js"
  asp-append-version="true"></script>
}
```

The JavaScript code for server-side and client-side is generated by Webpack from the TypeScript code that you write in the `ClientApp` folder.

In the `Controllers` folder, open `SampleDataController.cs`, and note that it is a Web API service with a single `GET` method that returns random weather forecast data using a simple `WeatherForecast` model class.

In the `ClientApp` folder, note the `boot.browser.ts` file that contains TypeScript statements that import an AppModule from `app/app.module.browser`, as shown in the following code:

```
import { AppModule } from './app/app.module.browser';
```

In the `ClientApp` folder, expand the `app` folder, open `app.module.brower.ts`, and note that it has a statement to import `AppModuleShared`, as shown in the following code:

```
import { AppModuleShared } from './app.module.shared';
```

Open `app.module.shared.ts`, and note that it imports five components, as shown in the following code:

```
import { AppComponent } from './components/app/app.component';
import { NavMenuComponent } from './components/navmenu/navmenu.component';
import { HomeComponent } from './components/home/home.component';
import { FetchDataComponent } from
'./components/fetchdata/fetchdata.component';
import { CounterComponent } from './components/counter/counter.component';
```

In the `ClientApp` folder, expand the `app` folder and the `components` folder, to see the five Angular components for this SPA, as shown in the following screenshot, and note the following:

- `app` is the main application component that has a menu on the left and a client-side router in the main part on the right
- `counter` is a component with a simple button that increments
- `fetchdata` is a component that requests data from the weather service
- `home` is the default component, and it shows some static HTML content
- `navmenu` is a component that allows client-side routing between the other components:

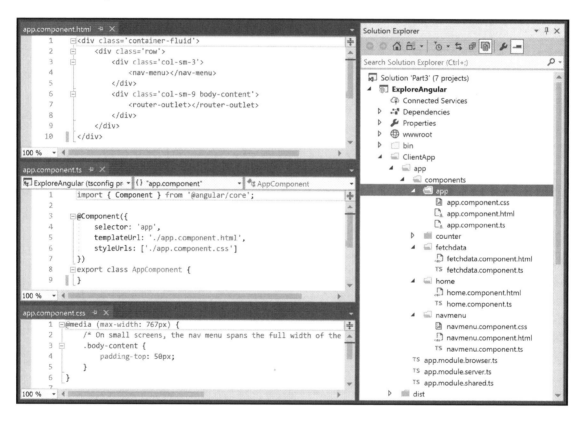

Open `home.component.ts` and `fetchdata.component.ts`, compare the two, as shown in the following code, and note the following:

- The `home` component has no code, but just static HTML content
- The `fetchdata` component imports the `Http` namespace, uses it in its constructor to make an HTTP GET request to the weather service, and stores the response in a public array of `WeatherForecast` objects, defined by an interface:

```
// home.component.ts
import { Component } from '@angular/core';

@Component({
    selector: 'home',
    templateUrl: './home.component.html'
})
export class HomeComponent {
}

// fetchdata.component.ts
import { Component, Inject } from '@angular/core';
import { Http } from '@angular/http';

@Component({
    selector: 'fetchdata',
    templateUrl: './fetchdata.component.html'
})
export class FetchDataComponent {
public forecasts: WeatherForecast[];

constructor(http: Http, @Inject('BASE_URL') baseUrl: string) {
    http.get(baseUrl + 'api/SampleData/WeatherForecasts')
    .subscribe(result => {
        this.forecasts = result.json() as WeatherForecast[];
        }, error => console.error(error));
    }
}

interface WeatherForecast {
    dateFormatted: string;
    temperatureC: number;
    temperatureF: number;
    summary: string;
}
```

Calling NorthwindService

Now that you understand a little of how Angular components fit together and can fetch data from services, we will modify the home component to load a list of customers from NorthwindService.

But first, it would be useful to explicitly specify the port numbers for the NorthwindService and ExploreAngular websites, and to enable **Cross-Origin Resource Sharing (CORS)** so that ExploreAngular can call NorthwindService.

 Default browser same-origin policy prevents code downloaded from one origin from accessing resources downloaded from a different origin to improve security. CORS can be enabled to allow requests from specified domains. Learn more about CORS and ASP.NET Core at the following link:
https://docs.microsoft.com/en-us/aspnet/core/security/cors

Using Visual Studio 2017

In **Solution Explorer**, right-click on **NorthwindService**, and select **Properties**.

Select **Debug** tab, in **Web Server Settings**, modify the **App URL** port number to 5001, as shown in the following code:

```
http://localhost:5001/
```

In **Solution Explorer**, right-click on **ExploreAngular**, and select **Properties**.

Select the **Debug** tab, in **Web Server Settings**, modify the **App URL** port number to 5002.

Using Visual Studio Code

In NorthwindService, open Program.cs, and in the BuildWebHost method, add an extension method call to UseUrls, to specify port number 5001, as shown highlighted in the following code:

```
public static IWebHost BuildWebHost(string[] args) =>
    WebHost.CreateDefaultBuilder(args)
    .UseStartup<Startup>()
    .UseUrls("http://localhost:5001")
    .Build();
```

In ExploreAngular, open Program.cs, and in the BuildWebHost method, add an extension method call to UseUrls, to specify port number 5002, as shown highlighted in the following code:

```
public static IWebHost BuildWebHost(string[] args) =>
    WebHost.CreateDefaultBuilder(args)
    .UseStartup<Startup>()
    .UseUrls("http://localhost:5002")
    .Build();
```

Using Visual Studio 2017 and Visual Studio Code

In NorthwindService, open Startup.cs, and add a statement to the top of the ConfigureServices method, to add support for CORS, as shown highlighted in the following code:

```
public void ConfigureServices(IServiceCollection services)
{
    services.AddCors();
```

Add a statement to the Configure method, before calling UseMvc, to use CORS and allow requests from the ExploreAngular site, as shown highlighted in the following code:

```
public void Configure(IApplicationBuilder app, IHostingEnvironment env)
{
    if (env.IsDevelopment())
    {
        app.UseDeveloperExceptionPage();
    }

    app.UseCors(c => c.WithOrigins("http://localhost:5002"));

    app.UseMvc();
```

 CORS must be used before MVC or it will not work!

Modifying the home component to call NorthwindService

Open `home.component.ts`, and modify it, as shown in the following code:

```
import { Component, Inject } from '@angular/core';
import { Http } from '@angular/http';

@Component({
    selector: 'home',
    templateUrl: './home.component.html'
})
export class HomeComponent {
    public customers: Customer[];

constructor(http: Http, @Inject('BASE_URL') baseUrl: string) {
    http.get('http://localhost:5001/api/customers').subscribe(result => {
        this.customers = result.json() as Customer[];
        }, error => console.error(error));
    }
}

interface Customer {
    customerID: string;
    companyName: string;
    contactName: string;
    contactTitle: string;
    address: string;
    city: string;
    region: string;
    postalCode: string;
    country: string;
    phone: string;
    fax: string;
}
```

Open `home.component.html`, and modify it, as shown in the following code:

```
<h1>Customers</h1>
<p>These customers have been loaded from the NorthwindService.</p>
<p *ngIf="!customers"><em>Loading customers... please wait.</em></p>
<table class='table' *ngIf="customers">
  <thead>
    <tr>
      <th>ID</th>
      <th>Company Name</th>
      <th>Contact Name</th>
```

```
        <th>City</th>
        <th>Country</th>
      </tr>
    </thead>
    <tbody>
    <tr *ngFor="let customer of customers">
      <td>{{ customer.customerID }}</td>
      <td>{{ customer.companyName }}</td>
      <td>{{ customer.contactName }}</td>
      <td>{{ customer.city }}</td>
      <td>{{ customer.country }}</td>
    </tr>
  </tbody>
</table>
```

Testing the Angular component calling the service

To test our changes, we should start the websites: `NorthwindService` and then `ExploreAngular`.

Using Visual Studio 2017

In **Solution Explorer**, select **NorthwindService**, and go to **Debug** | **Start Without Debugging,** or press *Ctrl + F5*.

Chrome will start and show the JSON document with all the customers from the `Northwind` database.

Leave Chrome running.

In **Solution Explorer**, select **ExploreAngular**, and go to **Debug** | **Start Without Debugging,** or press *Ctrl + F5*.

Using Visual Studio Code

In Visual Studio Code, open the `NorthwindService` folder, and in **Integrated Terminal**, enter the following command to set the hosting environment and start the website:

```
ASPNETCORE_ENVIRONMENT=Development dotnet run
```

In Visual Studio Code, go to **File | New Window**, open the `ExploreAngular` folder, and in **Integrated Terminal**, enter the following command to set the hosting environment and start the website:

```
ASPNETCORE_ENVIRONMENT=Development dotnet run
```

Start Chrome, and enter the address: `http://localhost:5002`.

Using Visual Studio 2017 and Visual Studio Code

The Angular component will execute first on the server and send a pre-rendered HTML page with all the customers, and then an asynchronous call will be made to `NorthwindService`. While it waits, the **Loading** message will briefly show, and then the table updates with the JSON response, as shown in the following screenshot:

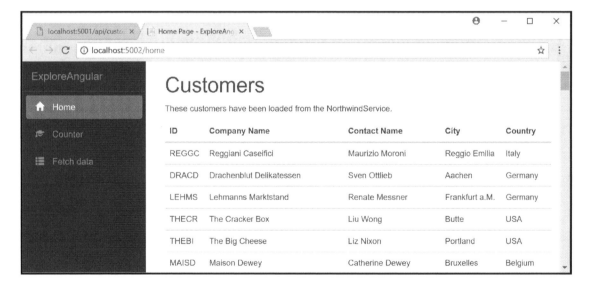

Using other project templates

When you install .NET Core SDK 2.0, there are many project templates included.

At Command Prompt or Terminal, enter the following command:

```
dotnet new --help
```

You will see a list of currently installed templates, as shown in the following screenshot:

```
  Terminal  Shell  Edit  View  Window  Help
                           markjprice — -bash — 128×41
[Marks-MBP-13:~ markjprice$ dotnet new --help
Usage: new [options]

Options:
  -h, --help         Displays help for this command.
  -l, --list         Lists templates containing the specified name. If no name is specified, lists all templates.
  -n, --name         The name for the output being created. If no name is specified, the name of the current directory is used.
  -o, --output       Location to place the generated output.
  -i, --install      Installs a source or a template pack.
  -u, --uninstall    Uninstalls a source or a template pack.
  --type             Filters templates based on available types. Predefined values are "project", "item" or "other".
  --force            Forces content to be generated even if it would change existing files.
  -lang, --language  Specifies the language of the template to create.


Templates                                    Short Name      Language      Tags
----------------------------------------------------------------------------------------------------
Console Application                          console         [C#], F#, VB  Common/Console
Class library                               classlib        [C#], F#, VB  Common/Library
Unit Test Project                           mstest          [C#], F#, VB  Test/MSTest
xUnit Test Project                          xunit           [C#], F#, VB  Test/xUnit
ASP.NET Core Empty                          web             [C#], F#      Web/Empty
ASP.NET Core Web App (Model-View-Controller) mvc            [C#], F#      Web/MVC
ASP.NET Core Web App                        razor           [C#]          Web/MVC/Razor Pages
ASP.NET Core with Angular                   angular         [C#]          Web/MVC/SPA
ASP.NET Core with React.js                  react           [C#]          Web/MVC/SPA
ASP.NET Core with React.js and Redux        reactredux      [C#]          Web/MVC/SPA
ASP.NET Core Web API                        webapi          [C#], F#      Web/WebAPI
global.json file                            globaljson                    Config
Nuget Config                                nugetconfig                   Config
Web Config                                  webconfig                     Config
Solution File                               sln                           Solution
Razor Page                                  page                          Web/ASP.NET
MVC ViewImports                             viewimports                   Web/ASP.NET
MVC ViewStart                               viewstart                     Web/ASP.NET


Examples:
    dotnet new mvc --auth Individual
    dotnet new xunit
    dotnet new --help
```

Installing additional template packs

Start a browser, and navigate to the `http://dotnetnew.azurewebsites.net` link, to see a searchable list of available templates, as shown in the following screenshot:

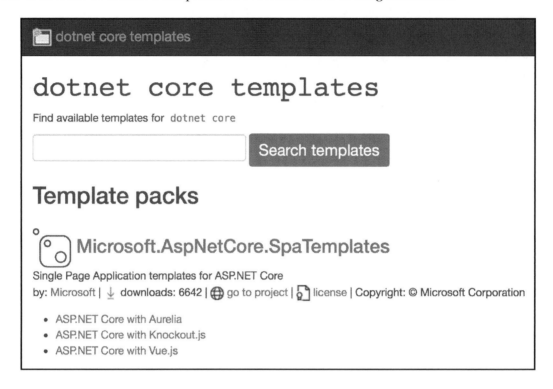

Click on **ASP.NET Core with Aurelia**, and note the instructions for installing and using this template, as shown in the following screenshot:

Summary

In this chapter, you learned how to build an ASP.NET Core Web API service that can be hosted cross-platform. You also learned how to test and document web service APIs with Swagger, and how to build a Single Page Application (SPA) using Angular that calls a web service, even if the service is on another domain.

In the next chapter, you will learn how to build cross-device apps for the Universal Windows Platform using XAML.

12
Building Windows Apps Using XAML and Fluent Design

This chapter is about seeing what can be achieved with XAML when defining the user interface for a graphical app, in particular, for **Universal Windows Platform (UWP)**. You will explore some of the new user interface features of Fluent Design, available in the Fall Creators Update of Windows 10.

In a single chapter, we will only be able to scratch the surface of everything that can be done with XAML and UWP. However, I hope to excite you into wanting to learn more about this cool technology and platform.

Think of this chapter as a whistle-stop tour of the coolest parts of XAML, UWP, and Fluent Design, including *template-able* controls, data binding, and animation!

Some important points about this chapter
UWP apps are not cross-platform, but they are cross-device if those devices run a modern flavor of Windows. You will need Windows 10 Fall Creators Update and Visual Studio 2017 version 15.4 or later to create the examples in this chapter. UWP supports .NET Native, which means that your code is compiled to native CPU instructions for a smaller memory footprint and faster execution.

In this chapter, we will cover the following topics:

- Understanding the modern Windows platform
- Creating a modern Windows app
- Using resources and templates
- Data binding
- Building apps using Windows Template Studio

Understanding the modern Windows platform

Microsoft continues to improve their Windows platform, which includes multiple technologies for building modern apps:

- Universal Windows Platform 6.0
- Fluent Design System
- XAML Standard 1.0

Understanding Universal Windows Platform

UWP is Microsoft's latest technology solution to build applications for its Windows suite of operating systems.

UWP provides a guaranteed API layer across multiple device types. You can create a single app package that can be uploaded to a single store to be distributed to reach all the device types your app can run on. These devices include Windows 10, Windows 10 Mobile, Xbox One, and Microsoft HoloLens.

Windows 10 Fall Creators Update, released on October 17, 2017, includes UWP 6.0, which is built on a custom-forked implementation of .NET Core 2.0.

XAML and UWP provide layout panels that adapt how they display their child controls to make the most of the device they are currently running on. It is the Windows app equivalent of web page responsive design.

XAML and UWP provide visual state triggers to alter the layout based on dynamic changes, such as the horizontal or vertical orientation of a tablet.

UWP provides standard mechanisms to detect the capabilities of the current device, and then activate additional features of your app to fully take advantage of them.

Understanding Fluent Design System

Microsoft's Fluent Design System will be delivered in multiple waves, rather than as a "Big Bang" all in one go, to help developers slowly migrate from traditional styles of user interface to more modern ones.

Wave 1, available in Windows 10 Fall Creators Update, includes the following features:

- Acrylic material
- Connected animations
- Parallax views
- Reveal lighting

Filling user interface elements with acrylic brushes

Acrylic material is a semi-transparent blur-effect brush that can be used to fill user interface elements to add depth and perspective to your apps. Acrylic can show through what is in the background behind the app, or elements within the app that are behind a pane. Acrylic material can be customized with varying colors and transparencies.

Learn about how and when to use Acrylic material at the following link:
`https://docs.microsoft.com/en-gb/windows/uwp/style/acrylic`

Connecting user interface elements with animations

When navigating around a user interface, animating elements to draw connections between screens helps users to understand where they are and how to interact with your app.

Learn about how and when to use Connected animations at the following link:
`https://docs.microsoft.com/en-gb/windows/uwp/style/connected-animation`

Parallax views and Reveal lighting

Parallax views give your apps a modern feel, and Reveal lighting helps the user understand what is an interactive element by *lighting up* the user interface to draw their focus as they move around it.

Learn about how and when to use Reveal to bring focus to user interface elements at the following link:
`https://docs.microsoft.com/en-gb/windows/uwp/style/reveal`

Understanding XAML Standard 1.0

In 2006, Microsoft released **Windows Presentation Foundation** (**WPF**), which was the first technology to use XAML. WPF is still used today to create Windows desktop applications, for example, Microsoft Visual Studio 2017 is a WPF application.

XAML can be used to create these:

- **Windows Store apps** for Windows 10, Windows 10 Mobile, Xbox One, and Microsoft HoloLens
- **WPF applications** for the Windows desktop, including Windows 7 and later

In a similar fashion to .NET, XAML has fragmented, with slight variations in capabilities between XAML for different platforms. So just as .NET Standard 2.0 is an initiative to bring various platforms of .NET together, XAML Standard 1.0 is an initiative to do the same for XAML.

Simplifying code using XAML

XAML simplifies C# code, especially when building a user interface.

Imagine that you need two or more buttons laid out horizontally to create a toolbar. In C#, you might write this code:

```
var toolbar = new StackPanel();
toolbar.Orientation = Orientation.Horizontal;
var newButton = new Button();
newButton.Content = "New";
newButton.Background = new SolidColorBrush(Colors.Pink);
toolbar.Children.Add(newButton);
var openButton = new Button();
openButton.Content = "Open";
openButton.Background = new SolidColorBrush(Colors.Pink);
toolbar.Children.Add(openButton);
```

In XAML, this could be simplified to the following lines of code. When this XAML is processed, the equivalent properties are set, and methods are called to achieve the same goal as the preceding C# code:

```
<StackPanel Name="toolbar" Orientation="Horizontal">
  <Button Name="newButton" Background="Pink">New</Button>
  <Button Name="OpenButton" Background="Pink">Open</Button>
</StackPanel>
```

XAML is an alternative (better) way of declaring and instantiating .NET types.

Choosing common controls

There are lots of predefined controls that you can choose from for common user interface scenarios. Almost all versions of XAML support these controls:

Controls	Description
`Button`, `Menu`, `Toolbar`	Executing actions
`CheckBox`, `RadioButton`	Choosing options
`Calendar`, `DatePicker`	Choosing dates
`ComboBox`, `ListBox`, `ListView`, `TreeView`	Choosing items from lists and hierarchical trees
`Canvas`, `DockPanel`, `Grid`, `StackPanel`, `WrapPanel`	Layout containers that affect their children in different ways
`Label`, `TextBlock`	Displaying read-only text
`RichTextBox`, `TextBox`	Editing text
`Image`, `MediaElement`	Embedding images, videos, and audio files
`DataGrid`	Viewing and editing bound data
`Scrollbar`, `Slider`, `StatusBar`	Miscellaneous user interface elements

Creating a modern Windows app

We will start by creating a simple Windows app, with some common controls and modern features of Fluent Design like acrylic material.

To be able to create apps for UWP, you must enable developer mode in Windows 10.

Enabling developer mode

Go to **Start** | **Settings** | **Update & Security** | **For developers**, and then click on **Developer mode**, as shown in the following screenshot:

Accept the warning about how it "could expose your device and personal data to security risk or harm your device," and then close the **Settings** app. You might need to restart your PC.

Creating a UWP project

In Visual Studio 2017, open the `Part3` solution, and choose **File** | **Add** | **New Project...**.

In the **Add New Project** dialog, in the **Installed** list, select **Visual C#** | **Windows Universal**. In the center list, select **Blank App (Universal Windows)**, type the name as `FluentUwpApp`, and then click on **OK**.

In the **New Universal Windows Platform Project** dialog, choose the latest version of Windows 10 for **Target Version** and **Minimum Version**, and click on **OK**, as shown in the following screenshot:

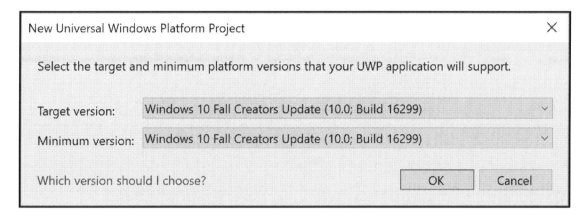

Good Practice

Developers writing UWP apps for a general audience should choose one of the latest builds of Windows 10 for **Minimum Version**. Developers writing enterprise apps should choose an older **Minimum Version**. Build 10240 was released in July 2015 and is a good choice for maximum compatibility, but you will not have access to modern features such as Fluent Design System.

In the **Solution Explorer** window, double-click on the **MainPage.xaml** file to open it for editing. You will see the XAML design window showing a graphical view and a XAML view. You will be able to make the following observations:

- The XAML designer is split horizontally, but you can toggle to a vertical split and collapse one side by clicking on the buttons on the right edge of the divider
- You can swap views by clicking on the double-arrow button in the divider

- You can scroll and zoom in both views:

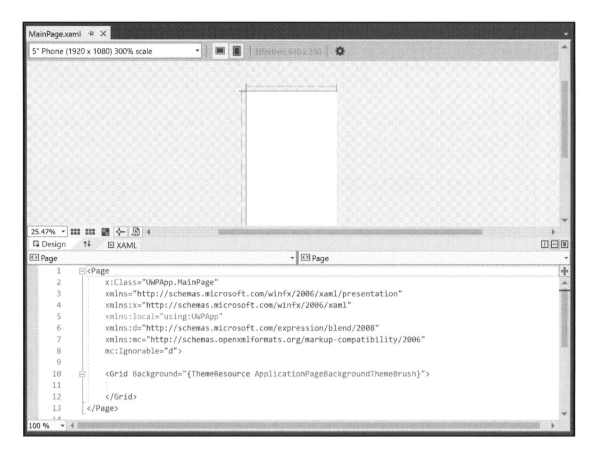

Change the zoom to 100%. Navigate to **View** | **Toolbox** or press *Ctrl + W, X*. Note that the toolbox has sections for **Common XAML Controls**, **All XAML Controls**, and **General**. At the top of the toolbox is a search box.

Enter the letters bu, and note that the list of controls is filtered.

Drag and drop the **Button** control from the toolbox onto the **Design** view. Resize it by clicking, holding, and dragging any of the eight square resize handles on each edge and in each corner. Note that the button is given a fixed width and height, and fixed left (30 units) and top (40 units) margins, to position and size it absolutely inside the grid, as shown in the following screenshot:

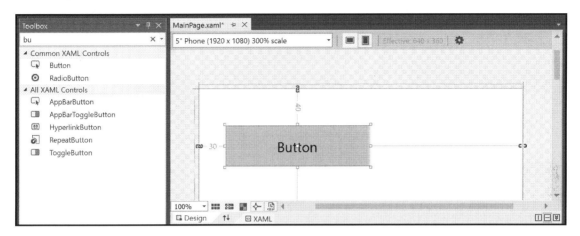

Although you can drag and drop controls, it is better to use the XAML view for layout so that you can position items relatively and implement more of a responsive design.

In the XAML view, find the Button element and delete it.

In the XAML view, inside the Grid element, enter the following markup:

```
<Button Margin="6" Padding="6" Name="clickMeButton">
  Click Me
</Button>
```

Change the zoom to 50%, and note that the button is automatically sized to its content, `Click Me`, aligned vertically in the center and aligned horizontally to the left, even if you toggle between vertical and horizontal phone layouts, as shown in the following screenshot:

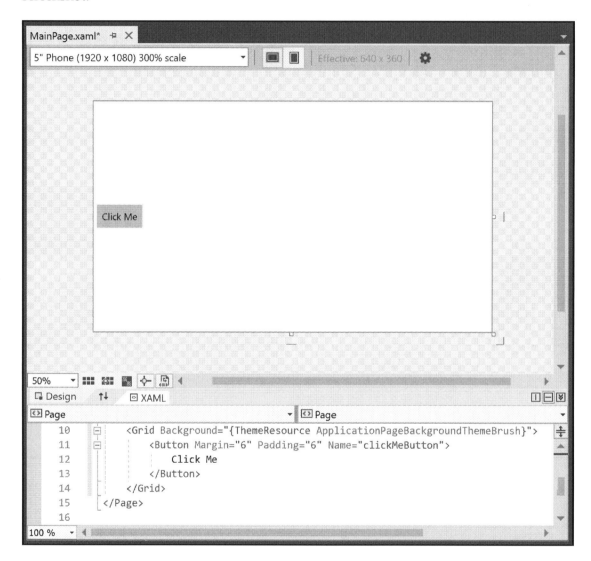

Modify the XAML to wrap the `Button` element inside a horizontally-orientated `StackPanel` with a light-gray background, that is inside a vertically orientated (by default) `StackPanel`, and note the change in its layout to be in the top-left of the available space:

```
<StackPanel>
  <StackPanel Orientation="Horizontal" Padding="4"
              Background="LightGray" Name="toolbar">
    <Button Margin="6" Padding="6" Name="clickMeButton">
      Click Me
    </Button>
  </StackPanel>
</StackPanel>
```

Modify the `Button` element to give it a new event handler for its `Click` event. When you see the IntelliSense showing `<New Event Handler>`, press *Enter*, as shown in the following screenshot:

Navigate to **View** | **Code**, or press *F7*.

In the `MainPage.xaml.cs` file, add a statement to the event handler that sets the content of the button to the current time, as shown highlighted in the following code:

```
private void clickMeButton_Click(object sender, RoutedEventArgs e)
{
    clickMeButton.Content = DateTime.Now.ToString("hh:mm:ss");
}
```

Navigate to **Build** | **Configuration Manager...**, for the **FluentUwpApp** project, select the **Build** and **Deploy** checkboxes, select **Platform** of **x64**, and then select **Close**, as shown in the following screenshot:

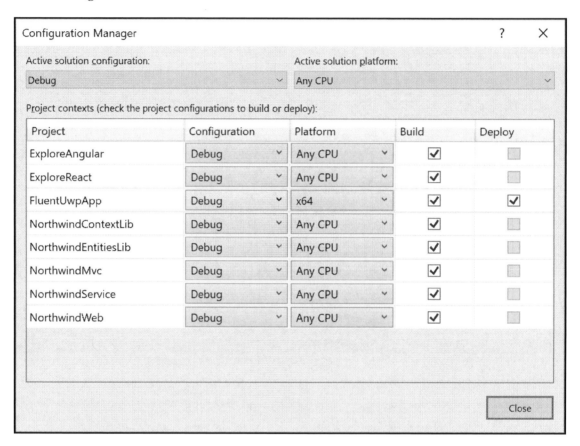

Run the application by navigating to **Debug** | **Start Without Debugging**, or pressing *Ctrl +
F5*.

Click on the **Click Me** button.

Every time you click on the button, the button's content changes to show the current time.

Exploring common controls and acrylic brushes

Open `MainPage.xaml`, set the grid's background to use the acrylic system window brush,
and add some elements to the stack panel after the button for the user to enter their name
and toggle acrylic material, as shown highlighted in the following markup:

```xml
<Grid Background="{ThemeResource SystemControlAcrylicWindowBrush}">
  <StackPanel>
    <StackPanel Orientation="Horizontal" Padding="4"
                Background="LightGray" Name="toolbar">
      <Button Margin="6" Padding="6" Name="clickMeButton"
              Click="clickMeButton_Click">
        Click Me
      </Button>
      <TextBlock Text="First name:"
                 VerticalAlignment="Center" Margin="4" />
      <TextBox PlaceholderText="Enter your name"
               VerticalAlignment="Center" Width="200" />
      <CheckBox IsChecked="True" Content="Enable acrylic background"
                Margin="20,0,0,0" Name="enableAcrylic" />
    </StackPanel>
  </StackPanel>
</Grid>
```

Run the application by navigating to **Debug** | **Start Without Debugging**, or pressing *Ctrl +* *F5*, and note the user interface, including the tinted acrylic material showing the orange rocks and blue sky through the app window background, as shown in the following screenshot:

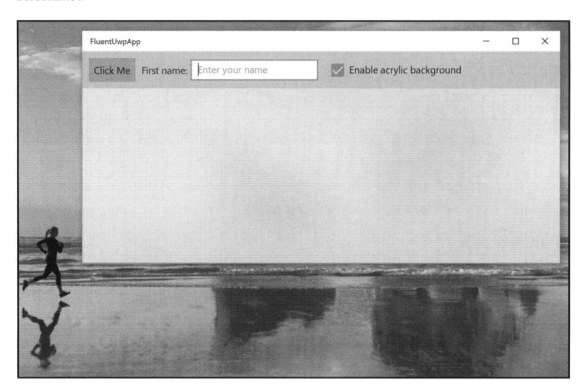

 Acrylic uses a lot of system resources, so if an app loses the focus, or your device is low on battery, then acrylic is disabled automatically.

Exploring Reveal

Reveal is built in to some controls, such as `ListView` and `NavigationView`, that you will see later. For other controls, you can enable it by applying a theme style.

Open `MainPage.xaml`, add a new horizontal stack panel under the one used as a toolbar, and add a grid with buttons to define a calculator, as shown in the following markup:

```
<StackPanel Orientation="Horizontal">
  <Grid Background="DarkGray" Margin="10"
        Padding="5" Name="gridCalculator">
    <Grid.ColumnDefinitions>
      <ColumnDefinition/>
      <ColumnDefinition/>
      <ColumnDefinition/>
      <ColumnDefinition/>
    </Grid.ColumnDefinitions>
    <Grid.RowDefinitions>
      <RowDefinition/>
      <RowDefinition/>
      <RowDefinition/>
      <RowDefinition/>
    </Grid.RowDefinitions>
    <Button Grid.Row="0" Grid.Column="0" Content="X" />
    <Button Grid.Row="0" Grid.Column="1" Content="/" />
    <Button Grid.Row="0" Grid.Column="2" Content="+" />
    <Button Grid.Row="0" Grid.Column="3" Content="-" />
    <Button Grid.Row="1" Grid.Column="0" Content="7" />
    <Button Grid.Row="1" Grid.Column="1" Content="8" />
    <Button Grid.Row="1" Grid.Column="2" Content="9" />
    <Button Grid.Row="1" Grid.Column="3" Content="0" />
    <Button Grid.Row="2" Grid.Column="0" Content="4" />
    <Button Grid.Row="2" Grid.Column="1" Content="5" />
    <Button Grid.Row="2" Grid.Column="2" Content="6" />
    <Button Grid.Row="2" Grid.Column="3" Content="." />
    <Button Grid.Row="3" Grid.Column="0" Content="1" />
    <Button Grid.Row="3" Grid.Column="1" Content="2" />
    <Button Grid.Row="3" Grid.Column="2" Content="3" />
    <Button Grid.Row="3" Grid.Column="3" Content="=" />
  </Grid>
</StackPanel>
```

In the `Page` element, add an event handler for `Loaded`, as shown highlighted in the following markup:

```
<Page
  x:Class="FluentUwpApp.MainPage"
  xmlns="http://schemas.microsoft.com/winfx/2006/xaml/presentation"
  xmlns:x="http://schemas.microsoft.com/winfx/2006/xaml"
  xmlns:local="using:FluentUwpApp"
  xmlns:d="http://schemas.microsoft.com/expression/blend/2008"
  xmlns:mc="http://schemas.openxmlformats.org/markup-compatibility/2006"
```

```
mc:Ignorable="d"
Loaded="Page_Loaded">
```

In `MainPage.xaml.cs`, add statements to the `Page_Loaded` method to loop through all of the calculator buttons, setting them to be the same size, and apply the Reveal style, as shown in the following code:

```
private void Page_Loaded(object sender, RoutedEventArgs e)
{
    foreach (Button b in gridCalculator.Children.OfType<Button>())
    {
        b.FontSize = 24;
        b.Width = 54;
        b.Height = 54;
        b.Style = Resources.ThemeDictionaries["ButtonRevealStyle"] as Style;
    }
}
```

Run the application by navigating to **Debug | Start Without Debugging**, or pressing *Ctrl + F5*, and note the calculator starts with a flat gray user interface, as shown in the following screenshot:

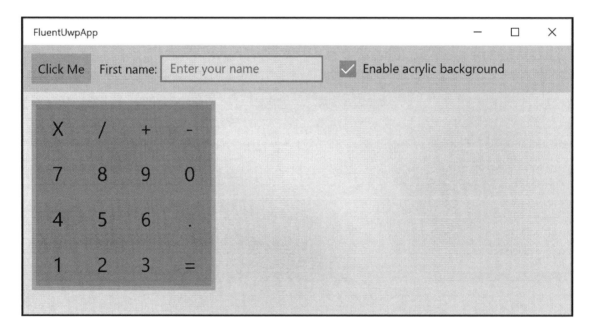

When the user moves their mouse pointer over the calculator, Reveal lights it up, as shown in the following screenshot:

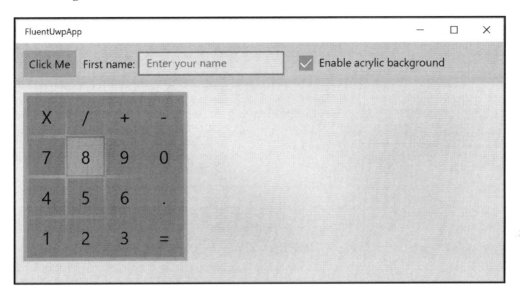

Installing more controls

In addition to dozens of built-in controls, you can install additional ones as NuGet packages. One of the best is the UWP Community Toolkit, which you can read more about at the following link:

```
http://www.uwpcommunitytoolkit.com/
```

In the **FluentUwpApp** project, right-click on **References**, and select **Manage NuGet Packages...**. Click on **Browse**, search for `Microsoft.Toolkit.Uwp.UI.Controls`, and click on **Install**, as shown in the following screenshot:

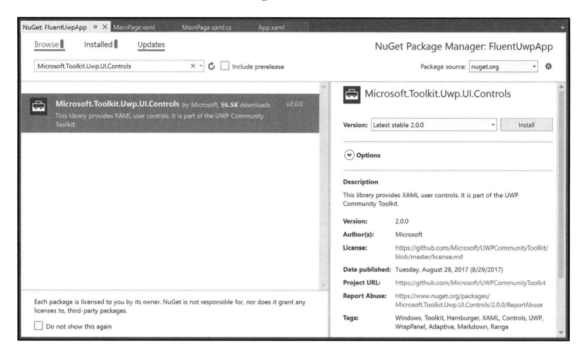

Review the changes and accept the license agreement.

Open `MainPage.xaml`, and in the `Page` element, import the toolkit namespace as a prefix named `kit`, as shown in the following markup:

```
<Page
  x:Class="FluentUwpApp.MainPage"
  xmlns="http://schemas.microsoft.com/winfx/2006/xaml/presentation"
  xmlns:x="http://schemas.microsoft.com/winfx/2006/xaml"
  xmlns:local="using:FluentUwpApp"
  xmlns:d="http://schemas.microsoft.com/expression/blend/2008"
  xmlns:mc="http://schemas.openxmlformats.org/markup-compatibility/2006"
  xmlns:kit="using:Microsoft.Toolkit.Uwp.UI.Controls"
  mc:Ignorable="d"
  Loaded="Page_Loaded">
```

After the calculator grid, add a textbox and a markdown text block, as shown in the following markup:

```
<TextBox Name="markdownSource" Text="# Welcome"
        Header="Enter some Markdown text:"
        VerticalAlignment="Stretch" Margin="5"
        AcceptsReturn="True" />
<kit:MarkdownTextBlock
        Text="{Binding ElementName=markdownSource, Path=Text}"
        VerticalAlignment="Stretch"
        HorizontalAlignment="Stretch" Margin="5"/>
```

Run the application by navigating to **Debug** | **Start Without Debugging**, or pressing *Ctrl +* *F5*, and note that the user can enter Markdown syntax in the textbox, and it is rendered in the Markdown text block, as shown in the following screenshot:

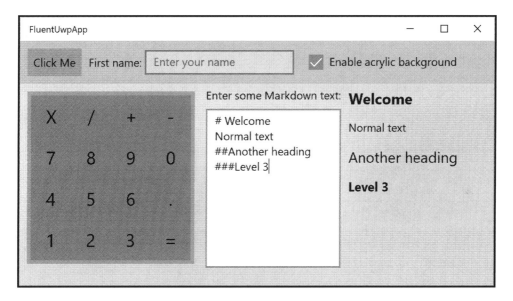

The UWP Community Toolkit includes dozens of controls, animations, extensions, and services.

Using resources and templates

When building graphical user interfaces, you will often want to use a resource, such as a brush, to paint the background of controls. These resources can be defined in a single place and shared throughout the app.

Sharing resources

In **Solution Explorer**, double-click on the **App.xaml** file, as shown in the following screenshot:

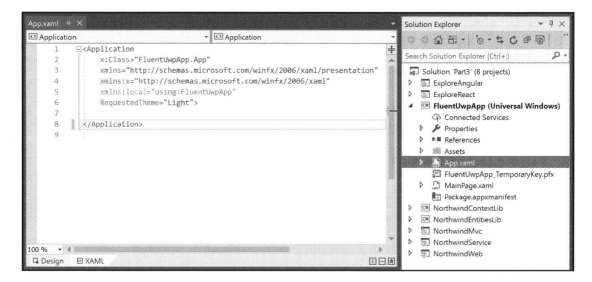

Add the following markup inside the existing `<Application>` element:

```xml
<Application.Resources>
  <LinearGradientBrush x:Key="rainbow">
    <GradientStop Color="Red" Offset="0" />
    <GradientStop Color="Orange" Offset="0.1" />
    <GradientStop Color="Yellow" Offset="0.3" />
    <GradientStop Color="Green" Offset="0.5" />
    <GradientStop Color="Blue" Offset="0.7" />
    <GradientStop Color="Indigo" Offset="0.9" />
    <GradientStop Color="Violet" Offset="1" />
  </LinearGradientBrush>
</Application.Resources>
```

In the `MainPage.xaml` file, modify the toolbar `StackPanel` element to have its background set to the `rainbow` brush that you just defined, as shown in the following markup:

```
<StackPanel Orientation="Horizontal" Padding="4"
            Background="{StaticResource rainbow}" Name="toolbar">
```

Design view will show your `rainbow` resource and the built-in resources in IntelliSense, as shown in the following screenshot:

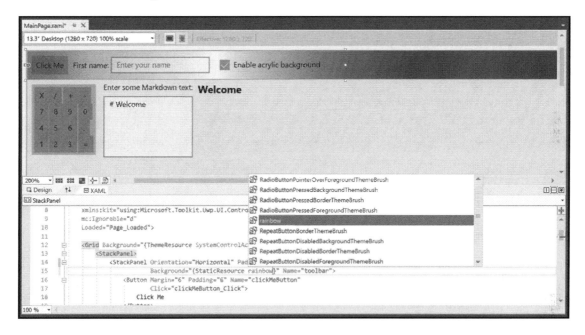

Good Practice

A resource can be an instance of any object. To share it within an application, define it in the `App.xaml` file and give it a unique key. To set an element's property to apply the resource, use `StaticResource` with the key.

Resources can be defined and stored inside any element of XAML, not just at the app level. So, for example, if a resource is only needed on `MainPage`, it can be defined there. You can also dynamically load XAML files at runtime.

Replacing a control template

You can redefine how a control looks by replacing its default template. The default control template for a button is flat and transparent.

One of the most common resources is a style that can set multiple properties at once. If a style has a unique key then it must be explicitly set, like we did earlier with the linear gradient. If it doesn't have a key then it will be automatically applied based on the TargetType property.

In the App.xaml file, add the following markup inside the `<Application.Resources>` element, and note that the `<Style>` element will automatically set the Template property of all controls that are TargetType, that is, buttons, to use the defined control template.

```xml
<ControlTemplate x:Key="DarkGlassButton" TargetType="Button">
  <Border BorderBrush="#FFFFFFFF"
          BorderThickness="1,1,1,1" CornerRadius="4,4,4,4">
    <Border x:Name="border" Background="#7F000000"
            BorderBrush="#FF000000" BorderThickness="1,1,1,1"
            CornerRadius="4,4,4,4">
      <Grid>
        <Grid.RowDefinitions>
          <RowDefinition Height="*"/>
          <RowDefinition Height="*"/>
        </Grid.RowDefinitions>
        <Border Opacity="0" HorizontalAlignment="Stretch"
                x:Name="glow" Width="Auto" Grid.RowSpan="2"
                CornerRadius="4,4,4,4">
        </Border>
        <ContentPresenter HorizontalAlignment="Center"
                          VerticalAlignment="Center" Width="Auto"
                          Grid.RowSpan="2" Padding="4"/>
        <Border HorizontalAlignment="Stretch" Margin="0,0,0,0"
                x:Name="shine" Width="Auto"
                CornerRadius="4,4,0,0">
          <Border.Background>
            <LinearGradientBrush EndPoint="0.5,0.9"
                                 StartPoint="0.5,0.03">
              <GradientStop Color="#99FFFFFF" Offset="0"/>
              <GradientStop Color="#33FFFFFF" Offset="1"/>
            </LinearGradientBrush>
          </Border.Background>
        </Border>
      </Grid>
    </Border>
  </Border>
</ControlTemplate>
```

```
<Style TargetType="Button">
  <Setter Property="Template"
          Value="{StaticResource DarkGlassButton}" />
  <Setter Property="Foreground" Value="White" />
</Style>
```

Rerun the application and view the results. Note the *black glass* effect on the button in the toolbar, as shown in the following screenshot:

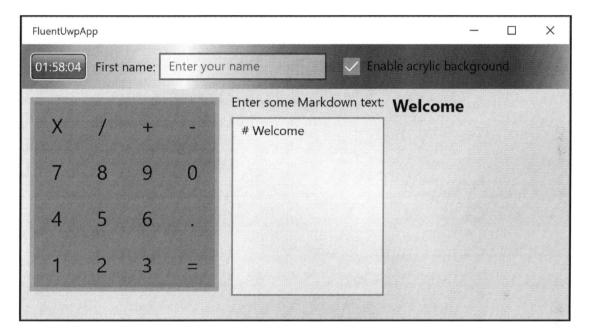

 The calculator buttons are not affected at runtime by this *black glass* effect because we replace their styles using code after the page has loaded.

Data binding

When building graphical user interfaces, you will often want to bind a property of one control to another or to some data.

Binding to elements

In the `MainPage.xaml` file, add a text block for instructions, a slider for selecting a rotation, a grid containing stack panel and text blocks to show the selected rotation in degrees, a radial gauge from the UWP Community Toolkit, and a red square to rotate, as shown in the following markup:

```
<TextBlock Grid.ColumnSpan="2" Margin="10">
  Use the slider to rotate the square:</TextBlock>
<Slider Value="180" Minimum="0" Maximum="360"
        Name="sliderRotation" Margin="10,0" />
<Grid>
  <Grid.ColumnDefinitions>
    <ColumnDefinition/>
    <ColumnDefinition/>
    <ColumnDefinition/>
  </Grid.ColumnDefinitions>
  <StackPanel Orientation="Horizontal"
              VerticalAlignment="Center"
              HorizontalAlignment="Center">
    <TextBlock
    Text="{Binding ElementName=sliderRotation, Path=Value}"
            FontSize="30" />
    <TextBlock Text="degrees" FontSize="30" Margin="10,0" />
  </StackPanel>
  <kit:RadialGauge Grid.Column="1" Minimum="0"
                   Maximum="360"
                   Value="{Binding ElementName=sliderRotation,
                   Path=Value}"
                   Height="200" Width="200" />
  <Rectangle Grid.Column="2" Height="100" Width="100" Fill="Red">
    <Rectangle.RenderTransform>
      <RotateTransform
        Angle="{Binding ElementName=sliderRotation, Path=Value}" />
    </Rectangle.RenderTransform>
  </Rectangle>
</Grid>
```

Note that the text of the text block, the value of the radial gauge, and the angle of the rotation transform are all data bound to the slider's value.

Run the app, and click, hold, and drag the slider to rotate the red square, as shown in the following screenshot:

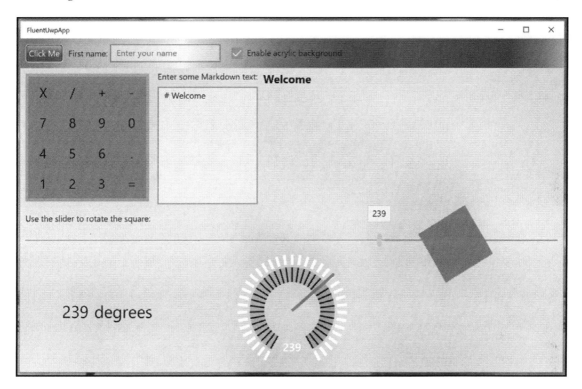

Binding to data sources

To illustrate binding to data sources, we will create an app for the Northwind database that shows categories and products.

Modifying the NorthwindService

Open the Part3 solution, and expand the **NorthwindService** project.

In the **Controllers** folder, right-click and choose **Add | New Item...**, select **Web API Controller Class**, name it as `CategoriesController.cs`, and modify it to have two `HttpGet` methods that use the `Northwind` database context to retrieve all categories, or a single category using its ID, as shown in the following code:

```
using Microsoft.AspNetCore.Mvc;
using Packt.CS7;
using System.Collections.Generic;
using System.Linq;

namespace NorthwindService.Controllers
{
    [Route("api/[controller]")]
    public class CategoriesController : Controller
    {
        private readonly Northwind db;

        public CategoriesController(Northwind db)
        {
            this.db = db;
        }

        // GET: api/categories
        [HttpGet]
        public IEnumerable<Category> Get()
        {
            var categories = db.Categories.ToArray();
            return categories;
        }

        // GET api/categories/5
        [HttpGet("{id}")]
        public Category Get(int id)
        {
            var category = db.Categories.Find(id);
            return category;
        }
    }
}
```

In the **Controllers** folder, right-click and choose **Add** | **New Item...**, select **Web API Controller Class**, name it as ProductsController.cs, and modify it to have two HttpGet methods that use the Northwind database context to retrieve all products, or the products in a category using the category ID, as shown in the following code:

```
using Microsoft.AspNetCore.Mvc;
using Packt.CS7;
using System.Collections.Generic;
using System.Linq;

namespace NorthwindService.Controllers
{
    [Route("api/[controller]")]
    public class ProductsController : Controller
    {
        private readonly Northwind db;

        public ProductsController(Northwind db)
        {
            this.db = db;
        }

        // GET: api/products
        [HttpGet]
        public IEnumerable<Product> Get()
        {
            var products = db.Products.ToArray();
            return products;
        }

        // GET api/products/5
        [HttpGet("{id}")]
        public IEnumerable<Product> GetByCategory(int id)
        {
            var products = db.Products.Where(
                p => p.CategoryID == id).ToArray();
                return products;
        }
    }
}
```

Test NorthwindService by entering the relative URL /api/products/1, and ensuring the service returns only beverages.

Creating the Northwind app

Open the `Part3` solution, and choose **File | Add | New Project....**

In the **New Project** dialog, in the **Installed** list, select **Visual C# | Windows Universal**. In the center list, select **Blank App (Universal Windows)**, type the location as `C:\Code\Part3\`, type the name as `NorthwindFluent`, and click on **OK**.

Select the latest Windows 10 build for both **Target Version** and **Minimum Version**.

In the `NorthwindFluent` project, add a **Blank Page** item named `NotImplementedPage`, and, inside the existing `Grid` element, add a text block saying, `"Not yet implemented"`, centered on the page, as shown in the following markup:

```
<Grid Background="{ThemeResource ApplicationPageBackgroundThemeBrush}">
  <TextBlock Text="Not yet implemented." VerticalAlignment="Center"
             HorizontalAlignment="Center" FontSize="20" />
</Grid>
```

In the `NorthwindFluent` project, add a reference to the `NorthwindEntities` project.

In the `NorthwindFluent` project, add some images to the `Assets` folder, named like this:

- `categories.jpeg`
- `category1-small.jpeg`
- `category2-small.jpeg`, and so on.

In the `NorthwindFluent` project, add a class named `CategoriesViewModel`, and populate its `Categories` property using the `Northwind` database context, as shown in the following markup:

```
using Packt.CS7;
using System;
using System.Collections.Generic;
using System.Collections.ObjectModel;
using System.Linq;
using System.Net.Http;
using System.Runtime.Serialization.Json;

namespace NorthwindFluent
{
    public class CategoriesViewModel
    {
        public class CategoryJson
        {
            public int categoryID;
```

```
            public string categoryName;
            public string description;
        }

        public ObservableCollection<Category> Categories { get; set; }

        public CategoriesViewModel()
        {
            using (var http = new HttpClient())
            {
                http.BaseAddress = new Uri("http://localhost:5001/");

                var serializer = new
                DataContractJsonSerializer(typeof(List<CategoryJson>));

                var stream = http.GetStreamAsync("api/categories").Result;

                var cats = serializer.ReadObject(stream) as List<CategoryJson>;

                var categories = cats.Select(c => new Category
                            { CategoryID = c.categoryID,
                              CategoryName = c.categoryName,
                              Description = c.description });

                Categories = new ObservableCollection<Category>(categories);
            }
        }
    }
}
```

 We had to define a class named `CategoryJson` because the `DataContractJsonSerializer` class is not smart enough to understand camel casing used in JSON and convert automatically to title casing used in C#. So the simplest solution is to do the conversion manually using LINQ projection.

In the `NorthwindFluent` project, add a class named `CategoryIDToImageConverter`, implement the `IValueConverter` interface, and convert the integer value for the category ID into a valid path to the appropriate image file, as shown in the following code:

```
using System;
using Windows.UI.Xaml.Data;
using Windows.UI.Xaml.Media.Imaging;

namespace NorthwindFluent
{
    public class CategoryIDToImageConverter : IValueConverter
```

```
    {
        public object Convert(object value, Type targetType,
                    object parameter, string language)
        {
            int n = (int)value;
            string path =
            $"{Environment.CurrentDirectory}/Assets/category{n}-small.jpeg";
            var image = new BitmapImage(new Uri(path));
            return image;
        }

        public object ConvertBack(object value, Type targetType,
                    object parameter, string language)
        {
            throw new NotImplementedException();
        }
    }
}
```

In the `NorthwindFluent` project, add a **Blank Page** item named `CategoriesPage`, as shown in the following markup:

```
<Page
  x:Class="NorthwindFluent.CategoriesPage"
  xmlns="http://schemas.microsoft.com/winfx/2006/xaml/presentation"
  xmlns:x="http://schemas.microsoft.com/winfx/2006/xaml"
  xmlns:local="using:NorthwindFluent"
  xmlns:nw="using:Packt.CS7"
  xmlns:d="http://schemas.microsoft.com/expression/blend/2008"
  xmlns:mc="http://schemas.openxmlformats.org/markup-compatibility/2006"
  mc:Ignorable="d">
  <Page.Resources>
    <local:CategoryIDToImageConverter x:Key="id2image" />
  </Page.Resources>

  <Grid Background="{ThemeResource ApplicationPageBackgroundThemeBrush}">
    <ParallaxView Source="{x:Bind ForegroundElement}" VerticalShift="50">
      <Image x:Name="BackgroundImage" Source="Assets/categories.jpeg"
             Stretch="UniformToFill"/>
    </ParallaxView>
    <ListView x:Name="ForegroundElement"
              ItemsSource="{x:Bind ViewModel.Categories}">
      <ListView.Header>
        <Grid Padding="20"
              Background="{ThemeResource
SystemControlAcrylicElementBrush}">
          <TextBlock Style="{StaticResource TitleTextBlockStyle}"
                     FontSize="24"
```

```
                        VerticalAlignment="Center"
                        Margin="12,0"
                        Text="Categories"/>
            </Grid>
        </ListView.Header>
        <ListView.ItemTemplate>
          <DataTemplate x:DataType="nw:Category">
            <Grid Margin="4">
              <Grid.ColumnDefinitions>
                <ColumnDefinition />
                <ColumnDefinition />
              </Grid.ColumnDefinitions>
              <Image Source="{x:Bind CategoryID,
                      Converter={StaticResource id2image}}"
                      Stretch="UniformToFill" Height="200"
                      Width="300" />
              <StackPanel
                      Background=
                      "{ThemeResource
 SystemControlAcrylicElementMediumHighBrush}"
                      Padding="10" Grid.Column="1">
                  <TextBlock Text="{x:Bind CategoryName}" FontSize="20" />
                  <TextBlock Text="{x:Bind Description}" FontSize="16" />
              </StackPanel>
            </Grid>
          </DataTemplate>
        </ListView.ItemTemplate>
      </ListView>
    </Grid>
</Page>
```

Note that the code does the following:

- Imports the `Packt.CS7` namespace using `nw` as the element prefix
- Defines a page resource that instantiates a converter for category IDs to images
- Uses a Parallax view to provide a large image as a scrolling background for the foreground element, which is the list view of categories, so when the list scrolls, the large background image moves slightly too
- Binds the list view to the view model's categories collection
- Gives the list view an in-app acrylic header
- Gives the list view an item template for rendering each category using its name, description, and image based on converting its ID into an image loaded from a path

Open `CategoriesPage.xaml.cs`, and add statements to define a `ViewModel` property, and then set it in the constructor, as shown in the following code:

```
public sealed partial class CategoriesPage : Page
{
    public CategoriesViewModel ViewModel { get; set; }

    public CategoriesPage()
    {
        this.InitializeComponent();
        ViewModel = new CategoriesViewModel();
    }
}
```

Open `MainPage.xaml` and add elements to define a navigation view, that automatically uses the new Acrylic material and Reveal highlight in its pane, as shown in the following markup:

```
<Page
  x:Class="NorthwindFluent.MainPage"
  xmlns="http://schemas.microsoft.com/winfx/2006/xaml/presentation"
  xmlns:x="http://schemas.microsoft.com/winfx/2006/xaml"
  xmlns:local="using:NorthwindFluent"
  xmlns:d="http://schemas.microsoft.com/expression/blend/2008"
  xmlns:mc="http://schemas.openxmlformats.org/markup-compatibility/2006"
  mc:Ignorable="d">

  <NavigationView x:Name="NavView"
                  ItemInvoked="NavView_ItemInvoked"
                  Loaded="NavView_Loaded">

  <NavigationView.AutoSuggestBox>
    <AutoSuggestBox x:Name="ASB" QueryIcon="Find"/>
  </NavigationView.AutoSuggestBox>

  <NavigationView.HeaderTemplate>
    <DataTemplate>
      <Grid>
        <Grid.ColumnDefinitions>
          <ColumnDefinition Width="Auto"/>
          <ColumnDefinition/>
        </Grid.ColumnDefinitions>
        <TextBlock Style="{StaticResource TitleTextBlockStyle}"
                   FontSize="28"
                   VerticalAlignment="Center"
                   Margin="12,0"
                   Text="Northwind Fluent"/>
          <CommandBar Grid.Column="1"
```

```
                    HorizontalAlignment="Right"
                    DefaultLabelPosition="Right"
                    Background=
                "{ThemeResource SystemControlBackgroundAltHighBrush}">
            <AppBarButton Label="Refresh" Icon="Refresh"
                    Name="RefreshButton" Click="RefreshButton_Click"/>
          </CommandBar>
        </Grid>
      </DataTemplate>
    </NavigationView.HeaderTemplate>

    <Frame x:Name="ContentFrame">
      <Frame.ContentTransitions>
        <TransitionCollection>
          <NavigationThemeTransition/>
        </TransitionCollection>
      </Frame.ContentTransitions>
    </Frame>

  </NavigationView>
</Page>
```

Open `MainPage.xaml.cs`, and modify its contents, as shown in the following code:

```
using System;
using Windows.UI.Xaml;
using Windows.UI.Xaml.Controls;

namespace NorthwindFluent
{
    public sealed partial class MainPage : Page
    {
        public MainPage()
        {
            this.InitializeComponent();
        }

        private void NavView_Loaded(object sender, RoutedEventArgs e)
        {
            NavView.MenuItems.Add(new NavigationViewItem
            { Content = "Categories",
              Icon = new SymbolIcon(Symbol.BrowsePhotos),
              Tag = "categories" });
            NavView.MenuItems.Add(new NavigationViewItem
            { Content = "Products",
              Icon = new SymbolIcon(Symbol.AllApps),
              Tag = "products" });
            NavView.MenuItems.Add(new NavigationViewItem
```

```csharp
            { Content = "Suppliers",
              Icon = new SymbolIcon(Symbol.Contact2),
              Tag = "suppliers" });
            NavView.MenuItems.Add(new NavigationViewItemSeparator());
            NavView.MenuItems.Add(new NavigationViewItem
            { Content = "Customers",
              Icon = new SymbolIcon(Symbol.People),
              Tag = "customers" });
            NavView.MenuItems.Add(new NavigationViewItem
            { Content = "Orders",
              Icon = new SymbolIcon(Symbol.PhoneBook),
              Tag = "orders" });
            NavView.MenuItems.Add(new NavigationViewItem
            { Content = "Shippers",
              Icon = new SymbolIcon(Symbol.PostUpdate),
              Tag = "shippers" });
        }

        private void NavView_ItemInvoked(
          NavigationView sender, NavigationViewItemInvokedEventArgs args)
        {
            switch (args.InvokedItem.ToString())
            {
                case "Categories":
                    ContentFrame.Navigate(typeof(CategoriesPage));
                    break;

                default:
                    ContentFrame.Navigate(typeof(NotImplementedPage));
                    break;
            }
        }

        private async void RefreshButton_Click(
              object sender, RoutedEventArgs e)
        {
            var notImplementedDialog = new ContentDialog
            {
                Title = "Not implemented",
                Content =
                    "The Refresh functionality has not yet been implemented.",
                    CloseButtonText = "OK"
            };
            ContentDialogResult result =
                        await notImplementedDialog.ShowAsync();
        }
    }
}
```

The **Refresh** button has not yet been implemented, so we can display a dialog. Like most APIs in UWP, the method to show a dialog is asynchronous.

We can use the `await` keyword for any `Task`. This means that the main thread will not be blocked while we wait, but will remember its current position within the statements so that, once the `Task` has completed, the main thread continues executing from that same point. This allows us to write code that looks as simple as synchronous, but underneath it is much more complex.

 Internally, `await` creates a state machine to manage the complexity of passing state between any worker threads and the user interface thread.

Note that, to use the `await` keyword, we must mark the `await` containing method with the `async` keyword. They always work as a pair.

Make sure that the web service is running and that you have configured the `NorthwindFluent` app to deploy, and then run the application by navigating to **Debug** | **Start Without Debugging**, or pressing *Ctrl + F5*.

Resize the window to show its responsive design, as explained in the following bullets:

- When narrow, the navigation hides and the user must click on the hamburger menu to show the navigation pane
- When mid-width, the navigation is thin and only shows the icons, and has a non-acrylic background
- When wide, the navigation shows with an acrylic background

As you move your mouse over the navigation, note the Reveal lighting, and when you click on a menu item, such as **Orders**, the highlight bar stretches and animates as it moves, and the **Not yet implemented** message appears, as shown in the following screenshot:

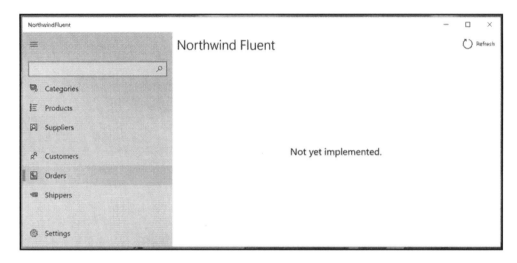

Click on **Categories**, and note the in-app acrylic of the **Categories** header, and the Parallax effect on the background image when scrolling up and down the list of categories, as shown in the following screenshot:

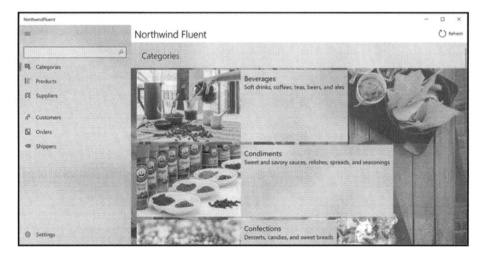

Click on the hamburger menu to collapse the navigation view and give more space for the categories list, as shown in the following screenshot:

I will leave it as an exercise, for the reader to implement a page for products that is shown when a user clicks on each category.

Building apps using Windows Template Studio

To quickly get started building UWP apps, Microsoft has created the Windows Template Studio extension for Visual Studio. We will use it to create a new app that shows some of its features and good practices.

Installing Windows Template Studio

Navigate to **Tools** | **Extensions and Updates...**, select **Online**, enter `Windows Template Studio` in the search box, and click on **Download**, and then **Close**, as shown in the following screenshot:

Exit Visual Studio 2017, and wait for the extension to install using the VSIX Installer.

Currently, Windows Template Studio gets confused when used in a solution with multiple projects, so I recommend that you always create projects with it in a new solution. After the project is created, you can then manually add it to another solution.

Selecting project types, frameworks, pages, and features

Start Visual Studio 2017, open the `Part3` solution, and go to **File** | **New** | **Project....**

In the **New Project** dialog, in the **Installed** list, select **Visual C# | Windows Universal**. In the center list, select **Windows Template Studio (Universal Windows)**, type the location as `C:\Code\Part3\`, type the name as `NorthwindUwp`, and click on **OK**.

In the **Select project type and framework** dialog, select **Navigation Pane** and **MVVM Basic**, and then click on **Next**, as shown in the following screenshot:

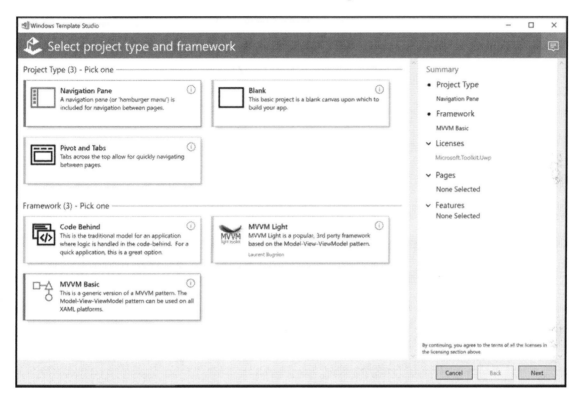

In the **Select pages and features** dialog, select the circle with a plus button in the **Settings** pane, leave its name as **Settings**, and then click on the tick button, as shown in the following screenshot:

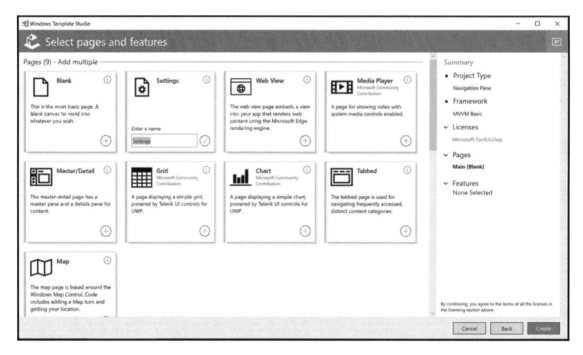

Repeat for the following panes:

- Add a **Blank** page named `AboutNorthwindApp`
- Add a **Web View** page named `AngularWebView`
- Add a **Master/Detail** page named `CategoryMasterDetail`
- Add a **Grid** page named `CustomersGrid`
- Add a **Map** page named `CustomerMap`
- Add **First Run Prompt**

In **Summary**, confirm you have created the pages, and click on **Create**, as shown in the following screenshot:

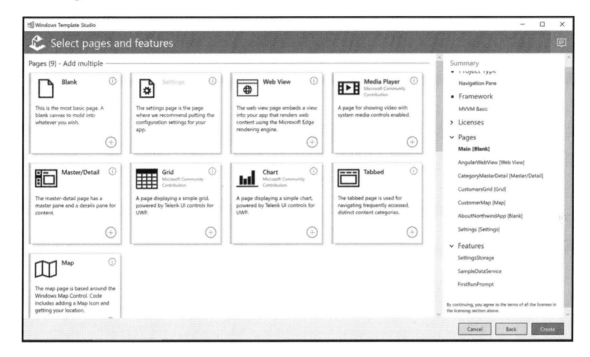

Once the new project has been successfully created, close the solution, and open the `Part3` solution.

Navigate to **File | Add | Existing Project**, and select **NorthwindUwp.csproj**.

Retargeting the project

In **Solution Explorer**, in **NorthwindUwp** project, open **Properties**, and change **Target version** and **Min version** to the latest build.

In **Solution Explorer**, right-click on the **Part3** solution, and choose **Properties**, or press *Alt + Enter*.

Set **Multiple startup projects**, with **ExploreAngular** set to **Start** first, then the **NorthwindService** project, and finally the **NorthwindUwp** project, as shown in the following screenshot:

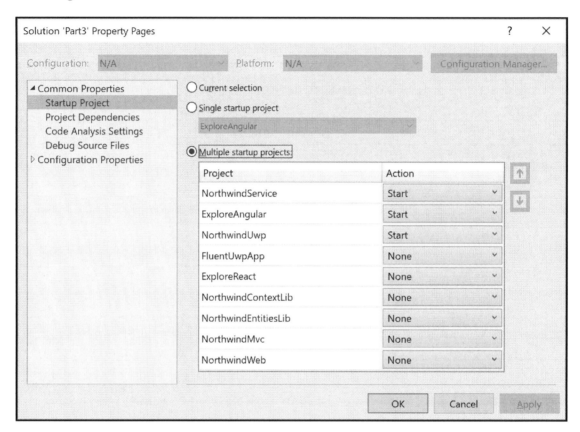

Customizing some views

In **Solution Explorer**, expand the NorthwindUwp project and the ViewModels folder, open AngularWebViewViewModel.cs, and modify the DefaultUrl string constant to use the Angular web application that you created earlier, which listens on port 5002, as shown in the following code:

```
private const string DefaultUrl = "http://localhost:5002";
```

In **Solution Explorer**, expand the `NorthwindUwp` project and the `ViewModels` folder, open `SHellViewModel.cs`, and modify the `PopulateNavItems` method to use some different symbols, as shown highlighted in the following code:

```
_primaryItems.Add(ShellNavigationItem.FromType<MainPage>("Shell_Main".GetLo
calized(), Symbol.Home));
_primaryItems.Add(ShellNavigationItem.FromType<AngularWebViewPage>("Shell_A
ngularWebView".GetLocalized(), Symbol.Globe));
_primaryItems.Add(ShellNavigationItem.FromType<CategoryMasterDetailPage>("S
hell_CategoryMasterDetail".GetLocalized(), Symbol.ContactInfo));
_primaryItems.Add(ShellNavigationItem.FromType<CustomersGridPage>("Shell_Cu
stomersGrid".GetLocalized(), Symbol.PhoneBook));
_primaryItems.Add(ShellNavigationItem.FromType<CustomerMapPage>("Shell_Cust
omerMap".GetLocalized(), Symbol.Map));
_primaryItems.Add(ShellNavigationItem.FromType<AboutNorthwindAppPage>("Shel
l_AboutNorthwindApp".GetLocalized(), Symbol.Help));
```

Expand the `Strings` and `en-us` folders, and open `Resources.resw`.

At the bottom of the grid, modify the **Value** for the resources that begin with the word `Shell` to be more appropriate, as shown in the following screenshot:

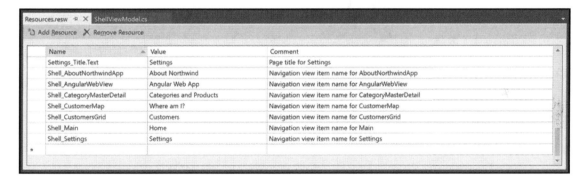

Navigate to **Build** | **Configuration Manager**, and select the **Build** and **Deploy** checkboxes for the **NorthwindUwp** project.

Testing the app's functionality

Start the app by navigating to **Debug** | **Start**, or press *F5*.

When the app has started, click on the hamburger menu, click on **Angular Web App**, and note that the web application is loaded, as shown in the following screenshot:

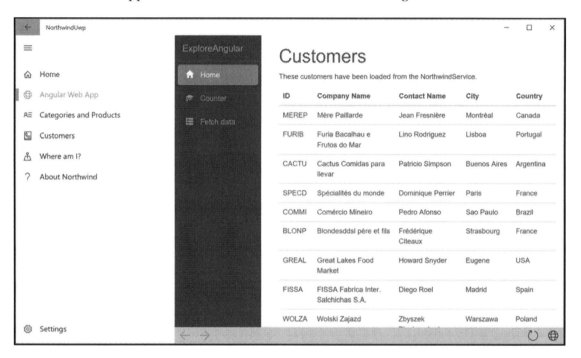

Click on **Where am I?**, and click on **Yes** to allow the app to access your precise location, as shown in the following screenshot:

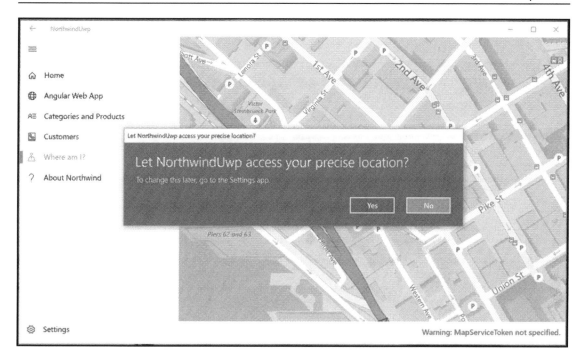

Note the back arrow button that navigates the user back to previous screens.

Click on **Settings** and select the **Dark** theme.

Click on **Customers** and note the grid of sample data.

Click on **Categories and Products** and note the sample data.

Close the app.

Summary

In this chapter, you learned how to build a graphical user interface using XAML and the new Fluent Design System, including features such as Acrylic material, Reveal lighting, and Parallax view. You also learned how to share resources in an app, how to replace a control's template, how to bind to data and controls, and how to prevent thread blocking with multitasking and the C# `async` and `await` keywords.

In the next chapter, you will learn how to build mobile apps using Xamarin.Forms.

13
Building Mobile Apps Using XAML and Xamarin.Forms

This chapter is about learning how to take C# mobile by building a cross-platform mobile app for iOS, Android, and other mobile platforms. The mobile app will allow the listing and management of customers in the Northwind database.

The mobile app will call the Northwind service that you built with ASP.NET Core Web API in Chapter 11, *Building Web Services and Applications Using ASP.NET Core*. If you have not built the Northwind service, go back and build it now.

The client-side Xamarin.Forms mobile app will be written with **Visual Studio for Mac**.

 You will need a computer with macOS, Xcode, and Visual Studio for Mac to complete this chapter.

In this chapter, we will cover the following topics:

- Understanding Xamarin and Xamarin.Forms
- Building mobile apps using Xamarin.Forms

Understanding Xamarin and Xamarin.Forms

Xamarin enables developers to build mobile apps for Apple iOS (iPhone and iPad), Google Android, and Windows Mobile using C#. It is based on a third-party open source implementation of .NET known as Mono. Business logic layer can be written once and shared between all mobile platforms. User interface interactions and APIs are different on various mobile platforms, so the user experience layer is often custom for each platform.

How Xamarin.Forms extends Xamarin

Xamarin.Forms extends Xamarin to make cross-platform mobile development even easier by sharing most of the user experience layer, as well as the business logic layer.

Like Universal Windows Platform apps, Xamarin.Forms uses XAML to define the user interface once for all platforms using abstractions of platform-specific user interface components. Applications built with Xamarin.Forms draw the user interface using native platform widgets, so the app's look-and-feel fits naturally with the target mobile platform.

A user experience built using Xamarin.Forms will never perfectly fit a specific platform as one custom built with Xamarin, but for enterprise mobile apps, it is more than good enough.

Mobile first, cloud first

Mobile apps are often supported by services in the cloud. Satya Nadella, CEO of Microsoft, famously said this:

> *To me, when we say mobile first, it's not the mobility of the device, it's actually the mobility of the individual experience. [...] The only way you are going to be able to orchestrate the mobility of these applications and data is through the cloud.*

As you have seen earlier in this book, to create the ASP.NET Core Web API service to support the mobile app, we can use any of the Visual Studio family of IDEs.

To create Xamarin.Forms apps, developers can use either Visual Studio 2017 or Visual Studio for Mac.

To compile Windows Mobile apps, you will require Windows and Visual Studio 2017. To compile iOS apps, you will require a Mac, Visual Studio for Mac, and Xcode. So, why did I choose the Mac platform for mobile development in this chapter?

Android runs on six times as many mobile phones compared to iOS; however, consider these things:

- For every dollar an Android user spends on apps, an iOS user spends ten dollars
- For every hour an Android user spends browsing the web, an iOS user spends two hours

So, market share numbers should be taken in the context that iOS users engage far more with their devices, which is important for monetizing mobile apps, either through up-front sales, in-app purchases, or advertising.

A summary of which IDE can be used to create and compile which type of app is shown in the following table:

	iOS	Android	Windows Mobile	ASP.NET Core Web API
Smartphone Market Share	14%	86%	< 0.1%	n/a
Visual Studio Code	No	No	No	Yes
Visual Studio for Mac	Yes	Yes	No	Yes
Visual Studio 2017	No	Yes	Yes	Yes

If you would like to learn more about Xamarin, then I recommend the *Xamarin: Cross-Platform Mobile Application Development* Learning Path, by *Jonathan Peppers, George Taskos,* and *Can Bilgin,* that you can read more about at the following link:
https://www.packtpub.com/application-development/xamarin-cross-platform-mobile-application-development

Building mobile apps using Xamarin.Forms

We will build a mobile app that runs on either iOS or Android for managing customers in Northwind.

If you have never run Xcode, run it now to ensure that all its required components are installed and registered.

Adding Android SDKs

To target Android, you must install at least one Android SDK. A default installation of Visual Studio for Mac already includes one Android SDK, but it is often an older version to support as many Android devices as possible. To use the latest features of Xamarin.Forms, you must install a more recent Android SDK.

Start Visual Studio for Mac, and navigate to **Visual Studio Community** | **Preferences**.

In **Preferences**, navigate to **Projects** | **SDK Locations**, and select the **Platforms** you want, for example, **Android 8.0 - Oreo**, as shown in the following screenshot:

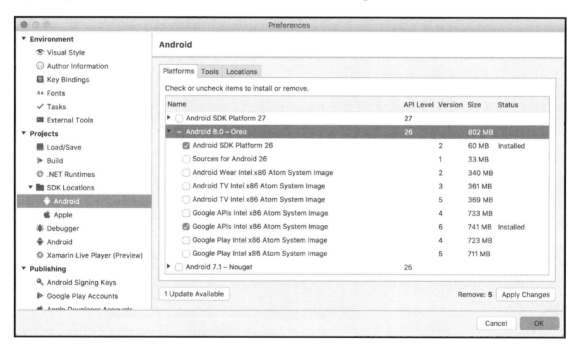

When installing an Android SDK, you must select at least one **System Image** to use as a virtual machine emulator for testing.

Creating a Xamarin.Forms solution

Navigate to **File | New Solution...**.

In the **New Project** dialog, choose **Multiplatform | App** in the left-hand column.

Choose **Xamarin.Forms | Blank Forms App** in the middle column, as shown in the following screenshot:

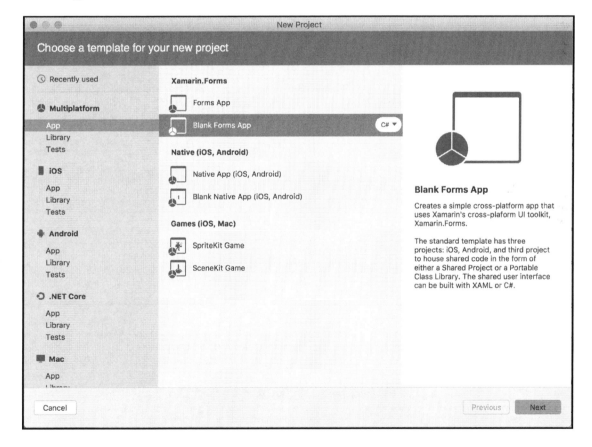

Click on **Next**.

Enter **App Name** as NorthwindMobile and **Organization Identifier** as com.packt, select **Shared Code** to **Use Shared Library**, and ensure that you use XAML for the user interface files, as shown in the following screenshot:

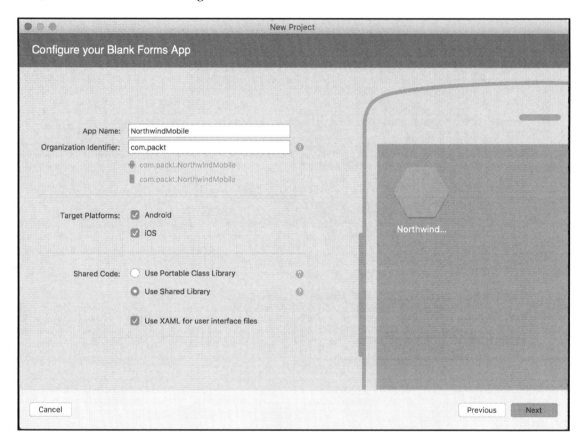

Click on **Next**.

Change **Solution Name** to `Part3Mobile`, and **Location** to `/Users/[user_folder]/Code`, as shown in the following screenshot:

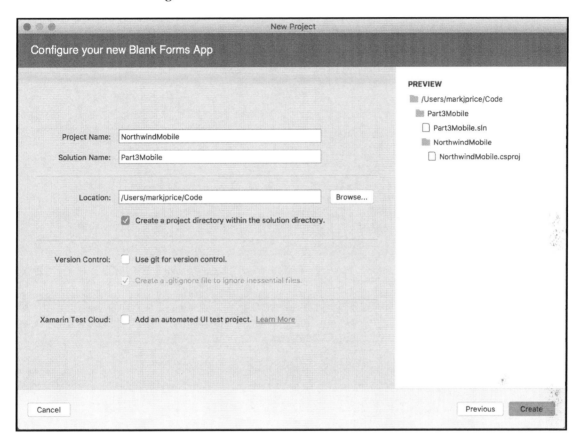

Click on **Create**.

After a few moments, the solution and all three projects will be created. In Visual Studio for Mac, navigate to **Build** | **Build All**, and wait for the solution to download any updated packages and build the projects, as shown in the following screenshot:

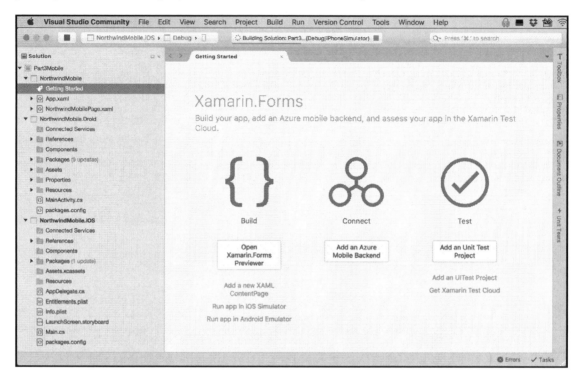

Right-click on **Part3Mobile**, and choose **Update NuGet Packages**.

Creating a model

Although we could reuse the .NET Standard 2.0 entity data model library that you created earlier, we want to implement two-way data binding, so we will create a new class to represent customer entities in the mobile app.

Right-click on the project named `NorthwindMobile`, go to **Add** | **New Folder**, and name it `Models`.

Right-click on the `Models` folder and go to **Add** | **New File....**

In the **New File** dialog, go to **General | Empty Class**, enter the name Customer, as shown
in the following screenshot, and click on **New**:

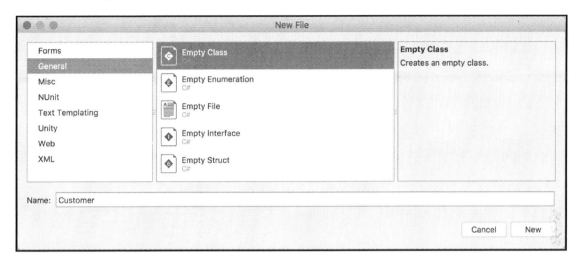

Modify the statements, as shown in the following code:

```
using System.Collections.Generic;
using System.Collections.ObjectModel;
using System.ComponentModel;

namespace NorthwindMobile.Models
{
    public class Customer : INotifyPropertyChanged
    {
        public static IList<Customer> Customers;

        static Customer()
        {
            Customers = new ObservableCollection<Customer>();
        }

        public event PropertyChangedEventHandler PropertyChanged;

        private string customerID;
        private string companyName;
        private string contactName;
        private string city;
        private string country;
        private string phone;

        public string CustomerID
```

```
      {
         get { return customerID; }
         set
         {
            customerID = value;
            PropertyChanged?.Invoke(this,
            new PropertyChangedEventArgs("CustomerID"));
         }
      }

      public string CompanyName
      {
         get { return companyName; }
         set
         {
            companyName = value;
            PropertyChanged?.Invoke(this,
            new PropertyChangedEventArgs("CompanyName"));
         }
      }

      public string ContactName
      {
         get { return contactName; }
         set
         {
            contactName = value;
            PropertyChanged?.Invoke(this,
            new PropertyChangedEventArgs("ContactName"));
         }
      }
      public string City
      {
         get { return city; }
         set
         {
            city = value;
            PropertyChanged?.Invoke(this,
            new PropertyChangedEventArgs("City"));
         }
      }

      public string Country
      {
         get { return country; }
         set
         {
            country = value;
```

```
            PropertyChanged?.Invoke(this,
            new PropertyChangedEventArgs("Country"));
      }
   }

   public string Phone
   {
      get { return phone; }
      set
      {
         phone = value;
         PropertyChanged?.Invoke(this,
         new PropertyChangedEventArgs("Phone"));
      }
   }

   public string Location
   {
      get
      {
         return string.Format("{0}, {1}", City, Country);
      }
   }

   // for testing before calling web service
   public static void SampleData()
   {
      Customers.Clear();

      Customers.Add(new Customer
      {
         CustomerID = "ALFKI",
         CompanyName = "Alfreds Futterkiste",
         ContactName = "Maria Anders",
         City = "Berlin",
         Country = "Germany",
         Phone = "030-0074321"
      });

      Customers.Add(new Customer
      {
         CustomerID = "FRANK",
         CompanyName = "Frankenversand",
         ContactName = "Peter Franken",
         City = "München",
         Country = "Germany",
         Phone = "089-0877310"
      });
```

```
            Customers.Add(new Customer
            {
                CustomerID = "SEVES",
                CompanyName = "Seven Seas Imports",
                ContactName = "Hari Kumar",
                City = "London",
                Country = "UK",
                Phone = "(171) 555-1717"
            });
        }
    }
}
```

Note the following:

- The class implements `INotifyPropertyChanged`, so a two-way bound user interface components such as `Editor` will update the property and vice versa. There is a `PropertyChanged` event that is raised whenever one of the properties is modified.

- After loading from the service, the customers will be cached locally in the mobile app using `ObservableCollection`. This supports notifications to any bound user interface components, such as `ListView`.

- In addition to properties for storing values retrieved from the REST service, the class defines a read-only `Location` property. This will be used to bind to, in a summary list of customers.

- For testing purposes, when the REST service is not available, there is a method to populate three sample customers.

Creating an interface for dialing phone numbers

Right-click on the `NorthwindMobile` folder and choose **New File...**.

Go to **General | Empty Interface**, name the file `IDialer`, and click on **New**.

Modify the `IDialer` contents, as shown in the following code:

```
namespace NorthwindMobile
{
    public interface IDialer
    {
        bool Dial(string number);
    }
}
```

Implement the phone dialer for iOS

Right-click on the `NorthwindMobile.iOS` folder and choose **New File...**.

Go to **General | Empty Class**, name the file as `PhoneDialer`, and click on **New**.

Modify its contents, as shown in the following code:

```
using Foundation;
using NorthwindMobile.iOS;
using UIKit;
using Xamarin.Forms;

[assembly: Dependency(typeof(PhoneDialer))]
namespace NorthwindMobile.iOS
{
    public class PhoneDialer : IDialer
    {
        public bool Dial(string number)
        {
            return UIApplication.SharedApplication.OpenUrl(
            new NSUrl("tel:" + number));
        }
    }
}
```

Implement the phone dialer for Android

Right-click on the `NorthwindMobile.Droid` folder and choose **New File...**

Choose **General** | **Empty Class**, name the file as `PhoneDialer`, and click on **New**.

Modify its contents, as shown in the following code:

```
using Android.Content;
using Android.Telephony;
using NorthwindMobile.Droid;
using System.Linq;
using Xamarin.Forms;
using Uri = Android.Net.Uri;

[assembly: Dependency(typeof(PhoneDialer))]
namespace NorthwindMobile.Droid
{
    public class PhoneDialer : IDialer
    {
        public bool Dial(string number)
        {
            var context = Forms.Context;
            if (context == null)
            return false;

            var intent = new Intent(Intent.ActionCall);
            intent.SetData(Uri.Parse("tel:" + number));

            if (IsIntentAvailable(context, intent))
            {
                context.StartActivity(intent);
                return true;
            }

            return false;
        }

        public static bool IsIntentAvailable(Context context, Intent
        intent)
        {
            var packageManager = context.PackageManager;

            var list = packageManager.QueryIntentServices(intent, 0)
            .Union(packageManager.QueryIntentActivities(intent, 0));

            if (list.Any())
            return true;
```

```
        var manager = TelephonyManager.FromContext(context);
        return manager.PhoneType != PhoneType.None;
      }
    }
  }
```

In `NorthwindMobile.Droid`, expand **Properties**, and open `AndroidManifest.xml`.

In **Required permissions**, check the **CallPhone** permission, as shown in the following screenshot:

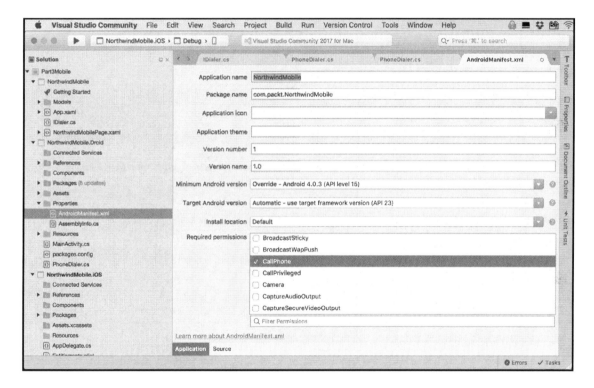

Creating views for the customers list and customer details

Right-click on `NorthwindMobilePage.xaml`, click on **Remove**, and then click on **Remove from Project**.

Right-click on the project named `NorthwindMobile`, go to **Add** | **New Folder**, and name it `Views`.

Right-click on the `Views` folder and choose **New File...**.

Go to **Forms** | **Forms ContentPage Xaml**, name the file as `CustomersList`, and click on **New**, as shown in the following screenshot:

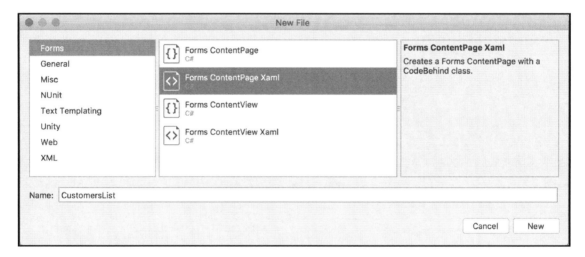

Creating the view for the list of customers

In `NorthwindMobile`, open `CustomersList.xaml`, and modify its contents, as shown in the following markup:

```xml
<?xml version="1.0" encoding="UTF-8"?>
<ContentPage xmlns="http://xamarin.com/schemas/2014/forms"
 xmlns:x="http://schemas.microsoft.com/winfx/2009/xaml"
 x:Class="NorthwindMobile.Views.CustomersList"
 Title="List">
  <ContentPage.Content>
    <ListView ItemsSource="{Binding .}"
      VerticalOptions="Center" HorizontalOptions="Center"
```

```
        IsPullToRefreshEnabled="True"
        ItemTapped="Customer_Tapped"
        Refreshing="Customers_Refreshing">
         <ListView.Header>
           <Label Text="Northwind Customers"
            BackgroundColor="Silver" />
         </ListView.Header>
         <ListView.ItemTemplate>
           <DataTemplate>
             <TextCell Text="{Binding CompanyName}"
              Detail="{Binding Location}">
                <TextCell.ContextActions>
                  <MenuItem Clicked="Customer_Phoned" Text="Phone" />
                  <MenuItem Clicked="Customer_Deleted"
                    Text="Delete" IsDestructive="True" />
                </TextCell.ContextActions>
             </TextCell>
           </DataTemplate>
         </ListView.ItemTemplate>
       </ListView>
    </ContentPage.Content>
    <ContentPage.ToolbarItems>
      <ToolbarItem Text="Add" Activated="Add_Activated"
       Order="Primary" Priority="0" />
    </ContentPage.ToolbarItems>
  </ContentPage>
```

Note the following:

- The `ContentPage` element has had its `Title` attribute set to `List`
- Event handlers have been written for this: loading the customers when the view appears, a customer being tapped (to show detail), the list being swiped down to refresh, and a customer being deleted by swiping left and then clicking on a **Delete** button
- A data template defines how to display each customer: large text for the company name and smaller text for the location underneath
- An **Add** button is displayed so that users can navigate to a detail view to add a new customer

Modify the contents of `CustomersList.xaml.cs`, as shown in the following code:

```
using System;
using System.Threading.Tasks;
using NorthwindMobile.Models;
using Xamarin.Forms;
```

```csharp
namespace NorthwindMobileApp.Views
{
    public partial class CustomersList : ContentPage
    {
        public CustomersList()
        {
            InitializeComponent();
            Customer.SampleData();
            BindingContext = Customer.Customers;
        }

        async void Customer_Tapped(object sender, ItemTappedEventArgs e)
        {
            Customer c = e.Item as Customer;
            if (c == null) return;
            // navigate to the detail view and show the tapped customer
            await Navigation.PushAsync(new CustomerDetails(c));
        }

        async void Customers_Refreshing(object sender, EventArgs e)
        {
            ListView listView = sender as ListView;
            listView.IsRefreshing = true;
            // simulate a refresh
            await Task.Delay(1500);
            listView.IsRefreshing = false;
        }

        void Customer_Deleted(object sender, EventArgs e)
        {
            MenuItem menuItem = sender as MenuItem;
            Customer c = menuItem.BindingContext as Customer;
            Customer.Customers.Remove(c);
        }

        async void Customer_Phoned(object sender, EventArgs e)
        {
            MenuItem menuItem = sender as MenuItem;
            Customer c = menuItem.BindingContext as Customer;
            if (await this.DisplayAlert("Dial a Number",
                "Would you like to call " + c.Phone + "?",
                "Yes", "No"))
            {
                var dialer = DependencyService.Get<IDialer>();
                if (dialer != null)
                dialer.Dial(c.Phone);
            }
        }
```

```
    async void Add_Activated(object sender, EventArgs e)
    {
        await Navigation.PushAsync(new CustomerDetails());
    }
  }
}
```

Note the following:

- `BindingContext` is set to the sample list of `Customers` in the constructor of the page
- When a customer in the list view is tapped, the user is taken to a details view (that you will create in the next step)
- When the list view is pulled down, it triggers a simulated refresh that takes one and a half seconds
- When a customer is deleted in the list view, it is removed from the bound collection of customers
- When a customer in the list view is swiped, and the **Phone** button is tapped, a dialog prompts the user if they want to dial the number, and if so, the platform-specific implementation will be retrieved using the dependency resolver and then used to dial the number
- When the **Add** button is tapped, the user is taken to the customer detail page to enter details for a new customer

Creating the view for the customer details

Add another **Forms ContentPage Xaml** file named `CustomerDetails`.

Open `CustomerDetails.xaml`, and modify its contents, as shown in the following markup, and note the following:

- `Title` of the `ContentPage` element has been set to `Edit Customer`
- `Grid` with two columns and six rows is used for the layout
- `Editor` elements are two-way bound to properties of the `Customer` class

```xml
<?xml version="1.0" encoding="UTF-8"?>
<ContentPage xmlns="http://xamarin.com/schemas/2014/forms"
 xmlns:x="http://schemas.microsoft.com/winfx/2009/xaml"
 x:Class="NorthwindMobile.Views.CustomerDetails" Title="Edit Customer">
  <ContentPage.Content>
    <StackLayout VerticalOptions="Fill"
     HorizontalOptions="Fill">
```

```
      <Grid BackgroundColor="Silver">
        <Grid.ColumnDefinitions>
          <ColumnDefinition/> <ColumnDefinition/>
        </Grid.ColumnDefinitions>
        <Grid.RowDefinitions>
          <RowDefinition/> <RowDefinition/> <RowDefinition/>
          <RowDefinition/> <RowDefinition/> <RowDefinition/>
        </Grid.RowDefinitions>
        <Label Text="Customer ID"
         VerticalOptions="Center" Margin="6" />
        <Editor Text="{Binding CustomerID, Mode=TwoWay}"
         Grid.Column="1" />
        <Label Text="Company Name" Grid.Row="1"
         VerticalOptions="Center" Margin="6" />
        <Editor Text="{Binding CompanyName, Mode=TwoWay}"
         Grid.Column="1" Grid.Row="1" />
        <Label Text="Contact Name" Grid.Row="2"
         VerticalOptions="Center" Margin="6" />
        <Editor Text="{Binding ContactName, Mode=TwoWay}"
         Grid.Column="1" Grid.Row="2" />
        <Label Text="City" Grid.Row="3"
         VerticalOptions="Center" Margin="6" />
        <Editor Text="{Binding City, Mode=TwoWay}"
         Grid.Column="1" Grid.Row="3" />
        <Label Text="Country" Grid.Row="4"
         VerticalOptions="Center" Margin="6" />
        <Editor Text="{Binding Country, Mode=TwoWay}"
         Grid.Column="1" Grid.Row="4" />
        <Label Text="Phone" Grid.Row="5"
         VerticalOptions="Center" Margin="6" />
        <Editor Text="{Binding Phone, Mode=TwoWay}"
         Grid.Column="1" Grid.Row="5" />
      </Grid>
      <Button x:Name="InsertButton" Text="Insert Customer"
       Clicked="InsertButton_Clicked" />
      </StackLayout>
    </ContentPage.Content>
  </ContentPage>
```

Open `CustomerDetails.xaml.cs`, and modify its contents, as shown in the following code:

```
using System;
using NorthwindMobile.Models;
using Xamarin.Forms;

namespace NorthwindMobile.Views
{
```

```
public partial class CustomerDetails : ContentPage
{
    private bool newCustomer = false;

    public CustomerDetails()
    {
        InitializeComponent();
        BindingContext = new Customer();
        newCustomer = true;
        Title = "Add Customer";
    }

    public CustomerDetails(Customer customer)
    {
        InitializeComponent();
        BindingContext = customer;
        InsertButton.IsVisible = false;
    }

    async void InsertButton_Clicked(object sender, EventArgs e)
    {
        if (newCustomer)
        {
            Customer.Customers.Add((Customer)BindingContext);
        }
        await Navigation.PopAsync(animated: true);
    }
}
```

Open App.xaml.cs.

Import the NorthwindMobile.Views namespace.

Modify the statement that sets MainPage to create an instance of CustomersList **wrapped** in NavigationPage, **as shown in the following code:**

```
MainPage = new NavigationPage(new CustomersList());
```

Testing the mobile app with iOS

Click on the mobile phone icon in the **Debug** toolbar, and select **iPhone X iOS 11.0**, as shown in the following screenshot:

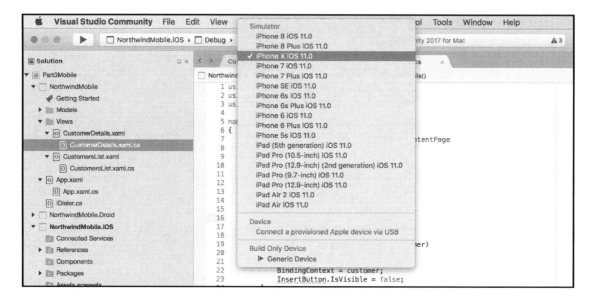

Click on the **Start** button in the toolbar, or go to **Run** | **Start Debugging**.

After a few moments, **Simulator** will show your running mobile app, as shown in the following screenshot:

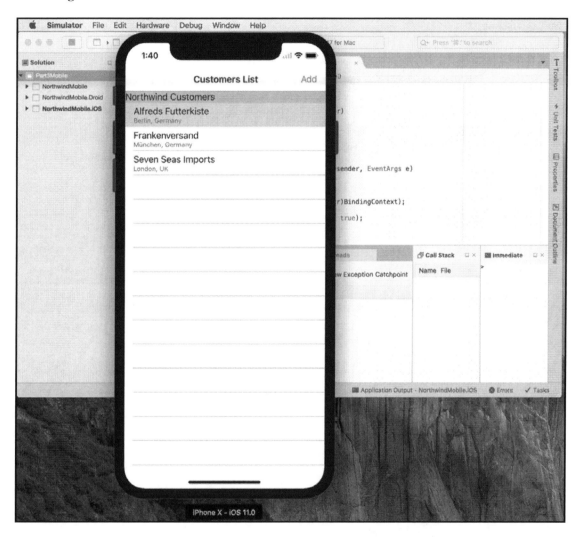

Click on a customer and modify its **Company Name**:

Click on **Back** to return to the list of customers and note that the company name has been updated.

Click on **Add**.

Fill in the fields for a new customer, as shown in the following screenshot:

Click on **Insert Customer** and note that the new customer has been added to the list.

Slide one of the customers to the left to reveal two action buttons, **Phone** and **Delete**:

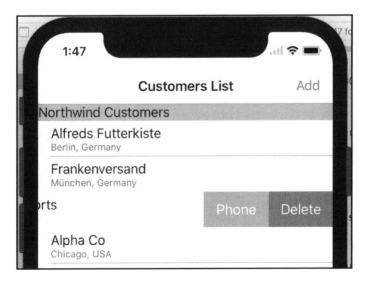

Click on **Phone** and note the prompt to the user, as shown here:

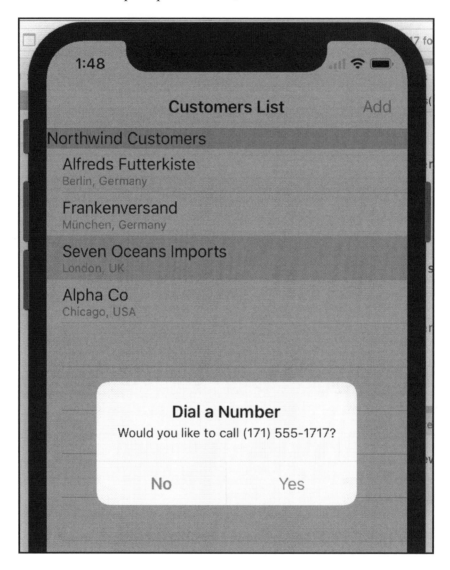

Slide one of the customers to the left to reveal two action buttons, **Phone** and **Delete**, and click on **Delete**, and note that the customer is removed.

Quit **Simulator**.

Adding NuGet packages for calling a REST service

In the project named `NorthwindMobile.iOS,` right-click on the folder named `Packages` and choose **Add Packages...**.

In the **Add Packages** dialog, enter `System.Net.Http` in the **Search** box. Select the package named **System.Net.Http** and click on **Add Package**, as shown in the following screenshot:

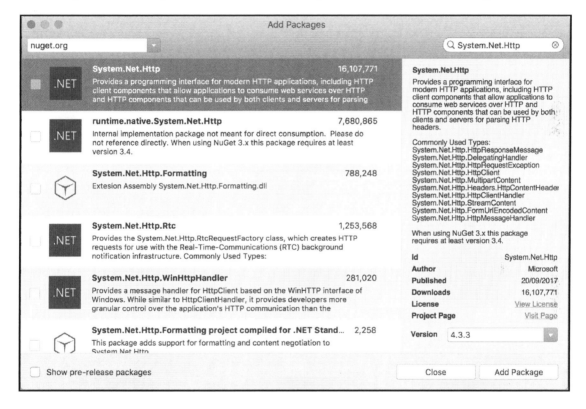

In the **License Acceptance** dialog, click on **Accept**.

In the project named `NorthwindMobile.iOS,` right-click on the folder named `Packages` and choose **Add Packages...**.

In the **Add Packages** dialog, enter `Json.NET` in the **Search** box. Select the package named **Json.NET** and click on **Add Package**, as shown in the following screenshot:

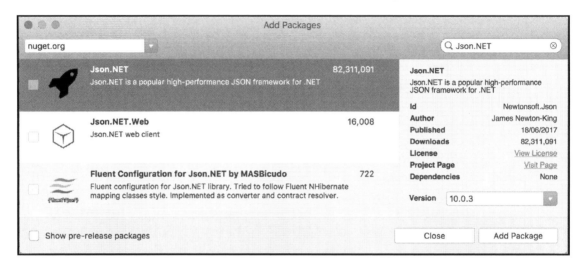

Accept the license.

Repeat these steps to add the same two NuGet packages to the project named `NorthwindMobile.Android`.

Getting customers from the service

Open `CustomersList.xaml.cs`, and import the following highlighted namespaces:

```
using System.Threading.Tasks;
using NorthwindMobile.Models;
using Xamarin.Forms;
using System;
using System.Linq;
using System.Collections.Generic;
using System.Net.Http;
using System.Net.Http.Headers;
using Newtonsoft.Json;
```

Modify the CustomersList constructor to load the list of customers using the service proxy instead of the SampleData method, as shown in the following code:

```
public CustomersList()
{
    InitializeComponent();

    //Customer.SampleData();

    var client = new HttpClient();
    client.BaseAddress = new Uri(
      "http://localhost:5001/api/customers");

    client.DefaultRequestHeaders.Accept.Add(
      new MediaTypeWithQualityHeaderValue("application/json"));

    HttpResponseMessage response = client.GetAsync("").Result;

    response.EnsureSuccessStatusCode();

    string content =
      response.Content.ReadAsStringAsync().Result;
    var customersFromService = JsonConvert.DeserializeObject
    <IEnumerable<Customer>>(content);

    foreach (Customer c in customersFromService
      .OrderBy(customer => customer.CompanyName)
    {
        Customer.Customers.Add(c);
    }

    BindingContext = Customer.Customers;
}
```

In Visual Studio Code, run the NorthwindService project.

In Visual Studio for Mac, run the `NorthwindMobile` project, and note that 91 customers are loaded from the web service, as shown in the following screenshot:

Summary

In this chapter, you learned how to build a mobile app using Xamarin.Forms, which is cross-platform for iOS and Android (and potentially other platforms), and consumes a REST/HTTP service using the `HttpClient` and `Newtonsoft.Json` packages.

14
Understanding .NET Core Internals and Measuring Performance

When developing application architecture, knowing the internals of how the .NET framework works plays a vital role in ensuring the quality of the application's performance. In this chapter, we will focus on the internals of .NET Core that can help us write quality code and architecture for any application. This chapter will cover some of the core concepts of .NET Core internals, including the compilation process, garbage collection, and **Framework Class Library (FCL)**. We will complete this chapter by going through the *BenchmarkDotNet* tool, which is mostly used in measuring code performance, and is highly recommended for benchmarking code snippets within an application.

In this chapter, you will learn the following topics:

- .NET Core internals
- Utilizing multiple cores of the CPU for high performance
- How releasing builds increases performance
- Benchmarking .NET Core 2.0 applications

.NET Core internals

.NET Core contains two core components—the runtime CoreCLR and the base-class libraries CoreFX. In this section, we will cover the following topics:

- CoreFX
- CoreCLR
- Understanding MSIL, CLI, CTS, and CLS

- How CLR works
- From compilation to execution—under the hood
- Garbage collection
- .NET Native and JIT compilation

CoreFX

CoreFX is the code name of .NET Core's set of libraries. It contains all the libraries that start with Microsoft.* or System.*and contains collections, I/O, string manipulation, reflection, security, and many more features.

The CoreFX is runtime agnostic, and it can run on any platform regardless of what APIs it supports.

> To learn more about each assembly, you can refer to the .NET Core source browser at `https://source.dot.net`.

CoreCLR

CoreCLR provides the common language runtime environment for .NET Core applications, and manages the execution of the complete application life cycle. It performs various operations when the program is running. Operations such as memory allocation, garbage collection, exception handling, type safety, thread management, and security are part of CoreCLR.

.NET Core's runtime provides the same **Garbage Collection (GC)** as .NET Framework and a new **Just In Time (JIT)** compiler that is more optimized, codenamed *RyuJIT*. When .NET Core was first released, it was only supported for 64-bit platforms, but with the release of .NET Core 2.0, it is now available for 32-bit platforms as well. However, the 32-bit version is only supported by Windows operating systems.

Understanding MSIL, CLI, CTS, and CLS

When we build our project, the code is compiled into the **Intermediate Language** (**IL**), also known as **Microsoft Intermediate Language** (**MSIL**). MSIL is compliant with the **Common Language Infrastructure** (**CLI**), where CLI is the standard that provides a common type system and a language specification, respectively known as the **Common Type System** (**CTS**) and **Common Language Specification** (**CLS**).

The CTS provides a common type system and compiles the language-specific types into the compliant data types. It standardizes all the .NET languages' data types to a common data type for language interoperability. For example, if the code is written in C#, it will be converted to the specific CTS.

Suppose we have two variables, defined in the following code fragment using C#:

```
class Program
{
  static void Main(string[] args)
  {
    int minNo = 1;
    long maxThroughput = 99999;
  }
}
```

On compilation, the compiler generates the MSIL into an assembly that will be available through the CoreCLR to perform the JIT and convert it into the native machine code. Note that the `int` and `long` types are converted to the `int32` and `int64` respectively:

```
.method private hidebysig static void  Main(string[] args) cil managed
{
  .entrypoint
  // Code size       11 (0xb)
  .maxstack  1
  .locals init (int32 V_0,
           int64 V_1)
  IL_0000:  nop
  IL_0001:  ldc.i4.1
  IL_0002:  stloc.0
  IL_0003:  ldc.i4      0x1869f
  IL_0008:  conv.i8
  IL_0009:  stloc.1
  IL_000a:  ret
} // end of method Program::Main
```

It is not necessary for every language to comply completely with the CTS, and it can support the smaller footprint of the CTS, too. For example, when VB.NET was first released in .NET Framework, it only supported the signed integer data types, and there was no provision to use unsigned integers. With later versions of .NET Framework, and now with .NET Core 2.0, we can use all managed languages, such as C#, F#, and VB.NET, to develop applications and easily reference any project's assembly.

How the CLR works

The CLR is implemented as a set of in-process libraries that are loaded with the application, and runs inside the context of the application process. In the following diagram, we have two .NET Core applications running, named **App1.exe** and **App2.exe**. Each black box represents the application process address space, where the applications **App1.exe** and **App2.exe** are running their own CLR version side by side:

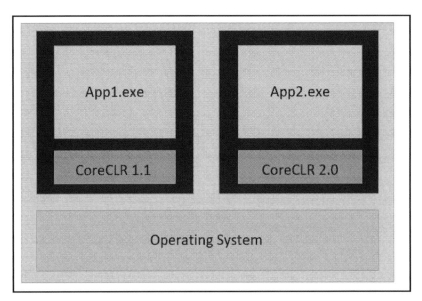

When packaging the .NET Core applications, we can either publish them as **framework-dependent deployments (FDDs)** or **self-contained deployments (SCDs)**. In FDDs, the published package does not contain the .NET Core runtime, and expects that the .NET Core is present on the target/hosting system. With SCDs, all the components, such as the .NET Core runtime and .NET Core libraries, are included in the published package, and the .NET Core installation on the target system is not required.

 To learn more about FDDs or SCDs, please refer to `https://docs.` `microsoft.com/en-us/dotnet/core/deploying/`.

From compilation to execution – Under the hood

The .NET Core compilation process is like the one used with the .NET Framework. When the project is built, the internal .NET CLI command is invoked by the MSBuild system, which builds the project and generates the assembly (`.dll`) or executable (`.exe`) file. This assembly contains the manifest that contains the assembly's metadata, and includes the version number, culture, type-reference information, information about the referenced assemblies, and a list of other files in the assembly and their association. This assembly manifest is stored either in the MSIL code or in a standalone **portable executable (PE)** file:

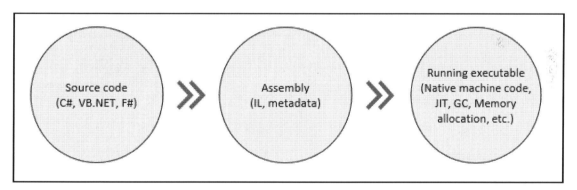

Now, when the executable is run, a new process is started and bootstraps the .NET Core runtime, which then initializes the execution environment, sets up the heap and thread pool, and loads the assembly into the process address space. Based on the program, it then executes the main entry point method (`Main`) and performs a JIT compilation. From here, the code starts executing and the objects start allocating memory on heap, where primitive types store on stack. For each method, the JIT compilation is done and the native machine code gets generated.

When JIT compilation is done, and before generating a native machine code, however, it also performs a few validations. These validations include the following:

- Verifying, that the MSIL was generated during the build process
- Verifying, whether any code was modified or new types added during the JIT compilation process
- Verifying, that the optimized code for the target machine has been generated

Garbage collection

One of the most important features of CLR is the garbage collector. Since the .NET Core applications are managed applications, most of the garbage collection is done automatically by the CLR. The allocation of objects in the memory is efficiently done by the CLR. The CLR not only tunes the virtual memory resources from time to time, but it also reduces the fragmentation of underlying virtual memory to make it more efficient in terms of space.

When the program is run, the objects start allocating memory on the heap and each object's address is stored on the stack. This process continues until the memory reaches its maximum limit. Then the GC comes into play and starts reclaiming memory by removing the unused managed objects and allocating new objects. This is all done automatically by the GC, but there is also a way to invoke the GC to perform garbage collection by calling the `GC.Collect` method

Let's take an example where we have a `Car` object called `c` in the `Main` method. When the function is executed, the `Car` object will be allocated by the CLR into the heap memory and the reference to that `c` object will be stored in the stack address pointing to the `Car` object on the heap. When the garbage collector runs, it reclaims the memory from the heap and removes the reference from the stack:

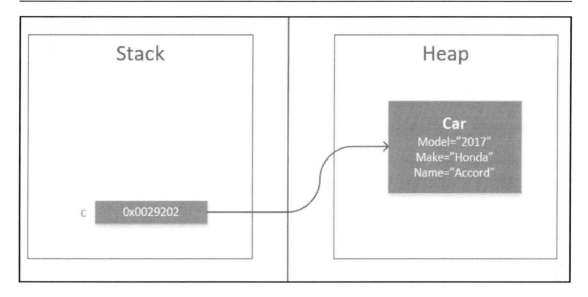

Some important points to note are that the garbage collection is done automatically by the GC on managed objects, and that if there are any unmanaged objects, such as database connections, I/O operations, and so on, they need to be garbage collected explicitly. Otherwise, GC works efficiently on managed objects and ensures that the application will not experience any decrease in performance when the GC is performed.

Generations in GC

There are three kinds of generation in garbage collection known as **Generation 0**, **Generation 1**, and **Generation 2**. In this section, we will look at the concept of generations and how it affects the performance of the garbage collector.

Let's suppose we run an application that creates three objects named **Object1**, **Object2**, and **Object3**. These objects will allocate the memory in **Generation 0**:

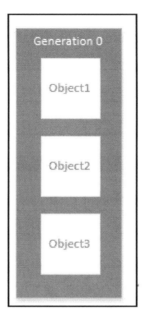

Now, when the garbage collector runs (this is an automatic process, unless you explicitly call the garbage collector from the code), it checks for the objects that are not needed by the application and have no reference in the program. It will simply remove those objects. For example, if the scope of **Object1** is not referenced anywhere, the memory for this object will be reclaimed. However, the other two objects, **Object1** and **Object2**, are still referenced in the program, and will be moved to **Generation 1**.

Now, let's suppose two more objects, called **Object4** and **Object5,** are created. We will store them in the **Generation 0** slot, as shown in the following diagram:

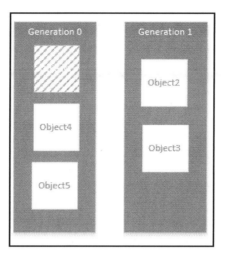

When garbage collection runs the second time, it will find two objects called **Object4** and **Object5** in **Generation 0** and two objects called **Object2** and **Object3** in **Generation 1**. Garbage collector will first check the reference of those objects in **Generation 0** and, if they are not used by the application, they will be removed. The same goes for the **Generation 1** objects. For example, if **Object3** is still referenced, it will be moved to **Generation 2** and **Object2** will be removed from **Generation 1**, as shown in the following diagram:

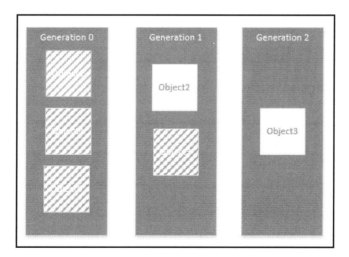

This concept of generations actually optimizes the performance of GC, and the objects stored in **Generation 2** are more likely to be stored for a longer period. GC performs fewer visits and gains time instead of checking each object again and again. The same goes for **Generation 1**, which is also less likely to reclaim the space than **Generation 0**.

.NET Native and JIT compilation

JIT compilation is done mostly at runtime, and it converts the MSIL code to the native machine code. This is when the code is run the first time, and it takes a little bit more time than its successive runs. In .NET Core today, we are developing applications for mobile and handheld devices that have limited resources in terms of CPU power and memory. Currently, the **Universal Windows Platform** (**UWP**) and the Xamarin platform run on .NET Core. With these platforms, .NET Core automatically generates that native assembly at compilation time or while generating the platform-specific packages. Though it does not require the JIT compilation process to be done at runtime, this eventually increases the performance of the application's boot-up time. This native compilation is done through a component known as .NET Native.

.NET Native begins the compilation process after the language-specific compiler finishes up the compilation process that is done at build time. The .NET Native toolchain reads the MSIL generated from the language compiler and performs the following operations:

- It eliminates the metadata from the MSIL.
- It replaces the code that relies on reflection and metadata with the static native code when comparing field values.
- It checks the code that is invoked by the application and includes only that in the final assembly.
- It replaces the full CLR with a refactored runtime that contains the garbage collector and no JIT compiler. The refactored runtime goes with the app and is contained in the assembly named `mrt100_app.dll`.

Utilizing multiple cores of the CPU for high performance

These days, the nature of applications focuses more on connectivity, and there are cases where their operations take more time to execute. We also know that nowadays, all computers come with a multi-core processor, and using these cores effectively increases the performance of the application. Operations such as network/IO have latency issues, and the synchronous execution of the application program may often lead to a long waiting time. If the long-running tasks are executed in a separate thread or in an asynchronous manner, the resulting operation will take less time and increase responsiveness. Another benefit is performance that actually utilizes multiple cores of the processor and executes the task simultaneously. In the .NET world, we can achieve responsiveness and performance by splitting the tasks into multiple threads and using classic multithreading programming APIs, or a more simplified and advanced model known as the **task programming library** (**TPL**). The TPL is now supported in .NET Core 2.0, and we will soon explore how it can be used to execute tasks on multiple cores.

The TPL programming model is based on the task. A task is a unit of work—an object's representation of an ongoing operation.

A simple task can be created by writing the following lines of code:

```
static void Main(string[] args)
{
  Task t = new Task(execute);
  t.Start();
  t.Wait();
}

private static void Execute() {
  for (int i = 0; i < 100; i++)
  {
    Console.WriteLine(i);
  }
}
```

In the preceding code, the task can be initialized using a `Task` object, where `Execute` is the computational method that is executed when the `Start` method is called. The `Start` method tells the .NET Core that the task can start and returns immediately. It forks the program execution into two threads that run concurrently. The first thread is the actual application thread and the second one is the one that executes the `execute` method. We have used the `t.Wait` method to wait for the worker task to show the result on the console. Otherwise, once the program exits the block of code under the `Main` method, the application ends.

The goal of parallel programming is to effectively use multiple cores. For example, we are running the preceding code in a single-core processor. These two threads will run and share the same processor. However, if the same program can run on a multi-core processor, it can run on multiple cores by utilizing each core separately, increasing the performance and achieving true parallelism:

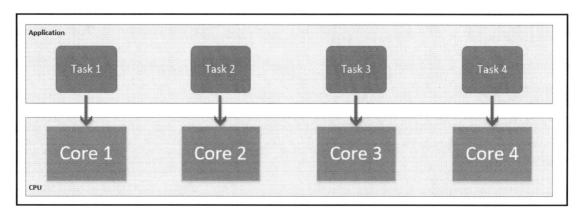

Unlike TPL, the classic `Thread` object doesn't guarantee that your thread will be running on distinct cores of the CPU. With TPL, however, it guarantees that each thread will run on the distinct thread unless it reaches the number of tasks as per the CPU and shares the cores.

To learn more about what TPL provides, please refer to
`https://docs.microsoft.com/en-us/dotnet/standard/parallel-programming/task-parallel-library-tpl`.

How releasing builds increases performance

Release and debug builds are two build modes provided in .NET applications. Debug mode is mostly used when we are in the process of writing code or troubleshooting errors, whereas release build mode is often used while packaging the application to deploy on production servers. When developing the deployment package, developers often miss updating the build mode to the release build, and then they face performance issues when the application is deployed:

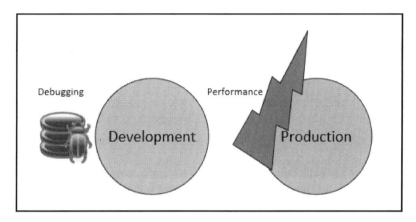

The following table shows some differences between the debug and release modes:

Debug	Release
No optimization of code is done by the compiler	Code is optimized and minified in size when built using release mode
Stack trace is captured and thrown at the time of exception	No stack trace is captured
The debug symbols are stored	All code and debug symbols under #debug directives are removed
More memory is used by the source code at runtime	Less memory is used by the source code at runtime

Benchmarking .NET Core 2.0 applications

Benchmarking applications is the process of evaluating and comparing artifacts with the agreed upon standards. To benchmark .NET Core 2.0 application code, we can use the BenchmarkDotNet tool, which provides a very simple API to evaluate the performance of code in your application. Usually, benchmarking at the micro-level, such as with classes and methods, is not an easy task, and requires quite an effort to measure the performance, whereas BenchmarkDotNet does all the low-level plumbing and the complex work associated with benchmark solutions.

Exploring BenchmarkDotNet

In this section, we will explore BenchmarkDotNet and learn how effectively it can be used to measure application performance.

It can simply be installed using a NuGet package manager console window or through the Project References section of your project. To install BenchmarkDotNet, execute the following command:

```
Install-Package BenchmarkDotNet
```

The preceding command adds a BenchmarkDotNet package from NuGet.org.

To test the BenchmarkDotNet tool, we will create a simple class that contains two methods to generate a Fibonacci series for a sequence of 10 numbers. The Fibonacci series can be implemented in multiple ways, which is why we are using it to measure which code snippet is faster and more performance efficient.

Here is the first method that generates the Fibonacci sequence iteratively:

```
public class TestBenchmark
{
  int len= 10;
  [Benchmark]
  public  void Fibonacci()
  {
    int a = 0, b = 1, c = 0;
    Console.Write("{0} {1}", a, b);

    for (int i = 2; i < len; i++)
    {
      c = a + b;
      Console.Write(" {0}", c);
      a = b;
```

```
      b = c;
    }
  }
}
```

Here is another method that uses the recursive approach to generate the Fibonacci series:

```
[Benchmark]
public  void FibonacciRecursive()
{
  int len= 10;
  Fibonacci_Recursive(0, 1, 1, len);
}

private void Fibonacci_Recursive(int a, int b, int counter, int len)
{
  if (counter <= len)
  {
    Console.Write("{0} ", a);
    Fibonacci_Recursive(b, a + b, counter + 1, len);
  }
}
```

Note that both of the main methods of the Fibonacci series contain a Benchmark attribute. This actually tells the BenchmarkRunner to measure methods that contain this attribute. Finally, we can call the BenchmarkRunner from the main entry point of the application that measures the performance and generates a report, as shown in the following code:

```
static void Main(string[] args)
{
  BenchmarkRunner.Run<TestBenchmark>();
  Console.Read();
}
```

Once the benchmark is run, we will get the report as follows:

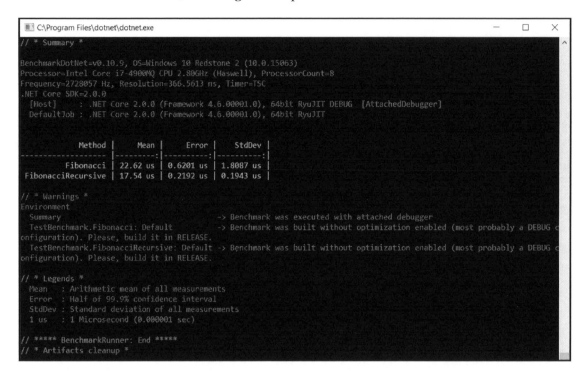

As well as this, it also generates files in the root folder of an application that runs the `BenchmarkRunner`. Here is the .html file that contains the information about the version of `BenchmarkDotNet` and the OS, the processor, frequency, resolution, and timer details, the .NET version (in our case, .NET Core SDK 2.0.0), host, and so on:

```
BenchmarkDotNet=v0.10.9, OS=Windows 10 Redstone 2 (10.0.15063)
Processor=Intel Core i7-4900MQ CPU 2.80GHz (Haswell), ProcessorCount=8
Frequency=2728057 Hz, Resolution=366.5613 ns, Timer=TSC
.NET Core SDK=2.0.0
  [Host]    : .NET Core 2.0.0 (Framework 4.6.00001.0), 64bit RyuJIT DEBUG  [AttachedDebugger]
  DefaultJob : .NET Core 2.0.0 (Framework 4.6.00001.0), 64bit RyuJIT
```

Method	Mean	Error	StdDev
Fibonacci	22.62 us	0.6201 us	1.8087 us
FibonacciRecursive	17.54 us	0.2192 us	0.1943 us

The table contains four columns. However, we can add more columns, which are optional by default. We can also add custom columns as well. The **Method** is the name of the method that contains the benchmark attribute, the **Mean** is the average time it takes for all the measurements to be taken (where **us** is microseconds), **Error** is the time taken to process errors, and **StdDev** is the standard deviation of the measurements.

After comparing both the methods, the `FibonacciRecursive` method is more efficient as the **Mean**, **Error**, and **StdDev** values are smaller than the `Fibonacci` method.

Other than the HTML, two more files are created, a **Comma Separated Value (CSV)** file and a **Markdown Documentation (MD)** file which contains the same information.

How it works

Benchmark generates a project at runtime for each benchmark method and builds it in release mode. It tries multiple combinations to measure the method's performance by launching that method multiple times. Once the multiple cycles are run, the report is generated, containing files and information about Benchmark.

Setting parameters

In the previous example, we tested the method with only one value. Practically, when testing an enterprise application, we want to test it with different values to estimate the method's performance.

First of all, we can define a property for each parameter, set the `Params` attribute, and specify the value(s) for which we need that method to be tested. Then we can use that property in the code. `BenchmarkRun` automatically tests that method with all of the parameters and generates the report. Here is the complete code snippet of the `TestBenchmark` class:

```
public class TestBenchmark
{

  [Params(10,20,30)]
  public int Len { get; set; }
  [Benchmark]
  public  void Fibonacci()
  {
    int a = 0, b = 1, c = 0;
    Console.Write("{0} {1}", a, b);
```

```
    for (int i = 2; i < Len; i++)
    {
      c = a + b;
      Console.Write(" {0}", c);
      a = b;
      b = c;
    }
  }


  [Benchmark]
  public  void FibonacciRecursive()
  {
    Fibonacci_Recursive(0, 1, 1, Len);
  }


  private void Fibonacci_Recursive(int a,  int b,  int counter,  int len)
  {
    if (counter <= len)
    {
      Console.Write("{0} ", a);
      Fibonacci_Recursive(b, a + b, counter + 1, len);
    }
  }
}
```

After running Benchmark, the following report is generated:

```
BenchmarkDotNet=v0.10.9, OS=Windows 10 Redstone 2 (10.0.15063)
Processor=Intel Core i7-4900MQ CPU 2.80GHz (Haswell), ProcessorCount=8
Frequency=2728057 Hz, Resolution=366.5613 ns, Timer=TSC
.NET Core SDK=2.0.0
  [Host]    : .NET Core 2.0.0 (Framework 4.6.00001.0), 64bit RyuJIT DEBUG
  DefaultJob : .NET Core 2.0.0 (Framework 4.6.00001.0), 64bit RyuJIT
```

Method	Len	Mean	Error	StdDev
Fibonacci	10	16.35 us	0.3267 us	0.3889 us
FibonacciRecursive	10	17.69 us	0.2207 us	0.2064 us
Fibonacci	20	36.52 us	0.6865 us	0.6742 us
FibonacciRecursive	20	38.50 us	0.7291 us	0.7488 us
Fibonacci	30	59.66 us	0.8321 us	0.7377 us
FibonacciRecursive	30	65.35 us	1.2867 us	1.1406 us

Memory diagnostics using BenchmarkDotnet

With `BenchmarkDotnet`, we can also diagnose any problems with the memory and measure the number of allocated bytes and garbage collection.

It can be implemented using a `MemoryDiagnoser` attribute at the class level. To start, let's just add the `MemoryDiagnoser` attribute to the `TestBenchmark` class that we created in the last example:

```
[MemoryDiagnoser]
public class TestBenchmark {}
```

Rerun the application. Now it will collect other memory allocation and garbage collection information and generate logs accordingly:

```
BenchmarkDotNet=v0.10.9, OS=Windows 10 Redstone 2 (10.0.15063)
Processor=Intel Core i7-4900MQ CPU 2.80GHz (Haswell), ProcessorCount=8
Frequency=2728057 Hz, Resolution=366.5613 ns, Timer=TSC
.NET Core SDK=2.0.0
  [Host]     : .NET Core 2.0.0 (Framework 4.6.00001.0), 64bit RyuJIT DEBUG
  DefaultJob : .NET Core 2.0.0 (Framework 4.6.00001.0), 64bit RyuJIT
```

Method	Len	Mean	Error	StdDev	Median	Gen 0	Gen 1	Allocated
Fibonacci	10	16.50 us	0.3281 us	0.7604 us	16.37 us	0.1984	-	848 B
FibonacciRecursive	10	25.46 us	3.2510 us	9.3799 us	20.97 us	0.1984	-	880 B
Fibonacci	20	62.13 us	3.8042 us	10.8537 us	62.22 us	0.4272	0.0012	1816 B
FibonacciRecursive	20	81.60 us	15.0942 us	44.5056 us	63.55 us	0.4272	-	1848 B
Fibonacci	30	99.37 us	9.4387 us	27.3834 us	97.40 us	0.6714	-	2856 B
FibonacciRecursive	30	103.11 us	7.1130 us	20.1784 us	103.42 us	0.6714	-	2888 B

In the preceding table, the **Gen 0** and **Gen 1** columns each contain the number of that particular generation per 1,000 operations. If the value is 1, then it means that the garbage collection was done after 1,000 operations. However, note that in the first row, the value is *0.1984*, which means that the garbage collection was done after *198.4* seconds, whereas for **Gen 1** of that row, no garbage collection took place. **Allocated** represents the size of the memory that is allocated while invoking that method. It does not include the Stackalloc/heap native allocations.

Adding configurations

Benchmark configuration can be defined by creating a custom class and inheriting it from the `ManualConfig` class. Here is an example of the `TestBenchmark` class that we created earlier containing some benchmark methods:

```
[Config(typeof(Config))]
public class TestBenchmark
{
  private class Config : ManualConfig
  {
    // We will benchmark ONLY method with names with names (which
    // contains "A" OR "1") AND (have length < 3)
    public Config()
    {
      Add(new DisjunctionFilter(
        new NameFilter(name => name.Contains("Recursive"))
      ));
    }
  }

  [Params(10,20,30)]
  public int Len { get; set; }
  [Benchmark]
  public  void Fibonacci()
  {
    int a = 0, b = 1, c = 0;
    Console.Write("{0} {1}", a, b);

    for (int i = 2; i < Len; i++)
    {
      c = a + b;
      Console.Write(" {0}", c);
      a = b;
      b = c;
    }
  }

  [Benchmark]
  public  void FibonacciRecursive()
  {
    Fibonacci_Recursive(0, 1, 1, Len);
  }

  private void Fibonacci_Recursive(int a, int b, int counter, int len)
  {
    if (counter <= len)
```

```
    {
      Console.Write("{0} ", a);
      Fibonacci_Recursive(b, a + b, counter + 1, len);
    }
  }
}
```

In the preceding code, we defined the `Config` class that inherits the `ManualConfig` class provided in the benchmark framework. Rules can be defined inside the `Config` constructor. In the preceding example, there is a rule that stipulates that only those benchmark methods that contain `Recursive` should be executed. In our case, we have only one method, `FibonacciRecursive`, that will be executed and whose performance we will measure.

Another way of doing this is through the fluent API, where we can skip creating a `Config` class and implement the following:

```
static void Main(string[] args)
{
  var config = ManualConfig.Create(DefaultConfig.Instance);
  config.Add(new DisjunctionFilter(new NameFilter(
    name => name.Contains("Recursive"))));
  BenchmarkRunner.Run<TestBenchmark>(config);
}
```

To learn more about `BenchmarkDotNet`, refer to `http://benchmarkdotnet.org/Configs.htm`.

Summary

In this chapter, we have learned about the core concepts of .NET Core, including the compilation process, garbage collection, how to develop high-performant .NET Core applications by utilizing multiple cores of the CPU, and publishing an application using a release build. We have also explored the benchmarking tool, which is highly used for code optimization, and provides results specific to class objects.

15
Data Structures and Writing Optimized Code in C#

Data structures are a particular way of storing data in software engineering. They play a vital role in storing data in a computer so that it can be accessed and modified efficiently, and they provide different storing mechanisms for storing different types of data. There are many types of data structure, and each one is designed to store a definite type of data. In this chapter, we will cover data structures in detail and learn which data structures should be used for particular scenarios in order to improve the performance of the system as regards data storage and retrieval. We will also learn how we can write optimized code in C# and what primary factors can affect performance, which is sometimes overlooked by developers when coding programs. We will learn some best practices that can be used to optimize code that is performance effective.

In this chapter, we will cover the following topics:

- What data structures are and their characteristics
- Choosing the right data structure for performance optimizations
- Understand the use of Big O notation to measure the performance and complexity of a program
- Best practices when writing code in .NET Core

What are data structures?

A data structure is a way of storing and unifying data in such a way that operations on that data can be performed in an efficient manner. The data can be stored in several ways. For example, we can have a `Person` object that contains a few properties, such as `PersonID` and `PersonName`, where `PersonID` is of the integer type and `PersonName` is of the *string* type. This `Person` object stores the data in memory, and can be further used to save that record in the database. Another example is an array called `Countries` of the `string` type that contains a list of countries. We can use the `Countries` array to retrieve a country name and use it in a program. Therefore, any type of object that stores data is called a data structure. All primitive types, such as integers, strings, chars, and Booleans, are different types of data structure, whereas other collection types, such as `LinkedList`, `ArrayList`, `SortedList`, and others, are also types of data structure that can store information in exclusive ways.

The following diagram illustrates the types of data structures and their relationship to each other:

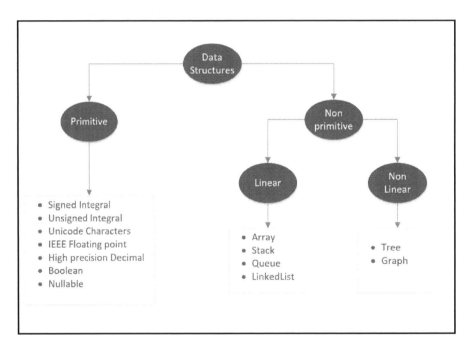

There are two types of data structure: *primitive* and *nonprimitive* types. Primitive types are value types that include *signed integral, unsigned integral, unicode characters, IEEE floating point, high-precision decimal, Boolean, enum, struct* and *nullable* value types.

Here is a list of the primitive data types available in C#:

Primitive types	
Signed integral	`sbyte, short, int, long`
Unsigned integral	`byte, ushort, uint, ulong`
Unicode characters	`Char`
IEEE floating point	`float, double`
High-precision decimal	`Decimal`
Boolean	`Bool`
String	`String`
Object	`System.Object`

Nonprimitive types are user-defined types, and further categorized as linear or nonlinear types. In a linear data structure, the elements are organized in a sequence, such as in *Array*, *Linked List*, and other related types, whereas in a nonlinear data structure, the elements are stored without any sequence, such as in *trees* and *graphs*.

The following table shows the types of linear and nonlinear classes available in .NET Core:

Nonprimitive types - linear data structures	
Array	`ArrayList, String[], primitive typed arrays, List, Dictionary, Hashtable, BitArray`
Stack	`Stack<T>, SortedSet<T>, SynchronizedCollection<T>`
Queue	`Queue<T>`
Linked list	`LinkedList<T>`

.NET Core does not provide any nonprimitive, nonlinear types to represent data in tree or graph formats. However, we can develop custom classes to support these kinds of types.

For example, here is the code to write a custom tree that stores data in the tree format:

```
class TreeNode
{
  public TreeNode(string text, object tag)
  {
    this.NodeText = text;
    this.Tag = tag;
    Nodes = new List<TreeNode>();
  }
  public string NodeText { get; set; }
  public Object Tag { get; set; }
  public List<TreeNode> Nodes { get; set; }
}
```

Finally, we can write a program to populate a tree view on the console window as follows:

```
static void Main(string[] args)
{
  TreeNode node = new TreeNode("Root", null);
  node.Nodes.Add(new TreeNode("Child 1", null));
  node.Nodes[0].Nodes.Add(new TreeNode("Grand Child 1", null));
  node.Nodes.Add(new TreeNode("Child 1 (Sibling)", null));
  PopulateTreeView(node, "");
  Console.Read();
}

//Populates a Tree View on Console
static void PopulateTreeView(TreeNode node, string space)
{
  Console.WriteLine(space + node.NodeText);
  space = space + " ";
  foreach(var treenode in node.Nodes)
  {
    //Recurive call
    PopulateTreeView(treenode, space);
  }
}
```

When you run the preceding program, it generates the following output:

```
Root
  Child 1
    Grand Child 1
  Child 1 (Sibling)
```

Understanding the use of Big O notation to measure the performance and complexity of an algorithm

Big O notation is used to define the complexity and performance of an algorithm with respect to time or space consumed during execution. It is an essential technique to express the performance of an algorithm and determine the worst-case complexity of the program.

To understand it in detail, let's go through some code examples and use Big O notation to calculate their performance.

If we calculate the complexity of the following program, the Big O notation will be equal to *O(1)*:

```
static int SumNumbers(int a, int b)
{
  return a + b;
}
```

This is because, however the parameter is specified, it is just adding and returning it.

Let's consider another program that loops through the list. The Big O notation will be determined as *O(N)*:

```
static bool FindItem(List<string> items, string value)
{
  foreach(var item in items)
  {
    if (item == value)
    {
      return true;
    }
  }
```

```
      return false;
   }
```

In the preceding example, the program is looping through the item list and comparing the value passed as a parameter with each item in the list. If the item is found, the program returns `true`.

The complexity is determined as *O(N)* because the worst-case scenario could be a loop towards *N* items where *N* could be either a first index or any index until it reaches the last index, which is *N*.

Now, let's look at an example of the *selection sort*, which is defined as *O(N2)*:

```
static void SelectionSort(int[] nums)
{
   int i, j, min;

   // One by one move boundary of unsorted subarray
   for (i = 0; i <nums.Length-1; i++)
   {
      min = i;
      for (j = i + 1; j < nums.Length; j++)
      if (nums[j] < nums[min])
      min = j;

      // Swap the found minimum element with the first element
      int temp = nums[min];
      nums[min] = nums[i];
      nums[i] = temp;
   }
}
```

In the preceding example, we have two loops that are nested. The first loop traverses from 0 to the last index, whereas the second loop traverses from the next item to the penultimate item and swaps the values to sort the array in ascending order. The number of nested loops is directly proportional to the power of *N*, hence the Big O notation is defined as *O(N2)*.

Next, let's consider a recursive function where the Big O notation is defined as *O(2N)*, where *2N* determines the time taken, which doubles with each additional element in the input dataset that runs for an exponential period of time. Here is an example of a `Fibonacci_Recursive` method that recursively calls the method until the counter becomes equal to the maximum number:

```
static void Main(string[] args){
   Fibonacci_Recursive(0, 1, 1, 10);
}
```

```
static void Fibonacci_Recursive(int a, int b, int counter, int maxNo)
{
   if (counter <= maxNo)
   {
      Console.Write("{0} ", a);
      Fibonacci_Recursive(b, a + b, counter + 1, len);
   }
}
```

Logarithms

A logarithm operation is the complete opposite of an exponential operation. The logarithm is a quantity representing the power to which a base number must be raised to produce a given number.

For example, *2x = 32*, where *x=5*, can be represented as *log2 32 =5*.

In this case, the logarithm of above expression is 5 that represents the power of a fixed number 2 which is raised to produce a given number 32.

Consider a binary search algorithm that works more effectively by splitting the list of an item into two datasets and uses a specific dataset based on the number. For example, say that I have a list of different numbers sorted in ascending order:

{1, 5, 6, 10, 15, 17, 20, 42, 55, 60, 67, 80, 100}

Say that we want to find number *55*. One way to do this is to loop through each index and check each item one by one. The more effective way is to split the list into two sets and check whether the number I am looking for is greater than the last item of the first dataset or to use the second dataset.

Here is an example of a binary search whose Big O notation will be determined as *O(LogN)*:

```
static int binarySearch(int[] nums, int startingIndex, int length, int
itemToSearch)
{
   if (length >= startingIndex)
   {
      int mid = startingIndex + (length - startingIndex) / 2;

      // If the element found at the middle itself
      if (nums[mid] == itemToSearch)
      return mid;

      // If the element is smaller than mid then it is
```

```
        // present in left set of array
        if (nums[mid] > itemToSearch)
        return binarySearch(nums, startingIndex, mid - 1, itemToSearch);

        // Else the element is present in right set of array
        return binarySearch(nums, mid + 1, length, itemToSearch);
    }

    // If item not found return 1
    return -1;
}
```

Choosing the right data structure for performance optimization

A data structure is a precise way of organizing data in a computer program. If data is not efficiently stored in the right data structure, it may lead to some performance issues that impact the overall experience of the application.

In this section, we will learn the advantages and disadvantages of the different collection types available in .NET Core and which ones are the better types for particular scenarios:

- Arrays and lists
- Stacks and queues
- LinkedLists (single, double, and circular)
- Dictionaries, hashtables, and hashsets
- Generic lists

Arrays

An array is a collection that holds similar types of elements. Arrays of both value types and reference types can be created.

Here are few circumstances where arrays are useful:

- If the data is of a fixed, set length, using an array is a better option as it is faster than other collections, such as `arraylists` and generic lists
- Arrays are good to represent data in a multidimensional way

- They take less memory compared to other collections
- With arrays, we can iterate through elements sequentially

The following table shows the Big O notation for each operation that can be performed in an array:

Operations	Big O notation
Access by Index	O(1)
Search	O(n)
Insert at the end	O(n)
Remove at the end	O(n)
Insert at a position before the last element	O(n)
Remove an element at an index	O(1)

As shown in the preceding table, the search for and insertion of an item in a specific position degrades performance, whereas accessing any item in an index or removing it from any position has a lower impact on performance.

Lists

Lists are extensively used by .NET developers. Although it is preferable to use it in many scenarios, there are some performance limitations, too.

Using lists is mostly advisable when you want to access the item using its index. Unlike a linked list, where you have to iterate over each node using an enumerator to search for the item, with a list, we can easily access it using an index.

Here are few recommendations where lists are useful:

- It is recommended that you use list when the collection size is not known. Resizing arrays is an expensive operation, and with lists we can easily grow the size of the collection by just adding to it as needed.
- Unlike arrays, lists do not reserve the total memory address space for the number of items when it is created. This is because, with lists, specifying the size of the collection is not needed. On the other hand, arrays depend on the type and the size at which it is initialized, and reserve the address space during initialization.

- With lists, we can use lambda expressions to filter out records, sort items in descending order, and execute other operations. Arrays do not provide sorting, filtering, or other such operations.
- Lists represent a single dimension collection.

The following table shows the Big O notation for each operation that can be performed on lists:

Operations	Big O notation
Access by index	O(1)
Search	O(n)
Insert at the end	O(1)
Remove from the end	O(1)
Insert at a position before the last element	O(n)
Remove an element at an index	O(n)

Stacks

Stacks maintain a collection of items in **Last In First Out** (**LIFO**) order. The last item to be inserted is retrieved first. Only two operations are allowed on stacks, namely push and pop. The real application of a stack is an undo operation that inserts the changes into the stack and, on undoing, removes the last action that was performed:

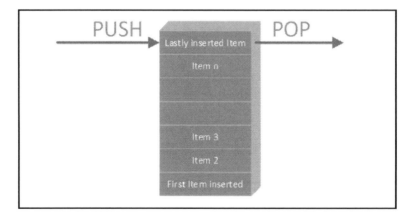

The preceding diagram illustrates how the items are added to the stack. The last inserted item pops out first, and to access the first item that was inserted, we have to pop out each element until it reaches the first one.

Here are a few of the circumstance where stacks are useful:

- Scenarios where the item should be removed when its value is accessed
- Where an undo operation needs to be implemented in a program
- To maintain navigation history on a web application
- Recursive operations

The following table shows the Big O notation for each operation that can be performed on stacks:

Operations	Big O notation
Access to the first object	O(1)
Search	O(n)
Push item	O(1)
Pop item	O(1)

Queue

Queues maintain a collection of items in a **First In First Out (FIFO)** order. The item inserted into the queue first is retrieved first from the queue. Only three operations are allowed in queues, namely Enqueue, Dequeue, and Peek.

Enqueue adds an element to the end of the queue, whereas Dequeue removes the element from the start of the queue. Peek returns the oldest elements in the queue but does not remove them:

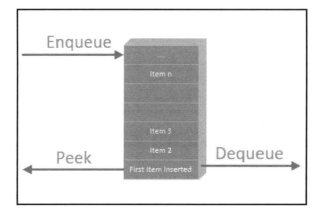

The preceding diagram illustrates how items are added to the queue. The item inserted first will be removed first from the queue and the pointer moves to the next item in the queue. Peek always returns the first item that was inserted or the item to which the pointer is set, based on whether the first item is removed.

Here are some of the circumstances where queues are useful:

- To process items in a sequence
- To serve an order based on a first-come-first-served basis

The following table shows the Big O notation for each operation that can be performed on queues:

Operations	Big O notation
Access to the first object inserted	O(1)
Search	O(n)
Queue item	O(1)
Enqueue item	O(1)
Peek item	O(1)

Linked lists

The linked list is a linear data structure where each node in the list contains the reference pointer to the next node, and the last node has a reference to null. The first node is known as the head. There are three types of linked list, known as *singly*, *doubly*, and *circular* linked lists.

Singly linked lists

Singly linked lists contain only the reference to the next node. The following diagram represents the singly linked list:

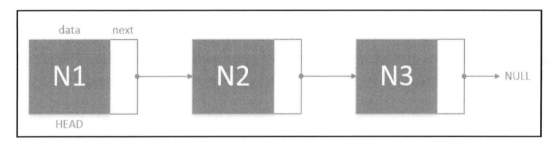

Doubly linked lists

In doubly linked lists, the nodes contain the references of both the next node and the previous node. The user can iterate forward and backward using reference pointers. The following image is a representation of a doubly linked list:

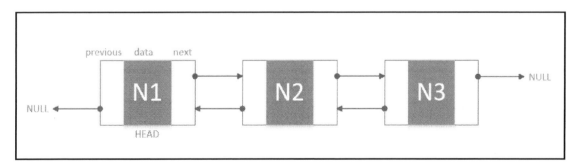

Circular linked lists

In circular linked lists, the last node points back to the first node. Here is a representation of a circular linked list:

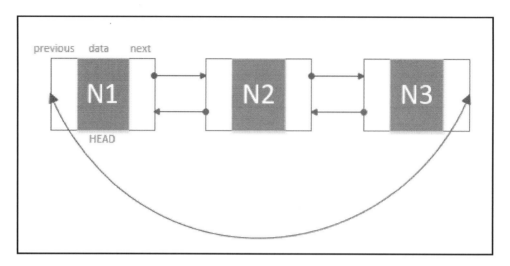

Here are a few circumstances where a linked list is useful:

- To provide access to an item in a sequential manner
- Insert an item in any position of the list
- Remove any item at any point or node
- When you need to consume less memory, as there is no array copy in the linked list

The following table shows the Big O notation value for each operation that can be performed on linked lists:

Operations	Big O notation
Access the item	*O(1)*
Search for the item	*O(n)*
Insert item	*O(1)*
Delete item	*O(1)*

Dictionaries, hashtables, and hashsets

Dictionary, hashtable, and hashset objects store items in key—value format. However, hashsets and dictionaries are good for scenarios where performance is key. Here are a few circumstances where these types are useful:

- To store an item in key–value format that can be retrieved based on a particular key
- To store unique values

The following table shows the Big O notation value for each operation that can be performed on these objects:

Operations	Big O notation
Access	*O(n)*
Search for the value if the key is not known	*O(n)*
Insert item	*O(n)*
Delete item	*O(n)*

Generic lists

The generic list is a strongly typed list of elements that is accessed using an index. In contrast to arrays, generic lists are expandable, and the list can grow dynamically; for this reason, they are known as dynamics arrays or vectors. Unlike arrays, generic lists are one dimensional, and are one of the best options for manipulating an in-memory collection of elements.

We can define a generic list as shown in the following code example. The code phrase `lstNumbers` allows only integer values to be stored, the phrase `lstNames` stores the `only` string, `personLst` stores `Person` objects, and so on:

```
List<int> lstNumbers = new List<int>();
List<string> lstNames = new List<string>();
List<Person> personLst = new List<Person>();
HashSet<int> hashInt = new HashSet<int>();
```

The following table shows the Big O notation value for each operation that can be performed on these objects:

Operations	Big O notation
Access by index	O(1)
Search	O(n)
Insert at the end	O(1)
Remove from the end	O(1)
Insert at a position before the last element	O(n)
Remove an element at an index	O(n)

Best practices in writing optimized code in C#

There are many factors that negatively impact the performance of a .NET Core application. Sometimes these are minor things that were not considered earlier at the time of writing the code, and are not addressed by the accepted best practices. As a result, to solve these problems, programmers often resort to ad hoc solutions. However, when bad practices are combined together, they produce performance issues. It is always better to know the best practices that help developers write cleaner code and make the application performant.

In this section, we will learn, the following topics:

- Boxing and unboxing overhead
- String concatenation
- Exceptions handling
- `for` **versus** `foreach`
- Delegates

Boxing and unboxing overhead

The boxing and unboxing methods are not always good to use and they negatively impact the performance of mission-critical applications. Boxing is a method of converting a value type to an object type, and is done implicitly, whereas unboxing is a method of converting an object type back to a value type and requires explicit casting.

Let's go through an example where we have two methods executing a loop of 10 million records, and in each iteration, they are incrementing the counter by 1. The AvoidBoxingUnboxing method is using a primitive integer to initialize and increment it on each iteration, whereas the BoxingUnboxing method is boxing by assigning the numeric value to the object type first and then unboxing it on each iteration to convert it back to the integer type, as shown in the following code:

```
private static void AvoidBoxingUnboxing()
{

  Stopwatch watch = new Stopwatch();
  watch.Start();
  //Boxing
  int counter = 0;
  for (int i = 0; i < 1000000; i++)
  {
    //Unboxing
    counter = i + 1;
  }
  watch.Stop();
  Console.WriteLine($"Time taken {watch.ElapsedMilliseconds}");
}

private static void BoxingUnboxing()
{

  Stopwatch watch = new Stopwatch();
  watch.Start();
  //Boxing
  object counter = 0;
  for (int i = 0; i < 1000000; i++)
  {
    //Unboxing
    counter = (int)i + 1;
  }
  watch.Stop();
  Console.WriteLine($"Time taken {watch.ElapsedMilliseconds}");
}
```

When we run both methods, we will clearly see the differences in performance. The `BoxingUnboxing` is executed seven times slower than the `AvoidBoxingUnboxing` method, as shown in the following screenshot:

For mission-critical applications, it's always better to avoid boxing and unboxing. However, in .NET Core, we have many other types that internally use objects and perform boxing and unboxing. Most of the types under `System.Collections` and `System.Collections.Specialized` use objects and object arrays for internal storage, and when we store primitive types in these collections, they perform boxing and convert each primitive value to an object type, adding extra overhead and negatively impacting the performance of the application. Other types of `System.Data`, namely `DateSet`, `DataTable`, and `DataRow`, also use object arrays under the hood.

Types under the `System.Collections.Generic` namespace or typed arrays are the best approaches to use when performance is the primary concern. For example, `HashSet<T>`, `LinkedList<T>`, and `List<T>` are all types of generic collections.

For example, here is a program that stores the integer value in `ArrayList`:

```
private static void AddValuesInArrayList()
{

  Stopwatch watch = new Stopwatch();
  watch.Start();
  ArrayList arr = new ArrayList();
  for (int i = 0; i < 1000000; i++)
  {
    arr.Add(i);
  }
  watch.Stop();
  Console.WriteLine($"Total time taken is
  {watch.ElapsedMilliseconds}");
}
```

Let's write another program that uses a generic list of the integer type:

```
private static void AddValuesInGenericList()
{

  Stopwatch watch = new Stopwatch();
  watch.Start();
  List<int> lst = new List<int>();
  for (int i = 0; i < 1000000; i++)
  {
    lst.Add(i);
  }
  watch.Stop();
  Console.WriteLine($"Total time taken is
  {watch.ElapsedMilliseconds}");
}
```

When running both programs, the differences are pretty noticeable. The code with the generic list `List<int>` is over 10 times faster than the code with `ArrayList`. The result is as follows:

```
Total time taken with ArrayList is 63
Total time taken with List<int> is 6
```

String concatenation

In .NET, strings are immutable objects. Two strings refer to the same memory on the heap until the string value is changed. If any of the string is changed, a new string is created on the heap and is allocated a new memory space. Immutable objects are generally thread safe and eliminate the race conditions between multiple threads. Any change in the string value creates and allocates a new object in memory and avoids producing conflicting scenarios with multiple threads.

For example, let's initialize the string and assign the `Hello World` value to the a string variable:

```
String a = "Hello World";
```

Now, let's assign the a string variable to another variable, b:

```
String b = a;
```

Both a and b point to the same value on the heap, as shown in the following diagram:

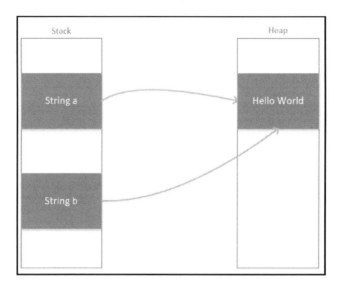

Now, suppose we change the value of b to Hope this helps:

```
b= "Hope this helps";
```

This will create another object on the heap, where a points to the same and b refers to the new memory space that contains the new text:

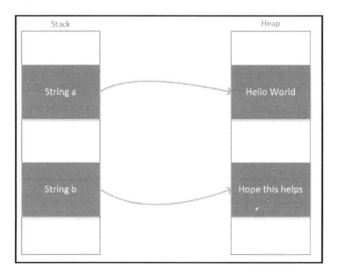

With each change in the string, the object allocates a new memory space. In some cases, it may be an overkill scenario, where the frequency of string modification is higher and each modification is allocated a separate memory space, creates work for the garbage collector in collecting the unused objects and freeing up space. In such a scenario, it is highly recommended that you use the `StringBuilder` class.

Exception handling

Improper handling of exceptions also decreases the performance of an application. The following list contains some of the best practices in dealing with exceptions in .NET Core:

- Always use a specific exception type or a type that can catch the exception for the code you have written in the method. Using the `Exception` type for all cases is not a good practice.
- It is always a good practice to use `try`, `catch`, and finally `block` where the code can throw exceptions. The final block is usually used to clean up the resources, and returns a proper response that the calling code is expecting.
- In deeply nested code, don't use `try catch` block and handle it to the calling method or main method. Catching exceptions on multiple stacks slows down performance and is not recommended.
- Always use exceptions for fatal conditions that terminate the program.
- Using exceptions for noncritical conditions, such as converting the value to an integer or reading the value from an empty array, is not recommended and should be handled through custom logic. For example, converting a string value to the integer type can be done by using the `Int32.Parse` method rather than by using the `Convert.ToInt32` method and then failing at a point when the string is not represented as a digit.
- While throwing an exception, add a meaningful message so that the user knows where that exception has actually occurred rather than going through the stack trace. For example, the following code shows a way of throwing an exception and adding a custom message based on the method and class being called:

```
static string GetCountryDetails(Dictionary<string, string>
countryDictionary, string key)
{
  try
  {
    return countryDictionary[key];
  }
  catch (KeyNotFoundException ex)
  {
```

```
        KeyNotFoundException argEx = new KeyNotFoundException("
        Error occured while executing GetCountryDetails method.
        Cause: Key not found", ex);
        throw argEx;
    }
}
```

- Throw exceptions rather than returning the custom messages or error codes and handle it in the main calling method.
- When logging exceptions, always check the inner exception and read the exception message or stack trace. It is helpful, and gives the actual point in the code where the error is thrown.

For and foreach

For and foreach are two of the alternative ways of iterating over a list of items. Each of them operates in a different way. The for loop actually loads all the items of the list in memory first and then uses an indexer to iterate over each element, whereas foreach uses an enumerator and iterates until it reaches the end of the list.

The following table shows the types of collections that are good to use for `for` and `foreach`:

Type	For/Foreach
Typed array	Good for both
Array list	Better with for
Generic collections	Better with for

Delegates

Delegates are a type in .NET which hold the reference to the method. The type is equivalent to the function pointer in C or C++. When defining a delegate, we can specify both the parameters that the method can take and its return type. This way, the reference methods will have the same signature.

Here is a simple delegate that takes a string and returns an integer:

```
delegate int Log(string n);
```

Now, suppose we have a `LogToConsole` method that has the same signature as the one shown in the following code. This method takes the string and writes it to the console window:

```
static int LogToConsole(string a) { Console.WriteLine(a);
  return 1;
}
```

We can initialize and use this delegate like this:

```
Log logDelegate = LogToConsole;
logDelegate ("This is a simple delegate call");
```

Suppose we have another method called `LogToDatabase` that writes the information in the database:

```
static int LogToDatabase(string a)
{
  Console.WriteLine(a);
  //Log to database
  return 1;
}
```

Here is the initialization of the new `logDelegate` instance that references the `LogToDatabase` method:

```
Log logDelegateDatabase = LogToDatabase;
logDelegateDatabase ("This is a simple delegate call");
```

The preceding delegate is the representation of unicast delegates, as each instance refers to a single method. On the other hand, we can also create multicast delegates by assigning `LogToDatabase` to the same `LogDelegate` instance, as follows:

```
Log logDelegate = LogToConsole;
logDelegate += LogToDatabase;
logDelegate("This is a simple delegate call");
```

The preceding code seems pretty straightforward and optimized, but under the hood, it has a huge performance overhead. In .NET, delegates are implemented by a `MutlicastDelegate` class that is optimized to run unicast delegates. It stores the reference of the method to the target property and calls the method directly. For multicast delegates, it uses the invocation list, which is a generic list, and holds the references to each method that is added. With multicast delegates, each target property holds the reference to the generic list that contains the method and executes in sequence. However, this adds an overhead for multicast delegates and takes more time to execute.

Summary

In this chapter, we have learned the core concepts about data structures, the types of data structures, as well as their advantages and disadvantages, followed by the best possible scenarios in which each can be used. We also learned about the Big O notation, which is one of the core topics to consider when writing code and helps developers to identify code performance. Finally, we looked into some best practices and covered topics such as boxing and unboxing, string concatenation, exception handling, `for` and `foreach` loops, and delegates.

In the next chapter, we will learn some guidelines and best practices that could be helpful when designing .NET Core applications.

Designing Guidelines for .NET Core Application Performance

16

Architecture and design are the core foundations for any application. Conforming to the best practices and guidelines makes the application highly maintainable, performant, and scalable. Applications can vary from a web-based application, Web APIs, a server/client TCP-based messaging application, a mission-critical application, and so on. However, all of these applications should follow certain practices that benefit in various ways. In this chapter, we will learn certain practices that are common in almost all of our applications.

Here are some of the principles we will learn in this chapter:

- Coding principles:
  - Naming convention
  - Code comments
  - One class per file
  - One logic per method
- Design principles:
  - KISS (Keep It Simple, Stupid)
  - YAGNI (You Aren't Gonna Need It)
  - DRY (Don't Repeat Yourself)
  - Separation of Concerns
  - SOLID principles
  - Caching
  - Data structures
  - Communication

- Resource management
- Concurrency

Coding principles

In this section, we will cover some of the basic coding principles that help in writing quality code that improves the overall performance and scalability of the application.

Naming convention

Always use the proper naming convention in every application, starting with the solution name, which should provide meaningful information about the project you are working on. The project name specifies the layer or component part of the application. Finally, classes should be nouns or noun phrases, and methods should represent the actions.

When we create a new project in Visual Studio, the default solution name is set to what you specify for the project name. The solution name should always be different from the project name as one solution may contain multiple projects. The project name should always represent the specific part of the system. For example, suppose we are developing a messaging gateway that sends different types of messages to different parties and contains three components, namely, listener, processor, and dispatcher; the listener listens for incoming requests, the processor processes the incoming message, and the dispatcher sends the message to the destination. The naming convention could be as follows:

- Solution name: `MessagingGateway` (or any code word)
- Listener project name: `ListenerApp`
- Processor project name: `ProcessorAPI` (if it's an API)
- Dispatcher project name: `DispatcherApp`

In .NET, the naming convention we usually follow is Pascal casing for class and method names. In Pascal casing, the first character of every word is a capital letter, whereas the parameters and other variables follow Camel casing. Here is some sample code showing how casing should be used in .NET.:

```
public class MessageDispatcher
{
  public const string SmtpAddress = "smpt.office365.com";

  public void SendEmail(string fromAddress, string toAddress,
  string subject, string body)
```

```
    {

    }
  }
```

In the preceding code, we have a constant field, `SmtpAddress`, and a `SendEmail` method that is cased using Pascal casing, whereas the parameters are cased using Camel casing.

The following table summarizes the naming conventions for different artifacts in .NET:

Attribute	Naming Convention	Example
Class	Pascal casing	`class PersonManager {}`
Method	Pascal casing	`void SaveRecord(Person person) {}`
Parameters/Member variables	Camel casing	`bool isActive;`
Interface	Pascal casing; starts with letter I	`IPerson`
Enum	Pascal casing	`enum Status {InProgress, New, Completed}`

Code comments

Any code that contains proper comments assists developers in many ways. It not only reduces the time to understand the code thoroughly, but can also give leverage with certain tools like *Sandcastle* or *DocFx* to generate complete code documentation on the fly that can be shared with other developers across the team. Also, when talking about APIs, Swagger is widely used and popular in the developer community. Swagger empowers API consumers by providing complete information about the API, available methods, parameters each method takes, and so on. Swagger also reads these comments to provide the complete documentation and interface to test any API.

One class per file

Unlike many other languages, in .NET we are not restricted to create separate files for each class. We can create one single `.cs` file and create numbers of classes inside it. Conversely, this is a bad practice and painful when working with large applications.

One logic per method

Always write methods to do one thing at a time. Let's suppose we have a method that reads the user ID from the database and then calls an API to retrieve the list of documents the user has uploaded. The best approach with this scenario is to have two separate methods, `GetUserID` and `GetUserDocuments`, to retrieve the user ID first and then the documents, respectively:

```
public int GetUserId(string userName)
{
  //Get user ID from database by passing the username
}

public List<Document> GetUserDocuments(int userID)
{
  //Get list of documents by calling some API
}
```

The benefit of this approach is that it reduces code repetition. In the future, if we wanted to change the logic of either method, we just have to change it in one place rather than replicating it everywhere and increasing the chances of error.

Design principles

Developing a clean architecture adhering to the best practices adds several benefits, and application performance is one of them. We have seen many times that the technologies used behind an application are robust and powerful, but the application's performance remains unsatisfactory or poor, which is usually because of bad architecture design and investing less time on the application's design.

In this section, we will discuss a few common design principles that should be addressed when designing and developing applications in .NET Core:

- KISS (Keep It Simple, Stupid)
- YAGNI (You Aren't Gonna Need It)
- DRY (Don't Repeat Yourself)
- Separation of Concerns
- SOLID principles
- Caching
- Data structures
- Communication

- Resource management
- Concurrency

KISS (Keep It Simple, Stupid)

Writing cleaner code and keeping it simple always helps developers understand and maintain it in the long run. Adding needless complexity in the code does not only make it less understandable, but also hard to maintain and change when required. This is what KISS states. In a software context, KISS can be considered while designing software architecture, using **Object Oriented Principles** (**OOP**), designing the database, user interfaces, integration, and so on. Adding unnecessary complexity complicates the software's design and may affect the application's maintainability and performance.

YAGNI (You Aren't Gonna Need It)

YAGNI is one of the core principles of XP (extreme programming). XP is a software methodology that contains short spans of iterations to meet customer requirements and welcomes changes when they are required or initiated by the customer. The primary goal is meeting the customer's expectation, and keeping the quality and responsiveness the customer needs. It involves pair programming and code reviews to keep the quality intact and to satisfy the customer's expectations.

YAGNI is best suited for the extreme programming methodology, which helps developers focus on the features that are part of the application's functionality or customer's requirements. Doing something extra that is not communicated to the customer or is not part of the iteration or requirement may end up needing a rework and being a waste of time.

DRY (Don't Repeat Yourself)

DRY (Don't Repeat Yourself) is also one of the core principles of writing cleaner code. It addresses the challenges developers face in big applications when they are constantly changing or extending with respect to functionality or underlying logic. As per the principle, it states that "*Every piece of knowledge must have a single dependable representation within the system.*"

When writing an application, we can use abstractions and avoid repetition of code to avoid redundancy. This benefits in accommodating changes and lets developers focus on one area where the change is required. If the same code is repeated in multiple areas, changes at one place need to be done in other places as well, and this eliminates good architecture practice, thus initiating higher risks of errors and making the application code more buggy.

Separation of Concerns (SoC)

One of the core principles for developing clean architecture is **Separation of Concerns (SoC)**. This pattern states that each distinct type of work application that is performing should be built separately as a separate component with little or no tight coupling with other components. For example, if a program saves the user message into the database and then a service randomly picks up the message and chooses the winner, you can see that these are two separate operations, and this is known as Separation of Concerns. With SoC, the code is considered a separate component and any customization, if needed, can be done at one place. Reusability is another factor that helps developers change code in one place so that they can use it in multiple places. Nevertheless, testing is far easier and bugs can be secluded and fixed later in case of predicament scenarios.

SOLID principles

SOLID is a collection of 5 principles, which are listed as follows. They are common design principles that are highly used when developing software design:

- **Single Responsibility Principle (SRP)**
- **Open Closed Principle (OCP)**
- **Liskov Substitution Principle (LSP)**
- **Interface Segregation Principle (ISP)**
- **Dependency Inversion Principle (DIP)**

Single Responsibility Principle

The Single Responsibility Principle states that the class should only have one particular objective and that responsibility should be entirely encapsulated from the class. If there is any change or a new objective has to be accommodated for, a new class or interface should be created.

Applying this principle in software design makes our code maintainable and easier to understand. Architects usually follow this principle when designing software architecture, but, with the passage of time when many developers work and incorporate changes into that code/class, it becomes bloated and disaffirms the single responsibility principle, thus eventually making our code unmaintainable.

This also relates to the concepts of Cohesion and Coupling. Cohesion refers to the measure of how strongly related the responsibilities in the class are, whereas coupling refers to the degree to which each class relies on one another. We should always focus on maintaining low coupling between classes and high cohesion within the class.

Here is the basic `PersonManager` class that contains four methods, namely `GetPerson`, `SavePerson`, `LogError`, and `LogInformation`:

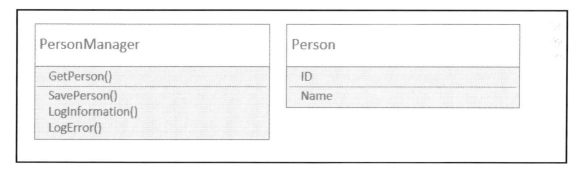

All of these methods use the database persistence manager to read/write the record into the database. As you may have noticed, `LogError` and `LogInformation` are not highly cohesive to the `PersonManager` class, and are tightly coupled with the `PersonManager` class. If we wanted to reuse these methods in other classes, we have to use the `PersonManager` class, and changing the logic of internal logging requires this `PersonManager` class to be changed as well. Hence, `PersonManager` violates the single responsibility principle.

To fix this design, we can create a separate `LogManager` class that can be used by the `PersonManager` to log information or errors when executing operations. Here is the updated class diagram representing the associations:

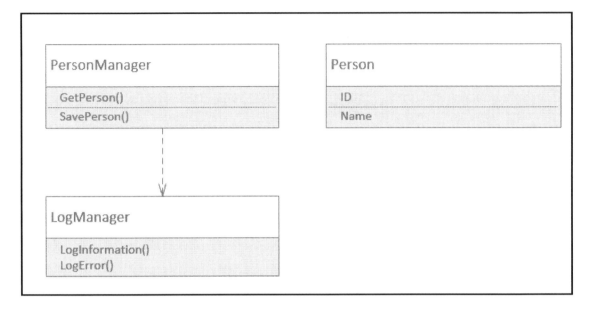

Open Closed principle

As per the definition, the Open Closed principle states that software entities like classes, methods, interfaces, and others should be closed for modification and open for extension. This means we cannot modify the existing code and extend the functionality by adding additional classes, interfaces, methods, and so on to address any changes.

Using this principle in any application solves various problems, which are listed as follows:

- Adding new functionality without changing existing code produces fewer errors and does not require thorough testing
- Less of a ripple effect that is usually experienced when changing existing code to add or update functionalities
- Extensions are mostly implemented using new interfaces or abstract classes where the existing code is unnecessary and has a lesser chance to break existing functionality

To implement the Open Closed Principle, we should use abstractions which is possible through parameters, inheritance, and composition approaches.

Parameters

Special parameters can be set in the methods, which can be used to control the behavior of the body written in that method. Suppose there is a `LogException` method that saves the exception into the database and also sends an email. Now, whenever this method is called, both the tasks will be performed. There is no way to stop sending an email for a particular exception from the code. However, if it is articulated in a way and uses some parameters to decide whether the email has to be sent out or not, it can be controlled. Nonetheless, if the existing code doesn't support this parameter, then customization is required, but, while designing, we can keep this approach to expose certain parameters so that we can handle the internal behavior of the method:

```
public void LogException(Exception ex)
{
  SendEmail(ex);
  LogToDatabase(ex);
}
```

The recommended implementation is as follows:

```
public void LogException(Exception ex, bool sendEmail, bool logToDb)
{
  if (sendEmail)
  {
    SendEmail(ex);
  }

  if (logToDb)
  {
    LogToDatabase(ex);
  }
}
```

Inheritance

With the inheritence approach, we can use the Template method pattern. Using the Template method pattern, we can create a default behavior in the root class and then create child classes to override the default behavior and implement new functionality.

For example, here is a `Logger` class that logs information into the file system:

```
public class Logger
{
  public virtual void LogMessage(string message)
  {
    //This method logs information into file system
    LogToFileSystem(message);
  }

  private void LogtoFileSystem(string message) {
    //Log to file system
  }
}
```

We have one `LogMessage` method that logs the message into the file system by calling the `LogToFileSystem` method. This method works fine until we wanted to extend the functionality. Suppose, later on, we come up with the requirement to log this information into the database as well. We have to change the existing `LogMessage` method and write the code into the same class itself. Later on, if any other requirement comes along, we have to add that functionality again and again and modify this class. As per the Open Closed Principle, this is a violation.

With the Template method pattern, we can redesign this code to follow the Open Closed Principle so that we can make it open for extension and closed for customization.

Following the OCP, here is the new design where we have one abstract class that contains the `LogMessage` abstract method, and two child classes that have their own implementations:

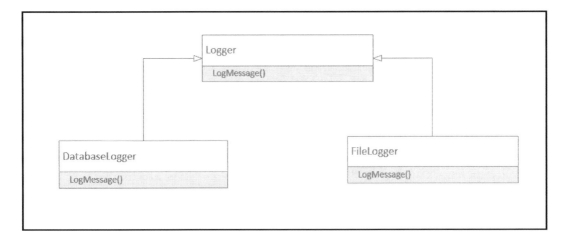

With this design, we can add the nth number of extensions without changing the existing `Logger` class:

```
public abstract class Logger
{
  public abstract void LogMessage(string message);

}

public class FileLogger : Logger
{
  public override void LogMessage(string message)
  {
    //Log to file system
  }
}

public class DatabaseLogger : Logger
{
  public override void LogMessage(string message)
  {
    //Log to database
  }
}
```

Composition

The third approach is composition, and this can be achieved using the Strategy pattern. With this approach, the client code is dependent on the abstraction, and the actual implementation is encapsulated in a separate class which is injected into the class exposed to the client.

Let's look into the following example that implements the strategy pattern. The basic requirement is to send messages that could be either emails or SMSes, and we need to construct it in a way so that new message types can be added in the future without any modification to the main class:

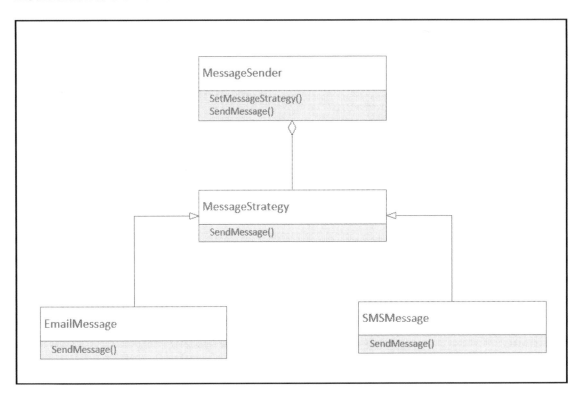

As per the strategy pattern, we have one `MessageStrategy` abstract class that exposes one abstract method. Each type of work is encapsulated into the separate class that inherits the `MessageStrategy` base abstract class.

Here is the code for the `MessageStrategy` abstract class:

```
public abstract class MessageStrategy
{
  public abstract void SendMessage(Message message);
}
```

We have two concrete implementations of `MessageStrategy`; one to send an email and another to send an SMS, which is shown as follows:

```
public class EmailMessage : MessageStrategy
{
  public override void SendMessage(Message message)
  {
    //Send Email
  }
}

public class SMSMessage : MessageStrategy
{
  public override void SendMessage(Message message)
  {
    //Send SMS
  }
}
```

Finally, we have the `MessageSender` class, which will be used by the client. In this class, the client can set the message strategy and call the `SendMessage` method that invokes the particular concrete implementation type to send the message:

```
public class MessageSender
{
  private MessageStrategy _messageStrategy;
  public void SetMessageStrategy(MessageStrategy messageStrategy)
  {
    _messageStrategy = messageStrategy;
  }

  public void SendMessage(Message message)
  {
    _messageStrategy.SendMessage(message);
  }

}
```

From the Main program, we can use `MessageSender`, which is shown as follows:

```
static void Main(string[] args)
{
  MessageSender sender = new MessageSender();
  sender.SetMessageStrategy(new EmailMessage());
  sender.SendMessage(new Message { MessageID = 1, MessageTo =
"jason@tfx.com",
  MessageFrom = "donotreply@tfx.com", MessageBody = "Hello readers",
  MessageSubject = "Chapter 5" });
```

```
     }
```

Liskov principle

As per the Liskov principle, the function that uses the references of derived classes through the base class object must comply with the behavior of the base class.

This means that the child classes should not remove the behavior of the base class since this violates the invariants of it. Typically, the calling code should completely rely on the methods exposed in a base class without knowing its derived implementations.

Let's take an example where we first violate the definition of the Liskov principle and then fix it to learn what it is particularly designed for:

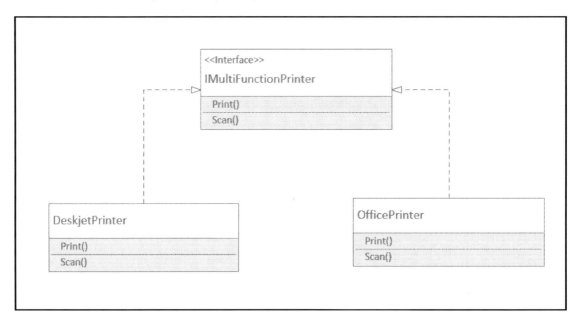

The IMultiFunctionPrinter interface exposes two methods as follows:

```
public interface IMultiFunctionPrinter
{
  void Print();
  void Scan();
}
```

This is an interface that can be implemented by different kinds of printers. The following are two kinds of printers that implement the IMultiFunctionPrinter interface, and they are as follows:

```
public class OfficePrinter: IMultiFunctionPrinter
{
  //Office printer can print the page
  public void Print() { }
  //Office printer can scan the page
  public void Scan() { }
}


public class DeskjetPrinter : IMultiFunctionPrinter
{
  //Deskjet printer print the page
  public void Print() { }
  //Deskjet printer does not contain this feature
  public void Scan() => throw new NotImplementedException();
}
```

In the preceding implementations, we have one OfficePrinter that provides printing and scanning functionalities, whereas the other home purpose DeskjetPrinter only provides the printing functionality. This DeskjetPrinter actually violates the Liskov principle as it throws the NotImplementedException when the Scan method is called.

As a remedy to the preceding problem, we can split the IMultiFunctionPrinter into two interfaces, namely IPrinter and IScanner, whereas IMultiFunctionPrinter can also implement both the interfaces to support both functionalities.

The `DeskjetPrinter` only implements the `IPrinter` interface as it does not support scanning:

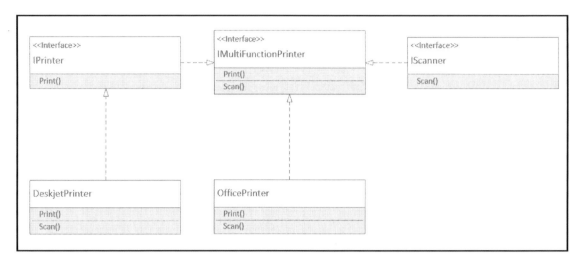

Here is the code for the three interfaces, `IPrinter`, `IScanner`, and `IMultiFunctionPrinter`:

```
public interface IPrinter
{
   void Print();
}

public interface IScanner
{
   void Scanner();
}

public interface MultiFunctionPrinter : IPrinter, IScanner
{

}
```

Finally, the concrete implementation will be as follows:

```
public class DeskjetPrinter : IPrinter
{
   //Deskjet printer print the page
   public void Print() { }
}

public class OfficePrinter: IMultiFunctionPrinter
```

```
{
    //Office printer can print the page
    public void Print() { }
    //Office printer can scan the page
    public void Scan() { }
}
```

The Interface Segregation principle

The Interface Segregation principle states that the client code should only depend on the things the client use and should not depend on anything they do not use. This means you cannot force client code to depend on certain methods which are not required.

Let's take an example that first violates the Interface Segregation principle:

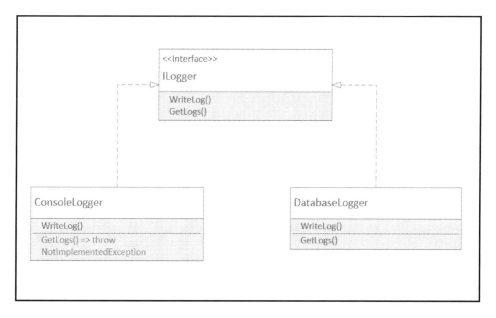

In the preceding diagram, we have the ILogger interface that contains two methods, namely `WriteLog` and `GetLogs`. The `ConsoleLogger` class writes the message into the application console window, whereas the `DatabaseLogger` class stores the message into the database. The `ConsoleLogger` prints the message on the console windows and does not persist it; it throws the `NotImplementedException` for the `GetLogs` method, and so this violates the Interface Segregation principle.

Here is the code for the preceding problem:

```
public interface ILogger
{
  void WriteLog(string message);
  List<string> GetLogs();
}

/// <summary>
/// Logger that prints the information on application console window
/// </summary>
public class ConsoleLogger : ILogger
{
  public List<string> GetLogs() => throw new NotImplementedException();
  public void WriteLog(string message)
  {
    Console.WriteLine(message);
  }
}

/// <summary>
/// Logger that writes the log into database and persist them
/// </summary>
public class DatabaseLogger : ILogger
{
  public List<string> GetLogs()
  {
    //do some work to get logs stored in database, as the actual code
    //in not written so returning null
    return null;
  }
  public void WriteLog(string message)
  {
    //do some work to write log into database
  }
}
```

To obey the **Interface Segregation Principle (ISP)**, we split the ILogger interface and make it more precise and pertinent with other implementers. The ILogger interface will only contain the `WriteLog` method and a new `IPersistenceLogger` interface is introduced that inherits the ILogger interface and provides the `GetLogs` method:

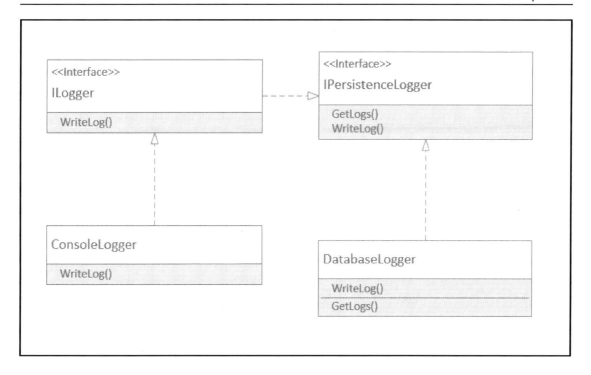

Here is the modified example, which is shown as follows:

```
public interface ILogger
{
  void WriteLog(string message);
}

public interface PersistenceLogger: ILogger
{
  List<string> GetLogs();
}

/// <summary>
/// Logger that prints the information on application console window
/// </summary>
public class ConsoleLogger : ILogger
{
  public void WriteLog(string message)
  {
    Console.WriteLine(message);
  }
}
```

```
/// <summary>
/// Logger that writes the log into database and persist them
/// </summary>
public class DatabaseLogger : PersistenceLogger
{
  public List<string> GetLogs()
  {
    //do some work to get logs stored in database, as the actual code
    //in not written so returning null
    return null;
  }
  public void WriteLog(string message)
  {
    //do some work to write log into database
  }
}
```

The Dependency Inversion principle

The Dependency Inversion principle states that high-level modules should not depend on low-level modules and both of them should depend on abstractions.

The software application contains numerous types of dependencies. A dependency could be a framework dependency, a third-party libraries dependency, a web service dependency, a database dependency, a class dependency, and so on. As per the Dependency Inversion principle, the dependencies should not be tightly coupled with one another.

For example, in the layered architecture approach we have a presentation layer where all the views are defined; the service layer that exposes certain methods used by the presentation layer; the business layer that contains core business logic of the system; and the database layer where the backend database connectors and the repository classes are defined. Consider this an ASP.NET MVC application where the controller invokes the service that references the business layer, where the business layer contains the core business logic of the system, and where it uses the database layer to perform CRUD (Create, Read, Update and Delete) operations on the database. The dependency tree will look as follows:

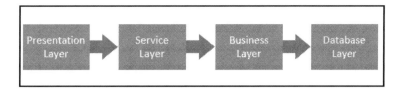

As per the Dependency Inversion principle, it is not recommended to instantiate the objects directly from each layer. This creates a tight coupling between the layers. To break this coupling, we can implement abstraction through interfaces or abstract classes. We may use some instantiation patterns like factory or dependency injection to instantiate objects. Moreover, we should always use interfaces rather than classes. Suppose in our service layer we have a reference to our business layer, and our service contract is using `EmployeeManager` to perform some CRUD operations. `EmployeeManager` contains the following methods:

```
public class EmployeeManager
{

  public List<Employee> GetEmployees(int id)
  {
    //logic to Get employees
    return null;
  }
  public void SaveEmployee(Employee emp)
  {
    //logic to Save employee
  }
  public void DeleteEmployee(int id)
  {
    //Logic to delete employee
  }

}
```

In the service layer, we can instantiate the business layer `EmployeeManager` object using the new keyword. Adding more methods in the `EmployeeManager` class will directly use the service layer based on the access modifiers being set at each method. Moreover, any changes in the existing methods will break the service layer code. If we expose the interface to the service layer and use some factory or **Dependency Injection (DI)** patterns, it encapsulates the underlying implementation and exposes only those methods that are needed.

The following code shows the IEmployeeManager interface being extracted from the EmployeeManager class:

```
public interface IEmployeeManager
{
  void DeleteEmployee(int id);
  System.Collections.Generic.List<Employee> GetEmployees(int id);
  void SaveEmployee(Employee emp);
}
```

Considering the preceding example, we can inject types using dependency injection, so whenever the service manager is invoked, the business manager instance will be initialized.

Caching

Caching is one of the best practices that can be used to increase application performance. It is often used with data where changes are less frequent. There are many caching providers available that we can consider to save data and retrieve it when needed. It is faster than the database operation. In ASP.NET Core, we can use in-memory caching that stores the data in the memory of the server, but for a web farm or a load balancing scenario where an application is deployed to multiple places, it is recommended to use a distributed cache. Microsoft Azure also provides a Redis cache which is a distributed cache that exposes an endpoint that can be used to store values on the cloud and can be retrieved when they are needed.

To use the in-memory cache in the ASP.NET Core project, we can simply add the memory cache in the ConfigureServices method, which is shown as follows:

```
public void ConfigureServices(IServiceCollection services)
{
  services.AddMvc();
  services.AddMemoryCache();
}
```

Then, we can inject IMemoryCache in our controllers or page models through dependency injection and set or get values using the Set and Get methods.

Data structures

Choosing the right data structure plays a vital role in application performance. Before choosing any data structure, it is highly recommended to think about whether it is an overhead or it literally solves a particular use case. Some key factors to be considered while choosing an appropriate data structure are as follows:

- Know about the type of data you need to store
- Know how the data grows and whether there is any drawback when it grows
- Know if you need to access your data through an index or key/value pairs and choose the appropriate data structure
- Know if you need synchronized access and choose thread-safe collections

There are many other factors when choosing the right data structure, and they have already been covered in the previous chapter.

Communication

Nowadays, communication has become an important epitome in any application, and the primary factor is the rapid evolution of technology. Applications such as web-based applications, mobile applications, IoT applications, and other distributed applications perform different types of communication over the wire. We can take an example of an application that has a web frontend deployed on some cloud instance, invoking some service deployed on a separate instance in the cloud and performing some backend connectivity to the database which is hosted locally. Besides this, we can have an IoT application that sends the room temperature by calling some service over the internet, and many more. Certain factors that need to be considered when designing distributed application are as follows:

Using lighter interfaces

Avoid multiple round trips to the server that adds more network latency and decreases application performance. Using the unit of work pattern avoids sending redundant operations to the server and performs one single operation to communicate to the backend service. The unit of work groups all the messages as a single unit and processes them as one unit.

Minimizing message size

Use as little data as possible to communicate to the service. For example, there is a Person API that provides some GET, POST, PUT, and DELETE methods to perform a CRUD operation on that backend database. To delete a person's record, we can just pass the ID (primary key) of the person as a parameter to the service rather than passing the whole object as a parameter. Moreover, use objects that are less bloated with properties or methods that offer a minimal set of artifacts. The best case is to use **POCO (Plain Old CLR object)** entities that have minimal dependencies on other objects which contain only those properties that are necessary to be sent across the wire.

Queuing communication

For larger object or complex operation, decoupling the single request/response channel from the distributed messaging channel increases the application's performance. For large, chunky operations, we can design and distribute communication into multiple components. For example, there is a website that calls a service to upload an image, and, once it is uploaded, it does some processing to extract a thumbnail and saves it in the database. One way is to do both uploading and processing in a single call, but at times when the user uploads a larger image or if the image processing takes a longer time, the user may face a request timeout exception, and the request will terminate.

With the queuing architecture, we can distribute these two operations into separate calls. The user uploads the image which is saved in the filesystem, and the image path will be saved into storage. A service running in the background will pick up that file and do the processing asynchronously. Meanwhile, when the backend service is processing, the control is returned to the user, where the user can see some in-progress notification. Finally, when the thumbnail is generated, the user will be notified:

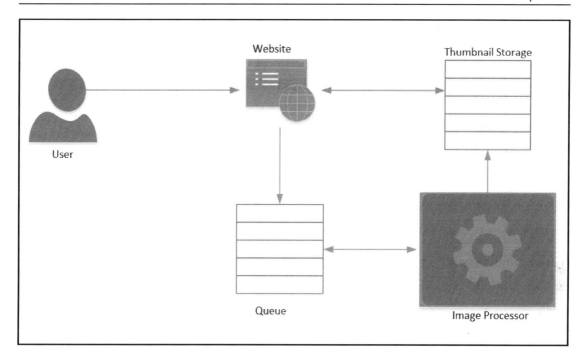

Resource management

Every server has a limited set of resources. No matter how good the server specification, if the application is not designed to utilize resources in an efficient manner, this leads to performance issues. There are certain best practices that need to be addressed to optimally use server resources when designing .NET Core applications.

Avoiding improper use of threads

Creating a new thread for each task without monitoring or aborting the lifecycle of the thread is a bad practice. Threads are good to perform multitasking and to utilize multiple resources of the server to run things in parallel. However, if the design is to create threads for each request, this can slow down the application's performance, as the CPU will take more time in the context of switching between the threads rather than executing the actual job.

Whenever we use threads, we should always try to keep a shared thread pool where any new item that needs to be executed waits in the queue if the thread is busy, and is acquired when it is available. This way, thread management is easy and server resources will be used efficiently.

Disposing objects in a timely fashion

CLR (**Common Language Runtime**) provides automatic memory management, and the objects instantiated with a new keyword do not require to be garbage collected explicitly; **GC** (**Garbage Collection**) does the job. However, non-managed resources are not automatically released by the GC and should be explicitly collected by implementing the IDisposable interface. Such resources could be database connections, file handlers, sockets, and so on. To learn more about disposing of unmanaged resources in .NET Core, please refer to Chapter 17, *Memory Management Techniques in .NET Core.*

Acquiring resources when they are required

Always acquire resources only when they are required. Instantiating objects ahead of time is not a good practice. It takes unnecessary memory and utilizes resources of the system. Furthermore, use *try, catch,* and *finally* to block and release objects in the *finally* block. This way, if any exception occurs, the objects which have been instantiated within the method will be released.

Concurrency

In concurrent programming, many objects may access the same resource at the same time, and keeping them thread-safe is the primary objective. In .NET Core, we can use locks to provide synchronized access. However, there are cases where a thread has to wait for a longer time to get access to resources, and this makes applications unresponsive.

The best practice is to apply for synchronized access only for those specific lines of code where the actual resource needs to be thread-safe, for example, where the locks can be used, which are the database operations, file handling, bank account access, and many other critical sections in the application. These need synchronized access so that they can be handled one thread at a time.

Summary

Writing cleaner code, following the architecture and design principles, and adhering to the best practices play a significant role in application performance. If the code if baggy and repetitive, it can increase the chances of errors, increase complexity, and affect performance.

In this chapter, we have learned some coding principles that make the application code look cleaner and easier to understand. If the code is clean, it offers other developers a way to understand it completely and helps in many other ways. Later on, we learned some basic design principles that are considered to be the core principles when designing applications. Principles such as KISS, YAGNI, DRY, Separation of Concerns, and SOLID are highly essential in software design, and caching and choosing the right data structure have a significant impact on performance and increase performance if they are used properly. Finally, we learned some best practices that should be considered when handling communication, resource management, and concurrency.

The next chapter is a detailed introduction to memory management, where we will explore some techniques of memory management in .NET Core.

.

17
Memory Management Techniques in .NET Core

Memory management significantly affects the performance of any application. When the application is run, .NET CLR (Common Language Runtime) allocates many objects in memory, and they stay there until they are not needed, until new objects are created and are allocated space, or until the GC runs (as it does occasionally) to release unused objects and make more space available for other objects. Most of the job is done by the GC itself, which runs intelligently and frees up space for the objects by removing those that are not needed. However, there are certain practices that can help any application to avoid performance issues and run smoothly.

In Chapter 14, *Understanding .NET Core Internals and Measuring Performance*, we already learned about how garbage collection works and how generations are maintained in .NET. In this chapter, we will focus on some recommended best practices and patterns that avoid memory leakage and make the application performant.

The following are the topics that we will learn:

- Memory allocation process overview
- Analysing memory through SOS debugging
- Memory fragmentation
- Avoiding finalizers
- Best practices to dispose of objects in .NET Core

Memory allocation process overview

Memory allocation is the process of allocating objects in memory when the application is running. It is done by the **Common Language Runtime (CLR)**. When the object is initialized (using a `new` keyword), the GC checks whether the generation reaches the threshold and performs garbage collection. This means that when the system memory reaches its limit, the GC is invoked. When an application runs, the GC register itself receives an event notification about the system memory, and when the system reaches its particular limit, it invokes garbage collection.

On the other hand, we can also programmatically invoke the GC using the `GC.Collect` method. However, as the GC is a highly fine-tuned algorithm and automatically behaves as per memory allocation patterns, calling it explicitly can affect performance, and so it is strongly recommended that you don't use it in production.

Analysing CLR internals through the SOS debugger in .NET Core

SOS is a debugging extension that is shipped with Windows and is available for Linux as well. It helps to debug .NET Core applications by providing information about CLR internals, especially memory allocation, the number of objects created, and other details about the CLR. We can use the SOS extension in .NET Core to debug the native machine code, which is specific to each platform.

 To install the SOS extension for Windows, install the **Windows Driver Kit (WDK)** from
https://developer.microsoft.com/en-us/windows/hardware/download-kits-windows-hardware-development.

When the Windows Driver Kit is installed, we can use various commands to analyze the CLR internals about the application and identify which objects are taking up the most memory in the heap and optimize them accordingly.

As we know that, in .NET Core, there is no executable file generated, we can use *dotnet cli* commands to execute the .NET Core application. The commands to run the .NET Core application are as follows:

- `dotnet run`
- `dotnet applicationpath/applicationname.dll`

We can run either of the preceding commands to run the .NET Core application. In the case of the ASP.NET Core application, we can go to the root of the application folder, where `Views`, `wwwroot`, `Models`, `Controllers` and other files reside, and run the following command:

```
Directory of D:\Authoring\C#7.0NetCore2.0\My Chapters\Chapter6\Chapter6\Chapter6WebApp

24-Dec-2017  09:55 PM    <DIR>          .
24-Dec-2017  09:55 PM    <DIR>          ..
24-Dec-2017  09:55 PM                36 .bowerrc
24-Dec-2017  09:55 PM               178 appsettings.Development.json
24-Dec-2017  09:55 PM               113 appsettings.json
24-Dec-2017  09:55 PM    <DIR>          bin
24-Dec-2017  09:55 PM               207 bower.json
24-Dec-2017  09:55 PM               628 bundleconfig.json
24-Dec-2017  09:55 PM               397 Chapter6WebApp.csproj
24-Dec-2017  09:55 PM    <DIR>          Controllers
24-Dec-2017  09:55 PM    <DIR>          Models
24-Dec-2017  11:12 PM    <DIR>          obj
24-Dec-2017  09:55 PM               631 Program.cs
24-Dec-2017  09:55 PM    <DIR>          Properties
24-Dec-2017  09:55 PM             1,472 Startup.cs
24-Dec-2017  09:55 PM    <DIR>          Views
24-Dec-2017  09:55 PM    <DIR>          wwwroot
               8 File(s)          3,662 bytes
               9 Dir(s)  41,166,479,360 bytes free
```

On the other hand, debugging tools usually require the `.exe` file or the process ID to dump information related to the CLR internals. To run the SOS debugger, we can go to the path where the Windows Driver Kit is installed (the directory path will be `{driveletter}:Program Files (x86)Windows Kits10Debuggersx64`) and run the following command:

```
windbg dotnet {application path}
```

Here is a screenshot that shows you how to run the ASP.NET Core application using the `windbg` command:

```
C:\Program Files (x86)\Windows Kits\10\Debuggers\x64>windbg dotnet D:\Authoring\C#7.0NetCore2.0\My Chapters\Chapter6
\Chapter6\Chapter6WebApp\bin\debug\netcoreapp2.0\chapter6webapp.dll
```

Once you run the preceding command, it will open up the Windbg window and the debugger, as follows:

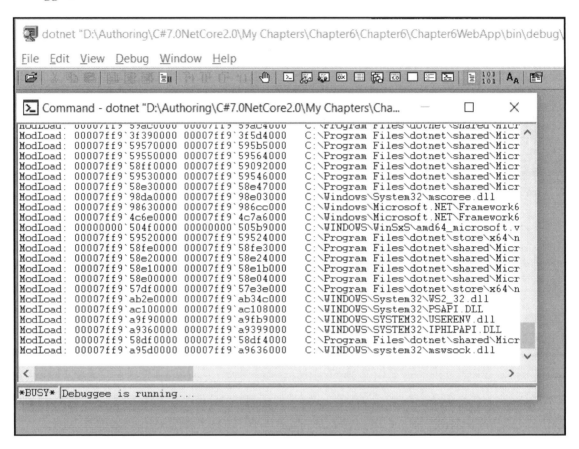

You can stop the debugger by clicking **Debug** | **Break** and running the sos command to load the information about .NET Core CLR.

Execute the following command from the Windbg window and hit *Enter*:

```
.loadby sos coreclr
```

The following screenshot is of the interface from which you can type and run the preceding command:

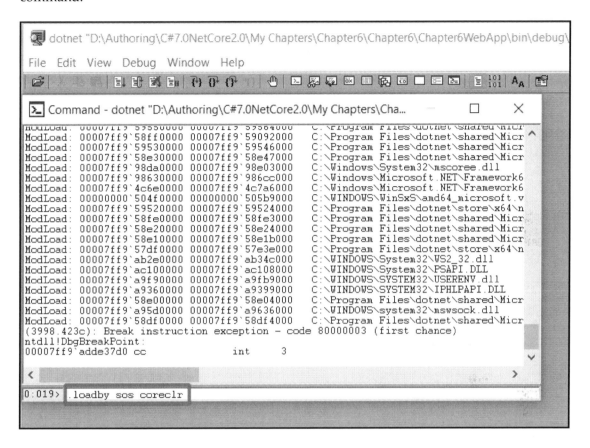

Finally, we can run the `!DumpHeap` command to see the complete statistical details of the objects heap:

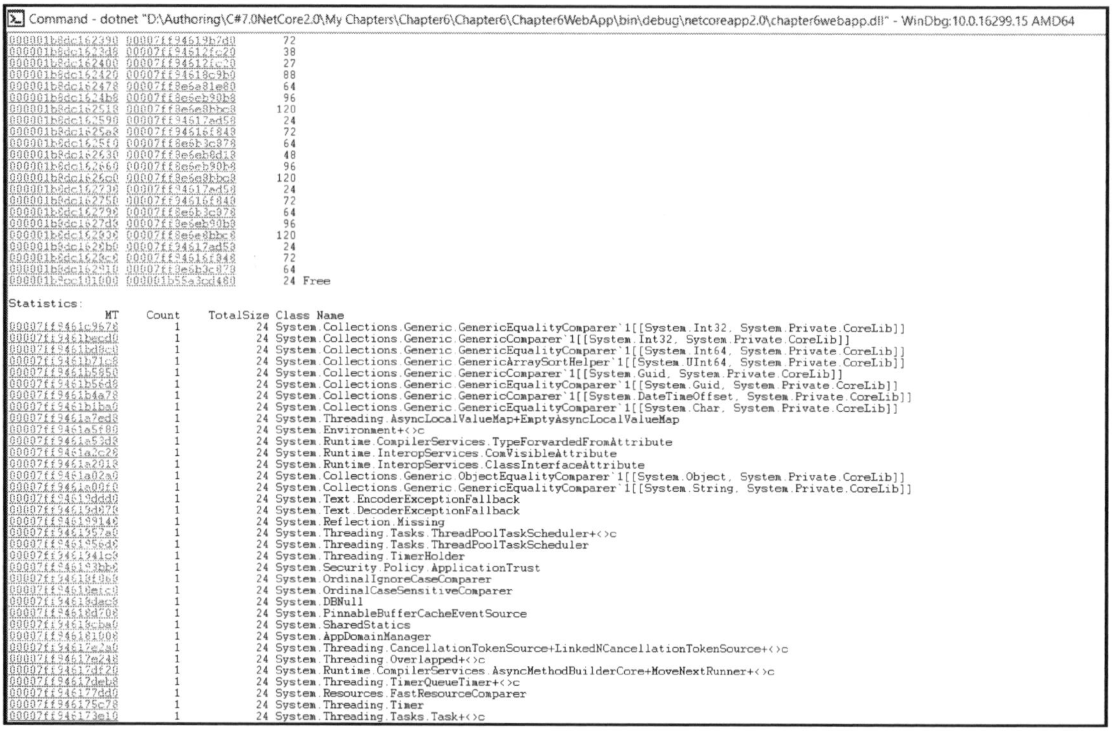

In the preceding screenshot, the first three columns as shown in the following screenshot, represent the `Address`, `Method` table and `Size` of each method:

Using the preceding information, it provides the statistics that classify the objects stored on the heap by their type. `MT` is the method table of that type, `Count` is the total number of instances of that type, `TotalSize` is the total memory size occupied by all the instances of that type, and `Classname` represents the actual type that takes up that space on the heap.

There are a few more commands that we can use to get specific details, listed as follows:

Switch	Command	Description
Statistics	`!DumpHeap -stat`	Shows only statistical details
Type	`!DumpHeap -type TypeName`	Shows the statistics for a particular type stored on the heap
Finalization queue	`!FinalizationQueue`	Show details about the finalizers

This tool helps developers to investigate how objects are allocated on the heap. In a practical scenario, we can run our application on a test or staging server by running this tool in the background and examining the detailed statistics about the objects stored on the heap for a particular point of time.

Memory fragmentation

Memory fragmentation is one of the primary causes of performance issues in .NET applications. When the object is instantiated, it occupies space in the memory, and when it is not needed, it is garbage collected, and that allocated memory block becomes available. This occurs when the object is allocated a larger space with respect to the size available in that memory segment/block and waits until space becomes available. Memory fragmentation is a problem that occurs when most of the memory is allocated in a larger number of non-contiguous blocks. When a larger size of object stores or occupies the larger memory block and the memory only contains smaller chunks of free blocks that are available, this causes fragmentation, and the system fails to allocate that object in memory.

.NET maintains two types of heap—namely the **small object heap (SOH)** and **large object heap (LOH)**. Objects that are greater than 85,000 bytes are stored in LOH. The key difference between SOH and LOH is that in LOH there is no compaction being done by the GC. Compaction is the process that is done at the time of garbage collection, where objects stored in the SOH are moved to eliminate the smaller chunks of free space available and increase the total space available as one form of large memory chunk that can be used by other objects, which reduces fragmentation. However, in LOH, there is no compaction being done by the GC implicitly. Objects that are large in size are stored in LOH and create fragmentation issues. Moreover, if we compare LOH with SOH, the compaction cost for LOH is moderately high and involves significant overhead, where the GC needs twice as much memory space to move objects for defragmentation. This is another reason why LOH is not defragmented implicitly by the GC.

The following is a representation of memory fragmentation, where the white blocks represent the unallocated memory space, and are followed by an allocated block:

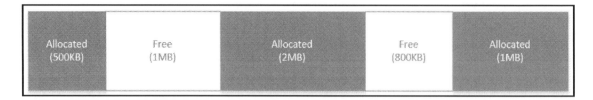

Suppose an object that has a size of 1.5 MB wants to be allocated some memory. It will not find any free space available, even though the total amount of memory available is 1.8 MB. The reason for this is memory fragmentation:

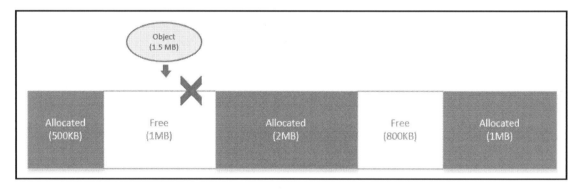

On the other hand, if the memory is defragmented, the object can easily use the space that is available and will be allocated:

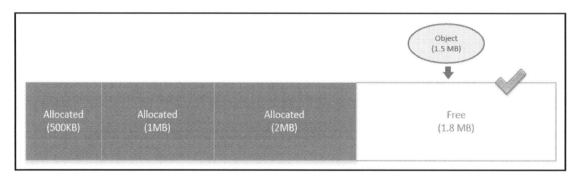

In .NET Core, we can perform compaction in LOH explicitly using `GCSettings`, as follows:

```
GCSettings.LargeObjectHeapCompactionMode =
GCLargeObjectHeapCompactionMode.CompactOnce;
GC.Collect();
```

Avoiding finalizers

Using finalizers is not a good practice to use in .NET Core applications. Objects that use finalizers stay in memory longer and ultimately affect the application's performance.

Objects that are not required by the application at a particular point in time stay in the memory so that their `Finalizer` method can be called. For example, if the object is considered dead by the GC in generation 0, it will always survive in generation 1.

In .NET Core, CLR maintains a separate thread to run the `Finalizer` method. All the objects that contain the `Finalizer` method are placed into the finalization queue. Any object that is no longer required by the application is placed in the F-Reachable queue, which is then executed by the dedicated finalizer thread.

The following diagram shows an `object1` object that contains a `Finalizer` method. The `Finalizer` method is placed in the finalization queue and the object occupies the memory space in the **Gen0** (generation 0) heap:

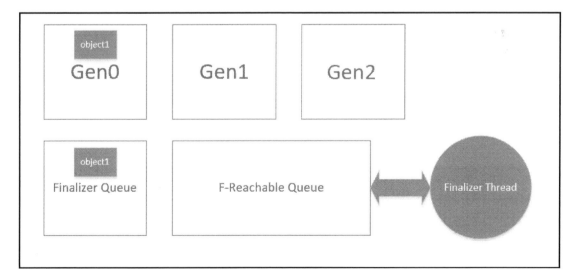

When the object is no longer required, it will be moved from **Gen0** (generation 0) to **Gen1** (generation 1) and from the **Finalizer Queue** to the **F-Reachable Queue**:

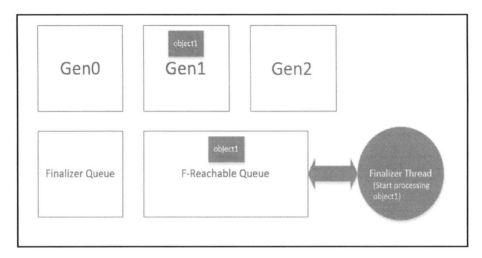

Once the finalizer thread runs the method in the **F-Reachable Queue**, it will be removed from the memory by the GC.

In .NET Core, the finalizer can be defined as follows:

```
public class FileLogger
{
  //Finalizer implementation
   ~FileLogger()
  {
    //dispose objects
  }
}
```

Usually, this method is used to dispose of unmanaged objects and contains some code. However, a code can contain bugs that affect performance. For example, we have three objects that are queued in a finalization queue, which then waits for the first object to be released by the finalizer thread so they can be processed. Now, suppose that a bug in the first `Finalizer` method causes a problem and delays the finalizer thread in returning and processing the rest of the methods. After some time, more objects will come into the finalization queue and wait for the finalizer thread to process, impacting the applications, performance.

The best practice to dispose of objects is to use the `IDisposable` interface rather than implementing the `Finalizer` method. If you are using the `Finalizer` method for some reason, it is always good to implement the `IDisposable` interface as well and suppress finalization by calling the `GC.SuppressFinalize` method.

Best practices for disposing of objects in .NET Core

We have learned in the previous section that object disposal in .NET Core is automatically done by the GC. Nevertheless, disposing of objects in your code is always a good practice, and is highly recommended when you are working with unmanaged objects. In this section, we will explore some best practices that can be used to dispose of objects while writing code in .NET Core.

Introduction to the IDisposable interface

`IDisposable` is a simple interface that contains one `Dispose` method, takes no parameter, and returns `void`:

```
public interface IDisposable
{
    void Dispose();
}
```

It is used to release unmanaged resources. So if any class implements the `IDisposable` interface, it means that the class contains unmanaged resources and these have to be released by calling the `Dispose` method of the class.

What are unmanaged resources?

Any resource that is outside of your application boundary is considered an unmanaged resource. It could be a database, filesystem, web service, or a similar resource. To access the database, we use the managed .NET API to open or close the connection and execute various commands. However, the actual connection to the database is not managed. The same is true for the filesystem and web services where we use managed .NET APIs to interact with them, but they use unmanaged resources in the backend that are not managed. The IDisposable interface is the best fit for all such scenarios.

Using IDisposable

Here is a simple DataManager class that uses a System.Data.SQL API to perform database operations on an SQL server database:

```
public class DataManager : IDisposable
{
  private SqlConnection _connection;
  //Returns the list of users from database
  public DataTable GetUsers()
  {
    //Invoke OpenConnection to instantiate the _connection object

    OpenConnection();

    //Executing command in a using block to dispose command object
    using(var command =new SqlCommand())
    {
      command.Connection = _connection;
      command.CommandText = "Select * from Users";

      //Executing reader in a using block to dispose reader object
      using (var reader = command.ExecuteReader())
      {
        var dt = new DataTable();
        dt.Load(reader);
        return dt;
      }

    }
  }
  private void OpenConnection()
  {
    if (_connection == null)
    {
```

```
        _connection = new SqlConnection(@"Integrated Security=SSPI;
        Persist Security Info=False;Initial Catalog=SampleDB;
        Data Source=.sqlexpress");
        _connection.Open();
    }
}

//Disposing _connection object
public void Dispose() {
    Console.WriteLine("Disposing object");
    _connection.Close();
    _connection.Dispose();
}
}
```

In the preceding code, we have implemented the IDisposable interface which, in turn, implemented the Dispose method to clean up the SQL connection object. We have also called the connection's Dispose method, which will chain up the process in the pipeline and close the underlying objects.

From the calling program, we can use the using block to instantiate the DatabaseManager object that invokes the Dispose method after calling the GetUsers method:

```
static void Main(string[] args)
{
    using(DataManager manager=new DataManager())
    {
        manager.GetUsers();
    }
}
```

The using block is a C# construct that is rendered by the compiler in a try finally block and calls the Dispose method in the finally block. So this means that when you are using a using block, we don't have to call the Dispose method explicitly. Alternatively, the preceding code can be written in the following way as well, and this particular code format is internally managed by the using block:

```
static void Main(string[] args)
{
    DataManager _manager;
    try
    {
        _manager = new DataManager();
    }
    finally
    {
```

```
      _manager.Dispose();
   }
}
```

When to implement the IDisposable interface

We already know that the `IDisposable` interface should be used whenever we need to release unmanaged resources. However, there is a standard rule that should be considered when dealing with the disposal of objects. The rule states that if the instance within the class implements the `IDisposable` interface, we should implement `IDisposable` on the consuming class as well. For example, the preceding class `DatabaseManager` class uses `SqlConnection`, where `SqlConnection` implements the `IDisposable` interface internally. To address this rule, we will implement the `IDisposable` interface and invoke the instance's `Dispose` method.

Here is a better example that invokes the `protected` `Dispose` method from the `DatabaseManager` `Dispose` method and passes a `Boolean` value indicating that the object is being disposed of. Ultimately, we will call the `GC.SuppressFinalize` method that tells the GC that the object is already cleaned up, preventing a redundant garbage collection from being called:

```
public void Dispose() {
   Console.WriteLine("Disposing object");
   Dispose(true);
   GC.SuppressFinalize(this);
}
protected virtual void Dispose(Boolean disposing)
{
   if (disposing)
   {
      if (_connection != null)
      {
         _connection.Close();
         _connection.Dispose();
         //set _connection to null, so next time it won't hit this block
         _connection = null;
      }
   }
}
```

The reason we have kept the parameterized Dispose method protected and virtual is so that the child classes if derived from the DatabaseManager class can override the Dispose method and clean up their own resources. This ensures that each class in the object tree will clean up its resources. Child classes dispose of their resources and call Dispose on the base class, and so on.

Finalizer and Dispose

The Finalizer method is called by the GC, whereas the Dispose method has to be called by the developer explicitly in the program. The GC doesn't know if the class contains a Dispose method, and it needs to be called when the object is disposing to clean up the unmanaged resources. In this scenario, where we need to strictly clean up the resources rather than relying on the caller to call the Dispose method of the object, we should implement the Finalizer method.

The following is a modified example of the DatabaseManager class that implements the Finalizer method:

```
public class DataManager : IDisposable
{
  private SqlConnection _connection;
  //Returns the list of users from database
  public DataTable GetUsers()
  {
    //Invoke OpenConnection to instantiate the _connection object

    OpenConnection();

    //Executing command in a using block to dispose command object
    using(var command =new SqlCommand())
    {
      command.Connection = _connection;
      command.CommandText = "Select * from Users";

      //Executing reader in a using block to dispose reader object
      using (var reader = command.ExecuteReader())
      {
        var dt = new DataTable();
        dt.Load(reader);
        return dt;
      }
    }
  }
  private void OpenConnection()
```

```
  {
    if (_conn == null)
    {
      _connection = new SqlConnection(@"Integrated Security=SSPI;
      Persist Security Info=False;Initial Catalog=SampleDB;
      Data Source=.sqlexpress");
      _connection.Open();
    }
  }

  //Disposing _connection object
  public void Dispose() {
    Console.WriteLine("Disposing object");
    Dispose(true);
    GC.SuppressFinalize(this);
  }

  private void Dispose(Boolean disposing)
  {
    if(disposing) {
      //clean up any managed resources, if called from the
      //finalizer, all the managed resources will already
      //be collected by the GC
    }
    if (_connection != null)
    {
      _connection.Close();
      _connection.Dispose();
      //set _connection to null, so next time it won't hit this block
      _connection = null;
    }

  }
  //Implementing Finalizer
  ~DataManager(){
    Dispose(false);
  }
}
```

In the preceding code snippet, we have modified the `Dispose` method and added the finalizer using a destructor syntax, `~DataManager`. When the GC runs, the finalizer is invoked and calls the `Dispose` method by passing a false flag as a Boolean parameter. In the `Dispose` method, we will clean up the `connection` object. During the finalization stage, the managed resources will already be cleaned up by the GC, so the `Dispose` method will now only clean up the unmanaged resources from the finalizer. However, a developer can explicitly dispose of objects by calling the `Dispose` method and passing a true flag as a Boolean parameter to clean up managed resources.

Summary

This chapter was focused on memory management. We learned some best practices and the actual underlying process of how memory management is done in .NET. We explored the debugging tool, which can be used by developers to investigate an object's memory allocation on the heap. We also learned about memory fragmentation, finalizers, and how to implement a dispose pattern to clean up resources by implementing the `IDisposable` interface.

In the next chapter, we will be creating an application following a microservices architecture. A microservice architecture is a highly performant and scalable architecture that helps the application to scale out easily. The following chapter provides you with a complete understanding of how an application can be developed following the best practices and principles.

18
Microservices Architecture

Microservices application development is growing at a rapid pace in the software industry. It is widely used for developing performant applications that are resilient, scalable, distributed, and cloud-ready. Many organizations and software companies are transforming their applications into the microservices architecture style. Amazon, eBay, and Uber are good examples of companies that have transformed their applications into microservices.

Microservices split the application horizontally and vertically into smaller components, where the components are independent of one another and communicate through an endpoint. With the recent development in the industry of containers, we can use containers to deploy/run microservices that can scale up or scale out independently without any dependency on other components of the application and are leveraged with the pay-as-you-go model.

Today, we can use **Azure Container Service (ACS)** or Service Fabric to deploy .NET Core applications in the cloud and provide a containerization model with the consortium of Docker, Kubernetes, and other third-party components.

In this chapter, we will learn the fundamentals of microservices architecture and its challenges, and create a basic application following microservices principles and practices.

The following are the topics we will learn in this chapter:

- Microservices architecture
- Benefits and standard practices
- Stateless versus stateful microservices
- Decomposing databases and its challenges
- Developing microservices in .NET Core
- Running .NET Core microservices on Docker

Microservices architecture

Microservices architecture is an architectural style in which the application is loosely coupled; it is divided into components based on business capability or domain, and scales independently without affecting other services or components of the application. This contrasts with the monolithic architecture, where a full application is deployed on a server or a **Virtual Machine** (**VM**) and scaling out is not a cost-effective or easy solution. For each scale-out operation, a new VM instance has to be cloned and the application needs to be deployed.

The following diagram shows the architecture of a monolithic application, where most of the functionality is isolated within a single process and scaling out to multiple servers requires the full deployment of the application on the other server:

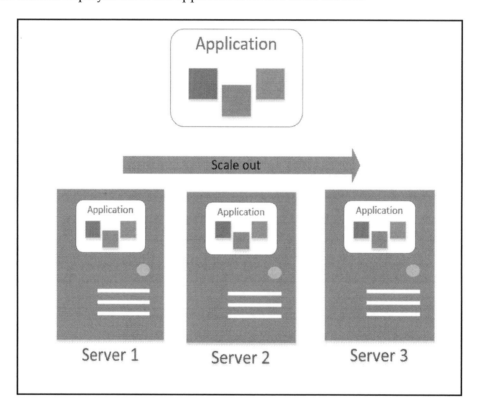

The following is a representation of microservices architecture, which separates an application into smaller services and, based on the workload, scales independently:

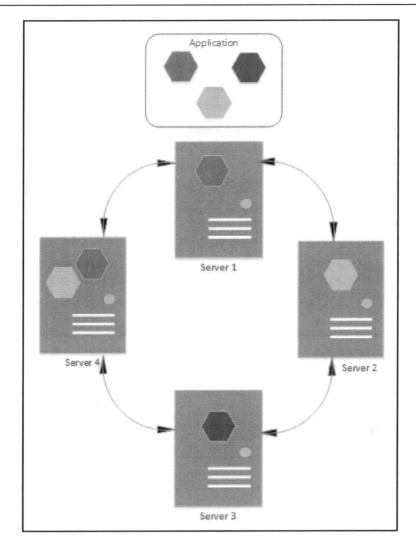

In microservices architecture, the application is divided into loosely coupled services, each of which exposes an endpoint and is deployed on a separate server or, most likely, container. Each service communicates with the other services through some endpoint.

Benefits of microservices architecture

There are various benefits of microservices architecture, which are as follows:

- Microservices are autonomous and expose a self-contained unit of functionality with loosely coupled dependencies on other services
- It exposes features to a caller via a well-defined API contract
- It degrades gracefully if any service fails
- It scales up and scales out independently
- It is best suited for containerized deployment, which is a cost-effective solution when compared to VMs
- Each component can be reused through an endpoint and modifying any service does not affect other services
- Development is faster when compared to monolithic architecture
- As each microservice provides a particular business capability, it is easily reusable and composable
- As each service is independent, using old architecture or technology is not a concern.
- It is resilient and eliminates monolith failover scenarios

Standard practice when developing microservices

As standard practice, microservices are designed and decomposed based on business capability or business domain. Business domain decomposition follows a **Domain-Driven Design (DDD)** pattern, where each service is developed to provide specific functionality of the business domain. This contrasts with a layered architecture approach, in which the application is divided into multiple layers, where each layer is dependent on another layer and has tight dependencies on it, and removing any layer breaks the whole application.

The following diagram illustrates the difference between layered architecture and microservices architecture:

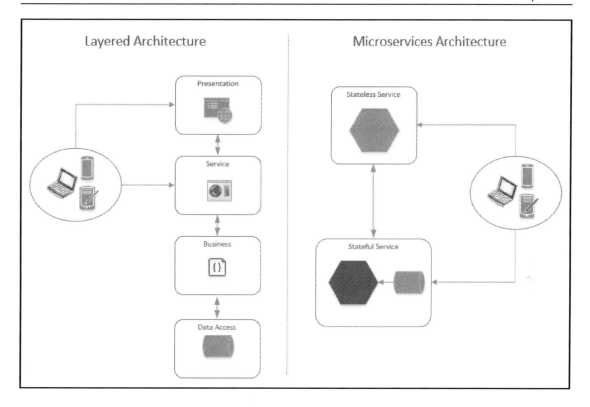

Types of microservices

Microservices are divided into two categories, which are as follows:

- Stateless microservices
- Stateful microservices

Stateless microservices

A stateless service has either no state or the state can be retrieved from an external data store. As the state is stored separately, multiple instances can run at the same time.

Stateful microservices

A stateful service maintains the state within its own context. Only a single instance is active at a time. However, the state is replicated to other inactive instances as well.

DDD

DDD is a pattern that emphasizes the business domain of the application. When building the application following a DDD pattern, we divide the application based on business domains, where each domain has one or more bounded contexts and the bounded context represents the business requirement. In technical terms, each bounded context has its own code and persistence mechanism and is independent of the others. Consider a vendor-management system where a vendor registers with the website, logs into the website, updates their profile, and attaches quotations. Each type of action will be termed the bounded context and is independent of the others. A set of vendor-operations can be termed a vendor domain.

DDD splits the requirement into domain-specific chunks known as bounded contexts, where each bounded context has its own model, logic, and data. There are chances that a single service is used by many services because of the core functionality it provides. For example, a vendor registration service uses an identity service to create a new user and the same identity service may be used by some other service to log into the system.

Data manipulation with microservices

As a general practice, each service provides specific business functionality to the user and involves **Create**, **Read**, **Update**, and **Delete (CRUD)** operations. In enterprise applications, we have one or more databases that have a number of tables. Following the DDD pattern, we can design each service that focuses on the specific domain. However, there are conditions where we need to extract the data from some other databases or tables that are out of scope from the service's domain. However, there are two options to address this challenge:

- Wrapping microservices behind an API gateway
- Decomposing data into a flat schema for read/query purposes

Wrapping microservices behind an API gateway

An enterprise application that is based on microservices architecture contains many services. An **Entity Resource Planning (ERP)** system contains many modules, such as **Human Resources (HR)**, financial, purchase requisition, and others. Each module may have a number of services providing specific business features. For example, the HR module may contain the following three services:

- Personal record management
- Appraisal management
- Recruitment management

The personal record management service exposes certain methods to create, update, or delete an employee's basic information. The appraisal-management service exposes certain methods to create appraisal requests for an employee, and the recruitment-management service performs new hiring decisions. Suppose we need to develop a web page that contains the basic employee information and the total number of appraisals done in the last five years. In this case, we will be calling two services, namely personal-record management and appraisal management, and two separate calls will be made by the caller to these services. Alternatively, we can wrap these two calls into a single call using an API gateway. The technique to address this scenario is known as **API composition** and is discussed in the *What is API composition?* section later in the chapter.

Denormalizing data into a flat schema for read/query purposes

This is another technique where we want to consume a service to read data from heterogeneous sources. It could be from multiple tables or databases. To transform multiple service calls into a single call, we can design each service and use patterns such as publisher/subscriber or mediator that listen for any CRUD operation to be performed on any service, save the data into a flat schema, and develop a service that only reads the data from that table(s). The technique to address this scenario is known as **Command Query Responsibility Segregation (CQRS)** and is discussed in the CQRS section later in the chapter.

Consistency across business scenarios

As we understand that each service is designed to serve a specific business functionality, let's take an example of an order-management system where a customer comes to the website and places an order. Once the order is placed, it is reflected in the inventory. In this scenario, we can have two microservices: one that places an order and creates a database record into the order database and an inventory service that performs CRUD on the inventory-related tables:

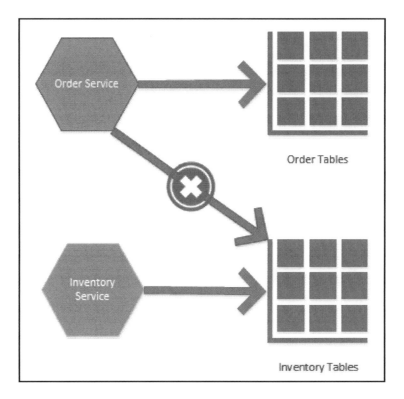

The important practice to follow when implementing an end-to-end business scenario and bringing consistency across multiple microservices is to keep the data and model specific to their domain. Considering the preceding example, the order placement service should not access or perform CRUD operations other than order tables, and if it is necessary to access any data which is out of the domain of that service, it should call that service directly.

An **Atomicity, Consistency, Integrity, and Durability (ACID)** transaction is another challenge. We may have multiple services serving one complete transaction, where each transaction is behind and operated by a separate service. To accommodate ACID transactions with the microservices architecture style, we can implement **asynchronous event-driven communication**, which is discussed later in the chapter.

Communication with microservices

In microservices architecture, each microservice is hosted at some server, most likely a container, and exposes an endpoint. These endpoints can be used to communicate to that service. There are many protocols that we can use but REST-based HTTP endpoints are most widely used due to their accessibility support on many platforms. In ASP.NET Core, we can create microservices using the ASP.NET Core MVC framework and use them through a RESTful endpoint. There are microservices that use other microservices as well to complete a particular operation and this can easily be done using the `HttpClient` class in .NET Core. However, we should design in such a way that our service offers resiliency and handles transient faults.

Database architecture in microservices

With microservices architecture, each service provides a certain functionality and has minimal dependencies on other services. However, porting the relational database into the smaller sets is a challenge, where each set represents a particular domain and contains tables related to that domain. Segregating tables based on domain and making them individual databases needs proper consideration.

Let's consider the vendor management system that provides **Business-to-Consumer (B2C)** and **Business-to-Business (B2B)** processes and involves the following operations:

- Vendor registers with the website
- Vendor adds products that can be purchased by other vendors or customers
- Vendor places orders to purchase products

To implement the preceding scenario, we can decompose the database based on the following two patterns:

- Tables per service
- Database per service

Tables per service

With this design, each service is designed to use specific tables in the database. In this scenario, the database is centralized and hosted at one place. Other microservices also connect to the same database but deal with their own domain-specific tables:

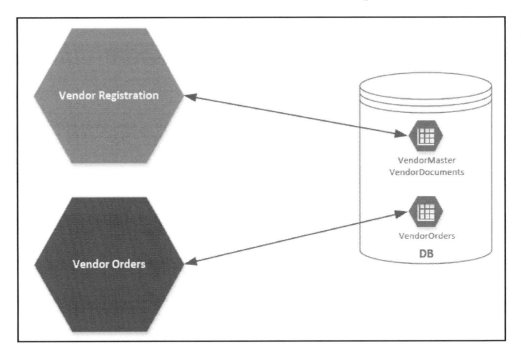

This helps us to use the central database but any modification in the schema may break or require an update for one or many microservices.

Database per service

With this design, each service has its own database and the application is loosely coupled. Modifications in the database do not harm or break any other service and offer complete isolation. This design is good for deployment scenarios, as each service contains its own database deployed in its own container:

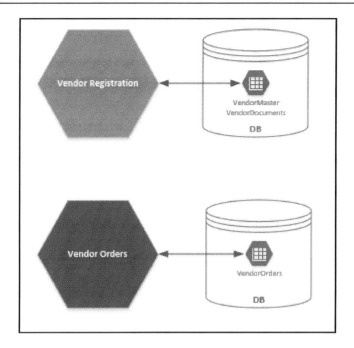

Challenges in segregating tables or databases per service

Segregating tables or databases as per business capability or business domain is recommended to limit dependencies and keep it intact with the domain model. But it also comes with some challenges. For example, we have two services: a vendor service and an order service. The vendor service is used to create a vendor record in its own vendor database, and the order service to place orders for a particular vendor. The challenge comes when we need to return the aggregated record of both the vendor and their orders to the user. To solve this problem, we can use either of the following two approaches:

- API composition
- CQRS

What is API composition?

API composition is a technique in which multiple microservices are composed to expose one endpoint to the user and provides an aggregated view. In a single database, this is easily possible by making a SQL query join and getting the data from different tables.

Let's consider the vendor management system, where we have two services. One is used to register a new vendor and has a corresponding database to persist vendor demographics, address, and other information. The other service is the order service, which is used to store the transactional data of the vendor and contains order information such as order number, quantity, and so on. Suppose we have a requirement to display the list of vendors with all the orders that are completed. With this scenario, we can provide a method in the vendor registration service that first loads the vendor details from its own data store, then loads their orders by calling the order service, and finally returns the aggregated data.

CQRS

CQRS is a principle in which application commands such as create, update, and delete are segregated by read operations. It works on the event-based model and when any create, update, or delete action is taken on the API, the event handler is invoked and stores that information into its own corresponding data store. We can implement CQRS in the previous vendor registration example, which will facilitate querying the vendor and their orders from a single service. When any command (create, update, delete) operation is performed on the vendor or order service, it will invoke the handler that invokes the query service to save the updated data into its store.

We can keep the data in a flat schema or used NoSQL database to hold all the information about the vendor and their orders and read them when required:

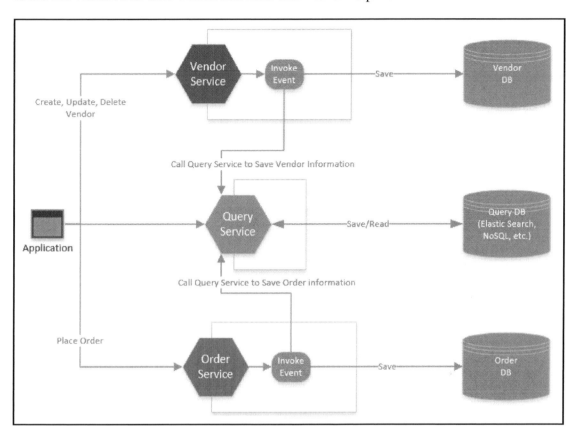

The preceding diagram represents three services: vendor service, order service, and query service. When any create, update, or delete operation is performed on the vendor service, the event is raised and the corresponding handler is invoked that makes the HTTP POST, PUT, or DELETE request on the query service to save or update its data store. The same goes for the order service, which calls the query service and stores the information related to orders. Finally, the query service is used to read the cumulative data of independent services in a single call.

The benefits of this approach are as follows:

- We can make optimize the query database by defining cluster and non-cluster indexes
- We can use some other database model, such as NoSQL, MongoDB, or Elasticsearch, to provide a faster retrieval and search experience to the user
- Each service has its own data store but, with this approach, we can aggregate the data in one place
- We can use the query data for reporting purposes

CQRS can be implemented using the mediator pattern, which we will discuss later in the chapter.

Developing microservices architecture with .NET Core

So far, we have learned the fundamentals of microservices and the importance of DDD. In this section, we will develop a microservices architecture for a sample application that contains the following features:

- Identity service
- Vendor service

Creating a sample app in .NET Core using microservices architecture

In this section, we will create a sample app in .NET Core and define services that include the authorization server, a vendor service, and an order service. To start with, we can use either Visual Studio 2017 or Visual Studio Code and create projects using dotnet **Command-Line Interface (CLI)** tools. The advantage of choosing Visual Studio 2017 is that it provides an option while creating the project to enable Docker support, add the Docker-related files, and make Docker the startup project:

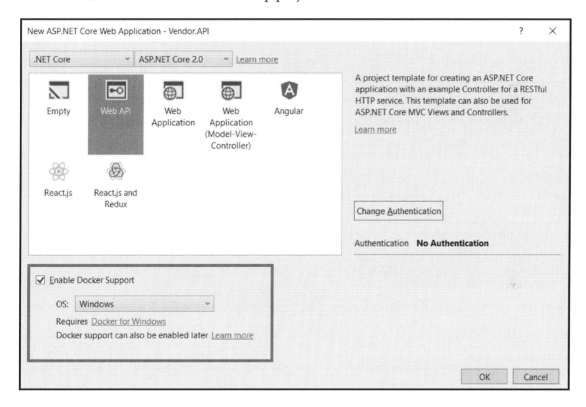

Solution structure

The structure of the solution will look like the following:

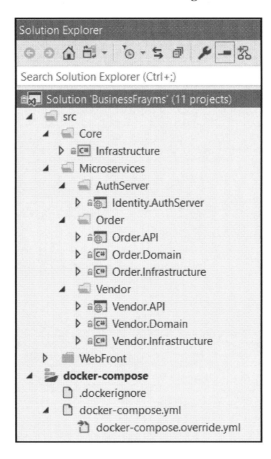

In the preceding structure, we have root folders, namely `Core`, `Microservices`, and `WebFront`. The common and core components reside in `Core`, all the microservices reside in the `Microservices` folder, and `WebFront` contains the frontend projects, most likely the ASP.NET MVC Core project, mobile application, and so on.

Creating projects inside designated folders gives proper meaning to the solution and makes it easy to understand the overall picture of the solution.

The following table shows the projects created inside each folder:

Folder	Project name	Project type	Description
Core	Infrastructure	.NET Standard 2.0	Contains repository classes, `UnitOfWork` and `BaseEntity`
Core	APIComponents	.NET Standard 2.0	Contains `BaseController`, `LoggingActionFilter` and `ResilientHttpClient`
Microservices > AuthServer	Identity.AuthServer	ASP.NET Core 2.0 web API	Authorization server using OpenIddict and ASP.NET Core Identity
Microservices > Vendor	Vendor.API	ASP.NET Core 2.0 web API	Contains vendor API controllers
Microservices > Vendor	Vendor.Domain	.NET Standard 2.0	Contains domain models specific to the vendor domain
Microservices > Vendor	Vendor.Infrastructure	.NET Standard 2.0	Contains vendor-specific repository and database context
WebFront	FraymsWebApp	ASP.NET Core 2.0 web app	Contains frontend views, pages, and client-side framework

Logical architecture

The logical architecture of the sample application represents two microservices, namely the identity service and vendor service. The identity service is used to perform user authentication and authorization, whereas the vendor service is used to perform vendor registration:

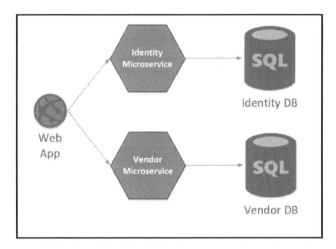

We will be using the DDD approach to articulate the data model, where each service will have its own corresponding tables.

The vendor service is based on business domain and is divided into three layers, namely the API that exposes HTTP endpoints and is used by the client, the domain that contains domain entities, aggregates, and DDD patterns, and the infrastructure layer that contains all common classes that include repository, **Entity Framework** (**EF**), Core context, and other helper classes.

The domain layer is the actual layer that defines the business logic and the entities, usually **Plain Old CLR Object** (**POCO**), for a particular business scenario. It should not have any direct dependency on any database framework or **Object Relationship Mapping** (**ORM**) such as EF, Hibernate, and others. However, with EF Core, we have a provision to keep entities separate from other assemblies and define them as POCO entities, removing dependencies from EF Core libraries.

When a request comes to an API, it uses the domain layer to execute a particular business scenario and pass the data it receives. The domain layer executes the business logic and uses the infrastructure layer to perform CRUD on the database. Finally, the response is sent back to the caller from an API:

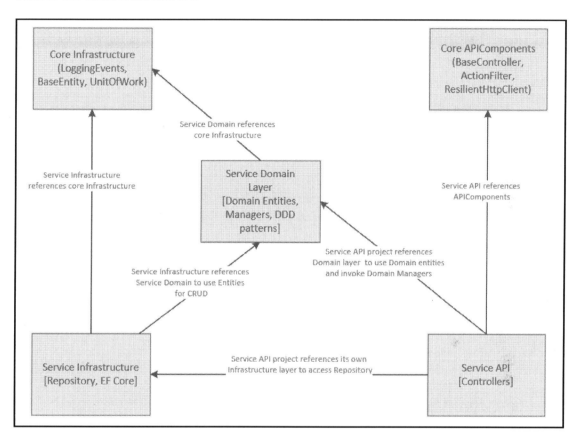

Developing a Core infrastructure project

This project contains the core classes and components used by the application. It will contain some generic or base classes, façade, and other helper classes that are common throughout the application.

We will create the following classes and discuss how they are useful for other projects specific to microservices.

Creating the BaseEntity class

The `BaseEntity` class contains common properties being used by all the domain models in our microservices projects. Usually, for all the transaction tables, we store `CreatedBy`, `CreatedOn`, `UpdatedBy`, and `UpdatedOn` fields. When designing the entity model for each service, we will inherit from the `BaseEntity` class so all these common properties will be added to the table when the migration is run. Here is the code snippet of the `BaseEntity` class:

```
public abstract class BaseEntity
{

  public BaseEntity()
  {
    this.CreatedOn = DateTime.Now;
    this.UpdatedOn = DateTime.Now;
    this.State = (int)EntityState.New;

  }
  public string CreatedBy { get; set; }
  public DateTime CreatedOn { get; set; }
  public string UpdatedBy { get; set; }
  public DateTime UpdatedOn { get; set; }
}
```

Any property being annotated with the `NotMapped` attribute does not create corresponding fields in the backend database.

The UnitOfWork pattern

We will implement the `UnitOfWork` pattern to save the context changes in a single call to the backend database. Updating the database on each object state change is not good practice and reduces the application performance. Consider an example of a form that contains a table where each row is editable. Committing a change in a database on each row update reduces application performance. The better way is to keep each row state in memory and update the database once the form is posted. With the Unit of Work pattern, we can define an interface that contains the following four methods:

```
public interface IUnitOfWork: IDisposable
{
  void BeginTransaction();

  void RollbackTransaction();
```

```
    void CommitTransaction();

    Task<bool> SaveChangesAsync();
}
```

The interface contains transaction-related methods, namely `BeginTransaction`, `RollbackTransaction`, and `CommitTransaction`, where `SaveChangesAsync` is used to save the changes to the database. Each service has its own database context implementation and implements the `IUnitOfWork` interface to provide transaction handling and save changes to a backend database.

Creating a repository interface

We will create a generic repository interface that will be implemented by each service's repository class, as each service will be following a DDD approach and has its own repository to give meaningful information to the developer based on the business domain. In this interface, we can keep generic methods such as `All` and `Contains` and a property to return `UnitOfWork`:

```
public interface IRepository<T> where T : BaseEntity
{
   IUnitOfWork UnitOfWork { get; }

   IQueryable<T> All<T>() where T : BaseEntity;
   T Find<T>(Expression<Func<T, bool>> predicate) where T : BaseEntity;
   bool Contains<T>(Expression<Func<T, bool>> predicate) where T :
BaseEntity;
}
```

Logging

Logging is an essential part of any enterprise application. Through logging, we can trace or troubleshoot actual errors when the application is running. In any good product, we usually see that each error has an error code. Defining error codes and then using them while logging exceptions intuitively tells the developers or the support team to troubleshoot and reach the point where the actual error occurred and provide a solution. For all application-level errors, we can create a `LoggingEvents` class and specify the constant values that can be further used during development. Here is the `LoggingEvents` class that contains a few `GET`, `CREATE`, `UPDATE`, and other event codes. We can create this class under a `Façade` folder inside the `Infrastructure` project:

```
public static class LoggingEvents
{
   public const int GET_ITEM = 1001;
```

```
        public const int GET_ITEMS = 1002;
        public const int CREATE_ITEM = 1003;
        public const int UPDATE_ITEM = 1004;
        public const int DELETE_ITEM = 1005;
        public const int DATABASE_ERROR = 2000;
        public const int SERVICE_ERROR = 2001;
        public const int ERROR = 2002;
        public const int ACCESS_METHOD = 3000;
    }
```

Next, we will add another class, `LoggerHelper`, which will be used throughout our application to get the exception stack trace from the exception. Here is the code snippet of the `LoggerHelper` class:

```
    public static string GetExceptionDetails(Exception ex)
    {

      StringBuilder errorString = new StringBuilder();
      errorString.AppendLine("An error occured. ");
      Exception inner = ex;
      while (inner != null)
      {
        errorString.Append("Error Message:");
        errorString.AppendLine(ex.Message);
        errorString.Append("Stack Trace:");
        errorString.AppendLine(ex.StackTrace);
        inner = inner.InnerException;
      }
      return errorString.ToString();
    }
```

Creating the APIComponents infrastructure project

The APIComponents project contains the components specific to microservices. In this project, we will create a `BaseController` class, which will add some classes related to logging and can also extend to add further common objects used by concrete controllers. Add a `BaseController` class under the `Controllers` folder inside the `APIComponents` project. Here is the code snippet of the `BaseController` class:

```
    public class BaseController : Controller
    {
      private ILogger _logger;
      public BaseController(ILogger logger)
      {
        _logger = logger;
      }
```

```
public ILogger Logger { get { return _logger; } }
public HttpResponseMessage LogException(Exception ex)
{
  HttpResponseMessage message = new HttpResponseMessage();
  message.Content = new StringContent(ex.Message);
  message.StatusCode = System.Net.HttpStatusCode.ExpectationFailed;
  return message;
}
}
```

BaseController takes ILogger in a parametrized constructor that will be injected through the built-in **Dependency Injection (DI)** component of ASP.NET Core.

The LogException method is used to log the exception and returns the HttpResponseMessage that will be returned by the derived controller to the user in case of any error.

Next, we will add the Filters folder inside the APIComponents project and add all the common filters that can be used by the microservices controllers. For now, we will just add the LoggingActionFilter that can be used by annotating the Action methods of the microservices controllers and automatically logging the information when the request comes in and response goes out. Here is the code snippet of the LoggingActionFilter class:

```
public class LoggingActionFilter: ActionFilterAttribute
{
  public override void OnActionExecuting(ActionExecutingContext context)
  {

    Log("OnActionExecuting", context.RouteData, context.Controller);

  }

  public override void OnActionExecuted(ActionExecutedContext context)
  {
    Log("OnActionExecuted", context.RouteData, context.Controller);

  }

  public override void OnResultExecuted(ResultExecutedContext context)
  {
    Log("OnResultExecuted", context.RouteData, context.Controller);
  }

  public override void OnResultExecuting(ResultExecutingContext context)
  {
```

```
      Log("OnResultExecuting", context.RouteData, context.Controller);
   }

   private void Log(string methodName, RouteData routeData, Object
controller)
   {
      var controllerName = routeData.Values["controller"];
      var actionName = routeData.Values["action"];
      var message = String.Format("{0} controller:{1} action:{2}",
      methodName, controllerName, actionName);
      BaseController baseController = ((BaseController)controller);
      baseController.Logger.LogInformation(LoggingEvents.ACCESS_METHOD,
message);
   }
}
```

Developing an identity service for user authorization

In ASP.NET Core, we have a choice of authenticating applications from various authentication providers. In microservices architecture, services are deployed and hosted separately in different containers. We can use ASP.NET Core Identity and add it as middleware in the service itself, or we can use IdentityServer and develop a central authentication server to perform authentication and authorization centrally, access all the services that are registered with the **Central Authentication Server** (**CAS**), and access protected resources by passing tokens.

The identity service basically acts as a CAS that registers all the services in the enterprise. When the request comes to the service, it asks for the token that can be obtained from the authorization server. Once the token is obtained, it can be used to access the resource service.

There are various libraries to build the authentication server, which are as follows:

- **IdentityServer4**: IdentityServer4 is an OpenID Connect and OAuth 2.0 framework for ASP.NET Core
- **OpenIddict**: Easy to plug in solution to implement OpenID Connect server in ASP.NET Core project

- **ASOS (AspNet.Security.OpenIdConnect.Server)**: ASOS is an advanced OpenID Connect server designed to offer a low-level protocol-first approach

We will be using OpenIddict in our identity service.

OpenIddict connect flows

OpenIddict offers various types of flows, including authorization code flow, password flow, client credentials flow, and others. However, we have used implicit flow in this chapter.

In implicit flow, the tokens are retrieved through the authorization endpoint by passing a username and password. All communication is done with the authorization server in a single round trip. Once the authentication is done, the token is added in the redirect URI and can be later used by passing in the request header for subsequent requests. The following diagram depicts how implicit flow works:

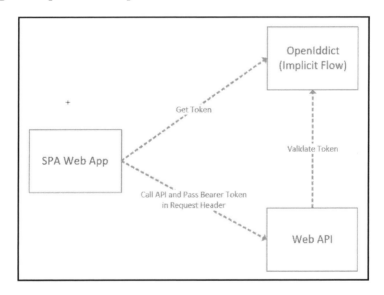

Implicit flow is widely used with **Single-Page Applications (SPAs)**. The process starts when an SPA web application wants to access the protected web API from the resource server. As the web API is protected, it needs a token to authenticate the request and validate the caller. To obtain the token (commonly known as a bearer token), the SPA web app first proceeds to the authorization server and enters the username and password. After successful authentication, the authorization server returns the token and appends it to the redirect URI itself. The web application parses the **Uniform Resource Locator** (URL) and retrieves the token and further used to access the protected resources.

Creating the identity service project

The identity service is an ASP.NET Core web API project. To use OpenIddict libraries, we have to add an `aspnet-contrib` reference to our Visual Studio package sources dialog. To add this source from Visual Studio, click on the NuGet Package Manager by right-clicking on the project and then hitting the settings button, as shown in the following screenshot:

Then add the entry of `aspnet-contrib` with the source as `https://www.myget.org/F/aspnet-contrib/api/v3/index.json`:

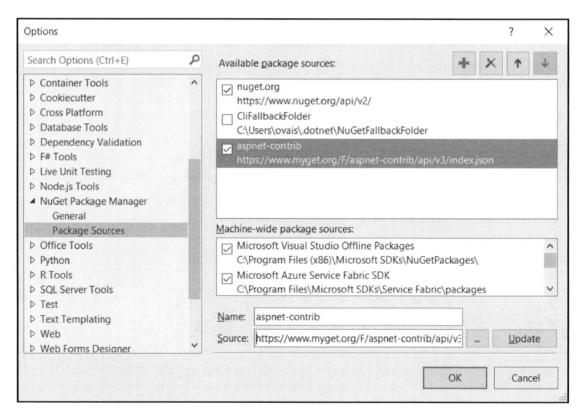

Once this is added, we can now easily add OpenIddict packages from the NuGet Package Manager window.

Remember to check that the **Include prerelease** checkbox is selected.

The following are the packages that we can add directly to our project file or from the NuGet Package Manager window in Visual Studio:

```
<PackageReference Include="AspNet.Security.OAuth.Validation"
Version="2.0.0-rc1-final" />
<PackageReference Include="AspNet.Security.OpenIdConnect.Server"
Version="2.0.0-rc1-final" />
<PackageReference Include="Microsoft.AspNetCore.Identity" Version="2.0.1"
/>
<PackageReference
Include="Microsoft.AspNetCore.Identity.EntityFrameworkCore" Version="2.0.1"
/>
<PackageReference
Include="Microsoft.VisualStudio.Web.CodeGeneration.Design" Version="2.0.2"
/>
<PackageReference Include="OpenIddict" Version="2.0.0-rc2-0797" />
<PackageReference Include="OpenIddict.Core" Version="2.0.0-rc2-0797" />
<PackageReference Include="OpenIddict.EntityFrameworkCore" Version="2.0.0-
rc2-0797" />
<PackageReference Include="OpenIddict.Models" Version="2.0.0-rc2-0797" />
<PackageReference Include="OpenIddict.Mvc" Version="2.0.0-rc2-0797" />
```

Add custom UserEntity and UserRole classes

ASP.NET Core Identity contains `IdentityUser` and `IdentityRole` classes and uses EF Core to create a backend database. However, if we want to customize the default tables, we can do so by inheriting from these base classes.

We will create a `Models` folder and customize `IdentityUser` by creating a custom `UserEntity` class and adding the following four fields:

```
public class UserEntity : IdentityUser<Guid>
{

  public int VendorId { get; set; }

  public string FirstName { get; set; }
  public string LastName { get; set; }

  public DateTimeOffset CreatedAt { get; set; }
}
```

We have added these fields so when a vendor registers, we will keep their first name, last name, and ID in this table. Next, we add another class, `UserRole`, which derives from `IdentityRole`, and add the parametrized constructor as follows:

```
public class UserRoleEntity : IdentityRole<Guid>
{
  public UserRoleEntity() : base() { }

  public UserRoleEntity(string roleName) : base(roleName) { }
}
```

We will add the custom database context class that derives from `IdentityDbContext` and specify `UserEntity` and `UserRoleEntity` types as follows:

```
public class BFIdentityContext : IdentityDbContext<UserEntity,
UserRoleEntity, Guid>
{
  public BFIdentityContext(Microsoft.EntityFrameworkCore.DbContextOptions
options) :
  base(options) { }
}
```

We can run EF Core migrations to create ASP.NET Identity tables, and we can run migration using EF CLI tooling. Before running the migration, we add the following entries in the `ConfigureServices` method of our `Startup` class:

```
public void ConfigureServices(IServiceCollection services)
{
  var connection= Configuration["ConnectionString"];

  services.AddDbContext<BFIdentityContext>(options =>
  {
    // Configure the context to use Microsoft SQL Server.
    options.UseSqlServer(connection);
  });

  services.AddIdentity<UserEntity,
UserRole>().AddEntityFrameworkStores<BFIdentityContext>();

  services.AddMvc();
}
```

You can run the EF migrations from the Visual Studio Package Manager Console window. To add migration, first run the following command:

```
Add-Migration Initial
```

Add-Migration is the command of EF CLI toolset, where Initial is the name of the migration. Once we run this command, it will add the Migrations folder into our project and the Initial class containing Up and Down methods to apply or remove changes to the database. Next, we can run the Update-Database command that loads the Initial class and apply the changes to the backend database.

Now we add the configuration related to the OpenIddict implicit flow in our Startup class. Here is the modified ConfigureServices method that adds the OpenIddict implicit flow:

```
public void ConfigureServices(IServiceCollection services)
{
  var connection = @"Server=.sqlexpress;Database=FraymsIdentityDB;
  User Id=sa;Password=P@ssw0rd;";

  services.AddDbContext<BFIdentityContext>(options =>
  {
    // Configure the context to use Microsoft SQL Server.
    options.UseSqlServer(connection);

    // Register the entity sets needed by OpenIddict.
    // Note: use the generic overload if you need
    // to replace the default OpenIddict entities.
    options.UseOpenIddict();
  });

  services.AddIdentity<UserEntity, UserRoleEntity>()
  .AddEntityFrameworkStores<BFIdentityContext>();

  // Configure Identity to use the same JWT claims as OpenIddict instead
  // of the legacy WS-Federation claims it uses by default (ClaimTypes),
  // which saves you from doing the mapping in your authorization
controller.
  services.Configure<IdentityOptions>(options =>
  {
    options.ClaimsIdentity.UserNameClaimType =
OpenIdConnectConstants.Claims.Name;
    options.ClaimsIdentity.UserIdClaimType =
OpenIdConnectConstants.Claims.Subject;
    options.ClaimsIdentity.RoleClaimType =
OpenIdConnectConstants.Claims.Role;
  });

  // Register the OpenIddict services.
  services.AddOpenIddict(options =>
  {
    // Register the Entity Framework stores.
```

```
        options.AddEntityFrameworkCoreStores<BFIdentityContext>();

        // Register the ASP.NET Core MVC binder used by OpenIddict.
        // Note: if you don't call this method, you won't be able to
        // bind OpenIdConnectRequest or OpenIdConnectResponse parameters.
        options.AddMvcBinders();

        // Enable the authorization, logout, userinfo, and introspection
    endpoints.
        options.EnableAuthorizationEndpoint("/connect/authorize")
        .EnableLogoutEndpoint("/connect/logout")
        .EnableIntrospectionEndpoint("/connect/introspect")
        .EnableUserinfoEndpoint("/api/userinfo");


        // Note: the sample only uses the implicit code flow but you can enable
        // the other flows if you need to support implicit, password or client
    credentials.
        options.AllowImplicitFlow();
        // During development, you can disable the HTTPS requirement.
        options.DisableHttpsRequirement();

        // Register a new ephemeral key, that is discarded when the application
        // shuts down. Tokens signed using this key are automatically
    invalidated.
        // This method should only be used during development.
        options.AddEphemeralSigningKey();

        options.UseJsonWebTokens();
    });

    services.AddAuthentication()
    .AddOAuthValidation();

    services.AddCors();
    services.AddMvc();
}
```

In the preceding method, we first add the `UseOpenIddict` method in the `AddDbContext` options that will create the OpenIddict-related tables in the database. Then, we configure Identity to use the same **JSON Web Tokens (JWT)** claims as OpenIddict by setting the `IdentityOptions` as follows:

```
services.Configure<IdentityOptions>(options =>
{
  options.ClaimsIdentity.UserNameClaimType =
OpenIdConnectConstants.Claims.Name;
  options.ClaimsIdentity.UserIdClaimType =
```

```
OpenIdConnectConstants.Claims.Subject;
  options.ClaimsIdentity.RoleClaimType =
OpenIdConnectConstants.Claims.Role;
});
```

Finally, we register the OpenIddict features and specify values by calling the `services.AddOpenIddict` method.

Here is the `Configure` method that first enables **Cross-Origin Resource Sharing (CORS)**, which allows requests from any header, origin, and method. Then, add authentication and call the `InitializeAsync` method to populate the OpenIddict tables with the application and resources (services) information:

```
public void Configure(IApplicationBuilder app)
{
  app.UseCors(builder =>
  {
    builder.AllowAnyOrigin();
    builder.AllowAnyHeader();
    builder.AllowAnyMethod();
  });

  app.UseAuthentication();

  app.UseMvcWithDefaultRoute();

  // Seed the database with the sample applications.
  // Note: in a real world application, this step should be part of a setup
script.
  InitializeAsync(app.ApplicationServices,
CancellationToken.None).GetAwaiter().GetResult();
}
```

Here is the `InitializeAsync` method shown as follows:

```
private async Task InitializeAsync(IServiceProvider services,
CancellationToken cancellationToken)
{
  // Create a new service scope to ensure the database context
  // is correctly disposed when this methods returns.
  using (var scope =
services.GetRequiredService<IServiceScopeFactory>().CreateScope())
  {
    var context =
scope.ServiceProvider.GetRequiredService<BFIdentityContext>();
    await context.Database.EnsureCreatedAsync();
```

```
        var manager = scope.ServiceProvider.GetRequiredService
        <OpenIddictApplicationManager<OpenIddictApplication>>();

        if (await manager.FindByClientIdAsync("bfrwebapp", cancellationToken)
== null)
        {
          var descriptor = new OpenIddictApplicationDescriptor
          {
            ClientId = "bfrwebapp",
            DisplayName = "Business Frayms web application",
            PostLogoutRedirectUris = { new
Uri("http://localhost:8080/signout-oidc") },
            RedirectUris = { new Uri("http://localhost:8080/signin-oidc") }
          };

          await manager.CreateAsync(descriptor, cancellationToken);
        }

        if (await manager.FindByClientIdAsync("vendor-api", cancellationToken)
== null)
        {
          var descriptor = new OpenIddictApplicationDescriptor
          {
            ClientId = "vendor-api",
            ClientSecret = "846B62D0-DEF9-4215-A99D-86E6B8DAB342",
            //RedirectUris = { new Uri("http://localhost:12345/api") }
          };

          await manager.CreateAsync(descriptor, cancellationToken);
        }

    }
}
```

In the preceding method, we have added the following three applications:

- bfrwebapp: An ASP.NET Core web application. When the user hits the web application, it checks whether the user is authenticated based on whether the token is provided. If the user is not authenticated, it will redirect it to the authorization server. The user enters the credentials and, with successful authentication, it will redirect back to the bfrwebapp. The redirect URI specified within this scope is the URI of bfrwebapp.
- vendor-api: A vendor microservice with a unique client secret key.

The preceding configuration is the server-side configuration and we will see what configuration needs to be added on the client side.

Finally, we will add `AuthorizationController` under the `Controllers` folder to implement endpoints defined for the authorization server in the `ConfigureServices` method in the `Startup` class. Here is the complete code snippet of the `AuthorizationController`:

```
public class AuthorizationController : Controller
{
  private readonly IOptions<IdentityOptions> _identityOptions;
  private readonly SignInManager<UserEntity> _signInManager;
  private readonly UserManager<UserEntity> _userManager;

  public AuthorizationController(
    IOptions<IdentityOptions> identityOptions,
    SignInManager<UserEntity> signInManager,
    UserManager<UserEntity> userManager)
  {
    _identityOptions = identityOptions;
    _signInManager = signInManager;
    _userManager = userManager;
  }

  [HttpGet("~/connect/authorize")]
  public async Task<IActionResult> Authorize(OpenIdConnectRequest request)
  {
    Debug.Assert(request.IsAuthorizationRequest(),
    "The OpenIddict binder for ASP.NET Core MVC is not registered. " +
    "Make sure services.AddOpenIddict().AddMvcBinders() is correctly
called.");

    if (!User.Identity.IsAuthenticated)
    {
      // If the client application request promptless authentication,
      // return an error indicating that the user is not logged in.
      if (request.HasPrompt(OpenIdConnectConstants.Prompts.None))
      {
        var properties = new AuthenticationProperties(new
Dictionary<string, string>
        {
          [OpenIdConnectConstants.Properties.Error] =
          OpenIdConnectConstants.Errors.LoginRequired,
          [OpenIdConnectConstants.Properties.ErrorDescription] =
          "The user is not logged in."
        });

        // Ask OpenIddict to return a login_required error to the client
application.
        return Forbid(properties,
```

```
OpenIdConnectServerDefaults.AuthenticationScheme);
    }

    return Challenge();
  }

  // Retrieve the profile of the logged in user.
  var user = await _userManager.GetUserAsync(User);
  if (user == null)
  {
    return BadRequest(new OpenIdConnectResponse
    {
      Error = OpenIdConnectConstants.Errors.InvalidGrant,
      ErrorDescription = "The username/password couple is invalid."
    });
  }

  // Create a new authentication ticket.
  var ticket = await CreateTicketAsync(request, user);

  // Returning a SignInResult will ask OpenIddict to issue
  the appropriate access/identity tokens.
  return SignIn(ticket.Principal, ticket.Properties,
ticket.AuthenticationScheme);
  }

  [HttpGet("~/connect/logout")]
  public async Task<IActionResult> Logout()
  {
    // Ask ASP.NET Core Identity to delete the local and external cookies
created
    // when the user agent is redirected from the external identity
provider
    // after a successful authentication flow (e.g Google or Facebook).
    await _signInManager.SignOutAsync();

    // Returning a SignOutResult will ask OpenIddict to redirect the user
agent
    // to the post_logout_redirect_uri specified by the client application.
    return SignOut(OpenIdConnectServerDefaults.AuthenticationScheme);
  }

  private async Task<AuthenticationTicket> CreateTicketAsync(
  OpenIdConnectRequest request, UserEntity user)
  {
    // Create a new ClaimsPrincipal containing the claims that
    // will be used to create an id_token, a token or a code.
    var principal = await _signInManager.CreateUserPrincipalAsync(user);
```

```
// Create a new authentication ticket holding the user identity.
var ticket = new AuthenticationTicket(principal,
new AuthenticationProperties(),
OpenIdConnectServerDefaults.AuthenticationScheme);

// Set the list of scopes granted to the client application.
ticket.SetScopes(new[]
{
  OpenIdConnectConstants.Scopes.OpenId,
  OpenIdConnectConstants.Scopes.Email,
  OpenIdConnectConstants.Scopes.Profile,
  OpenIddictConstants.Scopes.Roles
}.Intersect(request.GetScopes()));

ticket.SetResources("vendor-api");

// Note: by default, claims are NOT automatically included in
// the access and identity tokens.
// To allow OpenIddict to serialize them, you must attach them a
destination, that specifies
// whether they should be included in access tokens, in identity tokens
or in both.

foreach (var claim in ticket.Principal.Claims)
{
  // Never include the security stamp in the access and
  // identity tokens, as it's a secret value.
  if (claim.Type ==
_identityOptions.Value.ClaimsIdentity.SecurityStampClaimType)
  {
    continue;
  }

  var destinations = new List<string>
  {
    OpenIdConnectConstants.Destinations.AccessToken
  };

  // Only add the iterated claim to the id_token if
  // the corresponding scope was granted to the client application.
  // The other claims will only be added to the access_token,
  // which is encrypted when using the default format.
  if ((claim.Type == OpenIdConnectConstants.Claims.Name &&
  ticket.HasScope(OpenIdConnectConstants.Scopes.Profile)) ||
  (claim.Type == OpenIdConnectConstants.Claims.Email &&
  ticket.HasScope(OpenIdConnectConstants.Scopes.Email)) ||
  (claim.Type == OpenIdConnectConstants.Claims.Role &&
  ticket.HasScope(OpenIddictConstants.Claims.Roles)))
```

```
        {
destinations.Add(OpenIdConnectConstants.Destinations.IdentityToken);
        }

      claim.SetDestinations(destinations);
    }

    return ticket;
  }
}
```

`AuthorizationController` exposes two methods, namely `authorize` and `logout`. The `authorize` method checks whether the user is authenticated and returns a challenge that shows the login page, where the user can enter their username and password. Once the correct credentials are entered and the user is validated from the identity tables, the authorization server creates a new authentication token and returns it to the client application based on the redirect URI specified for `bfrwebapp`. To see the working example, please refer to the code repository.

Implementing the vendor service

The vendor service is a web API that exposes a method to perform vendor registration. This service implements the actual business domain of the vendor system where a vendor can register. As we learned in the previous section, we can decompose an application based on business capability or business domain. This service implements a DDD principle and decomposes based on business domain. It contains the following three projects:

- `Vendor.API`: An ASP.NET Core Web API project that exposes methods to register a vendor
- `Vendor.Domain`: .NET Standard 2.0 class library that contains POCO models such as `VendorMaster` and `VendorDocument`, and an `IVendorRepository` interface to define methods essential for a vendor domain.
- `Vendor.Infrastructure`: .NET Standard 2.0 class library that contains a `VendorRepository` that implements the `IVendorRepository` interface and a `VendorDBContext` to perform database operations.

Creating a vendor domain

Create a new .NET Standard library project and name it `Vendor.Domain`. We will reference our `Infrastructure` project created previously to derive our POCO entities from the `BaseEntity` class.

Create a `VendorMaster` class and derive it from the `BaseEntity` class. Here is the code snippet of `VendorMaster` class:

```
public class VendorMaster : BaseEntity
{
  [Key]
  public int ID { get; set; }
  public string VendorName { get; set; }
  public string ContractNumber { get; set; }
  public string Email { get; set; }
  public string Title { get; set; }
  public string PrimaryContactPersonName{ get; set; }
  public string PrimaryContactEmail { get; set; }
  public string PrimaryContactNumber { get; set; }
  public string SecondaryContactPersonName { get; set; }
  public string SecondaryContactEmail { get; set; }
  public string SecondaryContactNumber { get; set; }
  public string Website { get; set; }
  public string FaxNumber { get; set; }
  public string AddressLine1 { get; set; }
  public string AddressLine2 { get; set; }
  public string City { get; set; }
  public string State { get; set; }
  public string Country { get; set; }

  public List<VendorDocument> VendorDocuments { get; set; }

}
```

`VendorDocument` is another POCO class that contains document-related fields. Here is the code snippet of the `VendorDocument` class:

```
public class VendorDocument : BaseEntity
{

  [Key]
  public int ID { get; set; }
  public string DocumentName { get; set; }
  public string DocumentType { get; set; }
  public Byte[] DocumentContent { get; set; }
  public DateTime DocumentExpiry { get; set; }

  public int VendorMasterID { get; set; }

  [ForeignKey("VendorMasterID")]
  public VendorMaster VendorMaster { get; set; }
```

```
}
```

Next, we will add the `IVendorRepository` interface to expose methods specific to the vendor domain. Here is the code snippet of the `IVendorRepository` interface:

```
public interface IVendorRepository : IRepository<VendorMaster>
{
  VendorMaster Add(VendorMaster vendorMaster);

  void Update(VendorMaster vendorMaster);

  Task<VendorMaster> GetAsync(int vendorID);

  void Add(VendorDocument vendorDocument);

  void Delete(int vendorDocumentID);
}
```

Creating the vendor infrastructure

This project is a .NET Standard 2.0 class library project that reference the core `Infrastructure` and `Vendor.Domain` projects. This contains the actual implementation of the `VendorRepository` and a database context to connect with the backend SQL Server database.

Here is the `VendorDBContext` class that derives from the `DbContext` class of EF Core and defines `DbSet` for the `VendorMaster` and `VendorDocument` entities:

```
public class VendorDBContext : DbContext, IUnitOfWork
{

  public VendorDBContext(DbContextOptions options) : base(options)
  {

  }

  protected override void OnConfiguring(DbContextOptionsBuilder
optionsBuilder)
  {
    base.OnConfiguring(optionsBuilder);
    //  optionsBuilder.UseSqlServer(@"Data Source=.sqlexpress;
    Initial Catalog=FraymsVendorDB;Integrated Security=False; User Id=sa;
    Password=P@ssw0rd; Timeout=500000;");
  }

  protected override void OnModelCreating(ModelBuilder builder)
```

```
  {
    base.OnModelCreating(builder);
  }

  public void BeginTransaction()
  {
    this.Database.BeginTransaction();
  }
  public void RollbackTransaction()
  {
    this.Database.RollbackTransaction();
  }
  public void CommitTransaction()
  {
    this.Database.CommitTransaction();
  }
  public Task<bool> SaveChangesAsync()
  {
    return this.SaveChangesAsync();
  }

  public DbSet<VendorMaster> VendorMaster { get; set; }
  public DbSet<VendorDocument> VendorDocuments { get; protected set; }
```

We will also implement the `IUnitOfWork` interface, so when the `VendorRepository` is injected in a controller, we can perform transaction handling and save the changes to the associated database in a single call.

Here is the `VendorRepository` that implements the `IVendorRepository` interface:

```
public class VendorRepository : IVendorRepository
{

  VendorDBContext _dbContext;


  public VendorRepository(VendorDBContext dbContext)
  {
    this._dbContext = dbContext;
  }
  public IUnitOfWork UnitOfWork
  {
    get
    {
      return _dbContext;
    }
  }
```

```
  public VendorMaster Add(VendorMaster vendorMaster)
  {
    var res= _dbContext.Add(vendorMaster);
    return res.Entity;
  }
  public void AddDocument(VendorDocument vendorDocument)
  {
    var res = _dbContext.Add(vendorDocument);
  }

  public void Update(VendorMaster vendorMaster)
  {
    _dbContext.Entry(vendorMaster).State =
Microsoft.EntityFrameworkCore.EntityState.Modified;
  }

  public async Task<VendorMaster> GetAsync(int vendorID)
  {
    var vendorMaster = await _dbContext.VendorMaster.FindAsync(vendorID);
    if (vendorMaster != null)
    {
      await _dbContext.Entry(vendorMaster)
      .Collection(i => i.VendorDocuments).LoadAsync();
    }
    return vendorMaster;
  }


  public IQueryable<T> All<T>() where T : BaseEntity
  {
    return _dbContext.Set<T>().AsQueryable();
  }

  public bool Contains<T>(Expression<Func<T, bool>> predicate) where T :
BaseEntity
  {
    return _dbContext.Set<T>().Count<T>(predicate) > 0;
  }

  public T Find<T>(Expression<Func<T, bool>> predicate) where T :
BaseEntity
  {
    return _dbContext.Set<T>().FirstOrDefault<T>(predicate);
  }
}
```

Creating the vendor service

We will now create a vendor-service project that will expose methods for use by client applications to register a vendor. To start with, let's create a new ASP.NET Core web API project and name it `Vendor.API`.

Implementing the mediator pattern in the vendor service

In microservices architecture, an application is split into multiple services, where each service connects to the other services through an endpoint. There are possibilities that one service may invoke or interact with multiple services when the event is invoked. Segregating the interaction between services is always a recommended approach and solves tight dependencies on other services. For example, an application invokes this service to register a vendor and then invoke the identity service to create its user account and send an email by calling the messaging service. We can implement the mediator pattern to solve this scenario.

The mediator pattern is based on the event-driven topology that works as a publisher/subscriber model. When any event is invoked, the registered handlers are called and execute the underlying logic. This encapsulates the logic of how services interact with one another, keeping the actual logic separate for each interaction. Moreover, the code is clean and easy to change.

In `Vendor.API`, we will implement the mediator pattern using the `MediatR` library of .NET. `MediatR` is the implementation of the mediator pattern that supports command handling and domain event publishing. In the following section, we will implement mediator when the user registers and invoke the identity service to create a new user and send an email.

To use `MediatR`, we have to add the following two packages:

- `MediatR`
- `MediatR.Extensions.Microsoft.DependencyInjection`

After adding these packages, we can add it in the `ConfigureServices` method by calling the `services.AddMediatR` method. `MediatR` provides the following two types of messages:

- **Request/response**: Requests are commands that may or may not return a value
- **Notification**: Notifications are events that may not return a value

In our example, we will implement both request/response to save a vendor record into a database and, once it returns Boolean true as a response, we will invoke notification events to create a vendor user and send an email.

To implement request/response, we should define a class that implements the interface of IRequestHandler or IRequestHandlet<TRequest, TResponse>, where TRequest is the request object type and TResponse is the response object type.

Create a class CreateVendorCommand under the Commands folder in your Vendor.API project. Here is the code snippet of CreateVendorCommand:

```
public class CreateVendorCommand : IRequest<bool>
{

  [DataMember]
  public VendorViewModel VendorViewModel { get; set; }

  public CreateVendorCommand(VendorViewModel vendorViewModel)
  {
    VendorViewModel = vendorViewModel;
  }

}
```

It implements the IRequest class that returns a Boolean value as a response. We have also specified our VendorViewModel that will be injected by the MediatR library when we pass them while calling the send method in the VendorController class.

Next, we will create a command handler that implements the generic IRequestHandler<TRequest,TResponse>, where TRequest is the CreateVendorCommand and TResponse will be a Boolean type. Here is the code snippet of CreateVendorCommandHandler:

```
public class CreateVendorCommandHandler :
IRequestHandler<CreateVendorCommand, bool>
{
  private readonly IVendorRepository _vendorRepository;

  public CreateVendorCommandHandler(IVendorRepository vendorRepository)
  {
    _vendorRepository = vendorRepository;
  }

  public async Task<bool> Handle(CreateVendorCommand command,
  CancellationToken cancellationToken)
  {
```

```
_vendorRepository.UnitOfWork.BeginTransaction();
try
{
  _vendorRepository.Add(command.VendorMaster);
  _vendorRepository.UnitOfWork.CommitTransaction();
}catch(Exception ex)
{
  _vendorRepository.UnitOfWork.RollbackTransaction();
}
return await _vendorRepository.UnitOfWork.SaveChangesAsync();
  }
}
```

When this handler is invoked, it will call the `Handle` method and pass the command and the cancellation token. From the command object, we can get the object we have passed while calling the `Send` method of the `IMediator` object in the `VendorController` class. This method calls the `Add` method of the `VendorRepository` and saves the information into the database. With the request/response approach, only one command handler is executed even if you have multiple handlers defined for the command. To call all the handlers, we can use notifications. We will extend the preceding example and add notification events and corresponding handlers that will be invoked once the command is executed successfully.

First, we define the notification event by creating a class and implementing the `INotification` interface. Here is the code snippet of the `CreateVendorNotification` event that will be used by the notification handlers:

```
public class CreateVendorNotification : INotification
{
  public VendorMaster _vendorVM;
  public CreateVendorNotification(VendorMaster vendorVM)
  {
    _vendorVM = vendorVM;
  }
}
```

Here is the implementation of `CreateUserHandler`, which listens for the `CreateVendorNotification` event to be raised. Once the event is raised, it is invoked and executes the logic defined in the `Handle` method. We use `CreateUserHandler` to create a user in the ASP.NET Core Identity database by calling the identity service. Here is the code snippet of `CreateUserHandler`:

```
public class CreateUserHandler :
INotificationHandler<CreateVendorNotification>
{
  IResilientHttpClient _client;
```

```
   public CreateUserHandler(IResilientHttpClient client)
   {
     _client = client;
   }
   public Task Handle(CreateVendorNotification notification,
 CancellationToken cancellationToken)
   {
     string uri = "http://businessfrayms.com/api/Identity";
     string token = "";//read token from user session
     var response = _client.Post<VendorMaster>(uri,
 notification._vendorVM,"");
     return Task.FromResult(0);
   }
 }
```

Next, we will create a SendEmailHandler that listens for the
CreateVendorNotification and sends an email notification to the vendor about
registration. Here is the code snippet of SendEmailHandler:

```
 public class SendEmailHandler :
 INotificationHandler<CreateVendorNotification>
 {

   MessagingService _service;
   public SendEmailHandler(MessagingService service) : base()
   {
     _service = service;
   }

   public Task Handle(CreateVendorNotification notification,
 CancellationToken cancellationToken)
   {
     _service.SendEmail(notification._vendorVM.Email, "Registration",
     "Thankyou for registration");
     return Task.FromResult(0);
   }
 }
```

We can add more notification handlers based on the requirements. For example, if we want
to initiate a workflow notification once the vendor record is saved into the database, we can
create a vendor workflow notification handler, and so on.

From the VendorController side, we can invoke the mediator pattern by calling the Send and Publish methods. The Send method invokes command handlers and Publish is used to invoke notification handlers. Here is the code snippet of VendorController:

```
[Produces("application/json")]
[Route("api/Vendor")]
public class VendorController : BaseController
{
  private readonly IMediator _mediator;
  private ILogger _logger;

  public VendorController(IMediator mediator, ILogger logger) :
base(logger)
  {
    _mediator = mediator;
    _logger = logger;
  }

  [Authorize(AuthenticationSchemes =
OAuthIntrospectionDefaults.AuthenticationScheme)]
  // POST: api/VendorMaster
  [HttpPost]
  public void Post([FromBody]VendorMaster value)
  {
    try
    {
      bool result = _mediator.Send(new CreateVendorCommand(value)).Result;
      if (result)
      {
        //Record saved succesfully, publishing event now
        _mediator.Publish(new CreateVendorNotification(value));
      }
    }
    catch (Exception ex)
    {
      _logger.LogError(ex.Message);
    }
  }

}
```

In the preceding code, we have a `Post` method that will be called by the client application to create a new vendor. It first calls the `Send` method, which invokes the `CreateVendorCommandHandler` and saves the record in the database, and, once the record is created and the response is true, it will invoke the `SendEmailHandler` to send an email.

 You can access the complete sample application from the GitHub link provided with the book.

Deploying microservices on Docker containers

Microservices are best suited for containerization deployment. A container is a process that provides an isolated and controlled environment for an application to run without affecting the system or vice versa. Most of us have experienced hosting applications inside VMs, which provide an isolated space to install, configure, and run applications and use the dedicated resources without affecting the underlying system or application. In contrast to VMs, containers provide the same level of isolation but are more lightweight in terms of startup time and overhead. Unlike VMs, containers do not preallocate resources such as memory, disk, and CPU usage. We can run multiple containers on the same machine, where the containers are isolated from each other but share the memory, disk, and CPU usage. This enables any application running in a container to use the maximum resources available without having any preallocated or assigned.

The following diagram depicts how VMs run on the host OS:

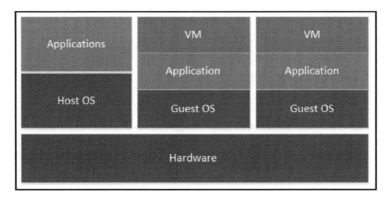

We run applications on the host OS and VMs on a guest OS. The virtualization is done at the hardware level, where VMs can talk to the host hardware using drivers available in the hypervisor virtualization system, as provided by the host OS.

Here is how containers run on the host OS:

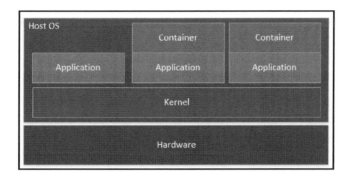

With containers, the kernel is shared between multiple containers. The kernel is a core component of the operating system that is responsible for interacting with different processes and hardware, and manages resources such as CPU cycles and virtual management. The kernel is the component that creates isolation between different containers.

What is Docker?

Docker is a software company that provides containers. Docker containers are very popular in the software industry to run microservices. They are best suited to microservices application development and provide a set of command-line tools that provide a unified way of building and maintaining different container images. We can create custom images or use existing ones from a registry such as Docker Hub (`http://hub.docker.com`).

Here are a few benefits of Docker:

Benefit	Description
Simplicity	Provides a powerful tool for application creation and orchestration
Openness	Built with open source technology and easy to integrate into existing environments
Independence	Creates separation of concerns between application and infrastructure

Using Docker with .NET Core

.NET Core is modular and faster when compared to the .NET framework and helps in running applications side by side, where each application is running its own set of CLR libraries and runtime. This makes it perfect for running on Docker containers. The image of .NET Core is far smaller when compared to the image having .NET framework installed. .NET Core uses a Windows Nano server or Linux image, which is a lot smaller than the Windows service core image. As .NET Core runs cross-platform, we can also create Docker images of other platforms and run applications on them.

With Visual Studio 2017, we can choose Docker while creating a .NET Core or ASP.NET Core project, and it auto scaffolds the Docker files and sets up the basic configuration to run applications on Docker. The following screenshot shows the Docker options available in Visual Studio 2017 to provision Docker containers:

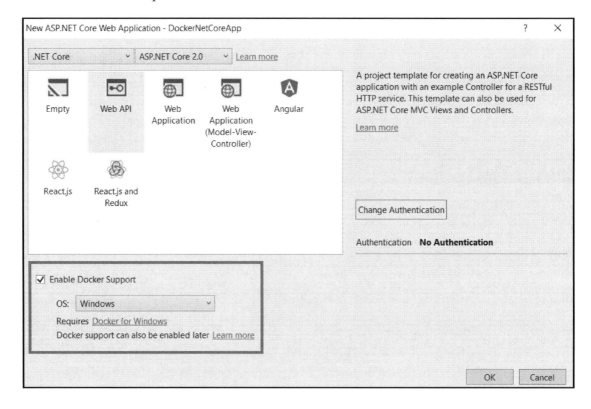

Alternatively, if the project is already created, we can add Docker support by right-clicking on the .NET Core project and clicking on the **Add | Docker Support** option.

Once we create or enable Docker support in our application, it creates the Docker files in our project and also adds another project, named `docker-compose`, as follows:

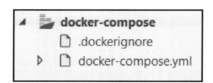

The `docker-compose` project contains set of YAML (`.yml`) files that contain the configuration related to the application hosted in the container and a reference to the path of the Dockerfile created for the project when Docker support was added. Here is the sample `docker-compose.yml` file that contains two services having details such as the image name, `dockerfile` path, and so on. This file is from the sample application we discussed previously:

```
version: '1'

services:
  vendor.api:
    image: vendor.api
    build:
      context: .
      dockerfile: srcmicroservicesVendorVendor.APIDockerfile

  identity.api:
    image: identity.api
    build:
      context: .
      dockerfile: srcmicroservicesAuthServerIdentity.AuthServerDockerfile
```

The following is the content of the `Dockerfile` residing inside the `Vendor.API` project we created in the sample application above:

```
FROM microsoft/aspnetcore:2.0-nanoserver-1709 AS base
WORKDIR /app
EXPOSE 80

FROM microsoft/aspnetcore-build:2.0-nanoserver-1709 AS build
WORKDIR /src
COPY *.sln ./
COPY src/microservices/Vendor/Vendor.API/Vendor.API.csproj
src/microservices/Vendor/Vendor.API/
```

```
RUN dotnet restore
COPY . .
WORKDIR /src/src/microservices/Vendor/Vendor.API
RUN dotnet build -c Release -o /app

FROM build AS publish
RUN dotnet publish -c Release -o /app

FROM base AS final
WORKDIR /app
COPY --from=publish /app .
ENTRYPOINT ["dotnet", "Vendor.API.dll"]
```

The preceding `Dockerfile` starts referencing a base image `microsoft/aspnetcore:2.0-nanoserver-1709` that will be used to create a Docker container. The `COPY` command is the actual path where the project files reside. It will then use dotnet CLI commands such as `dotnet restore` to restore all the NuGet packages inside the container, `dotnet build` to build the application, and `dotnet publish` to build and publishes the compiled output into a publish folder inside the container.

Running Docker images

We can run Docker images either from the command line or from Visual Studio directly. As we saw in the previous section, a new `docker-compose` project is created on adding Docker support into our project. Running the `docker-compose` project reads the `docker-compose` YAML file and hooks up containers for the services defined. Docker is a first-class citizen in Visual Studio. It not only supports running the Docker containers but fully-fledged debugging capabilities are also provided.

Alternatively, from the command line, we can run Docker containers by going to the root path where the `docker-compose.yml` file resides and running the following command:

```
docker-compose up
```

Once the containers are up, each application has its own IP assigned at runtime. To inspect the actual IP of each service running on a separate container, we can run the `docker inspect` command to retrieve it. However, the `docker inspect` command requires the container ID as a parameter. To get the list of the containers running, we can first call the `docker ps` command as follows:

```
docker ps
```

The preceding command displays the list of containers as shown in the following screenshot:

```
C:\Users\ovais>docker ps
CONTAINER ID        IMAGE          COMMAND              CREATED         STATUS         PORTS
          NAMES
a12d3a37a644       vendor.api:dev    "C:\\remote_debugger\\…"  6 minutes ago   Up 5 minutes    0.0.0.0:40277
->80/tcp    dockercompose17175663515996174189_vendor.api_1
```

Finally, we can use the container ID and execute `docker inspect` command to get its IP address as follows:

```
docker inspect -f "{{range
.NetworkSettings.Networks}}{{.IPAddress}}{{end}}" containerid
```

The preceding command displays the IP address as follows:

```
C:\Users\ovais>docker inspect -f "{{range .NetworkSettings.Networks}}{{.IPAddress}}{{end}}" a12d3a37a644
192.168.44.35
```

Summary

In this chapter, we learned about the microservices architecture for developing highly performant and scalable applications for the cloud-based on microservices. We learned some of the fundamentals of microservices, their benefits, and patterns and practices used when designing the architecture. We discussed certain challenges in decomposing enterprise applications into the microservices architecture style and learned patterns such as API composition and CQRS to address them. Later in the chapter, we developed a basic application in .NET Core and discussed the solution structure and components of microservices, and developed identity and vendor services.

Other Books You May Enjoy

If you enjoyed this book, you may be interested in these other books by Packt:

Hands-On Full-Stack Web Development with ASP.NET Core
Tamir Dresher, Amir Zuker, Shay Friedman

ISBN: 978-1-78862-288-2

- Build RESTful APIs in C# with ASP.NET Core, web APIs, and Entity Framework
- See the history and future horizons of the web development field
- Bring static-typing to web apps using TypeScript
- Build web applications using Angular, React, and Vue
- Deploy your application to the cloud
- Write web applications that scale, can adapt to changes, and are easy to maintain
- Discover best practices and real-world tips and tricks
- Secure your backend server with Authentication and Authorization using OAuth 2.0

Hands-On TypeScript for C# and .NET Core Developers
Francesco Abbruzzese

ISBN: 978-1-78913-028-7

- Organize, test, and package large TypeScript code base
- Add TypeScript to projects using TypeScript declaration files
- Perform DOM manipulation with TypeScript
- Develop Angular projects with the Visual Studio Angular project template
- Define and use inheritance, abstract classes, and methods
- Leverage TypeScript-type compatibility rules
- Use WebPack to bundle JavaScript and other resources such as CSS to improve performance
- Build custom directives and attributes, and learn about animations

Leave a Review - Let Other Readers Know What You Think

Please share your thoughts on this book with others by leaving a review on the site that you bought it from. If you purchased the book from Amazon, please leave us an honest review on this book's Amazon page. This is vital so that other potential readers can see and use your unbiased opinion to make purchasing decisions, we can understand what our customers think about our products, and our authors can see your feedback on the title that they have worked with Packt to create. It will only take a few minutes of your time, but is valuable to other potential customers, our authors, and Packt. Thank you!

Index

IP addresses
    working with 218
iteration statements
    about 15
    do statement 16
    for statement 16
    foreach statement 17
    while statement 15

J

JavaScript 299
JavaScript Object Notation (JSON) 186, 258
JIT compilation 494
JSON Web Tokens (JWT) 606
JSON
    serializing with 262
Just In Time (JIT) compiler 486

K

Kestrel 302, 345
KISS (Keep it Simple, Stupid) 535

L

language compilers 160
large object heap (LOH) 565
Last In First Out (LIFO) 516
last-in, first-out (LIFO) 213
layered architecture
    versus microservices architecture 580
libraries
    packaging, for NuGet distributions 184, 188
linked list
    about 519
    benefits 520
    circular linked list 520
    doubly linked lists 519
    singly linked list 519
Linux
    Microsoft Visual Studio Code, using on 10
Liskov Substitution Principle (LSP) 544
lists
    about 212, 515
    benefits 515
    working with 214
local functions

defining 125, 126
localization 226
lock statement 286
logarithm operation 513
logging
    during development 57
    during runtime 57

M

macOS
    filesystem, managing 232
    Microsoft Visual Studio Code, using on 10
Mads Kristensen's extensions, for VS code
    reference 300
Markdown Documentation (MD) 501
mathematical functions
    writing 44
memory allocation
    overview 560
memory diagnostics
    with BenchmarkDotnet 503
memory fragmentation 565, 566
memory
    managing, with reference type 140
    managing, with value types 140
    usage, monitoring 267
metadata 220
metapackages 173
method signature 105
methods
    about 40, 79, 126
    calling 100
    calling, delegates used 127
    defining, with tuples 102
    functionality, implementing 122
    named arguments 106
    optional parameters 106
    overloading 105, 106
    parameters, defining to 104
    parameters, passing to 104
    simplifying, with operators 121
    writing 100
microservices architecture
    about 578
    benefits 580

formatting, for output 44
rounding 21
working with 199

O

object disposition, in .NET Core
best practices 569
object graphs, serializing
about 258
with JSON 262
with other formats 264
with XML 258
Object Oriented Principles (OOP) 535
Object Relationship Mapping (ORM) 594
object-oriented programming (OOP)
about 75, 76
abstraction 76
aggregation 76
composition 76
encapsulation 76
inheritance 76
polymorphism 76
objects
comparing, when sorting 132
Open Closed Principle (OCP)
about 538
composition 541
inheritance 539
parameters 539
OpenAPI Specification 385
OpenIddict 601
operators
about 79
functionality, implementing 124
methods, simplifying with 121
ordinal numbers 44
overflow
checking for 28
checking, checked statement used 28, 29
overriding
preventing 150

P

package reference
adding 186

adding, Visual Studio 2017 used 187
adding, Visual Studio Code used 186
package
benefits 172
testing 192
testing, Visual Studio 2017 used 193
testing, Visual Studio Code used 193
parameters
defining, to methods 104
passing, query string used 366, 367, 368
passing, route value used 364
passing, to method 108
passing, to methods 104, 109
partial keyword
used, for splitting class 111
used, for splitting classes 110
paths
managing 239
pattern matching
reference 14
with if statement 11
with regular expressions 206, 207
with switch statement 13, 14
performance
monitoring 267
Plain Old CLR Object (POCO) 554, 594
polymorphic inheritance 150
polymorphism 76, 150, 151
Portable Class Libraries (PCL) 169
portable executable (PE) file 489
primitive data types, C# 509
processes 272
processing strings
efficiency, measuring 271
project templates
additional packs, installing 406
reference 406
using 405
properties
about 79
access, controlling with 111
read-only properties 112
settable properties 113, 114

Q

query string
  used, for passing parameters 365, 367, 368
queue
  about 517
  benefits 518
queues 213

R

Razor 354
Razor Pages
  code-behind files, using 317
  defining 312
  enabling 312
  exploring 311
  shared layout, defining 314
  shared layout, setting 314
  shared layouts, using 313
read mode 289
read-only properties
  defining 112
recursion
  factorials, calculating with 46
  versus iteration, reference 46
reflection 220, 226
regular expressions
  examples 208
  pattern matching 206, 207
  syntax 208
release build 497
release mode
  versus debug mode 497
Representational State Transfer (REST) 370
resource management
  objects, disposing 556
  resources, acquiring 556
  threads misuse, avoiding 555
resources
  sharing 428
  usage, monitoring 265
  using 428
REST service
  calling, with NuGet packages 481
Reveal

reference 411
route value
  used, for passing parameters 364
Runtime IDentifier (RID)
  about 178
  reference link 178

S

Safari 296
sample app, in .NET Core
  creating, microservices architecture used 591
  logical architecture 594
  mediator pattern, implementing in vendor service 617, 619
  solution structure 592
  vendor domain, creating 612
  vendor infrastructure, creating 614
  vendor service implementation 612
  vendor service, creating 617
Secure Sockets Layer (SSL)
  about 11
  reference 11
segments 350
selection statements
  about 9
  if statement 10
  Microsoft Visual Studio 2017, using 10
  Microsoft Visual Studio Code, using on Linux 10
  Microsoft Visual Studio Code, using on macOS 10
  Microsoft Visual Studio Code, using on Windows 10
  switch statement 12
self-contained deployments (SCDs) 489
semantic versioning
  reference 221
separate comparer
  defining 134, 135
Separation of Concerns (SoC) 536
serialization 258
sets
  about 213
settable properties
  defining 113, 114
shared resources